Afro-European Trade in the Atlantic World

THE WESTERN SLAVE COAST
c. 1550–c. 1885

Silke Strickrodt

JAMES CURREY

James Currey
is an imprint of
Boydell & Brewer Ltd
PO Box 9, Woodbridge
Suffolk IP12 3DF (GB)
www.jamescurrey.com
and of
Boydell & Brewer Inc.
668 Mt Hope Avenue
Rochester, NY 14620-2731 (US)
www.boydellandbrewer.com

© Silke Strickrodt 2015 and 2017

First published in hardback 2015

All rights reserved. No part of this book may be reproduced in any form, or by electronic or mechanical means, including information storage and retrieval systems, without permission in writing from the publishers, except by a reviewer who may quote brief passages in a review.

The right of Silke Strickrodt to be identified as
the author of this work has been asserted in accordance with
sections 77 and 78 of the Copyright, Designs and Patents Act 1988

British Library Cataloguing in Publication Data
A catalogue record for this book is available on request from the British Library

ISBN 978-1-84701-110-7 (James Currey cloth)
ISBN 978-1-84701-178-7 (James Currey paperback)

The publisher has no responsibility for the continued existence or accuracy of URLs for external or third-party internet websites referred to in this book, and does not guarantee that any content on such websites is, or will remain, accurate or appropriate.

Typeset in 11/13 Bembo with Albertus MT display
by Avocet Typeset, Somerton, Somerset TA11 6RT

Afro-European Trade IN THE Atlantic World
THE WESTERN SLAVE COAST
c. 1550–c. 1885

WESTERN AFRICA SERIES

The Economics of Ethnic Conflict:
The Case of Burkina Faso
Andreas Dafinger

Commercial Agriculture, the Slave Trade
& Slavery in Atlantic Africa
Edited by Robin Law, Suzanne Schwarz
& Silke Strickrodt

Afro-European Trade in the Atlantic World:
The Western Slave Coast c. 1550–c. 1885
Silke Strickrodt

The Politics of Peacemaking in Africa:
Non-State Actors' Role in the Liberian Civil War
Babatunde Tolu Afolabi

Sects & Social Disorder:
Muslim Identities & Conflict in Northern Nigeria
Edited by Abdul Raufu Mustapha

★Creed & Grievance:
Muslim-Christian Relations & Conflict Resolution in Northern Nigeria
Edited by Abdul Raufu Mustapha & David Ehrhardt

★forthcoming

To the memory of Lutz Wiederhold
(1963–2012)

Contents

List of Maps	ix
List of Abbreviations	xi
Acknowledgements	xii

Introduction   1

1
The regional setting   28

2
The Atlantic connection: Little Popo & the rise of Afro-European trade on the western Slave Coast, c.1600 to 1702   65

3
The era of the warrior kings: 1702 to 1772   102

4
The era of the traders: 1772 to c.1807   134

5
Disintegration & reconstitution: Political developments, 1820s to 1870s   157

6
From slaves to palm oil: Afro-European trade, c.1807 to 1870s   195

Epilogue: The colonial partition & its
consequences, 1870s to c.1900 225

Bibliography 237
Index 254

List of Maps

1. The Slave Coast and the Gold Coast — xiv
2. The western Slave Coast (including the Anlo region) — 2
3. The lagoon system — 32
4. Grand Popo and the Bouche du Roi in the late seventeenth century, as drawn by Jean Barbot — 47
5. The western Slave Coast in 1879 as drawn by W. T. G. Lawson — 49

List of Abbreviations

ADCM	Archives Départementales de Charente-Maritime, La Rochelle
ANB	Archives Nationales du Bénin, Porto-Novo
ANF	Archives Nationales de la France, Aix-en-Provence
ANT	Archives Nationales du Togo, Lomé
BIFAN	*Bulletin de l'Institut Fondamental d'Afrique Noir*
BNP	Bibliothèque Nationale, Paris
CEA	*Cahiers d'Études Africaines*
DNA	Danish National Archives, Copenhagen
ED	*Études dahoméennes*
GLL	'Le Grand Livre Lolamé' (Aného, Togo)
GNA	Ghana National Archives, Accra
HiA	*History in Africa*
IJAHS	*International Journal of African Historical Studies*
JAH	*Journal of African History*
MSOSB	*Mitteilungen des Seminars für Orientalische Sprachen zu Berlin*
NAN	National Archives of the Netherlands, The Hague
PP	Parliamentary Papers (UK)
RGCG	*Royal Gold Coast Gazette and Commercial Intelligencer*
RIHS	Rhode Island Historical Society, Rhode Island
TA	*Thaarups Archiv*
TGCTHS	*Transactions of the Gold Coast and Togoland Historical Society*
THSG	*Transactions of the Historical Society of Ghana*
TNA	The National Archives, London
UaH	Unitätsarchiv Herrnhut
UKHO	United Kingdom Hydrographic Office, Taunton
WMMS	Wesleyan Methodist Missionary Society Archives, London

Acknowledgements

This book has been a long time in the making. It derives from a PhD thesis submitted to the Department of History of the University of Stirling in 2002. Following completion, the thesis was left to rest for several years, while I was engaged in other projects. It was then rewritten, cut down in some parts and extended in others, with new material and ideas integrated. In producing first the thesis and then the book I have profited from the work, advice and support of many people. I want to use this opportunity to thank them.

Before all others, my thanks are due to Robin Law and Adam Jones, two distinguished historians of West Africa whom it has been my great privilege to work with. Robin Law has supervised the PhD thesis and advised on its transformation into a book. Adam Jones, with whom I did my undergraduate studies, was a constant source of encouragement and information. Their experience, knowledge and friendship have been indispensable to the production of the book, and my scholarly development more generally.

I owe a debt of gratitude to the historians who have shared their knowledge and material with me. In West Africa, I should particularly thank Nicoué Lodjou Gayibor of the Université du Bénin in Togo and Elisée Soumonni, Joseph Adande, Michel Videgla, Régina Byll-Catária and Félix Iroko of the Université de Abomey-Calavi (formerly the Université Nationale du Bénin), in Bénin. I have also benefitted from their assistance during my fieldtrips to West Africa, where they took care of me. I am grateful to George E. Brooks, Natalie Everts, the late Christopher Fyfe, Per O. Hernaes, Ole Justesen, Sydney Kanya-Forstner, John Parker and Esther Ries for providing valuable information. I thank Tony Hopkins and Joël Glasman for reading and commenting on drafts of the introduction. I am grateful to Paul Lovejoy for his generous support and for providing access to his wide network of people studying African history, among whom I have made many friends. I also want to thank the colleagues who by producing critical editions of documents have rendered an invaluable but often underrated service to research on West Africa's precolonial past and who have facilitated – indeed, enabled! – my work. Apart from some of the individuals already mentioned, these are particularly the late Selena Axelrod Winsnes and the late Albert van Dantzig.

Further, I am indebted for support and information to colleagues and friends at the institutions where I have worked during the production of the thesis and the book. Apart from those already mentioned, particular thanks are due to Annabelle Hopkins, John McCracken and George Peden, all formerly of the History Department of the University of Stirling, Andreas Gestrich and Markus Mößlang of the German Historical Institute London, and Stefan Hoffmann of the Department of African Studies of the Humboldt-Universität zu Berlin.

I am grateful to the people who have facilitated my fieldwork in West Africa. In addition to those already mentioned, I thank especially Martine de Souza, Léon da Silveira and the staff of CODIAM in Cotonou.

I also want to record my thanks to the staff of the archives and libraries in which I have worked in the course of my research, particularly the staff of the Archives Nationales du Bénin in Porto-Novo, the Archives Nationales du Togo in Lomé, the Ghana National Archives in Accra, the archives of the United Kingdom Hydrographic Office in Taunton, and, in London, the National Archives of the UK, the SOAS Library and the British Library.

For financial support, my thanks are due to the following organizations and individuals. The research for the thesis was funded by the History Department of the University of Stirling, the Nigerian Hinterland Project, the German Academic Exchange Service, the German Historical Institute London, the Royal History Society, the Checkland Memorial Fund and, last but not least, Jana Strickrodt, my sister. The production of the book manuscript was assisted by the German Historical Institute London, which among other things contributed towards the cost of the maps, and the Commission for Women's Advancement of the former Philosophical Faculty III of the Humboldt-Universität zu Berlin.

I thank Damien Bove for making the maps, as well as for inspiring and entertaining discussions about cartography and history.

Finally, I am grateful to my family and my friends, whose encouragement and support have been constant and indispensable. Apart from Jana, my parents Heidi and Gerd Strickrodt, and my partner, René Kriegler, I particularly want to thank Alison and the late Alan Kennedy, Alexandra Lembert-Heidenreich, Tim Lovering, Ulrike Renker and Kathrin Wiederhold. This book is dedicated to the memory of Lutz Wiederhold, a great friend and brilliant scholar who has been important to my world in many respects, including my intellectual development and the accomplishment of the PhD project.

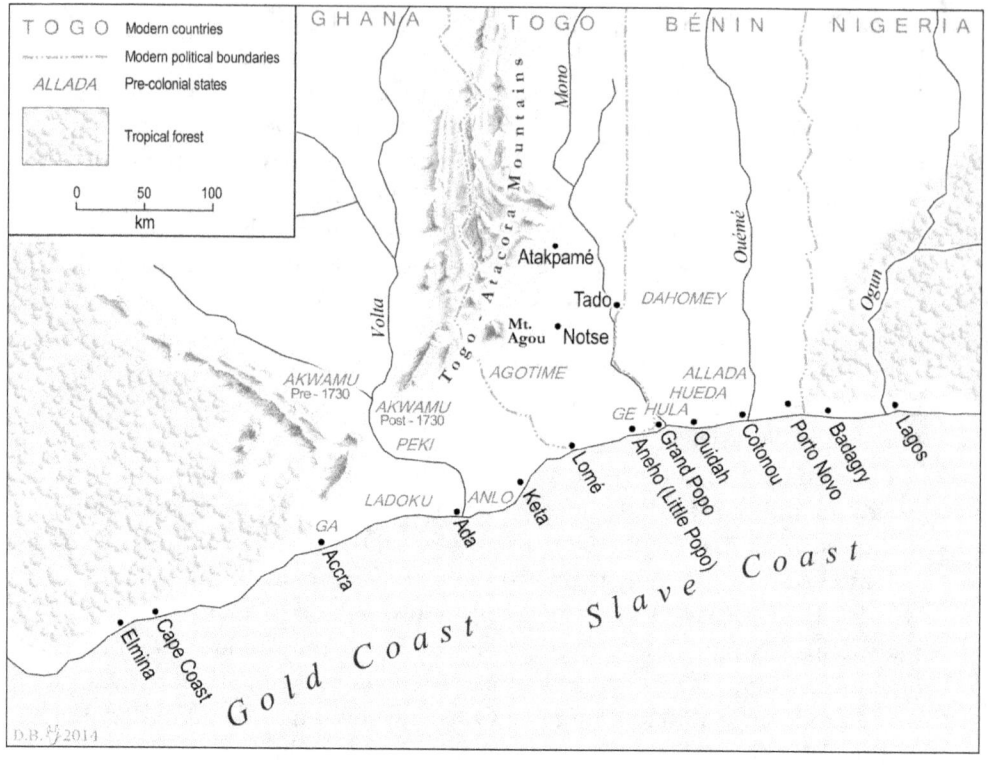

Map 1 The Slave Coast and the Gold Coast

Introduction

In 1553 Portuguese traders arrived at the mouth of the Mono river (in today's Republic of Bénin) and initiated commercial relations with the resident Hula people. As fishermen and salt-makers, the Hula had experience of inter-regional trade and had developed structures to support it, but the arrival of the Europeans signified something radically new for them.[1] The Atlantic Ocean, which until then had been a barrier, now became a gateway, bringing the Hula into contact with other communities and cultures located on the edges of the various continents bounding the Atlantic. This contact was mainly commercial and economic, but also entailed social, cultural and political transformations, including, by the end of the period examined in this study, the colonial takeover by the French.

Although intensifying over time, this was no linear process; nor was its outcome predetermined. It involved changing trading partners, arrangements and networks as well as stops and starts and reversals, as in the latter half of the eighteenth century, when the Hula virtually dropped out of the Afro-European trade. However, even if they decided to step back from the trade or were pushed out of it by competitors, the world around them was transformed, directly or indirectly, by its influence. The ensuing changes included the arrival of new neighbours (Akan- and Ga-Adangme-speaking immigrants from the Gold Coast to the west, and, to the east, Fon from the interior), new technologies (such as firearms and sea-going canoes), and new plants, animals, diseases, currency and commodities from Asia, Europe and the Americas, to mention only a few. Less visible to historians but no less important were changes in outlook, values and taste, social organisation and religious practice.

This book is a study of the Afro-European commercial encounter on the

---

[1] Robin Law, 'West Africa's Discovery of the Atlantic', *IJAHS*, 44/1 (2011), 1–25, pp.1–6.

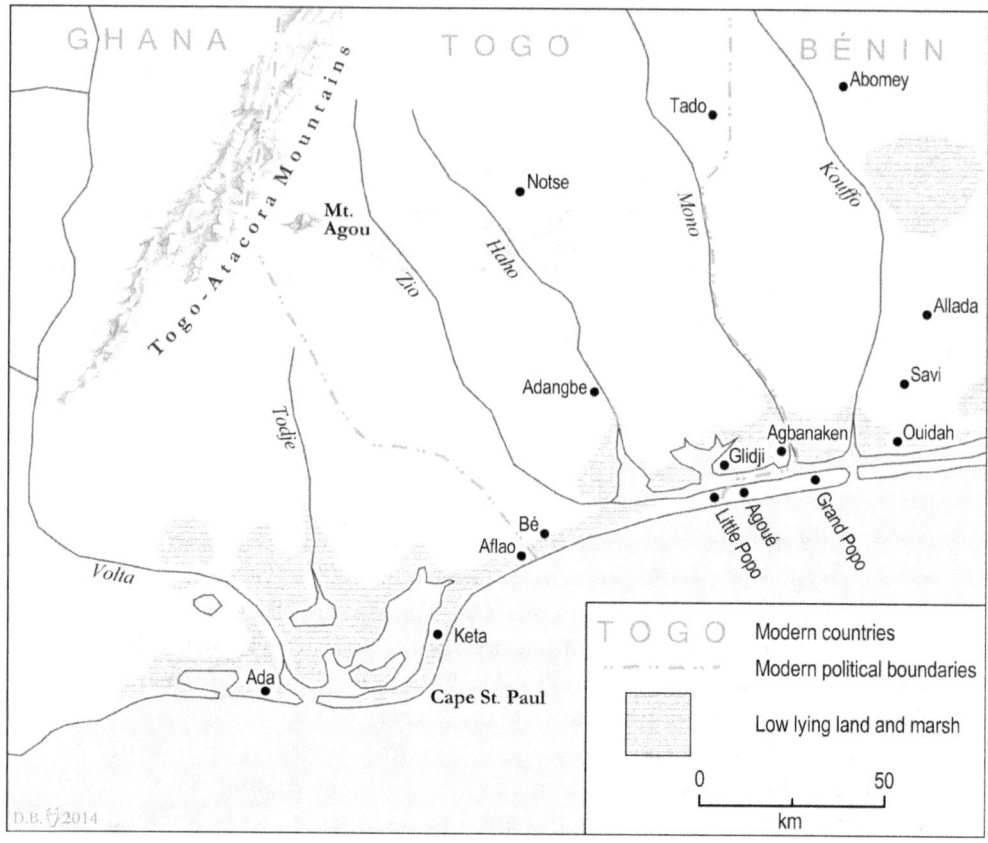

Map 2 The western Slave Coast (including the Anlo region)

western Slave Coast from its beginnings around 1550 to the colonial partition in the 1880s, particularly the slave trade but also that in ivory and agricultural produce. It focuses on the role which local communities played in this trade and how the trade affected them. The western or 'upper' Slave Coast comprises the coastal areas of present-day Togo and adjacent parts of the coasts of Ghana and the Republic of Bénin, extending from west of Ouidah (in the Republic of Bénin) to the end of the coastal lagoon in the west. This is the western part of the area that was originally settled by the Hula people. However, for most of the pre-colonial period for which there is documentation, this area was divided between two states: the kingdom of the Hula, which was known to Europeans traders by the name of its port, Great or Grand Popo (in Bénin), and the kingdom of Ge (Gen/ Genyi/ Guin), known as Little Popo after its main port (present-day Aného in Togo). In the nineteenth century two more ports of trade appeared in the region, Porto Seguro (present-day Agbodrafo, in Togo) and Agoué (in Bénin). The Bouche du Roi, that is the outlet of the joint waters of the Mono river and the lagoon, constituted Grand Popo's eastern boundary, which it shared first with the Hueda kingdom and then with Dahomey. The western limits of Little Popo's authority were fluid, as was the extent of the lagoon in this direction. In the nineteenth century, the westernmost place to have permanent access to water communication to the east via the lagoon was Baguida (in Togo), lying nearly 45 miles/roughly 72km from the Bouche du Roi. However, for most of the period under consideration, Little Popo's authority extended to Aflao (in Ghana), which lies further west and beyond the limits of the lagoon, roughly 53 miles/ 85km from the Bouche du Roi. Aflao also appears to have been the westernmost place to be settled by the Hula.

This definition of the region excludes the Anlo area at the extreme western end of the Slave Coast, usually considered part of the western Slave Coast. Arguably, it belonged more to the Gold Coast sphere, particularly after the take-over of Fort Prindsensten by the British in 1850. In 1874 Anlo was incorporated into the Gold Coast colony and became part of the Anglophone world, unlike the area controlled by the Ge and the Hula which subsequently fell to the Germans and the French. This may partly explain why its history has been studied extensively, unlike that of the Ge and Hula kingdoms.[2]

For European slave traders, the western Slave Coast was an intermediate area between regions of greater interest, the Gold Coast to the west and the eastern Slave Coast, particularly Dahomey, to the east. There were no permanent European trading establishments, 'castles' or forts in this area,[3] as the supply of slaves from its ports was unreliable and intermittent (and is difficult to quantify). Nevertheless, the western Slave Coast did play an important part in the operation of the Atlantic slave trade, providing crucial services to the slave merchants. These services included communication between the trading companies' headquarters on the Gold Coast and their 'factories' (trading posts) on the eastern Slave Coast, particularly at Ouidah, Dahomey's major port, which was facilitated by the existence of coastal lagoons and the employment of African canoemen. The lagoons also served as feeders for the Atlantic trade, slaves from the western Slave Coast being transported by canoe to Ouidah for embarkation in slave ships to the Americas. Further, the region was a major source of provisions, both for European traders and enslaved Africans during their stay on the coast

---

[2] Emmanuel Kwaku Akyeampong, *Between the Sea and the Lagoon: An Eco-Social History of the Anlo of Southeastern Ghana, c.1850 to Recent Times* (Athens and Oxford, 2001); Anne C. Bailey, *African Voices and the Atlantic Slave Trade: Beyond the Silence and the Shame* (Boston, 2005); Sandra E. Greene, *Gender, Ethnicity and Social Change on the Upper Slave Coast: A History of the Anlo-Ewe* (Portsmouth, NH and London, 1996); Greene, *Sacred Sites and the Colonial Encounter: A History of Meaning and Memory in Ghana* (Bloomington and Indianapolis, 2002).
[3] Unless one counts the forts at Keta, which during the eighteenth century sometimes fell under Little Popo's control: the Dutch fort Singelenburg, which existed in the mid-1730s, and the Danish fort Prindsensten, built in 1784. See Chapters 3 and 4.

and during the Middle Passage.⁴ Finally, it gave the slave traders an alternative outlet when there were problems at the more established slave ports, notably in the nineteenth century, when the region became a hotspot of the illegal slave trade. This was due to the disruption of Ouidah's trade by the men-of-war of the British navy's anti-slave trade squadron, prompting Ouidah's slave merchants to send slaves via the lagoon to the ports on the western Slave Coast to be embarked there for shipment (see Chapter 6).

Whatever its role for the Europeans, the trade was significant for the coastal communities. As 'middlemen' they participated in it in various roles, mainly as brokers, selling enslaved Africans from the interior (as well as other commodities and services, as noted above) to European merchants, but also, in the case of the Ge, as captors of slaves in the immediate hinterland. Sometimes slaves for sale to Europeans were drawn from these communities themselves, particularly following their defeat in military conflicts with neighbouring groups, such as the Anlo and Dahomey.⁵

Historiographical debates and the case study of the western Slave Coast

While providing a detailed account of the trading communities of the western Slave Coast, I also address wider historiographical issues which make this book relevant to historians whose interests lie beyond the western Slave Coast. First, it contributes to debates on the history of the Atlantic world, conceived as a historical unit which is constructed by the interactions of the states and communities on its shores.⁶ The active participation of African communities and individuals in the creation and maintenance of the Atlantic world has been recognised since John Thornton published his study in 1992.⁷ These Atlantic connections were mainly commercial,

---

⁴ The importance of the provisions trade has recently been drawn attention to by David Eltis, 'The Slave Trade and Commercial Agriculture in an African Context', *Commercial Agriculture, the Slave Trade and Slavery in Atlantic Africa*, ed. Robin Law, Suzanne Schwarz and Silke Strickrodt (Woodbridge and Rochester, NY, 2013), 28–53.

⁵ For recent studies of other coastal trading communities, see Mariana P. Candido, *An African Slaving Port and the Atlantic World: Benguela and its Hinterland* (Cambridge, 2013); Christopher R. DeCorse, *An Archaeology of Elmina: Africans and Europeans on the Gold Coast, 1400–1900* (Washington and London, 2001); Toby Green, *The Rise of the Trans-Atlantic Slave Trade in Western Africa, 1300–1589* (Cambridge, 2012); Green (ed.), *Brokers of Change: Atlantic Commerce and Cultures in Pre-Colonial Western Africa* (New York, 2012); Robin Law, *Ouidah: The Social History of an African Slaving 'Port', 1727–1892* (Athens and Oxford, 2004); Kristin Mann, *Slavery and the Birth of an African City: Lagos, 1760–1900* (Bloomington and Indianapolis, 2007), Rebecca Shumway, *The Fante and the Transatlantic Slave Trade* (Rochester, 2011); Pierluigi Valsecchi, *Power and State Formation in West Africa: Appolonia from the Sixteenth to the Eighteenth Century* (New York, 2011).

⁶ Bernard Baylin, 'The Idea of Atlantic History', *Itinerario*, 20/1 (1996), 38–44; Nicholas Canny and Philip Morgan (eds), *The Oxford Handbook of the Atlantic World, 1450–1850* (Oxford, 2011).

⁷ John Thornton, *African and Africans in the Making of the Atlantic World, 1400–1800* (1992, 2nd

forged by the export of more than 12.5 million enslaved Africans, of whom roughly 10.7 million arrived in the Americas.[8] The commercial encounter between African sellers and European buyers of slaves took place mainly in the African coastal communities. The trade also fostered social and cultural networks in which ruling and commercial elites were involved.[9] For example, Christianus Jacob Protten, a Eurafrican born at Christiansborg (Accra) who was related through his mother to the rulers of the Ga at Accra and the Ge at Little Popo, went to Europe in 1727, associated with the German Herrnhuter Brüdergemeinde and converted to Christianity in the mid-1730s. He returned to the West African coast, including Little Popo, and also went to the Danish West Indies.[10] A son of Ashampo, King of Little Popo (c.1737 – c.1767), went to England for education in the 1750s, likewise returning as a Christian seven years later (see Chapter 4). Several members of the Lawson family of Little Popo spent periods in Europe and/or on slave vessels from the 1780s. Among them was George Lawson, who became an important actor in the region's commercial and political life (see Chapter 5). A further example is the liberated slaves from Brazil and Cuba who immigrated and settled at Agoué from the 1830s onwards.[11]

Our understanding of the connections forged between the Atlantic ports that participated in the slave trade has been steadily advanced by the trans-Atlantic slave trade database.[12] But while this quantitative approach helps us to deal with broad trends and wide regions, it is less useful for detailed analysis of minor ports. This is partly because the database relies on imputed numbers when no others are available. More pertinently, as there were no permanent European factories on the western Slave Coast, information about its ports was often second-hand and therefore unreliable, deriving from traders at Ouidah or on the Gold Coast. The database's focus on ports of embarkation also tends to obscure the role of the commu-

(cont.) ed. Cambridge, 1998); Thornton, *A Cultural History of the Atlantic World, 1250–1820* (Cambridge, 2012). See also Robin Law and Kristin Mann, 'West Africa in the Atlantic Community: The Case of the Slave Coast', *William and Mary Quarterly*, 56/2 (1999), 307–34; Kristin Mann and Edna G. Bay (eds), *Rethinking the African Diaspora: The Making of a Black Atlantic World in the Bight of Benin and Brazil* (London and Portland, OR, 2001); David Northrup, *Africa's Discovery of Europe 1450–1850* (2002, 2nd ed., New York, 2009).

[8] For these estimates, see 'Voyages: The Trans-Atlantic Slave Trade Database' (2009): http://www.slavevoyages.org/tast/assessment/estimates.faces (accessed 25 May 2014).

[9] E.g. Law/ Mann, 'West Africa'; Thornton, *Cultural History*; Paul E. Lovejoy and David Richardson, 'Letters of the Old Calabar Slave Trade 1760–1789', in *Genius in Bondage: Literature of the Early Black Atlantic*, ed. Vincent Carretta and Philip Gould (Lexington, KY, 2001), 89–115.

[10] H. W. Debrunner, *Presence and Prestige: Africans in Europe: A History of Africans in Europe before 1918* (Basel, 1979), 82–86; Jon F. Sensbach, *Rebecca's Revival: Creating Black Christianity in the Atlantic World* (Cambridge, MA, 2005).

[11] See Chapter 5; Silke Strickrodt, '"Afro-Brazilians" of the Western Slave Coast in the Nineteenth Century', in *Enslaving Connections: Changing Cultures of Africa and Brazil during the Era of Slavery*, ed. José C. Curto and Paul E. Lovejoy (Amherst, NY, 2004), 213–44.

[12] 'Voyages: The Trans-Atlantic Slave Trade Database' (2009): http://slavevoyages.org/tast/index.faces.

nities on the western Slave Coast as feeders of the trade, slaves from there being transported by canoes along the lagoon to Ouidah for embarkation (as already noted) and also collected by boats belonging to European traders at Ouidah or on the Gold Coast. In addition, the practice of European vessels of sailing along the West African coast and collecting slaves at various ports sometimes makes it difficult to know exactly how many slaves were purchased at each particular port. Finally, confusion arises as the names of ports referred to in European documents change over time (as well as according to spelling conventions in the various European languages), which can lead to wrong assumptions about their role. For instance, prior to the 1680s, 'Popo' refers to the port that subsequently became called Grand Popo. Little Popo entered the trade in 1683 and in the following decade was called various names, including 'Abree'/ 'Abrow' and 'Poccahonna'/ 'Paokahnee' as well as 'Little Paw Paw'/ 'Little Po Po' (see Chapter 2). From the 1690s it was sometimes simply called 'Popo', which became regular usage in the second half of the eighteenth century when Grand Popo temporarily dropped out of the trade. The database does not adequately reflect such ambiguities. Case studies of the communities from which the slaves were embarked are therefore of critical importance if we are to understand how the trade actually operated. Following the 'quantitative' turn which began with Philip Curtin's *The Atlantic Slave Trade: A Census* (1969), of which the trans-Atlantic slave trade database is the crowning achievement, there has been a qualitative backlash. This has, however, found expression mainly in an increased interest in slave biographies (with Joseph Miller postulating a 'biographical turn').[13]

Second, this study is anchored in the historiography of globalisation, that is, the increasing interconnectedness of different places and regions of the world. Historians have been concerned with the concept of globalisation for the last two decades.[14] Not all have found it useful, with criticism ranging from its alleged theoretical vagueness, teleological and Eurocentric nature, and disregard for the limits of and obstructions to globalising flows

---

[13] Joseph C. Miller, 'A Historical Appreciation of the Biographical Turn', in *Biography and the Black Atlantic*, ed. Lisa A. Lindsay and John Wood Sweet (Philadelphia, 2014), 19–47. Curtin himself published a collective biography of former slaves: *Africa Remembered: Narratives by West Africans from the Era of the Slave Trade* (Madison Wisc.,1967). Recent studies include Alice Bellagamba, Sandra E. Greene, Martin A. Klein (eds.), *African Voices on Slavery and the Slave Trade*, vol.1 (Cambridge, 2013). For examples relating to the Slave Coast, see Mahommah Gardo Baquaqua, *The Biography of Mahommah Gardo Baquaqua: His Passage from Slavery to Freedom in African and America*, ed. Robin Law and Paul Lovejoy (Princeton, 2001); Robin Law, 'Individualising the Atlantic Slave Trade: The Biography of Mahommah Gardo Baquaqua of Djougou (1854)', *Transactions of the Royal Historical Society*, 12 (2002), 113–40; Silke Strickrodt, 'Aballow's Story: The Experience of Slavery in Mid-Nineteenth Century West Africa, as Told by Herself', in *African Voices*, ed. Bellagamba, Greene, Klein, 387–403.

[14] A. G. Hopkins (ed.), *Globalization in World History* (London, 2002); Hopkins (ed.), *Global History: Interactions between the Universal and the Local* (Basingstoke, 2006).

and connections.¹⁵ However, the Atlantic slave trade can be regarded as a 'global' phenomenon, which is not to say that it impinged on every corner of the globe but rather that its scope went beyond the local and the regional. At any rate, this adjective is a useful reminder that the trade's range was bigger than the Atlantic basin, involving, among others, beads from Venice and Bohemia, cowries from the Maldives and Zanzibar, textiles from South Asia and enslaved Africans from East Africa. Moreover, the slave trade was intertwined with other trades and exchanges, including the trans-Saharan and Indian Ocean slave trades, the trade in gold (from Brazil as well as from West Africa), ivory and agricultural produce, and a more general exchange of diseases and plants (including those cultivated on American plantations by enslaved Africans).

The study of the western Slave Coast illuminates several aspects in the debates on globalisation. One is the question of the relationship between the universal and the local. Large-scale global processes, such as the Atlantic slave trade, are articulated through the local, that is, their influence is negotiated, adapted and reformulated in interaction with local factors.¹⁶ The history of the western Slave Coast serves as an illustration of the complex relationship between the global, local – and regional – influences which determine the trade's development in any one particular region of Africa, or at any one particular African slave port. The question here is: How does the general development of the Atlantic slave trade with its periods of expansion and contraction relate to the rhythm of the trade on the western Slave Coast or at any one port there?¹⁷ Minor ports such as Little Popo illustrate more clearly than straightforward success cases, such as Ouidah, the difficulties and strains involved in the struggle to prevail, or at least survive, in the extremely competitive environment fostered by the trade.

Another aspect concerns the chronology of globalisation. Hopkins has identified four categories of globalisation – archaic, proto-, modern and post-colonial – which are to be conceived as 'a series of overlapping and interacting sequences rather than a succession of new stages'. According to him, 'One form co-existed with another or others which it may have nurtured, absorbed, or simply complemented. The relationship, whether

---

¹⁵ Frederick Cooper, 'What is the Concept of Globalization Good for? An African Historian's Perspective', *African Affairs*, 100/399 (2001), 189–213; Ulrike Freitag and Achim von Oppen, '"Translocality": An Approach to Connection and Transfer in Area Studies', in *Translocality: The Study of Globalising Processes from a Southern Perspective*, ed. Freitag and Oppen (Leiden, 2010), 1–21; Sebastian Conrad, *Globalgeschichte: Eine Einführung* (München, 2013), 18–19.

¹⁶ This is aptly expressed by the title of Donald R. Wright's book: *The World and a Very Small Place in Africa: A History of Globalization in Niumi, The Gambia* (1997, 3rd ed., Armonk, NY and London, 2010).

¹⁷ See Silke Strickrodt, 'The Atlantic Slave Trade and a Very Small Place in Africa: Global Processes and Local Factors in the History of Little Popo, 1680s to 1860s', in *The End of Slavery in Africa and the Americas: A Comparative Approach*, ed. Ulrike Schmieder, Katja Füllberg-Stolberg and Michael Zeuske (Berlin, 2011), 15–26.

symbiotic or competitive, does therefore not foreclose on the future.'[18] In this scheme, the Atlantic system was part of proto-globalisation, defined by the reconfiguration of state systems and the growth of finance, services and pre-industrial manufacturing between 1600 and 1800. Modern globalisation is characterised by the rise of the nation state and the spread of industrialisation after 1800.[19]

What can the case study of the western Slave Coast contribute to this? The time frame of this study, comprising more than three centuries, may offer a chance to test such models. Can the western Slave Coast's shift from the Atlantic slave trade to 'legitimate' commerce in agricultural produce (the 'crisis of adaptation') be interpreted as a shift from proto-globalisation to modern globalisation: two systems overlapping and linked, one holding back, the other pushing forward? The case of the western Slave Coast shows that in the nineteenth century there were several realignments of connections with the wider world: first, following the abolition of the British slave trade in 1807, European traders (apart from the Portuguese) left the coast; then, following the Equipment Act of 1839, there was an influx of 'illegal' traders from Brazil and Portugal; the closure of the Brazilian slave market in the 1850s prompted many of these traders to leave, only to be replaced by slave-traders from Cuba with ships from the US; the end of the trade in the 1860s also weakened links to Brazil, particularly in connection with the arrival of European firms engaged in the palm oil trade (although on the western Slave Coast this new trade had begun much earlier). Thus, the suppression of the Atlantic slave trade in the early nineteenth century first strengthened the links of coastal communities with Brazil due to their role in the illegal trade and the arrival of liberated slaves from Brazil and Cuba after 1835 (although Britain continued to play a role); but after the 1860s there was a reorientation towards Europe, specifically Britain, France and Germany (see Chapter 6).

A further aspect is the role of the Atlantic slave trade in African state-building.[20] The western Slave Coast, particularly the Ge kingdom, illustrates the complex effects of this trade on political centralisation. On the one

---

[18] Hopkins, 'Introduction: Globalization', in *Globalization in World History*, ed. Hopkins., 1–10, p. 3.

[19] Ibid., 5–6.

[20] C. A. Bayly encourages historians to pay more regard to the role of external, globalising phenomena, such as international trade, in the development of early states: '"Archaic" and "Modern" Globalization in the Eurasian and African Arena, c.1750–1850', *Globalization in World History*, ed. Hopkins, 47–73, p.63. Conversely, Gérard L. Chouin and Christopher R. DeCorse, in their discussion of the early history of agricultural communities in the Ghanaian forest region, warn against an overemphasis on the influence of the Atlantic trade on African peoples: 'Prelude to the Atlantic Trade: New Perspectives on Southern Ghana's Pre-Atlantic History', *JAH*, 51/2 (2010), 123–45. For a comparative debate on the relative weight of internal (African) and external (non-African) factors in the history of an East African coastal civilization, see Thomas Spear,'Early Swahili History Reconsidered', *IJAHS*, 33/2 (2000), 257–90; Randall Lee Pouwels,'A Reply to Spear on Early Swahili History', *IJAHS*, 34/3 (2001), 639–46.

hand, the slave trade can be seen to have assisted the emergence of the Ge state from groups of immigrant Ga warriors from the Gold Coast ('those Rob[b]ers the Accras', in the words of a European trader) in the late seventeenth and early eighteenth centuries.[21] Imported firearms and trade goods made it easier to accumulate dependants and allies (see Chapters 2 and 3). On the other, the slave trade encouraged upstart traders in the port of Little Popo in the 1780s who challenged established authority, and the eclipse of the kings of Glidji testifies to the potentially destructive influence of the trade (see Chapter 4).

Globalisation also reflects on urbanisation. Hopkins argues that in early forms of globalisation cities were junctions between the universal and the local, the connections between them being made by migrants and mobile diasporic networks.[22] On the western Slave Coast, Little Popo and Agoué were examples of multi-ethnic urban communities that thrived on the trade, attracting immigrants from different places. Within a century Little Popo developed into a settlement consisting of several juxtaposed 'towns', which in the 1780s impressed a European visitor with its evident prosperity and first multi-storey houses (see Chapters 2 and 4). Agoué, founded in the 1820s, grew rapidly due to the influx of liberated slaves from Brazil after 1835, who settled in different quarters according to ethnicity and religion (see Chapter 5). The African immigrants in these towns included slaves, some of whom would have remained in the community as domestic workers while many were destined for export.[23] The European traders who visited the coastal towns in the era of the slave trade were joined in the nineteenth century by missionaries, naval officers and explorers. Family ties, commercial networks and ritual as well as diplomatic connections linked these communities to other towns on the Atlantic rim, particularly Gold Coast towns (Accra, Elmina, Cape Coast), Ouidah and Lagos on the eastern Slave Coast and Freetown, London and Bahia. The development of cosmopolitanism is another aspect of globalisation.[24]

---

[21] Robin Law (ed.), *Correspondence of the Royal African Company's Chief Merchants at Cabo Corso Castle with William's Fort, Whydah, and the Little Popo Factory, 1727–1728: An annotated transcription of Ms Francklin 1055/1 in the Bedfordshire County Record Office* (African Studies Program, University of Wisconsin-Madison, 1991) [hereafter: *Ms Francklin 1055/1*], no.22: Thomas Wilson, William's Fort Whydah, 12 July 1728.

[22] Hopkins, 'Introduction: Globalization', 4.

[23] There is hardly any information about domestic slaves or other low status groups in these communities for the era of the slave trade, as the reports of visiting Europeans focus on local authorities and trading partners. For an exception from the nineteenth century, see Strickrodt, 'Aballow's Story'. The existence of Tchamba, a slave cult, among the Ge today indicates the role which domestic slavery played in their society. See Judy Rosenthal, *Possession, Ecstasy, and Law in Ewe Voodoo* (Charlottesville and London, 1998), 103–11; Tobias Wendl, 'Slavery, Spirit Possession and Ritual Consciousness: The *Tchamba* Cult among the Mina of Togo', *Spirit Possession, Modernity and Power in Africa*, ed. Heike Behrendt and Ute Luig (Oxford, 1999), 111–23.

[24] Hopkins, 'Introduction: Globalization', 3–6; David Hancock, *Citizens of the World: London Merchants and the Integration of the British Atlantic Community, 1735–1785* (Cambridge, 1997).

This study also deals with the issue of cross-cultural trade, specifically the institutional framework of the operation of European trade in Africa.[25] How did traders manage to create a climate of confidence that enabled trade across cultural divides? Thirty years ago, Philip Curtin defined cross-cultural trade as one between strangers 'not to be trusted in the same full sense that neighbors and kinfolk can be trusted'. This lack of trust, he argued, poses a challenge, which means that trade across cultural borders 'has almost always been carried out through special institutional arrangements to help guarantee the mutual security of the two sides.'[26] One model to explain cross-cultural understanding between traders is the 'moral community'. Hopkins conceptualises the relationship between Europeans and Africans on the West African coast in the era of the Atlantic slave trade as one of 'two complementary and more or less equal trading partners, whose mutual business interests were cemented by a mixture of goodwill and extensive credit obligations.'[27] More recent research has focused on other arrangements for the security of contracts. Paul Lovejoy and David Richardson, who studied credit protection mechanisms in the Bight of Biafra in the eighteenth century, argue that African and European merchants tried to engender trust by forging personal relations but these ties were insufficient to protect credit. Therefore, they developed mechanisms that were supplementary to trust, such as letters of recommendation or endorsement for local traders. African institutions, most importantly debt pawnship, were also appropriated and adapted to this purpose, However, Lovejoy and Richardson conclude that the use of local state institutions was a more effective means of credit protection.[28] On the Slave Coast, Dahomey is an example of a strong state where contracts were guaranteed by the state's law-enforcing authority.[29] Other historians have identified further indigenous institutions adapted by European and African slave traders to underpin their credit, including

---

[25] For a more general discussion of the new institutional approach to the history of Africa, see A. G. Hopkins, 'The New Economic History of Africa', *JAH*, 50 (2009), 155–77.
[26] Philip D. Curtin, *Cross-Cultural Trade in World Perspective* (Cambridge, 1984), 1.
[27] A. G. Hopkins, *An Economic History of West Africa* (Harlow, 1973), 108–9.
[28] Paul E. Lovejoy and David Richardson, 'Trust, Pawnship, and Atlantic History: The Institutional Foundations of the Old Calabar Slave Trade', *American Historical Review*, 104/2 (1999), 333–55; Lovejoy and Richardson., 'The Business of Slaving: Pawnship in Western Africa, c.1600–1810', *JAH*, 42/1 (2001), 67–89; Lovejoy and Richardson., 'This Horrid Hole': Royal Authority, Commerce and Credit at Bonny, 1690–1840', *JAH*, 45/3 (2004), 363–92. See also Lovejoy and Richardson, 'African Agency and the Liverpool Slave Trade', in *Liverpool and Transatlantic Slavery*, ed. David Richardson, Suzanne Schwarz and Anthony Tibbles (Liverpool, 2007), 43–65, which adds some information for Sierra Leone and Windward Coast.
[29] Robin Law, 'Finance and Credit in Pre-Colonial Dahomey', *Credit, Currencies and Culture: African Financial Institutions in Historical Perspective*, ed. Endre Stiansen and Jane I. Guyer (Stockholm, 1999), 15–37; Law, 'On Pawning and Enslavement for Debt in the Precolonial Slave Coast', *Pawnship, Slavery, and Colonialism in Africa*, ed. Paul E. Lovejoy and Toyin Falola (Trenton, NJ and Asmara, 2003), 55–69.

the landlord-stranger relationship[30] and marriage of European traders to African women.[31]

Afro-European commercial relations on the western Slave Coast are interesting because they illustrate how difficult it was in practice for traders, in the absence of both strong state institutions and effective private order mechanisms, to establish a working relationship that allowed trade to flourish. This becomes clear from an examination of the development of trade relations at Little Popo during the rule of Ashampo, who cheated and robbed European traders in order to gain access to their goods (see Chapter 3). By contrast, during the last two decades of the eighteenth century, when the authority of the Ge rulers over Little Popo was waning and a group of powerful African traders emerged in the coastal settlement, lasting relations of trust were created and trade flourished (see Chapter 4).

This study also contributes to the existing historiography of the Slave Coast by taking the physical environment seriously as a factor in the history of human communities. Lagoons have played a role in studies of the economic and political life of the region, but the connection between the sea and the lagoons as well as the dynamic character of the lagoon environment in the precolonial period have not been fully appreciated.[32]

At the most fundamental level, this is the history of two West African states over roughly 330 years, reconstructed mainly on the basis of information from contemporary written documents but occasionally complemented by information drawn from oral traditions. The history of the Afro-European trade serves as an entry point both because it affected the development of these states and because it generated documents providing rich information. The focus is on the reconstruction of commercial/ economic, political and social life not because these spheres are more important than others but because the nature of the sources privileges them. If this book stimulates discussion and encourages further studies on other aspects of the region's history, it has served its purpose.

---

[30] V. R. Dorjahn and Christopher Fyfe, 'Landlord and Stranger: Change in Tenancy Relations in Sierra Leone', *JAH*, 3 (1962), 391–7.
[31] For Upper Guinea, see George E. Brooks, *Eurafricans in Western Africa: Commerce, Social Status, Gender, and Religious Observance from the Sixteenth to the Eighteenth Century* (Athens and Oxford, 2003); Christopher Fyfe, *A History of Sierra Leone* (Oxford, 1962). For the Gold Coast, see Margaret Priestley, *West African Trade and Coast Society: A Family Study* (London, 1969); Natalie Everts, 'A Motley Company: Differing Identities among Euro-Africans in Eighteenth-Century Elmina', in *Brokers of Change*, ed. Green, 53–69; Everts, 'Incorporating Euro-Africans in Akan Lineages and a Modest Development towards a Euro-African Identity in Eighteenth-Century Elmina', *THSG*, new series, 14 (2012), 79–104. For an interesting comparative case, relating to the Swahili in East Africa, see John Middleton, 'Merchants: An Essay in Historical Ethnography', *The Journal of the Royal Anthropological Institute*, 9/3 (2003), 509–26.
[32] Robin Law, 'Between the Sea and the Lagoons: The Interaction of Maritime and Inland Navigation on the Precolonial Slave Coast', *CEA*, 114/29-2 (1989), 209–37; Akyeampong, *Between the Sea*; Greene, *Sacred Sites*.

Historiography and sources

The western Slave Coast has attracted relatively little attention from academic historians, unlike the eastern Slave Coast and the Gold Coast which were more important to the slave traders.[33] There are a number of general studies of the Slave Coast which concentrate on Dahomey but also make some reference to the western Slave Coast. The first to appear was C. W. Newbury's study, which however does not offer much on the precolonial history of the region and focuses on the European commercial and political activities, rather than the African side.[34] Ade Akinjogbin's book deals with the western Slave Coast, intermittently at least, as far as it was involved in military and diplomatic relations with Dahomey.[35] The most comprehensive and detailed discussion of trade relations in the region comes from Robin Law's study on the history of the Slave Coast, which has laid the groundwork for this study, at least as regards the period before 1750.[36] However, although it purports to deal with the whole Slave Coast, the study focuses on Allada, Hueda and Dahomey and deals with the societies on the western Slave Coast mainly in relation with them. There is an alternative narrative to be told, from the point of view of, or at least with focus on the western Slave Coast.

In the last two decades there has also been archaeological research relating to the history of the Slave Coast, mainly concerned with the relationship between long-distance trade and urban-rural dynamics on the Slave Coast. However, this too focuses on the central region, with Kenneth Kelly and Neil Norman working on the Hueda kingdom and Cameron Monroe on Dahomey, and mainly Cana.[37] I have found no published results of archaeo-

[33] On the Gold Coast, see Kwame Yeboa Daaku, *Trade and Politics on the Gold Coast, 1600–1720: A Study of the African Reaction to European Trade* (Oxford, 1970); Ray A. Kea, *Settlements, Trade, and Polities in the Seventeenth-Century Gold Coast* (Baltimore, 1982); Shumway, *Fante*; Valsecchi, *Power*. See also Adam Jones and Silke Strickrodt, 'Introduction: Recent Research on the Early Modern History of Atlantic Africa', *THSG*, new series, 14 (2012), 1–12.
[34] C. W. Newbury, *The Western Slave Coast and its Rulers: European Trade and Administration among the Yoruba and Adja-Speaking Peoples of South-Western Nigeria, Southern Dahomey and Togo* (Oxford: 1961). Newbury's title is somewhat misleading as his book deals with the whole of the Slave Coast and, indeed, mainly with its eastern part. What is evidently meant is the 'Slave Coast of West Africa'.
[35] I. A. Akinjogbin, *Dahomey and its Neighbours 1708–1818* (Cambridge, 1967).
[36] Robin Law, *The Slave Coast of West Africa, 1550–1750: The Impact of the Atlantic Slave Trade on an African Society* (Cambridge, 1991).
[37] See e.g. Kenneth G. Kelly, 'Change and Continuity in Coastal Bénin', *West Africa during the Atlantic Slave Trade: Archaeological Perspectives*, ed. Christopher deCorse (London and New York, 2001), 81–100; Neil L. Norman, 'Hueda (Whydah) Country and Town: Archaeological Perspectives on the Rise and Collapse of an African Atlantic Kingdom', *IJAHS*, 42/3 (2009), 387–410; J. Cameron Monroe, 'Continuity, Revolution or Evolution on the Slave Coast of West Africa? Royal Architecture and Political Order in Precolonial Dahomey', *JAH*, 48/3 (2007), 349–73;

logical work on the western Slave Coast, apart from a doctoral dissertation dealing with Notsé, which however does not deal with Afro-European trade.[38]

Very few studies have focused on the western Slave Coast (east of Anlo) in particular, none of which have shown much interest in the history of Afro-European commercial enterprise. Nicoué Lodjou Gayibor's history of Little Popo, which so far is the only monograph devoted exclusively to the region's history, is mainly concerned with the kingdom's political development.[39] Félix Iroko has examined the Hula in the precolonial period but is mainly interested in traditions of origins, on the one hand, and, on the other, synchronic descriptions of political institutions and religious and economic practices.[40] Seth Wilson's discussion of the 'Mina' at Aného, that is the people who trace their origins to the Gold Coast canoemen and traders who immigrated from the mid-seventeenth century onwards, is mainly a cultural history.[41] There are also two student's dissertations which deal with societies or communities in the region, Jérôme Kassa's on the early history of the Hula and Imbert Akibode's on Agoué.[42] However, they are not concerned with the trade, nor do they use archival material. Instead, they rely largely on recently recorded local traditions, which for the reconstruction of the precolonial history is problematic.

Finally, there are works dealing with the individual European colonies in the region. The most substantial among these are Patrick Manning's study of the French colony of Dahomey, published in 1982, and Peter Sebald's study of German Togoland, published in 1988.[43] Both make reference to the coastal communities dealt with in this book, each to those which lay

(cont.) Monroe, 'Building the State in Dahomey: Power and Landscape on the Bight of Benin', *Power and Landscape in Atlantic West Africa: Archaeological Perspectives*, ed. Monroe and Akinwumi Ogundiran (Cambridge, 2012), 192–221.

[38] D. A. Aguigah, 'La Site de Notsé: Contribution a l'archeologie du Togo' (thèse de Doctorat de troisème cycle, Université de Paris I, 1985). There is also a prospectus for projected research on the lower Mono valley, but apparently this has not been followed-up: Obare Bagodo, 'Archaeological Reconnaissance of the Lower Mono Valley: A Preliminary Report', *West African Journal of Archaeology*, 22 (1993), 24–36.

[39] Nicoué Lodjou Gayibor, *Le Genyi: Un royaume oublié de la Côte de Guinée au temps de la traite des noirs* (Lomé, 1990).

[40] A. Félix Iroko, *Les Hula du XIVe au XIXe siècle* (Cotonou, 2001).

[41] Seth Wilson, 'Aperçu historique sur les peuples et cultures dans le Golfe du Bénin: le cas des "Mina" d'Anécho', *Peuples du Golfe du Bénin (Aja-Ewè)*, ed. François de Medeiros (Paris, 1984), 127–50.

[42] Imbert B. Oswin Akibode, *Contribution à l'étude de l'histoire de l'ancien royaume d'Agoué (1821–1885)* (mémoire de maîtrise, FLASH, Université Nationale du Bénin, 1988–89); Jérôme Koffi Kassa, 'Le Foyer Xwla de Xwlagan: Migrations et traits de culture (des probables origines au XVème siècle)' (mémoire de maîtrise, FLASH, Université Nationale du Bénin, 1993–94).

[43] Patrick Manning, *Slavery, Colonialism and Economic Growth in Dahomey, 1640–1960* (Cambridge, 1982); Peter Sebald, *Togo 1884–1914: Eine Geschichte der deutschen "Musterkolonie" auf der Grundlage amtlicher Quellen* (Berlin, 1988).

within the territory of the respective colony: Agoué and Grand Popo in Dahomey and Little Popo and Porto Seguro in Togoland. They also give some relevant information about the precolonial history of the region. However, a discussion of these communities from the point of view of the European colonies is necessarily limited, especially because the colonial borders did not follow those of the kingdoms of Grand Popo and Little Popo but cut across them.

There is a great variety of documentary material for the history of the coastal communities on the western Slave Coast and their trade relations with the Europeans. This can be divided into two broad categories: material generated by the African communities themselves (i.e. internal sources) and material by European visitors and other outsiders (i.e. external sources). As regards the latter, several sub-categories can be distinguished according to the nature and the purpose for which the documents were produced: commercial records, missionary records, accounts by explorers, documents generated by British agencies engaged in the anti-slave trade campaign in the region and records of the colonial administrations.

NON-AFRICAN (EUROPEAN AND AMERICAN) SOURCES

Commercial records. The main source for the history of the region and the Afro-European trade there are the records of the various European companies that were active there. These records constitute the only large-scale body of material relating to the period before the nineteenth century. At least seven European countries and two (former) American colonies traded in the region in the precolonial period: the Brandenburgers, the Danes, the Dutch, the English/ Americans, the French, the Germans and the Portuguese/ Brazilians. The records of their activities are scattered over archives in at least twelve countries and on three continents: Bénin, Ghana, Togo, São Tomé, Denmark, France, Germany, the Netherlands, Portugal, the UK, Brazil and the USA. It is beyond the capacity of an individual scholar to visit all these archives, due to financial, linguistic and temporal constraints, but I have used as wide a range of source material as possible, profiting also from published source editions and the generosity of colleagues who have shared their material with me.

The Portuguese were the first to trade on the western Slave Coast and continued to do so until the end of the slave trade in the 1860s. However, documentation for their activities is limited due to the large-scale destruction of Portuguese and Brazilian documents in the Lisbon earthquake of 1755 and by official action after the abolition of the slave trade respectively.[44] For the early period of Portuguese trade in the region, the collection of documents published by António Brásio contains some infor-

[44] See A.F.C. Ryder, *Materials for West African History in Portuguese Archives* (London, 1965), 3.

mation.[45] For the eighteenth and nineteenth centuries, information about Portuguese (and Brazilian) activities comes mainly from reports of other European traders in the region.[46] An exception is the account of C. H. van Zütphen, a trader from Bahia who in 1831 visited the West African coast, including Agoué, to explore the possibility and profitability of engaging in the illegal slave trade. The account, based on a journal written during the trip and published in 1835 in German, is particularly valuable because it is the first from Agoué and the only one from the 1830s. It gives information about the political situation and also identifies important individuals.[47]

The bulk of the material on which this study is based was generated by the activities of English traders, who started to engage in trade on the western Slave Coast in the 1680s. This mainly comprises the records of the English African companies, most of which is preserved in the British National Archives in Kew/ London (TNA). Among them are the papers of Thomas Miles, which documents the activity of the factory of the London firm of Messrs Miles & Weuves at Little Popo in the 1790s.[48] However, there are also several collections of relevant material outside the TNA. One is the Rawlinson Collection at the Bodleian Library, which contains information the western Slave Coast in the 1680s and 1690s.[49] Particularly rich is the correspondence of the RAC chief factor at Ouidah, John Carter, who visited Little Popo in 1687 and gave a description of the place (see Chapter 2). Another is the Ms Francklin 1055/1 at Bedford County Record Office, comprising a letter-book of the RAC. It contains copies of 29 letters that were exchanged between the RAC's chief merchant at Cape Coast Castle and its subordinate settlement on the Slave Coast between October 1727 and August 1728, among them five letters exchanged with the factory at Little Popo.[50] Further, there are a number of published accounts by British traders relating to the eighteenth and early nineteenth centuries which give information. Among them is the account by G. A. Robertson, published in

---

[45] António Brásio, ed., *Monumenta Missionaria Africana*, 1st series 14 vols., 2nd series 5 vols. (Lisbon, 1952–85).
[46] Verger gives extensive quotes from Portuguese and Brazilian documents, which however are not relevant for the western Slave Coast (*Flux et reflux de la traite des Négres entre le Golfe du Bénin et Bahia de Todos os Santos de 17è au 19è siècle*, Paris, 1968).
[47] C. H. van Zütphen, *Tagebuch einer Reise von Bahia nach Afrika* (Düsseldorf, 1835).
[48] See Silke Strickrodt, 'A Neglected Source for the History of Little Popo: The Thomas Miles Papers *ca.* 1789–1796', *HiA*, 28 (2001), 293–330.
[49] This material has recently been published: see Robin Law, ed., *The English in West Africa 1681–1683; The Local Correspondence of the Royal African Company of England 1681–1699*, part 1 (London, 1997); *The English in West Africa 1685–1688*, part 2 (Oxford, 2001), *The English in West Africa 1691–1699*, part 3 (Oxford, 2006). A selection of documents from the Rawlinson collection, relating to the RAC over the whole period from 1681–99, has also been published in Law, ed., *Further Correspondence of the Royal African Company of England relating to the 'Slave Coast', 1681–99: Selected Documents from Ms. Rawlinson c. 745–747 in the Bodleian Library, Oxford* (African Studies Program, University of Wisconsin-Madison, 1992).
[50] *Ms Francklin 1055/1.*

1819 but referring mainly to his experiences on the coast in the 1790s and 1800s. It has been largely neglected by historians of the Slave Coast although he gives detailed information for a period otherwise little documented.[51]

The Dutch West India Company was active on the western Slave Coast from the 1630s to the 1790s, particularly when there was trouble at the more established trade ports. For its activities I have made use of documents from the Dutch National Archive provided and translated by Natalie Everts, as well as accounts and documents published in English translation.[52]

The French showed intermittent interest in the western Slave Coast during the period of the slave trade. They generally practised 'floating trade' there, that is they traded directly from vessels without the intermediary services of a local agent. Nevertheless, the French archives do contain some relevant material for the period, such as the reports by Bauduchiron and Champagny in the 1770s and 1780s respectively, describing the settlements in the region and their commercial potential.[53] In the nineteenth century, French interest in the western Slave Coast revived, when the Marseille firm of Victor Régis established factories for the palm oil trade there. I have not myself been able to look at the records generated by Régis's activities in the region, but the impression given by studies of scholars who did is that there is not much for my purposes anyway.[54] There are also published accounts by French traders which refer to the western Slave Coast, most importantly that by Jean Barbot describing his visit to the region in 1682.[55]

The Danes became a major force in the trade on the western Slave Coast in the eighteenth century, especially the 1770s and 1780s, although there was some activity already in the late seventeenth century. Relevant documents

---

[51] G. A. Robertson, *Notes on Africa, particularly those parts which are situated between Cape Verde and the River Congo* (1819, repr. n.p., 2007).

[52] Adam Jones, ed., *West Africa in the Mid-Seventeenth Century: An Anonymous Dutch Manuscript* (The African Association Press, 1995); Albert van Dantzig, comp. and transl., *The Dutch and the Guinea Coast 1674–1742: A Collection of Documents from the General State Archive at The Hague* (Accra, 1978); William Bosman, *A New and Accurate Description of the Coast of Guinea: Divided into The Gold, The Slave, and The Ivory Coasts* (1705), introd. John Ralph Willis, ed. John D. Fage and R. E. Bradbury (London, 1967), 337. This English translation has been criticised by van Dantzig, whose corrections are used in this study when quoting from the account '(English Bosman and Dutch Bosman: A Comparison of Texts –V', *HiA*, 6 [1979], 265–85).

[53] ANF: C.6/26, Sr Bauduchiron, 'Mémoire pour servir à faire de nouveaux établissemens à la Côte de Guinée', 23 July 1777; ibid., Sr Bauduchiron, 'Mémoire d'Observations sur ceux faits par Sr Baud Duchiron, pour les noveaux Etablissmens à faire à la Côte de Guinée', Fontainebleu, 28 Sept. 1777; C6/27, M. de Champagny, 'Mémoire contenant des observations sur quelque points de la Côte de Guinée, visités en mil sept cent quatre vingt six par la Corvette le Pandour, et sur la possibilité d'y faire des Etablissemens'.

[54] John D. Hargreaves, *Prelude to the Partition of West Africa* (London, 1963); Bernard Schnapper, *La politique et le commerce français dans le Golfe de Guinée de 1838 à 1871* (Paris, 1961); Elisée Akpo Soumonni, 'Trade and politics in Dahomey 1841–1892, with particular reference to the house of Régis' (PhD thesis, University of Ife, Ile-Ife, June 1983).

[55] Jean Barbot, *Barbot on Guinea: the Writings of Jean Barbot on West Africa, 1678–1712*, ed. Paul Hair, Adam Jones and Robin Law, 2 vols. (London, 1992).

from the Rigsarkiv in Copenhagen have recently been published in English translation by Ole Justesen.[56] This material includes several documents relating to the establishment of a Danish lodge at Keta in 1744 by Ludewig Ferdinand Rømer. Rømer's negotiations for this lodge took him to Keta and to Little Popo, Keta's overlord in the period, and in his report to his superior at Christiansborg (Accra) he gave a first-hand account of his negotiations with Little Popo's ruler, Ashampo. A description of this visit was also given in Rømer's published account, which has been recently published in an English translation, but perpetuates some inaccuracies (including the date of his visit to Little Popo).[57] There are also a number of published accounts by traders, in English translation, the most important of which is by Paul Erdmann Isert who was active on the coast in the 1780s.[58] Also, I have made use of relevant documents cited in the studies of Sandra Greene and Ray Kea.[59]

The western Slave Coast was especially attractive to the smaller European powers in the slave trade, due to the relative absence of competition in the trade there. The Brandenburg African Company was active there in the last two decades of the seventeenth century, but little documentation of their activities has survived. Information about their activities comes mainly from references made in the records of other traders in the region. The collection of Brandenburg documents published by Adam Jones does not contain accounts of trade on the western Slave Coast, but there is nevertheless some detail (such as names of vessels and numbers of slaves shipped in them) which in combination with information from elsewhere can be pieced together to throw a little more light on the Brandenburgers' trade in the region.[60] In the early nineteenth century, American traders also visited the region and left documentation, some of which has been made available to me by George E. Brooks.[61]

Missionary records. A significant amount of documentation was also generated by the various Christian missionary societies that were active on the western Slave Coast. These relate mainly to the nineteenth century, although there are rare exceptions for the earlier period. Grand Popo was visited in 1660/61 by three of the Spanish Capuchin missionaries who for a brief period worked in Allada. However, beyond this bare fact nothing is

---

[56] Ole Justesen, ed., *Danish Sources for the History of Ghana, 1657–1754*, 2 vols. (Copenhagen, 2005). He already made documents available to me while in the process of editing them.
[57] Ludewig Ferdinand Rømer, *A Reliable Account of the Coast of Guinea (1760)*, transl. and ed. Selena Axelrod Winsnes (Oxford, 2000).
[58] Paul Erdmann Isert, *Letters on West Africa and the Slave Trade: Paul Erdmann Isert's Journey to Guinea and the Caribbean Islands in Columbia (1788)*, transl. and ed. Selena Axelrod Winsnes (Legon-Accra, 2007).
[59] Greene, *Gender*; Ray Kea, 'Akwamu-Anlo Relations, c. 1750–1813', *THSG* 10 (1969), 29–63.
[60] Adam Jones, transl. and ed., *Brandenburg Sources for West African History 1680–1700* (Wiesbaden, 1985).
[61] RIHS: Carrington Papers: Samuel Banks, Little Popo, Africa, 20 Dec. 1818.

recorded.[62] More informative are the Christianus Jacob Protten's journals (1737–41, 1757–1761).[63] During his three sojourns on the West African coast he was based at Christiansborg, but also visited Little Popo. He gives rare information about the relations between Glidji and Accra in the 1750s.

For the nineteenth century, the records of the Wesleyan Methodist Missionary Society of London and Catholic missionaries from the seminary at São Tomé and the Société des Missions Africaines of Lyon are important. The Wesleyan Methodist Missionary Society became active on the Slave Coast in the 1840s and in the 1850s established stations at Little Popo, Glidji, Agoué and Grand Popo. Its records include the correspondence of various missionaries and, most importantly, the papers of Thomas Birch Freeman, the pioneer missionary resident at Cape Coast.[64] He visited the western Slave Coast several times, notably in 1843 on his return from Dahomey and in April 1847, when he travelled overland from Badagry to Accra. His account of the former trip exists in two versions, his unpublished diary and a published version.[65] In the latter, which is usually cited by historians, small but significant changes have been made to the original account (among others, a reference to Agoué has been deleted), apparently not by Freeman himself.[66] The 1847 trip is described in his unpublished manuscript of a history of West Africa.[67]

The first Catholic priests to arrive on the western Slave Coast in the nineteenth century came from the seminary on São Tomé and were attached to the Portuguese Fort at Ouidah.[68] They visited Agoué, Little Popo and Porto Seguro from 1846 to 1860 and carried out baptisms of the children and slaves of the Afro-Brazilians. They were followed by the missionaries of the Société des Missions Africaines of Lyon, which established itself at

---

[62] See Robin Law, 'Religion, Trade and Politics on the "Slave Coast". Roman Catholic Missions in Allada and Whydah in the Seventeenth Century', *Journal of Religion in Africa*, 21/1 (1991), 42–77, p. 49.

[63] UaH: R.15.N.2 no.11, Prottens Diarium, 1737–41; R.15.N.8, 'Guinea Prottens Reise-Diarium' (1756–1761). Protten's journals are currently being translated into English and edited for publication by Adam Jones and Peter Sebald, who have made transcripts available to me.

[64] Most of the papers of the Wesleyan Methodist Missionary Society are preserved in its archives at SOAS in London. However, there are also some in the GNA: SC4, Freeman Papers.

[65] WMMS: Special Series Biographical, West Africa: Papers of Thomas Birch Freeman, 'Journal December 1842– December 1845'; Thomas Birch Freeman, *Journal of Various Visits to the Kingdoms of Ashanti, Aku, & Dahomi, in Western Africa* (1844, repr. London, 1968).

[66] Freeman's journals were prepared for publication by John Beecham, one of general secretaries of the Wesleyan Methodist Missionary Society who had no first-hand experience of the coast. See Harrison M. Wright, 'Introduction', in Freeman, *Journal*, vii-xxxix, p. xxi. It is possible that Freeman made the changes himself, with hindsight, but more likely they were made by Beecham due to stylistic or political considerations.

[67] WMMS: Special Series Biographical, West Africa: Papers of Thomas Birch Freeman, 'West Africa'.

[68] For a brief summary of the Catholic missionary activity on the Western Slave Coast, see Robert Codjo Sastre, *Le premier siège de la préfecture apostolique du Dahomey: Survol de l'histoire religieuse d'Agoué* ([Mission d'Agoué], 2000).

Ouidah in 1861 and in 1874 founded a mission at Agoué. The documentary material generated by their activities falls into two categories, baptismal registers and accounts. Parts of the former have been reproduced in the works of various authors. Most importantly, Isidore Pélofy used them to compile a register of families who had come to Agoué from Brazil, Cuba and Sierra Leone. This register, which contains almost 150 entries (that is family names), is a unique source of information about the first generation of returnees at Agoué.[69] Simone de Souza also reproduces extracts from the baptismal registers in her work about the de Souza family.[70] The priests of the Société des Missions Africaines also produced a large number of accounts, some of which were published as books.[71] One of these is the journal of Francesco Borghero (1861–65), which contains a detailed description of his visit to Agoué and Little Popo in February 1863 to mediate in the conflict between the two communities.[72] He also travelled along the lagoon to Porto Seguro, which he described.[73] A book and an article by Pierre Bouche, who between May 1874 and July 1875 directed the Société's station at Agoué, also give valuable information for the history of the western Slave Coast.[74]

Apart from these main missionary influences, other missionaries visited the western Slave Coast and made brief references to it in their published accounts. Among them was the Danish missionary H. C. Monrad, who between 1805 and 1809 was based on the Gold Coast but made a few references to Little Popo in his book.[75] The American Baptist missionary T. J. Bowen visited Agoué in 1850 and gave an unsympathetic account of it.[76]

Explorers' accounts. There is the published account of John Duncan, who between 1844 and 1847 visited the West African coast in the service of the

---

[69] Isidore Pélofy, *Histoire d'Agoué (République du Bénin)*, ed. Régina Byll-Cataria (Leipzig, 2002), 13–32: 'Liste des Brésiliens et affranchis résidant à Agoué'.
[70] Simone de Souza, *La famille de Souza du Bénin – Togo* (Cotonou, 1992).
[71] Some accounts by the Catholic missionaries appeared in the form of articles in the publications of the Société, such as *Echo des Missions Africaines* and *Annales de la Propagation de la Foi* (Sastre, *Le premier siège*, 8–10).
[72] Francesco Borghero, *Journal de Francesco Borghero, premier missionaire du Dahomey, 1861–1865*, ed. Renzo Mandirola and Yves Morel (Paris, 1997), 122–7.
[73] This trip is described in his journal and in greater detail in a letter published in the *Bulletin de la Société de Géographie* (July 1866), reprinted in (M. l'Abbé) Laffitte, *Le Dahomé, souvenirs de voyage et de mission* (Tours, 1873), xi–xxvii: 'Lettre au sujet d'une carte de la Côte des Esclaves adressée à M. d'Avezac par M. l'abbé Borghéro, missionaire', Lyon, 14 April 1866.
[74] Bouche, *Sept ans en Afrique occidentale: la Côte des Esclaves et le Dahomey* (Paris, 1885); Bouche, 'Notes sur les républiques minas de la Côte des Esclaves', ed. J. E. Bouche, *Bulletin de la Société de Géographie*, 6th series, 10 (July-Dec. 1875), 93–100.
[75] H. C. Monrad, *A Description of the Guinea Coast and its Inhabitants*, transl. S. Axelrod Winsnes (1822, Legon, 2008). According to Monrad, the Portuguese also made at least one early missionary attempt at Little Popo, which however ended when the priest was poisoned after a quarrel with the locals (163).
[76] T. J. Bowen, *Central Africa. Adventures and Missionary Labours in Several Countries in the Interior of Africa, from 1849 to 1856* (1857, repr. London, 1968).

Royal Geographical Society.[77] During his stay on the coast he visited the western Slave Coast twice, first in mid-February 1845, when he visited Agoué, Little Popo and Glidji, and second in early March 1845, when he explored the lagoons from Ouidah to Porto Seguro and from there crossed Lake Togo to go a few miles up the Haho river. Although parts of his account have been shown to be exaggerated and unreliable, it nevertheless is an important source for the history of the western Slave Coast, especially as regards the local economy.[78] As the son of a smallholder, Duncan had a good eye for details relating to agriculture, animal husbandry and local markets, which regrettably was not matched by his abilities when it came to dealing with the local people. A description of his first visit to the western Slave Coast is also given in a letter written to the Royal Geographical Society while he was still on the coast and published in the society's journal, serving as a check on the more embellished version in the book.[79]

The accounts by Thomas Edward Bowdich and Hugh Clapperton also contain some relevant information, although they did not actually visit the region. Bowdich, a servant of the English African Company on the Gold Coast, visited Asante in 1817. He also collected information about neighbouring regions, including the western Slave Coast, from Africans and Europeans.[80] Clapperton passed the western Slave Coast by ship on his way to Badagry in November 1825. His account suggests that he was off Little Popo for three or four days but there is no evidence that he visited it. In his journal, he gives of an account of Little Popo and the civil war there two years earlier, probably based on information from European traders or naval officers.[81]

Government records. The records of the various government agencies that were active on the West African Coast comprise another important body of documentary material for the nineteenth century. Most relevant are the records generated by British government agencies that were engaged in the suppression of the slave trade there, including the Royal Navy and the consular agents.[82] Among the records of the Royal Navy, two categories are

---

[77] John Duncan, *Travels in Western Africa in 1845 & 1846: Comprising a Journey from Whydah, through the Kingdom of Dahomey, to Adofoodia, in the Interior*, 2 vols. (1847, repr. London, 1968).
[78] Marion Johnson, 'News from Nowhere: Duncan and "Adofoodia"', *HiA*, 1 (1974), 55–66.
[79] John Duncan, 'Note of a Journey from Cape Coast to Whydah, on the West Coast of Africa', *Journal of the Royal Geographical Society of London*, 16 (1846), 143–153.
[80] Thomas Edward Bowdich, *Mission from Cape Coast Castle to Ashantee*, ed. W. E. F. Ward (1819, repr. London, 1966), 221–2. Unlike most explorers in the period, Bowdich collected data methodically and also described his method (161–2).
[81] Hugh Clapperton, *Hugh Clapperton into the Interior of Africa: Records of the Second Expedition, 1825–27*, ed. Jamie Bruce Lockhart and Paul E. Lovejoy (Leiden: Brill, 2005), 88–90. The source of information about Little Popo may have been John Houtson, a Liverpool trader based at Badagry who is mentioned in the text. N.B. Clapperton mistakenly dates the war to 1822.
[82] The original documents produced by the Royal Navy and the consular correspondence are preserved in the TNA in the FO84, FO2 and ADM series. A large number of them have been published, although sometimes in abridged form (which is not always indicated), in the *PP*, Slave

especially informative: first, the documents relating to cases of ships that had been arrested on suspicion of being engaged in the slave trade and subsequently had been adjudged by the Mixed Commission's Courts at Sierra Leone, Luanda or St Helena and second, the correspondence of Royal Navy officers, which includes accounts of visits to the coastal settlements in the region, reports of captures of slave ships and annual reports on the state of the trade. Among these, arguably the most important documents for developments on the western Slave Coast are the reports from the naval officer T. G. Forbes, who in 1852 concluded the anti-slave trade treaties with the chiefs in the region, and from the naval officers who attempted to negotiate peace treaties in the conflict between Agoué and Little Popo in 1862 and 1864.[83] Another source of information is Ferdinand Struvé's report of his residence at Little Popo from December 1849 to November 1850. Although a civilian not a naval officer, he was sent out by the Admiralty to survey the lagoons on the western Slave Coast. This failed for several reasons, including illness and lack of canoemen, but his report gives descriptions of trips to Porto Seguro and Lake Togo and throws light on the political situation at Little Popo.[84] None of these documents has previously been used by historians of the region.

In 1849 and 1851–2 a British Vice-Consul for the kingdom of Dahomey resided at Ouidah, and subsequently there was a British Consul for the Bight of Benin who was based at Lagos. Their correspondence gives information concerning the illegal slave trade and the Afro-Brazilians.[85]

Official records from the British settlements on the Gold Coast and at Sierra Leone also contain some relevant material for nineteenth-century developments on the western Slave Coast. As regards the former, this is because prior to the establishment of the consulate at Ouidah in 1849, British relations with the local authorities on the Slave Coast were handled from Cape Coast. Most important in this group is the body of documents relating to the fire at Thomas Hutton's factory at Agoué in 1843, which gives an abundance of detail about the political situation at Agoué in the

---

(cont.) Trade series, reprinted by the Irish Universities Press. They are now also available online: http://parlipapers.chadwyck.co.uk/marketing/index.jsp.
[83] TNA: FO84/893, incls. in Hamilton, [London] 10 April 1852: T. G. Forbes, HMS 'Philomel', at Whydah, 5 Feb. 1852; 'Schedule of Treaties concluded between 23 Jan. and 2 Feb. 1852'. For the 1862 agreements, see TNA: FO84/1184, incls. in Admiralty, [London], 15 April 1862; *PP* Slave Trade 1862, Class A, incls. in no. 91, Commodore Edmonstone, 'Arrogant', Fernando Po, 3 March 1862. For the 1864 agreements, see TNA: ADM123/66, incls. in no.2, Commodore A. P. Eardley Wilmot, 'Rattlesnake', off Whydah, 11 July 1864; (another copy:) CO96/66, incls. in Hammond, [London] 20 Sept. 1864; *PP*, Slave Trade 1864, Class A, incls. in no.128, Commodore A.P.E. Wilmot, 'Rattlesnake', off Whydah, 11 July 1864.
[84] UKHO: OD 9A, Ferdinand Struvé, 'Report on the results obtained by the expedition [...] in the years 1849 and 1850' (5 Oct. 1850); L7791, Struvé, 'West Coast of Africa: Plan of the Coastal Lagoon between Whydah and Cape St. Paul, Bight of Benin, surveyed in the years 1849 and 1850'.
[85] The papers of the Vice-Consul have recently been published: Louis Fraser, *Dahomey and the Ending of the Trans-Atlantic Slave Trade: The Journals and Correspondence of Vice-Consul Louis Fraser, 1851–1852*, ed. Robin Law (Oxford, 2012).

period.[86] The Sierra Leone series is interesting for the records relating to the trial of the British trader John Marman in 1852 for slave dealing.[87] Marman, who was based at Accra, had been an important palm oil trader on the western Slave Coast with factories at various places, including Little Popo. Particularly interesting is the detailed testimony by his local agent, George Latty Lawson, which is included in these records and allows a rare insight into the local operation of the trade, both in palm oil as well as in slaves. Further, the report from the Parliamentary Select Committees of 1842 gives detailed information concerning Marman's early activities at Little Popo and the commercial and political situation there more generally.[88]

Official records relating to the colonial partition of the region are also relevant for the pre-colonial period.[89] Of particular interest is W. T. G. Lawson's report of his survey of the western Slave Coast in 1879, which comprises the first detailed description of the physical characteristics and the settlements in the region, complete with a map.[90]

Apart from these official records, there are published accounts by individuals engaged in government activities which relate to the western Slave Coast. The most important – and most frequently cited – English-language account is that by the naval officer Frederick E. Forbes, who visited Agoué and Little Popo in March 1850.[91] Less well known but equally

---

[86] The records relating the British Gold Coast settlements (from 1843) are preserved in the TNA, in the CO96 series. For the correspondence relating to the fire at Hutton's Agoué factory, see TNA: CO96/2, W.B. Hutton & Sons, [London], 20 Dec. 1843 (encls.); CO96/4, no.8, Gov. Hill, Cape Coast Castle, 21 March 1844 (incls.), CO96/4, no.31, Gov. Hill, Cape Coast Castle, 1 June 1844 (incls.); CO96/5, Canning, [London] 13 Jan. 1844 (incls.).

[87] The records relating to Sierra Leone are preserved the CO267 series in the TNA. For documentation of the Marman trial, see TNA: CO267/228, incls. in Gov. Macdonald, Sierra Leone, 21 April 1852: 'Copy of depositions taken before the Police Magistrate, Freetown, Sierra Leone, 10 March 1852'; 'Chief Justice's notes taken at the trial of Marman indicted for Slave dealing'. For the documents generated by the preliminary investigation of Marman, at Accra, see CO96/23, incl. in Stephen J. Hill, Cape Coast Castle, 24 Nov. 1851: B. Cruickshank, Cape Coast Castle, 24 Nov. 1851 (with inclosures). See Silke Strickrodt, 'British Abolitionist Policy on the Ground in West Africa in the Mid-Nineteenth Century', *The Changing Worlds of Atlantic Africa: Essays in Honour of Robin Law*, ed. Toyin Falola and Matt D. Childs (Durham, NC, 2009), 183–200.

[88] See PP, Colonies Africa 1842, i, Report of the Select Committee on the West Coast of Africa.

[89] For British records, see TNA: PRO.30/29.269, Confidential 4955, 4994, 5020. See also Yves Marguerat, ed., *La naissance du Togo selon les documents de l'époque; premier periode: l'ombre de l'Angleterre* (Lomé, 1993). Relevant French and German records are preserved in the national archives in Benin and Togo, see bibliography. Some French documents have been published in *Mémoires du Bénin*, e.g. 'Rapport de Monsieur Pornain Lieutenant de vaisseau, Adjudant du Commandant Superieur sur sa mission aux Popos pour y etablir le protectorat de la France' [April 1885], *Mémoires du Bénin*, 1 (1993), 45–67.

[90] GNA: ADM 1/2/361, incl. in no. 26: W.T. G. Lawson, Lagos 22 Aug. 1879: 'Report descriptive of the towns, lagoons, rivers &c, lying between the Volta and Peida Rivers'; TNA: CO700/ Gold Coast13: W.T.G. Lawson, 'Sketch Map of the Towns, Lagoons, Rivers, &c., of the Countries lying between the Volta and Peida Rivers, April 1879'.

[91] Frederick E. Forbes, *Dahomey and the Dahomans, being the Journal of two Missions to the Kingdom of the King of Dahomey and Residence at his Capital in the Years 1849 and 1850*, 2 vols. (1851, repr. London, 1966), i, 96–130.

important are the accounts by German officials who visited the region in the 1880s and 1890s. The first of these was Hugo Zöller, a journalist who in late 1884 visited the West African coast as an agent for the German government.[92] He travelled from Lomé (Bé Beach) via Grand Popo to Ouidah, and went into the interior as far as to Agome, on the western bank of the Haho opposite Hahoté. He was followed by Ernst Henrici, who in August and September 1887 visited the stretch of coast between Baguida and Little Popo, that is the new German Togo protectorate, and the immediate hinterland.[93] In 1894 Heinrich Klose visited the places from Lomé to Little Popo and travelled along the lagoon and up the Haho river before turning to the interior.[94] The accounts of these travellers contain a wealth of detail especially as regards the lie of the land, the lagoons, and the local economy and trade.

AFRICAN SOURCES

The African or 'internal' sources fall into three broad categories: first, documents produced from within the African and Afro-Brazilian commercial community, such as business papers and wills; secondly, oral traditions, and thirdly, local and family histories. In fact, however, the latter two categories often overlap because traditions are usually preserved in the local and family histories.

Documents from African and Afro-Brazilian traders began to appear in the nineteenth century with the spread of literacy. A major source is the business correspondence of the Lawson family of Little Popo/Aného, part of which has been preserved, in English, in the 'GLL' and has recently been published.[95] The first part comprises commercial correspondence mainly from 1843 to 1853, written by or to George Lawson, a prominent trader and chief at Little Popo/Aného, and his son, George Latty Lawson (who as noted above acted as an agent for John Marman). These letters throw light on the day-to-day business of palm-oil traders, the operation of the trade and the trade networks on the coast and are particularly valuable for the purposes of this study.

Other important 'internal' documents include the wills of Joaquim

---

[92] Hugo Zöller, *Das Togoland und die Sklavenküste* (Berlin and Stuttgart, 1885). See also Zöller, *Als Jurnalist* [sic] *und Forscher in Deutschlands großer Kolonialzeit* (Leipzig, 1930), 128–58.
[93] Ernst Henrici, *Das Deutsche Togogebiet und meine Afrikareise 1887* (Leipzig, 1888).
[94] Heinrich Klose, *Togo unter deutscher Flagge* (Berlin, 1899).
[95] Adam Jones and Peter Sebald, eds, *An African Family Archive: The Lawsons of Little Popo/Aneho (Togo), 1841–1938* (Oxford, 2005). For descriptions, see Adam Jones, 'Little Popo and Agoué at the End of the Atlantic Slave Trade: Glimpses from the Lawson Correspondence and Other Sources', *Ports of the Slave Trade*, ed. Law/ Strickrodt, 122–34; Peter Sebald, '7,5 Kilogramm westafrikanische Korrespondenz, 1843–1887: Der Foliant der Königsfamilie Lawson, Aneho, Togo,' *Sprachkulturelle und historische Forschungen in Afrika; Beiträge zum 11. Afrikanistentag in Köln 1994* (Köln, 1995), 267–81.

d'Almeida (d. 1857) and Antonio d'Almeida (d. 1890), both of whom were liberated slaves who settled at Agoué and Ouidah.[96] The will of the former, which was made at Bahia in 1844 shortly before he finally returned to Africa, throws light on his career up to this point but disappointingly gives little information about his activities on the West African coast. The will of Antonio d'Almeida was written at Ouidah in 1864 and is more informative as regards his life at Agoué and Ouidah. The business correspondence of José Francisco dos Santos, part of which has survived and was published in a French translation by Pierre Verger, is another valuable source.[97] Dos Santos was a Brazilian slave trader who was based at Ouidah but in the 1840s extended his activities to the western Slave Coast. His correspondence includes three letters written by him at Agoué (November 1844) and five letters at Little Popo (August 1847 and December 1847), apart from a number of letters that were written elsewhere but refer to his affairs at these places.

Oral traditions also give information about the history of the societies in the region, from an internal perspective. Some of these are preserved in the accounts of European visitors, such as those by Rømer, Bouche and Henrici.[98] A major source for them, which has hitherto been neglected because it is in German, is Diedrich Westermann's ethnographic study of the Ge of Little Popo.[99] Others, that is the majority, are preserved or rather reworked in the local and family histories, which were mainly written in the early colonial period. A number have been published, such as Agbanon II's *Histoire du Petit-Popo et du royaume guin* (1934), while others exist in manuscript form.[100] As has been discussed by others, these local histories present the historian with complex problems and need to be used with caution. Rather than comprising collections of oral traditions in written form, they are results of an attempt 'to create something completely new out of the existing oral material (and sometimes out of written sources)'.[101]

---

[96] The wills of Joaquim d'Almeida and Antonio d'Almeida as well as that of their former master, Manoel Joaquim d'Almeida, are published in Pierre Verger, *Os libertos: Sete caminhos na liberdade de escravos da Bahia no século XIX* (São Paulo, 1992), 114–24. For a French translation of Joaquim d'Almeida's will, see Verger, *Flux et reflux*, 540–1.
[97] Pierre Verger, *Les afro-américains* (Dakar, 1952), 53–100.
[98] Rømer, *Reliable Account*, 118; Bouche, *Sept ans*, 305; Ernst Henrici, *Lehrbuch der Ephe-Sprache [Ewe]. Anlo-, Anecho- und Dahome-Mundart mit Glossar und einer Karte der Sklavenküste* (Stuttgart & Berlin, 1891), 4.
[99] Diedrich Westermann, *Die Glidyi-Ewe in Togo: Züge aus ihrem Gesellschaftsleben* (supplement to *Mitteilungen des Seminars für orientalische Sprachen an der Universität Berlin* 38, 1935). See also Westermann, 'Kinderheitserinnerungen des Togonegers Bonifatius Foli', *Mitteilungen des Seminars für orientalische Sprachen zu Berlin. Dritte Abteilung: Afrikanische Sprachen,* 34 (1931), 1–69.
[100] See bibliography under 'Local and family histories'. The unpublished manuscripts have been made available to me by Nicoué Lodjou Gayibor.
[101] Adam Jones, *Zur Quellenproblematik der Geschichte Westafrikas 1450–1900* (Frankfurt, 1990), 28 (my translation). See also N. L. Gayibor, ed., *Les traditions historiques du Bas-Togo* (Niamey, 1992), pp. 6–11: 'Introduction'.

In the process of creation, contradictory traditions were harmonised for the sake of a coherent (hi-)story and gaps were filled with information from other texts, sometimes without acknowledgement of the source. Further, these works were written for a particular purpose, usually the legitimation of claims to political authority, which also influences the text. Nevertheless, they do give important information which sometimes fleshes out the evidence from the contemporary written sources.

The major challenge in the reconstruction of the history of the region is the discontinuity and uneven nature of the source material. On the one hand, there are long periods which are hardly documented, while, on the other, there are brief periods for which there is an abundance of detail. This influences the way in which this study is organised.

CHAPTER OUTLINES

Chapter 1 provides the setting, dealing with the physical environment, the first settlers of the region and their local economy and trade before the arrival of the Europeans and the area's development in connection with Afro-European trade. Due to the lack of contemporary sources for the earlier period, this chapter is largely extrapolated from evidence from the seventeenth to the nineteenth century, and mainly the latter. I occasionally use 'informed speculation', inferring what would most likely have been the case in the region through examining similar communities elsewhere in West Africa that are better documented. Emphasis is placed on the central importance of the lagoon for the local economy of the region, which continued in the period of the Afro-European trade.

Chapter 2 places the region in the context of the wider Atlantic world. It discusses the immigration of Gold Coast people in the seventeenth century, first Akan-speaking canoemen and traders and then Ga and Adangme refugees, and the beginning of Afro-European trade on the western Slave Coast. The last part of the chapter comprises a detailed discussion of political developments and trade in the region during the last two decades of the seventeenth century, for which there is a relative abundance of detailed documentation.

Chapter 3 deals with the period from 1702 to 1772, which is again unevenly documented. Documentation is generally poor for the first half of the period, although there are exceptions, particularly a detailed description of the region by a European visitor in 1717. To make the best use of this, I use it as a 'snapshot', giving extensive quotes and a detailed discussion. Documentation is more abundant for the rule of the warrior king Ashampo of Little Popo (c.1737–c.1767), which was characterised by the military struggle for dominance with the Adangme in the Anlo region to the west and Dahomey to the east. A major issue discussed here is the question of the relationship between war and the Atlantic slave trade, by examining Ashampo's success as a warrior and a trader.

Chapter 4 is concerned with the period between the establishment of a Danish lodge at Little Popo in 1772 and the abolition of the slave trade. This period is exceptionally well documented, reflecting the increasing interest of European traders in the region. The chapter is divided into three parts: political developments in the region, the development of Afro-European trade and a discussion of political changes within the coastal settlement of Little Popo, which can be seen as a prelude to the events discussed in Chapter 5.

Chapters 5 and 6 are devoted to the nineteenth century. Chapter 5 deals with political developments, preceding a discussion of economic and commercial developments in Chapter 6. This order is adopted not because I think it reflects cause and effect – indeed, the argument is rather that trade and the efforts to share its profits were the driving forces which led to political transformations – but because it facilitates the exposition of what happened. The first half of the nineteenth century was a period of important political developments in the region, which, among other things, led to the foundation of the coastal trading settlements of Agoué and Porto Seguro. From the 1840s the period is well-documented, allowing a detailed discussion of the political situation, especially at Little Popo and Agoué. Chapter 5 closes with a reconstruction of the war between Agoué and Little Popo in the 1860s. This has not been fully studied before and is commonly held to have ended in 1863, although in fact it did continue some years thereafter. Chapter 6 deals with the transition from the slave trade to the so-called 'legitimate' commerce in agricultural produce. It examines Little Popo's prominent role in the illegal slave trade, which it owed to the lagoon connection with Ouidah, and the region's pioneering role in the palm oil trade, which has been overlooked in previous studies dealing with the transition.

The epilogue deals, concisely, with the colonial partition and its consequences for communities in the region. Drawing mainly on earlier studies, the main question I am concerned with here is whether the partition can be seen as arising from earlier history, especially the breakdown of political and commercial order in coastal towns, or whether it derived from external pressures.

Note on terminology and spelling

Some of the communities on the western Slave Coast used different names in the past from those current today. There are also many different spellings, reflecting the variety of languages spoken by the European traders as well as idiosyncrasies and the change of spelling conventions over time. Generally, this study uses the names that were current in the period, e.g. Little Popo (rather than Aného) and Porto Seguro (rather than Agbodrafo). However, in cases where the names have remained the same today, the modern spelling (or language version) is preferred, e.g. Grand Popo (rather than Great Popo, for the coastal settlement and the state) and Ouidah (rather than Whydah).

A special case is the ethnonym used to refer to the people of the kingdom of Little Popo descending from the various groups of Gold Coast immigrants. In scholarly literature, the term 'Mina' is sometimes used, reflecting current local usage when the people speak French (the official language of Togo and Bénin). The term derives from the Gold Coast town of Elmina and originally referred specifically to immigrants from there but its meaning has been extended to include the descendants of all Gold Coast settlers.[102] The term used in this study, 'Ge', is the indigenous name and a variant of 'Ga', the indigenous name of Accra (see Chapter 2). Due to the continuing links between the Ga immigrants on the western Slave Coast and their homeland, Accra (as discussed in Chapter 2), it is difficult to establish when the immigrants became 'Ge'. Therefore, I have chosen a pragmatic approach and call them 'Ge' from Chapter 3.

The case of individual and family names is even more complex, as there are not only many different spellings but African traders sometimes used different names in different spheres, e.g. in their local community and in their interactions with Europeans. Furthermore, they are sometimes given different names in retrospective family and local histories.[103] In this study, I generally use the name and the spelling as it first appears in the contemporary sources.

Given the paucity of contemporary information on indigenous titles, it is not easy to decide how to refer to rulers and office holders. For example, recent Hula rulers in Agbanaken have used the title 'Hulaholu', whilst Ge rulers in Glidji have used 'Fio'; yet neither designation is documented before the twentieth century.[104] In nineteenth-century sources rulers are usually referred to, both by Europeans and by Africans in their correspondence with Europeans, as 'king' and subordinate office holders as 'caboceer' or 'chief'. To avoid anachronism, I use these terms. In cases where information on indigenous titles exists, this is discussed (see index s. v. 'titles').

---

[102] See Robin Law, 'Ethnicities of Enslaved Africans in the Diaspora: On the Meanings of "Mina" (Again)', *HiA*, 32 (2005), 247–67, pp.248–56.
[103] For a detailed discussion of the complex Ge system of naming, see Westermann, *Die Glidyi-Ewe*, 18–27.
[104] For 'Hulahulo', see Iroko, *Les hula*, 106; for 'Fio', see Westermann, *Die Glidyi-Ewe*, 180.

1

The regional setting

The western Slave Coast can be regarded as a sub-region of the Slave Coast, the latter being conventionally defined as comprising the coastal area between the Volta river in the west and the Lagos channel in the east.[1] The term 'Slave Coast' was being used by the seventeenth century. The Slave Coast was mainly defined externally, in terms of the European activities affecting it, as a source of enslaved Africans for shipment to the Americas.[2] It has been argued, however, that there were also internal characteristics that justified its treatment as a unit. In terms of physical geography, two features stand out: the Benin (or Dahomey) Gap, a stretch of savannah (rather than tropical forest) which affected the microclimate, and a system of lagoons which extended along almost the whole of the coast, connecting the various places and serving as an integrating factor. Also, there was a degree of cultural and linguistic unity, as the Slave Coast was settled mainly by Gbe-speaking peoples who trace their origins to Tado, with the exception of the Yoruba in the extreme east and northeast.[3]

The western Slave Coast was an integral part of the Slave Coast, sharing all the characteristics mentioned above. There were also however features that set it apart, justifying its treatment as a distinct entity. First, while the eastern part of the Slave Coast enjoyed easy communication with the far interior due to the relative openness of the country, putting it at the mercy of Oyo's invasions in the late seventeenth and eighteenth centuries but also enabling the establishment of trade connections that were crucial for regular and abundant supplies of enslaved Africans for the trade with Europeans, the

---

[1] The boundaries of the Slave Coast are sometimes disputed. See Law, *Slave Coast*, 14; A. Félix Iroko, 'La Côte des Esclaves: Un espace regional pour une histoire internationale', *Toponomie historique et glossonymes actuels de l'ancienne Côte des Esclaves (XVe-XIXe s.)*, ed. N. L. Gayibor (Lomé, 1990), 43–54.
[2] Law, *Slave Coast*, 13–14.
[3] Ibid., 19–32.

importance of the hinterland of the western Slave Coast was limited by the Togo-Atacora mountain ranges, restricting communication and exchange with the far interior.[4] Second (and perhaps linked with the first point), unlike the eastern Slave Coast, which from the 1720s was controlled by the kingdom of Dahomey, there was no single large state that dominated the western Slave Coast. Third, the western Slave Coast was affected by the immigration and settlement of various groups of Gold Coast people, notably Akan-speaking canoemen, who were engaged in the trade, and Ga and Adangme refugees, whose kingdoms of Accra and Ladoku, on the eastern Gold Coast, had been conquered by the inland power of Akwamu in the 1680s and 1690s (see Chapter 2). This resulted in the foundation of the Ge kingdom at Little Popo by Ga immigrants. However, these settlers remained in contact with their homelands on the Gold Coast through family ties, political alliances and ritual links, and regular visits and exchanges took place throughout the period of the Atlantic slave trade (see Chapters 2–6). These communities should be thought of as leading translocal existences, living on the western Slave Coast but partaking in the political, economic, social and cultural life of the Gold Coast. This was a real factor in the development of Afro-European trade on the western Slave Coast as the European traders learnt, for example, that their actions at Accra had repercussions for their business at Little Popo and Keta. Therefore, it can be argued that the western Slave Coast was an intermediate region during the Atlantic slave trade, being as much part of the Gold Coast as of the Slave Coast.

The natural environment

The western Slave Coast forms part of the portion of the West African coast that is affected by the 'Benin Gap'. This is a gap in the belt of tropical forest, stretching along the West African coast from Accra (in Ghana) in the west to Porto Novo (in Bénin) in the east, with significant consequences for the climate and vegetation of the region. It is a 'dry corridor' where Sudanic climatic influences reached the coast, resulting in milder rainy seasons and longer and more rigorous dry seasons than in the neighbouring forest zones.[5] There are two rainy seasons, the great

---

[4] For Oyo's activities on the Slave Coast, see *ibid.*, 236–38, 281–82, 287–95, 318–24.
[5] See Hopkins, *Economic History*, 11; Law, *The Slave Coast*, 19; Dominique Juhé-Beaulaton, 'History of a controversy between social sciences: The origin of the Dahomey Gap (Togo-Benin) or the complementary of history and archaeology', unpublished paper (conference 'Common Ground, Different Meanings: Archaeology, History, and the Interpretation of the African Past', Syracuse University, 8–10 Oct. 2009); W. B. Morgan and J. C. Pugh, *West Africa* (London, 1969), 216–7; Karl Polanyi with Abraham Rotstein, *Dahomey and the Slave Trade: An Analysis of an Archaic Economy* (Seattle and London, 1966), 5–8, 116–7; Jaques Richard-Molard, *Afrique Occidentale Française* (Paris, 1949), 18–9.

rains which last from about mid-March to mid-July and the little rains which last from about September to October.[6] This climate is suitable both for root crops (such as cassava and yams) and cereals, which need moderate annual rainfall, and for tree crops (such as oil palms), which prefer higher rainfall.[7]

It has been argued that the Benin Gap might be a result of another feature of this region, the Togo-Atacora mountain ranges, which deflect the dry harmattan winds from the interior.[8] These ranges are a belt of highland stretching from the mouth of the Densu river on the Gold Coast (i.e. to the west of the Volta river), where they are called the Akuapem hills, in a northeasterly direction towards the Niger river, crossing part of the hinterland of the western Slave Coast. They comprise a series of parallel ridges and steep valleys, rising to a maximum height of 1,025 metres at Mount Agou. They had an indirect consequence for the economic life on the western Slave Coast as they formed an obstacle to communication between the coast and the interior. In effect, they limited the hinterland to the west, with trade routes running along their back rather than across them, except where the Volta cuts through them. Further, they offered protection and hiding places to local people and other refugees, as illustrated by the case of a number of Adangme refugees who settled at Mount Agou in the late seventeenth and early eighteenth centuries.[9]

To the mariner, the western Slave Coast, like the Slave Coast in general, presented problems.[10] It lacked natural harbours or navigable openings of rivers (apart from the Lagos channel on the eastern limits of the Slave Coast) and, unlike the Gold Coast to the west, consisted entirely of sandy beaches. Sand bars ran parallel to the coast and there were strong easterly currents and heavy surf. The easterly currents prevailed especially in the period between April and September, which overlapped with the time when the surf was particularly violent, from April to July.[11] The only exception was

---

[6] Adoté Blivi, 'Vulnerabilité de la côte togolais à l'elevation du niveau marin: une analyse de prévision et d'impact', *Le tricentenaire d'Aného*, ed. Gayibor, vol. 2, 643–60, p. 644. Cf. Ellis, *The Ewe-Speaking Peoples of the Slave Coast of West Africa* (Chicago, 1965), 5; R. Grivot, 'La pêche chez les Pedah du lac Ahémé', *BIFAN*, 11 (1949), 85; Henrici, *Das Deutsche Togogebiet*, 118; Zöller, *Das Togoland*, 214.
[7] R. J. Harrison Church, *West Africa: A Study of the Environment and of Man's Use of It* (London, 1974), 97, 99–117; Morgan/ Pugh, *West Africa*, 73, 75, 92–3, 110, 112.
[8] See Morgan/ Pugh, *West Africa*, 216–7, 276–7; Jakob Spieth, *Die Ewe-Stämme: Material zur Kunde des Ewe-Volkes in Deutsch-Togo* (Berlin, 1906), 16, 19–20.
[9] A. R. Biørn, 'Biørns beretning 1788 om de Danske Forter og Negerier', *Archiv for Statistik, Politik og Huusholdnings-Videnskaber, et Hefteskrivt*, ed. Friderik Thaarup, vol. iii (Copenhagen, 1797–98), 193–231, p. 224.
[10] See Law, 'Between the Sea', 210–7.
[11] John Adams, *Remarks on the Country extending from Cape Palmas to the River Congo* (London, 1823), 168; Edward Bold, *The Merchants' and Mariners' African Guide: The Coast, Bays, Harbours and Adjacent Islands of West Africa* (London, 1822), 60; Bosman, *New and Accurate Description*, 337; van Dantzig, 'English Bosman', 276.

the harmattan season, which occurred in January and February and lasted for about two or three weeks, when a dry wind blew from a north-easterly direction and currents went from east to west.[12]

These difficult conditions had repercussions for the local economy as well as for the development of Afro-European trade in the region. For the local people they served as a deterrent from engaging in maritime navigation and sea-fishing, especially as the calm waters of the coastal lagoons and rivers abounded with fish.[13] For European traders the lack of natural harbours meant that their vessels were unable to approach the coast but had to stand some distance offshore. Since European boats were unable to cross the surf and the local people did not engage in maritime navigation, Europeans had to bring Gold Coast canoemen and canoes into the region in order to have them ferry people and goods from ship to shore and back. Some of these Gold Coast canoemen came to stay in the region and founded their own settlements (see Chapter 2). Further, outside the harmattan season European vessels found it difficult to sail from east to west due to the prevailing currents and winds, which made them further reliant on the Gold Coast canoemen for communication between the Slave Coast and the Gold Coast (although the canoemen also preferred to make the return trip to the Gold Coast in the harmattan season). This inability to sail against the current shaped the way in which Afro-European trade was operated on the coast. From the Gold Coast, European vessels would go eastwards along the coast, trading at the various ports. Having finished their trade, they proceeded to the Gabon area, where they caught the 'trade winds' and sailed through the open sea to the Americas, Europe or to return to the Gold Coast, which they hit at its western limit.[14]

The violent sea also shaped the region itself. Most importantly, the sand that was constantly washed up by the sea formed dunes which the rivers were unable to penetrate, resulting in the formation of coastal lagoons.[15] Since the dunes, like the sea current, run in a north-easterly direction, the rivers were deflected eastward, leaving sediment on their western banks. This resulted in the creation of the sandspit separating the lagoons from the sea, which became the location of the coastal settlements where the Afro-European trade took place: Grand Popo, Little Popo (present-day Aneho), Agoué and Porto Seguro (present-day Agbodrafo). To the north of the lagoon stretches a low plateau of loams and clay sands, rising gently

[12] Adams, *Remarks*, 169; Ellis, *Ewe-Speaking Peoples*, 5; UKHO: OD8, H. M. Denham, 'Remarks and Sailing Directions for the Bight of Benin, West Coast of Africa […] 1846', 31, 37.
[13] Law, 'Between the Sea', pp. 212–13.
[14] See e.g. Erick Tilleman, *En kort og enfoldig Beretning om det landskab Guinea og dets beskaffenhed (1697). A Short and Simple Account Account of the Country of Guinea*, ed. Selena Axelrod Winsnes (African Studies Program, University of Wisconsin-Madison, 1994), 44.
[15] See Klose, *Togo*, 77–8.

32 • *The regional setting*

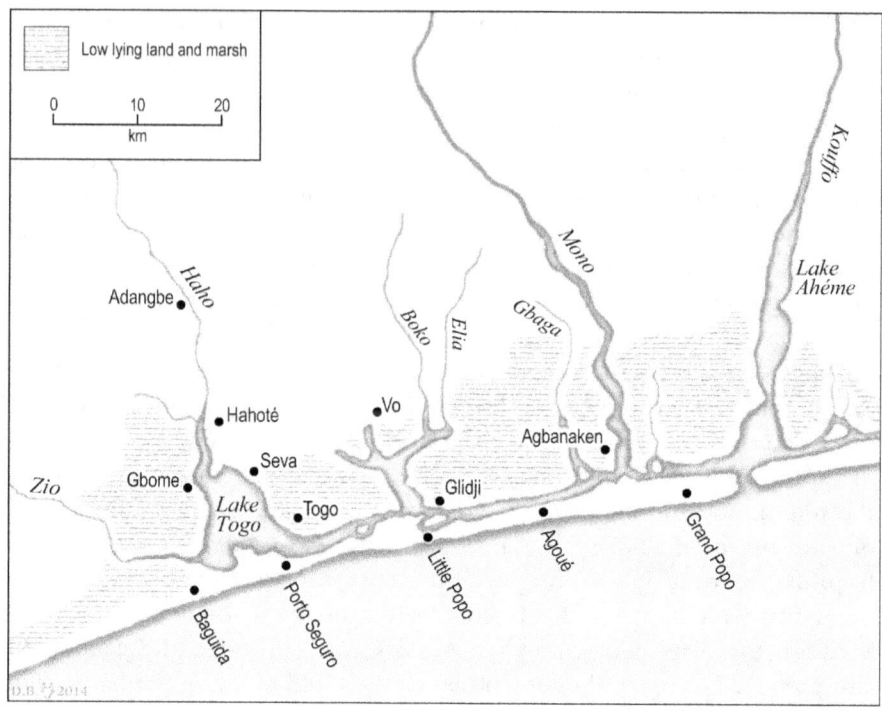

Map 3 The lagoon system

northwards for some 30–40 miles/48–64 km, then passing into the plains of the interior.[16]

The lagoons generally consist of channels of varying width running more or less parallel to the coast, but on the western Slave Coast they expand into large bodies of water in three places.[17] At the western end of the navigable lagoon system, to the north of Porto Seguro, is Lake Togo, the indigenous name of which is Haco or Haho lagoon.[18] It is fed from the southwest by the Zio river, rising north of Kpalime in the plateau of Dayes, and from the north by the Haho. The Aného and Zowla lagoons expand north of Little Popo, the Zowla lagoon being fed by the Boko and Elia rivers. Finally, at

---

[16] Harrison Church, *West Africa*, 400–01, 409; Morgan and Pugh, *West Africa*, 297.
[17] For a detailed description of the lagoons and rivers from the late nineteenth century, see GNA: ADM 1/2/361, incl. in no. 26: Lawson, 'Report' (1879); TNA: CO700/ GoldCoast13: Lawson, 'Sketch Map' (1879); Zöller, *Das Togoland*, 99–127; Klose, *Togo*, 77–107.
[18] See Borghero's map from 1865 (reproduced in Laffitte, *Le Dahomé*; Newbury, *Western Slave Coast*, fig. 4); Bouche, *Sept ans*, 306; Zöller, *Das Togoland*, 104. British charts from the nineteenth century call it 'Avon waters', after the naval vessel that carried out the coastal survey of 1846. This name was also used in W. T. G. Lawson's report, besides 'Pomeh' or 'Apomeh Waters', deriving from the market town Gbome on its north-western shore (GNA: ADM 1/2/361, incl. in no. 26: Lawson, 'Report' (1879); TNA: CO700/ GoldCoast13: Lawson, 'Sketch Map' (1879). The modern name was coined by Zöller and his companions, who explored the lagoon in 1885, and derives from the town which at this time was the capital of the new German protectorate (*Das Togoland*, 119).

the eastern extremity of the western Slave Coast, Lake Ahéme, which is fed from the north by the Kouffo river, is to be found.[19] The largest river in the region is the Mono, which has its source some 218 miles/ 350km in the interior, north of Tchamba, and joins the lagoon at Agbanaken point just south of Agbanaken. A large number of small rivers feed the lagoon, especially in the region between the Gbaga river and Lake Ahéme, comprising the Hula heartland. The superabundance of water in this region is reflected in its name on early Portuguese maps, 'Terra Anegada', meaning 'drowned land'.[20] W.T.G. Lawson, who in 1879 carried out the first systematic survey of the region between the Volta and Lake Ahéme, described it as 'a very swampy Country' which was 'so much intersected by numerous creeks and rivulets some drying up in the dry season and others perennial that the whole of it might be described as one mass of Islands.'[21]

These lagoons offset the difficulties presented by the sea to some extent. To the local population, they offered rich fishing and saltmaking grounds, and a means of transport, communication and defence against invaders. For the Europeans they also played an important role. As will be discussed in greater detail later, Afro-European trade in the region was dependent on the lagoons for the transport of goods and slaves. This became especially important in the period of the illegal slave trade in the nineteenth century, when slaves were ferried along the lagoon from Ouidah to be embarked from settlements on the western Slave Coast (see Chapter 7). Further, Europeans were reliant on the lagoons for communication between the central ports on the Slave Coast and their headquarters on the Gold Coast. Canoes were sent from the latter places along the lagoon to Little Popo, where they were put to sea and continued their voyage along the shore to the Gold Coast (see Chapter 2).

The extent of the navigable lagoon system is an important question, since it has been argued that Little Popo's initial importance was due to its position towards the western end of the navigable lagoon system.[22] In recent times there has been an interruption of the lagoon system between the Keta lagoon and Lake Togo, but the question is whether this already existed in the earlier period or whether it is the result of recent changes. According to Lawson's report, Baguida was the westernmost place to have access to water communication to the east, via Lake Togo and the Zio river.[23] This is

---

[19] Lawson calls Lake Ahéme 'Pedah/ Peida Waters' and its outlet into the lagoon 'Pedah River', derived from the name of Hueda people ('Pedah' in the local dialect) who settled there after the Dahomian conquest of their kingdom in 1727 (GNA: ADM 1/2/361, incl. in no. 26: Lawson, 'Report' [1879], 56, 60–1).
[20] Barbot, *Barbot*, ii, 621, 626–7, n. 9. On Barbot's map the country is described as 'flat and swampy' ('Pais Plat & Marêcageux').
[21] GNA: ADM 1/2/361, incl. in no. 26: Lawson, 'Report' (1879), 72, 63. See also Isert, *Letters*, 127: 'morass-like ground'.
[22] Law, 'Between the Sea', 214.
[23] GNA: ADM 1/2/361, incl. in no. 26: Lawson, 'Report' (1879), 26; TNA: CO700/ GoldCoast13: Lawson, 'Sketch Map' (1879).

corroborated by the accounts of European observers from the 1880s and 1890s.[24] As regards the limits of the Keta lagoon, Lawson stated that it was 'navigable for boats and large canoes as far as Brokosu [= Blekesu] and for small canoes as far as Amutinu. In the rains canoes ascend to Adafio [= Adafia] where it terminates in a swamp which extends almost to Denu.'[25] Accounts for the period before the 1870s offer conflicting evidence. On the one hand, some European accounts and maps from the eighteenth and early nineteenth century show the lagoon system as continuous from the Lagos channel to the Volta. John M'Leod, who visited the coast in 1803, claimed that from Cape St Paul (near Woe, south-west of Keta) to Cape Formosa (east of Benin) 'an easy communication is afforded by means of lakes and rivers, which run in a direction nearly parallel to the coast'.[26] This is corroborated by the map accompanying Robert Norris's account of 1789.[27] The reliability of this information is questionable, however, because it probably did not derive from first-hand information. Nevertheless, it is supported by local traditions which recall the former existence of an uninterrupted lagoon route along the Slave Coast. According to Lieutenant Lind, a Danish official who in the 1820s explored the mouth and lower course of the Volta, the Keta ('Guitta') channel, which ran long the coast from the river to Keta and then turned northeast, was 'said earlier on to have been connected with the big river which runs into the Benin Bay [= Bight of Benin].'[28]

On the other hand, however, there is first-hand information from the early and mid-eighteenth century which indicates that there was an interruption between the Keta lagoon and Lake Togo. The Dutch trader Philip Eytzen, who made an overland trip from Ouidah to Accra in December 1717, in the early dry season, noted that east of Aflao ('Offra Lade') he travelled for 'more than 13 [Dutch] miles', i.e. 52 English miles/ 84km, 'without water' through a 'desert-like' region.[29] A few hours' march west of Offra Lade there was 'a big dry water-hold [*sic*]', suggesting that during the rainy season there were bodies of waters, if perhaps disconnected ones.

---

[24] Zöller, *Das Togoland*, 100; Henrici, *Das Deutsche Togogebiet*, 23; Klose, *Togo*, 96; Ellis, *Ewe-Speaking Peoples*, 4.

[25] GNA: ADM 1/2/361, incl. in no. 26: Lawson, 'Report' (1879), 7. Cf. Bouche, *Sept ans*, 8, 305, map.

[26] John M'Leod, *A Voyage to Africa, with Some Account of the Manners and Customs of the Dahomian People* (London, 1971), 135.

[27] See 'A Map of the Slave Coast' in Robert Norris, *Memoirs of the Reign of Bossa Ahadee, King of Dahomy* (London, 1789). This map was reproduced, with 'a few additions', in Archibald Dalzel, *The History of Dahomy, An Inland Kingdom of Africa* (London, 1793).

[28] H. G. Lind, 'Undersøgelser foretagne op ad Flodan Volta i 1827 og 1828', *Archiv for Sovaesenet* VI (Copenhagen, 1834), 1–6, p.3, quoted in Jean M. Grove and A. M. Johansen, 'The Historical Geography of the Volta Delta, Ghana, during the period of Danish Influence', *BIFAN.* 30, series B, n.4 (1968), 1376–1421, p.1410.

[29] Van Dantzig, *Dutch and the Guinea Coast*, no. 228, WIC 124: Minutes of Council-meeting, Elmina, 17 Feb. 1718.

An employee of the Danish trading company, Ferdinand Ludewig Rømer, made an overland journey from Little Popo to Keta in early August 1744, that is just after the end of the great rainy season. He stated that the Keta lagoon came within two Danish miles, i.e. 9.2 English miles/ roughly 15km, of Little Popo.[30] According to Paul Erdmann Isert, who visited the region in the 1780s, the Keta lagoon extended from the Volta 'to Pottebra, and in the rainy season may well stretch further.'[31] According to him, Pottebra lay three Danish miles, i.e. roughly 13.8 English miles/ 22km east of Keta.[32] If Pottebra is identifiable with Blekesu, this would corroborate the information given by Lawson in 1879, indicating that little had changed during the century which lay between their respective visits to the region.

An explanation that would make sense of this contradictory evidence is that there was once a connection which however was not permanent but subject to seasonal variations and long-term changes. This is indicated by the evidence of Isert and Lawson, who noted the seasonal variations of the lagoon's extent. Topographical characteristics of the area also suggest this. The basin of the Keta lagoon continues eastwards in the form of a hollow, which, according to a visitor from the late nineteenth century, was about 100m wide and extended to the outlet of the Zio into Lake Togo.[33] The modern map shows this hollow as marshy, and there are several smallish bodies of water, such as the lagoon at Lomé.[34] It is possible that in years of extraordinary rainfall this hollow was flooded and a connection made between the Keta lagoon and Lake Togo. Even the normal variation between the high and low watermarks of the lagoons was significant; Zöller reported it to be 'about four to five metres'.[35] An indication of the possible extent of such variations was given by Lind, according to whom the water level in the Aklapa channel (upstream the Volta, beyond Mefe) rose more than seven metres, during floods of a type said by the locals to occur every seven or eight years.[36] However, by the end of the nineteenth century these cyclical floods apparently failed to occur, which may have been due to long-term changes in the climate. Information from the 1880s and 1890s show that the Keta lagoon was getting drier over the long term, suggesting that it may have flooded more often in the earlier

---

[30] Rømer, *Reliable Account*, 208. One Danish mile of the time equalled 4.6 English miles (Grove and Johansen, 'The Historical Geography', 382 n.1). See also Justesen, *Danish Sources*, vol.1, xix.
[31] Isert, *Letters*, 82.
[32] *Ibid.*, 59.
[33] Klose, *Togo*, 80, 115. This is possibly what Grove/ Johansen refer to as 'the Aka, the eastern prolongation of the Keta lagoon' ('Historical Geography', 1403 n.1).
[34] *Togo: Carte générale au 1: 500 000* (Lomé: IGN, 1989). Cf. Klose, *Togo*, map.
[35] Zöller, *Das Togoland*, 101. For a similar information concerning Lake Nokoue, see ANB: Roget to Ministre de la Marine et des Colonies, Cotonou, 17 & 27 Sept. 1885, in Verger, *Flux*, 285. Cf. Bourgoignie, *Les hommes de L'eau: Ethno-écologie au Dahomey lacustre* (Paris, 1973), 16.
[36] Grove/ Johansen, 'Historical Geography', 1412, 1414 and 1373 map (reproduced in Isert, *Letters*, 329, map 2).

period.[37] Therefore, it seems reasonable to assume that sometime after the mid-seventeenth century, when the Akan-speaking canoemen settled at Little Popo, no permanent and navigable connection existed between Lake Togo and the Keta lagoon. However, such a connection may have existed in an earlier period, and in years of exceptionally heavy rainfall and flooding it may have been formed even after this date.

There was only one, semi-permanent, outlet of the lagoons into the sea on the western Slave Coast, forced by the joint waters of the lagoon, the Mono and Lake Ahéme. This was the Bouche du Roi (a corruption of the Portuguese 'boca do rio', meaning 'mouth of the river'), which in the seventeenth century had been known as 'River of the Popos'.[38] It was situated to the east of the coastal settlement of Grand Popo, although information as to its exact position varies, suggesting that it changed. The only first-hand information for the pre-nineteenth century period comes from Barbot who visited there in 1682. According to the map which accompanies his account, Grand Popo ('Popo') lay directly at the opening, with settlements on both sides of it as well as to the north.[39] (See Map 4). Information from the nineteenth century suggests that it sometimes silted up and changed its position, moving from west to east, which also corresponds to the direction of the currents of the sea and the inland rivers.[40] Grivot, a French colonial administrator who studied the lagoons in the mid-twentieth century, described it as 'a wandering opening' by which the lagoon communicated intermittently with the sea.[41]

The role of the Bouche du Roi in the development of maritime trade appears to have been very limited. Although the earliest record of European trade in the region, from 1553, refers to 'the river called the Papoues', implying that this was what the Portuguese first thought worth exploring, the trade soon centred elsewhere, suggesting that this outlet was not very useful for communication from the sea.[42] Barbot observed that the outlet was blocked by a sand bar, and the fact that he does not explicitly mention

[37] Klose, *Togo*, 78; Zöller, *Das Togoland*, 196.
[38] See Law, 'Between the Sea', 215–6; Law, 'Problems of Plagiarism, Harmonization and Misunderstanding in Contemporary European Sources; Early (pre-1680s) Sources for the "Slave Coast" of West Africa', in *European Sources for Sub-Saharan Africa before 1900: Use and Abuse (Paideuma 33)*, ed. Beatrix Heintze and Adam Jones (1987), 337–358; pp.339, 341; Law, *The Slave Coast*, 118.
[39] Barbot, *Barbot*, ii, plate 51: 'Popo Lagoon' (opp. p. 620). The map accompanying Norris' account from 1789 shows Grand Popo to be lying east of the opening, which however is of doubtful reliability (*Memoirs*).
[40] *African Pilot, or Sailing Directions for the Western Coast of Africa, Part 1: From Cape Spartel to the River Cameroons* (5th ed., London, 1890), 332; Borghero, 'Lettre', xxiv; GNA: ADM 1/2/361, incl. in no. 26: Lawson, 'Report' (1879), 61, 66. For an example from the eighteenth century, see Norris' map which comments that the outlet was 'open only in the Rains' (*Memoirs*).
[41] Grivot, 'La pêche', p.110.
[42] Brásio, *Monumenta*, 1st series, ii, no.97: Relatório de Jácome Leite a El-Rei, 8 Aug. 1553. Cf. Law, 'Between the Sea', 216.

canoes entering the lagoon through the outlet, while noting that '[t]he coastal shore is very easy for a bar canoe [to approach]', further implies that this was not generally practicable.[43] There is no record of vessels entering via the Bouche du Roi in the later period either, indicating that this was not feasible. According to the *African Pilot*, in 1893 'the channel appeared to be impassable for boats.'[44]

Although the lagoons in the region were of vital importance for the development of the Afro-European trade in the region, their limitations were also noted. Their depth varied greatly according to the season, making them unsuitable for any vessels except canoes, and in some parts even these could be used only in the rainy season. This is illustrated by a report from the British Vice-Consul at Ouidah from 1852: 'The Lagoon, is open from [Ouidah] to Arguey [= Agoué], but in some places, in the dry season, there is not more than six inches of water, consequently you must get out, while the canoe is hauled over the shallows.'[45] Lawson observed of the lagoon at Grand Popo, 'In the rains boats of a good size easily pass but in the dries it requires the aid of a pilot to travel conveniently.'[46] Zöller reported that a canoe trip from Little Popo to Glidji took twenty minutes in the rainy season but forty-five in the dry season, owing to the impossibility of going there by the direct route.[47] Also, he noted how differently the rising water level affected economic activity in different parts of the region. Flooding of the Keta lagoon meant that the palm oil trade flourished because the situation of the oil producing-places was such that a high watermark facilitated transport. In contrast, the flooding of the lagoon at Little Popo halted the trade because it cut off the paths that were preferred by the market women.[48] Due to the shallowness of the lagoons, the canoes were propelled by poles, up to six metres long, rather than by paddles.[49]

As regards the rivers, apart from the Mono they played only a secondary role for transport and communication, due to their relatively small size and seasonal variations, which meant that during the dry season they often were too shallow even for canoes. The Zio, for example, was navigable no further than Baguida (Town), and in the dry season not even to there.[50] The Haho may have been navigable by canoes during the rainy season, but information from the nineteenth century shows that this was not normally done. Zöller tried to ascend the river during the dry season but turned back when he encountered 'a barrier of waterplants and magnif-

[43] Barbot, *Barbot*, 620, plate 51: 'Popo Lagoon', plate 52: 'Popo Lagoon – printed version'.
[44] *African Pilot* (7th ed., London, 1907), 451.
[45] Louis Fraser, 'the daily journal', 30 July 1851, in: Fraser, *Dahomey*, 41.
[46] GNA: ADM 1/2/361, incl. in no. 26: Lawson, 'Report' (1879), 58.
[47] Zöller, *Das Togoland*, 175.
[48] Ibid., 196.
[49] Duncan, *Travels*, i, 109, 157; Klose, *Togo*, 112; Zöller, *Das Togoland*, 101.
[50] Ibid., 153; Henrici, *Das Deutsche Togogebiet*, 23; Klose, *Togo*, 95–6.

icently flowering waterflowers, which I thought it impossible to break through.'[51] Klose, who explored the Haho during the little rains, first had to free the river from branches which impeded his passage and then found it barred by fishtraps. He requested a local fisherman to show him 'the right path' to Hahoté, which turned out to be overland through the forest.[52] In 1845, Duncan ascended the river a few miles until he came to a fishermen's camp on the bank of the river: 'these people frequently came down the river as far as [this] place [...] to catch fish, but never ventured lower, declaring, that if they proceeded farther, one large fetish alligator destroyed every person, as well as smashed the canoe.'[53] When he wanted to proceed further up the river, they indicated 'equal difficulties in ascending, unless great sacrifices were made to propitiate the river-spirit or fetish.'[54] This was echoed five years later by Struvé, who was unable to convince his canoemen to proceed up the river, 'in consequence of the opening being guarded by a strong "Fetish" or if I might be better understood it is considered sacred by the Natives.'[55] Evidently, the river was not used for communication between the coast and the interior, but there was a boundary that was respected by the locals. Produce from the interior was presumably carried overland to the market at Gbome, on the north-western shores of Lake Togo, and from there transported to the coast. The Mono, the region's major link with the interior, was navigable to Atakpame, lying some 95 miles/152km inland.[56]

The sea and the lagoons should not be regarded as separate entities but as interacting parts of a single system, to which the indigenous people not only adapted but which they also actively managed. This system was complex, dynamic and continually changing, both periodically according to season and in the long term. Its hub was the Bouche du Roi and it is no coincidence that it was there that the original settlers of the country, the Hula people, first settled. Depending on the season and tide, the Bouche du Roi functioned either as an outlet of the inland waters or as an inlet for the sea. During the season when the rivers were swollen, the level of the lagoons rose and they contained fresh water. At the time of the highest water mark, the rivers and lagoons flooded the surrounding land, turning large parts of it into swamps. Lawson reported that during the rainy season more than one third of the Hula country was 'under water'.[57] With reference to Little Popo,

---

[51] Zöller, *Das Togoland*, 111.
[52] Klose, *Togo*, 107.
[53] Duncan, *Travels*, i, 154–63.
[54] Ibid., 158.
[55] UKHO: OD 9A, Struvé, 'Report' (5 Oct. 1850).
[56] Klose, *Togo*, 454.
[57] GNA: ADM 1/2/361, incl. in no. 26: Lawson, 'Report' (1879), 56.

Westermann noted that the people fished in the flood water.[58] Paradoxically, however, as was noted by observers from the late eighteenth and nineteenth centuries, the floods did not occur during the rainy season but in the early part of the great dry season. According to Burton, the lagoon at Ouidah was 'deeper in December of the "dries" than I had seen it in June.'[59] Westermann also noted that the floods occurred in November and December, while Struvé reported them in early October.[60] This delayed flooding was also observed with regard to the Volta which functioned in a similar way.[61] The explanation is that after the dry season, much of the early rains are absorbed into the ground and do not reach the lagoons. It is only after the ground has been sufficiently saturated that the rivers begin to flow and the water levels (and the salinity) of the lagoons are affected.[62]

The force of the floodwaters discharging from the Bouche du Roi was considerable and at times parts of the banks were swept away by the force of the water.[63] Occasionally the pressure of the floodwaters was so great that they burst through the sandspit separating the lagoon from the sea, creating temporary outlets. This occurred at places where the lagoons closely approached the sea, including at Little Popo.[64] The locals sometimes also pierced the sandspit in order to draw off the surplus water.[65] With reference to the western Slave Coast, this is first documented at Little Popo in 1850, although this particular attempt failed due to 'the loose running nature of the soil'.[66] Information concerning the Volta indicates that the floods did not last very long, only about two or three weeks, after which they quickly receded.[67]

During the season when the lagoons were at the low water mark because

[58] Westermann, *Die Glidyi-Ewe*, 92, 100.
[59] Richard Burton, *A Mission to Gelele, King of Dahomey*, 2 vols. (London, 1864), i, 33. Cf. Henrici, *Das Deutsche Togogebiet*, 25.
[60] Westermann, *Die Glidyi-Ewe*, 92; UKHO: OD 9A, Struvé, 'Report' (5 Oct. 1850).
[61] Rømer, *Reliable Account*, 207. For a discussion, see Grove and Johansen, 'Historical Geography', 1383. Cf. Isert, *Letters*, 108–9, 110.
[62] M. B. Hill and J. E. Webb, 'The ecology of Lagos Lagoon, II. The Topography and Physical Features', *Philosophical Transactions of the Royal Society of London*, B, 241, 683 (4 Sept. 1958), 319–33, p.324. Cf. Burton, *Mission*, i, 33.
[63] For the Bouche du Roi, see Robertson, *Notes*, 237–38. For the Volta and the Lagos Channel, where conditions were similar, see Thomas Phillips, *A Journal of a Voyage Made in the Hannibal of London, Ann. 1693, 1694, from England, to Cape Monserradoe, in Africa* (London, 1746), 230; Bosman, *New and Accurate Description* (London,1967), 328; van Dantzig, 'English Bosman', 273; Rømer, *Reliable Account*, 207; *African Pilot* (1856), 197, cf. 174 and (5th ed., 1890), 336–8.
[64] Klose, *Togo*, 73, 81 (for Keta and Little Popo); *African Pilot* (1856), 197 (for the eastern Slave Coast).
[65] Westermann, *Die Glidyi-Ewe*, 92, 100 n.3.
[66] UKHO: OD 9A, Struvé, 'Report' (5 Oct. 1850). According to Zöller, in 1884 the sandspit at Little Popo was 'artificially cut several times' but he does not say whether this was done by Africans or Europeans (*Das Togoland*, 100). In 1887, Henrici reported that there was an opening that was maintained by the European factories. Its width varied but sometimes reached 70 or 80 metres (*Das Deutsche Togogebiet*, 130, also 23, 25). However, this must have been temporary, as it is not mentioned in Klose's detailed description of the lagoon in the mid-1890s (*Togo*, 77–85).
[67] Rømer, *Reliable Account*, 207; Grove/Johansen, 'Historical Geography', 1383.

the rivers from the interior fed little or no fresh water into the system, the Bouche du Roi acted as an inlet for the sea. This was observed by the British Vice-Consul Fraser in 1852, who reported that at the opening 'the sea [...] at times breaks on the north bank of the Lagoon'.[68] Seawater also poured in through the temporary openings that had been created by the floods or by the locals, until they were closed again by sand washed up by the sea.[69] In this period, the lagoons and the lower courses of the rivers turned salty and harboured sea-fish. This was documented for the Bouche du Roi by Duncan, who reported, 'Near Whydah, the sea flows into the lagoon at high water, consequently it is very salt.'[70] There is more abundant contemporary documentation for the Volta and the Lagos Channel.[71] For example, Adams, who was active on the coast in the late eighteenth century, observed that the water of the Porto Novo lagoon was 'impregnated with salt, and unfit for domestic purposes, except during the rainy season.'[72] With reference to the Volta, Isert noted in the 1780s that during the season when the sea enters the river, 'there is the advantage that it is even richer in fish. In this salty water the fisherman [sic] catch a particular species of fish called hardis [= grey mullet, probably]'.[73] Some twenty years later, Monrad observed, 'At times ocean fish swim up the Rio Volta, especially at certain times of the year when its water, for a distance of several miles, is mixed with seawater'. There were even reports of 'battles' between the crocodile and the shark.[74] Sharks were also reported in the lagoons on the western Slave Coast in 1879, showing that things were similar there. Lawson suggests that this was a recent development, which may or may not have been the case.[75] During this period of the low watermark, parts of the lagoons turned into stagnant pools that evaporated by the heat of the sun and even dried up completely. This was the time for salt-making, which will be discussed below.

The Hula People

The western Slave Coast coincides with the western part of the area which was originally the Hula cultural and ethnic space. Their kingdom was

---

[68] Fraser, 'Windward Treaties', 22 June 1852, in: Fraser, *Dahomey*, 149.
[69] Westermann, *Die Glidyi-Ewe*, 100 n.3.
[70] Duncan, *Travels*, i, 190–1. Cf. Burton, *Mission*, i, 33n.; Klose, *Togo*, 78–80.
[71] Sandra Barnes, 'The Economic Significance of Inland Coastal Fishing in Seventeenth-Century Lagos', *The Changing Worlds of Atlantic Africa: Essays in Honor of Robin Law*, ed. Toyin Falola and Matt D. Childs (Durham, North Carolina, 2009), 51–66, pp. 54–5; Walther Manshard, 'Die Küsten- und Flußfischerei Ghanas', *Die Erde: Zeitschrift der Gesellschaft für Erdkunde zu Berlin*, 89/1 (1958), 21–33, 28.
[72] Adams, *Remarks*, 79. Cf. Duncan, *Travels*, i, 190–1; Lawson, 'Report', 35.
[73] Isert, *Letter*, 108–9.
[74] Monrad, *Description*, 139–40.
[75] GNA: ADM 1/2/361, incl. in no. 26: Lawson, 'Report' (1879), 32.

known to European traders as 'Popo' or, from the mid-seventeenth century, 'Grand Popo' or 'Great Popo'. The origin of this name is not certain, but it appears that it is neither an indigenous term nor derived from the Portuguese.[76] There has been much discussion about it in the scholarly literature.[77] The most convincing argument is offered by Law, who suggests that this term was borrowed by the first European traders, the Portuguese, from the Yoruba-speaking people at the eastern end of the Slave Coast, particularly the kingdom of Ijebu, where they had traded before making direct commercial contact with the central Slave Coast.[78] This seems plausible because the Yoruba are documented (in recent times at least) to have used this term to refer to their Gbe-speaking western neighbours. The question where the Yoruba derived this term from is more complex. Law argues that it may come from the name or title of the king of Tado, a state situated roughly 62 miles/100km in the interior, which the Hula, and the Gbe-speaking peoples more generally, regard as their ancestral homeland and which used to be the overlord of the region. This is suggested by an account of 1627 by the Spanish missionary Alonso de Sandoval, who uses the term as the title or name of a king, 'el Popo' ('the Popo'), as well as the name of the state which he ruled.[79] This king is said to have resided 60 leagues, i.e. 180 miles/roughly 290km in the interior but also possessed a coastal port which lay on the river 'Aguato' and was ruled by 'the Fidalgo' (Port. fidalgo, meaning nobleman but commonly applied in West Africa to subordinate governors). As Law has suggested, the powerful state in the interior can best be identified with Tado, the traditional overlord of the region, while its coastal port on the river Aguato probably corresponds to Grand Popo on the Mono/ the Bouche du Roi. The former is supported by Tado tradition which recalls a powerful ruler called 'Kpokpo', while the latter is suggested by the fact that Portuguese documents from the second half of the sixteenth-century commonly referred to the Mono/ Bouche du Roi as the 'River of the Popos'.[80]

However, from the second quarter of the eighteenth century European visitors to the coastal settlement began to note that 'Popo' was not what

---

[76] See Law, 'Problems', 337–58; 347; Luis Nicolau Parés, 'The Hula "Problem": Ethnicity on the Pre-Colonial Slave Coast', *Changing Worlds*, ed. Falola/ Childs, 323–346; Yves Person, 'La toponymie ancienne de la côte entre le Volta et Lagos', *CEA*, 60, 15–4 (1975), 715–21, p.716; André Pognon, 'Le Problème "Popo"', *ED*, 8 (1955), 11–14, p.11 n.1.

[77] For a survey of the various arguments, see Iroko, *Les Hula*, 25–8; Kassa, 'Le Foyer Xwla', 23–7. However, they both ignore Law's contribution to the discussion.

[78] See Law, 'Problems', 347–9; Law, *The Slave Coast*, 15–6; Law, 'The Earliest European Descriptions', 1–2. Cf. Diedrich Westermann, *Wörterbuch der Ewe-Sprache* (Berlin 1954), 577 *s.v.* popô.

[79] Alonso de Sandoval, *Naturaleza, policia sagrada I profana, costumbres I ritos, disciplina I catechismo evangelico de todos Etiopes* (Seville, 1627), cited in Law, 'Problems', 342, 348. Sandoval was active in the South America and had derived his information presumably 'either from correspondence with contemporaries in West Africa or from questioning African slaves in America' (342).

[80] Law, 'Problems', 341, 347–8; Law, *The Slave Coast*, 16, 118.

the indigenous people called the place or themselves, but 'Pla' or 'Fla'. In the 1720s, the Danish governor on the Gold Coast referred to it as 'Afra or Popo, as the Whites call it.'[81] In the 1780s, Isert noted that 'Great Popo [...] is nowadays generally called in these parts Afla.'[82] In the early nineteenth century, the English trader Robertson referred to it as 'Grand Popo, or Iffla.'[83] In the 1850s, the British Vice-Consul at Ouidah quoted a complaint by a servant of an English trader, an Agoué man, who had been made to pay a toll at a place called 'Plar', evidently referring to the toll station at Grand Popo.[84] According to Bouche, who visited the region in the 1870s, 'Grand-Popo is called by [the locals] Pla.'[85] Lawson refers to the kingdom as the 'Plah country' while calling its main sea port 'Grand Popo.'[86] German officials from the early colonial period likewise noted that the indigenous name of the settlement was 'Pla'/'Plah' or 'Phla', while a French official referred to the people as 'Kplas'.[87] According to Mouléro, a local clergyman who collected oral traditions in the 1960s, Pla is derived from 'pou' or 'apou', meaning 'sea' in their language.[88]

In the scholarly literature, however, the name that has been generally adopted for the people is 'Hula' (sometimes transcribed as 'Xwla'), which is what they are called by their eastern neighbours, the Fon. Like 'Pla', 'Hula' is derived from the local term for 'sea', which in Fon is 'hu'.[89] The adoption of the Fon form, rather than the indigenous one, can be explained by the scholarly focus on the Fon kingdom of Dahomey in the first half of the twentieth century and appears to derive from Le Herissé's influential study of 1911.[90] As it has become the conventional term, it will also be used in this study.

While the use of 'Hula' for the people is a puzzle, the use of 'Hulagan', that is 'Great Hula', as the indigenous name for Grand Popo, the coastal

---

[81] Justesen, *Danish Sources*, no. VIII.39, V.-g.K. 122: Pahl et al., Christiansborg, 10 Sept. 1727.
[82] Isert, *Letters*, 121. Biørn uses the same term ('Beretning 1788', 225, 227).
[83] Robertson, *Notes*, 237.
[84] Fraser, 'Scraps from the daily memoranda', 7 Nov. 1851, in: Fraser, *Dahomey*, 124.
[85] Bouche, 'Notes', 99. Cf. *id.*, *Sept ans*, 301: 'Grand Popo (nome indigéne, Pla).'
[86] GNA: ADM 1/2/361, incl. in no. 26: Lawson, 'Report', 56, 69.
[87] ANT: FA1/197, J. P. to Fürst von Bismarck, Klein Popo, 8 March 1888; Henrici, *Lehrbuch*, XVI; Zöller, *Das Togoland*, 175. See also Westermann, *Die Glidyi-Ewe*, 230 n.1. For the French official, see ANB: 1E12.8, no.28, Rapport de l'administrateur de Grand Popo, Grand-Popo, 4 Jan. 1910.
[88] Th. Mouléro, 'Histoire et légendes des Djêkens', *ED*, 8 (Oct. 1966), 39–56, p.56 n.2.
[89] 'Hu' is the sea divinity and head of a group of divinities which include lagoon and river spirits (e.g. Tokpodun, the crocodile). See Law, *The Slave Coast*, 109.
[90] A. le Herissé, *L'Ancien royaume du Dahomey* (Paris 1911), 109. Cf. Gayibor, 'L'aire culturelle'; Iroko, *Les Hula*; Emmanuel Karl-Augustt, 'Les populations du Mono béninois', *Peuples du Golfe du Bénin*, ed. Medeiros, 243–68; Kassa, 'Le Foyer Xwla'; Law, 'Problems', 347; *id.*, *The Slave Coast*; Roberto Pazzi, 'Aperçu sur l'implantation actuelle et les migrations anciennes des peuples de l'aire culturelle Aja-Tado', *Peuples du Golfe du Bénin*, 10–19, pp.13–4; Pognon, 'Le Problème', 11–4; Pierre Verger, *Notes sur le culte des orisa et vodun à Bahia, la Baie de tous les Saints, au Brésil et à l'ancienne Côte des Esclaves en Afrique* (Dakar, 1957), 537. However, there are exceptions: Capo, 'Le Gbe' ('Phla'); Mouléro, 'Histoire', 41 ('Pla').

settlement, is clearly wrong. As shown above, contemporary sources show that 'Pla'/'Fla' was the indigenous name for the coastal settlement and the country. Le Herissé uses Hula ('Houala'), the Fon form. Since the 1980s, however, the term 'Hulagan' (sometimes transcribed as 'Xwlagan') has gained currency.[91] It appears to have been inadvertently coined to match the use of Grand Popo in distinction from Little Popo. In the early period of trade, Europeans called the settlement of Grand Popo simply 'Popo'. Subsequently, when trade was opened further west at another Pla settlement, which the indigenous people called 'Aplaviho', i.e. 'Little Pla' (+ -ho/ -x☐, which is a locative translated as 'house'),[92] Europeans called it Little Popo in distinction from Popo, which at the same time became 'Grand Popo'. This pattern now appears to be applied (by some scholars) to 'Hula', which becomes 'Hulagan'.[93]

The Hula immigration and settlement on the western Slave Coast

The Hula, like the other Gbe-speaking peoples inhabiting the Slave Coast, trace their origins to the ancestral city of Tado. Their emigration from Tado and subsequent settlement on the coast near the Bouche du Roi is recalled in their traditions. According to a version recorded by Mouléro in the 1960s, the ancestor of the Hula was the eldest of three royal brothers who fled from the town after one of them had killed a rival in the competition for succession to the throne.[94] They founded a settlement called 'Adja-honoue', which on the modern map lies some 15 miles/25km south-east of Tado. However, they were discovered by their pursuers and forced to move on. They decided to split up; Avlêkpon, the ancestor of the Hula, fled to Adamé on the banks of the Mono, while his brothers fled to Dôdômê and Allada, becoming the ancestors of the Fon.[95] The pursuers from Tado followed Avlêkpon to Adamé, forcing him to flee yet again. He moved further south along the river and founded a new settlement, Agbanaken, where he decided to stay for good.

Once he had arrived at Agbanaken, Avlêkpon is said to have heard a loud

---

[91] Pazzi, 'Aperçu sur l'implantation', 13–4. Cf. Gayibor, *Le Genyi*; Law, 'Problems', 347; *id.*, *The Slave Coast*; Kassa, 'Le Foyer Xwla.' Iroko takes the discussion a step further by questioning whether 'Hulagan', 'cette fameux cité insulaire', is really synonymous with 'Grand Popo' and trying to identify it with other places (*Les Hula*, 61).
[92] Westermann, *Wörterbuch*, 335 *s.v.* x☐.
[93] Pazzi commits another error along the same lines by referring to 'Aplaviho' as 'Hulavi' ('Xlwàví'). This, too, has been repeated in recent scholarly literature. See e.g. Gayibor, *Le Genyi*, 167 (misquoting Bouche); Law, 'Problems', 347; Gayibor, *Slave Coast*, 25.
[94] Mouléro, 'Histoire', 39–43. Cf. Law, 'Between the Sea', 218–9.
[95] This however is an anachronism because the people of Allada were not Fon but conquered by them in the 1720s.

noise that was unfamiliar. He requested information from his diviner and was told in response: 'This noise which you hear and which worries you is something liquid like water and is not to be feared.' Avlêkpon then went to the place where the noise came from and saw that it was caused by the violent sea beating on the shore. This was the very first time that he saw the sea. A settlement was founded there, which became Grand Popo. The king washed himself in the seawater, which his diviner told him would bring him 'immense wealth.' Since this time the sea has been worshipped by the Hula. However, according to the traditions, Avlêkpon waited in vain for the arrival of the wealth promised to him, as did his son. It was only during the reign of his grandson, Kpossi, that European traders arrived. They were received well and promised to return. When they did so, they brought with them many presents: cloth, farming implements and seeds which they requested to be planted. Kpossi planted the seeds some twelve kilometres from Agbanaken at Agoué, which was founded for this purpose. The European traders returned, bringing cowries (which were used for money) and kitchen salt in exchange for agricultural produce (the 'kitchen salt' evidently being a reflection of conditions in the later nineteenth century, when European salt was imported into the region).[96]

According to this version of the traditions, the reason for the emigration of the Hula ancestor was competition for the throne. This is a common motif in such traditions and can be interpreted as a metaphor for the competition for control of resources, suggesting that the ancestors of the Hula were forced out from their homeland or chose to make a (better) living elsewhere. Since they were fishermen, their case is probably similar to that of other inland African communities who for centuries have made their living by fishing, such as the Duala of Cameroon who have been discussed by Ralph Austen and Jonathan Derrick.[97] According to Austen and Derrick, the Duala were unable to expand their sphere beyond the immediate vicinity of their ancestral town, Piti, because the area was controlled by other peoples, while remaining at Piti was equally problematic as it was not a location that could support a large population. It seems reasonable to assume that the case of the Hula was similar, and that population pressure and 'the needs of fishing' forced them to leave their ancestral home.[98] The foundation of settlements on their way to the coast, as recorded in the traditions, suggests that they pressed forward in stages until they reached the coast. They founded their kingdom near the Bouche du Roi and spread along the coastal lagoons to the east and the west, making their living by fishing and saltmaking.

By the time Portuguese traders first visited the coast in the late fifteenth

---

[96] Mouléro, 'Histoire', 43.
[97] Ralph A. Austen and Jonathan Derrick, *Middlemen of the Cameroons Rivers: The Duala and their Hinterland c. 1600–1960* (Cambridge, 1999), 19–20.
[98] *Ibid.*, 20.

century, the Hula had already settled on the coast. This was prior to the establishment of direct commercial contacts between Europeans and the region, when the Portuguese were trading on the Gold Coast to the west and in Benin to the east, passing the Slave Coast by sea. A Portuguese navigational guide from the late fifteenth century refers to two settlements that were visible from the sea, called in Portuguese 'Villa Franca' (from 'Fra' = Pla?) and 'Villa Longa', that is 'Free Town' and 'Long Town'. These have been identified as Grand Popo and Apa (near Badagry, in modern Nigeria) respectively.[99]

From Grand Popo, the Hula spread along the lagoons to the west and east and founded other settlements. These can be identified either by their traditions of origin or by their names, which often are a variant of 'Pla' or 'Fla'.[100] To the west of Grand Popo, they include Aplaviho (which survives as the name of the original quarter of modern Aneho), Aflao, Agbodrafo and possibly Agouégan. Aflao's name, which in 1717 was documented as 'Offra Lade' and in the nineteenth century variously as 'Afflou', 'Afflahoo', 'Flohow', 'Aflaha', is evidently a version of 'Fla' in combination with the locative '-ho', meaning 'place' or 'home of the Fla/ Pla'.[101] The same applies to 'Aplaviho', for which local traditions furthermore recall the foundation by (Hula) fishermen. According to versions recorded in the late nineteenth century, the first Akan-speaking immigrants from the Gold Coast founded their settlement as a resting place close to a fishing settlement. They had been attracted to the place by 'smoke rising there from fishermen's camps and hoped that there would be good drinking water.'[102] (See Chapter 2). In the case of Agbodrafo, known in the nineteenth century as 'Porto Seguro', recent traditions recall its foundation by Huesu Agbo, a son of a king of Grand Popo.[103] As regards Agouégan, Hula traditions as recorded by Mouléro state that it was originally a Hula settlement.[104] Although contested by Ge traditions, which claim that it had been founded by a Ga immigrant, this seems likely given that there are several settlements on Lake Nokoué, in the eastern Hula area, with similar names such as 'Aguégué' and 'Kpodji-Agué'.[105] However, in the absence of further information this remains uncertain.

[99] 'Roteiro Quatrocentista', in *Os mais antigos roteiros da Guiné,* ed. Damião Peres (Lisbon, 1952), 26, cited in Law, 'Problems', 341; *id.*, *Slave Coast,* 31–2. Cf. Person, 'La toponymie', 715–21.
[100] See Law, 'Problems', 350–1, 353–4.
[101] Van Dantzig, *Dutch and the Guinea Coast,* no.228, WIC 124: Minutes of Council-meeting, Elmina, 17 Feb. 1718; Bowdich, *Mission,* 221; Robertson, *Notes,* 232; TNA: FO84/893 incl. in Hamilton, [London] 10 Apr. 1852: Lieut. T. G. Forbes, 'Schedule of Treaties'. Cf. Gayibor, *Le Genyi,* 50–1; Iroko, *Les hula,* 69–70.
[102] Henrici, *Lehrbuch,* 5. Cf. Bouche, 'Notes', 99 (who mistakenly identifies 'Plavikho' with Fish Town, i.e. today's Gun Kope).
[103] Gayibor, *Le Genyi,* 50–1; Iroko, *Les hula,* 70.
[104] Mouléro, 'Histoire', 42–3. Agouégan is possibly first documented by Barbot in the 1680s: 'The village of Oy is between Little and Great Popo, a quarter of a league East of a little river which discharges itself into the sea' (Barbot, *Barbot,* 621).
[105] Agbanon, *Histoire,* 66. See also J[aques] L[ombard], 'A propos de l'etymologie d'Agoué', *ED,* 16 (1956), 3–6.

To the east of Grand Popo (and outside the area with which this study is concerned), the Hula settlements include Glehue/ Ouidah, Avrekete/ Avlékété, Jakin (present-day Godomé), Offra (destroyed in 1692), Cotonou (the earliest quarter of which is Plakondji), Ekpe (east of Cotonou, founded by refugees from Jakin), 'Ba' (which is a Hula clan name) and the 'Whara' (Hula) ward of Badagry.[106] This means that the Hula ethnic and cultural space extended at least from Aflao in the west to Badagry in the east, spanning a distance of more than 95 miles/152 km.[107] However, by the time contemporary documentation started, in the second half of the seventeenth century, the region had become politically fragmented and at least the settlements in the east were no longer under the authority of the king at Tado or that at Grand Popo. By then the coastal kingdom of Allada had emerged as the major state of the Slave Coast and replaced Tado as the overlord of the region.[108] Delbée's account from 1670 implies that Grand Popo itself had fallen under the Allada's control, which was corroborated by some later writers.[109]

The kingdom of Grand Popo

Little is known about the early history of the Hula state and its Ewe and Aja neighbours due to the paucity of documentation before the nineteenth century. Therefore, the following reconstruction will take information from the nineteenth century as its starting point. This will then be compared to evidence from the earlier period, to establish whether conditions were similar or different.

Nineteenth-century observers noted that Grand Popo was not unified but consisted of a number of separate settlements. According to Borghero, who visited in 1863, it was 'not one homogeneous country' but 'an assemblage of several villages spread around the opening of the sandspit which separates the lagoon from the sea [= the Bouche du Roi].'[110] Bouche, who visited the region in the 1870s, likewise observed that Grand Popo was

[106] See Law, 'Problems', 351, 353–5. For the quarter Plakondji at Cotonou: Robin Law, p.c. 16 Jan. 2002. For 'Ba', see Bourgoignie, *Les hommes*, 54–9. Law has formerly identified 'Ba' with 'Apa' but now doubts this (*The Slave Coast*, 122–3; p.c. 16 Jan. 2002). For Badagry, see Law, 'A Lagoonside Port on the Eighteenth-Century Slave Coast: The Early History of Badagri', *Canadian Journal of African Studies*, 28 (1994), 35–59, 41.
[107] Law, 'Between the Sea', 218.
[108] See Law, 'Earliest European Descriptions', 2.
[109] Delbée, 'Journal du voyage du Sieur Delbée', in vol. 2 of Jean Clodoré, *Relation de ce qui s'est passé dans les isles & terre-ferme de l'Amerique, pendant la dernière guerre avec l'Angleterre* (Paris, 1671), 347–558, p.382; Jean-Baptiste Labat, *Voyage du Chevalier des Marchais en Guinée, isles voisines, et à Cayenne, fait en 1725, 1726, et 1727*, 4 vols. (Amsterdam, 1731), ii, 6–7. Cf. Barbot, *Barbot*, ii, 628 n.12; Robin Law, *The Kingdom of Allada* (Leiden, 1997), 15–7, 21–7.
[110] Borghero, *Journal*, 122 (2 Feb. 1863). Cf. l'Abbé Laffitte, *Le pays des nègres et la Côte des Esclaves* (Tours, 1885), 26–7.

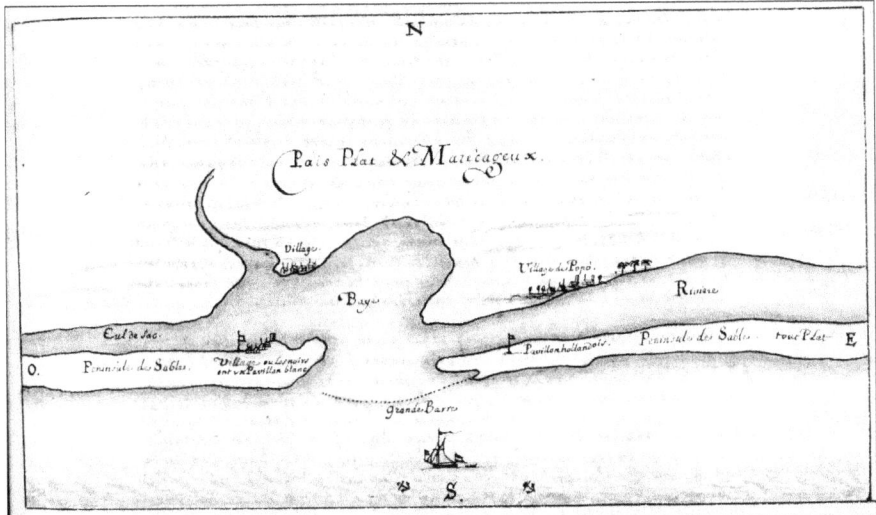

Map 4 Grand Popo and the Bouche du Roi in the late seventeenth century, as drawn by Jean Barbot (Source: The National Archives: ADM 7/830B: Description des Côte d'Afrique depuis le Cap Bojador, jusque au Cap de Lopo Gonzalves, 1688, vol.2, p. 76: 'Popo Lagoon')

'an assemblage of houses scattered on the islands in the lagoon and on the beach. One cannot say that this is a town; it is a people ["une peuplade"]'[111] In 1879, Lawson gave a detailed description of the country, complete with a map.[112] (See Map 5). He lists a large number of settlements, situated either on the banks of the lagoon or the rivers that feed it. The most important of these were Grand Popo, 'the Chief Sea Port of the Plah Country', situated on the beach to the south of the lagoon and 4 miles/roughly 6.4km to the west of the Bouche du Roi. Opposite Grand Popo on the northern bank of the lagoon lay 'Hevé', which according to him was 'the original sea port town of the Country.' Agbanaken, 'the capital of the Plah Country and residence of the king of the Country' lay on the western bank of Mono just north of its confluence with the lagoon.

The description of Grand Popo as a place consisting of a number of separate settlements is confirmed by information given by Barbot, referring to 1682. According to him, the place, which he called 'Tary or Popo', was 'divided into three parts, which are on the mouth of the river', that is the Bouche du Roi. This is also shown on the map accompanying his account, according to which two villages were situated on the northern bank of the lagoon and one on the beach to the south of the lagoon.[113] (See Map 4). Of the two villages to the north, the eastern one

[111] Bouche, *Sept ans*, 301.
[112] GNA: ADM 1/2/361, incl. in no. 26: Lawson, 'Report' (1979), 56–76.
[113] Barbot, *Barbot*, ii, 619–21 (incl. plate 51: 'Popo Lagoon'). The name 'Tary' is copied from Delbée and involves confusion with Tori, inland of Ouidah. See *ibid.*, 626–7, n. 9; Law, 'Problems', 351–2.

48 • *The regional setting*

is called 'Village de Popo' and can probably be identified with the royal seat, corresponding to what was later to become Agbanaken, although this was not necessarily in exactly the same place.[114] The second village is simply marked as 'village.' The third settlement was opposite this place to the south of the lagoon, i.e. on the beach, and to the west of the Bouche du Roi. It is described as the 'village where the blacks have a white flag.' Further, on the beach east of the Bouche du Roi, that is opposite the 'Village de Popo', a Dutch flag is shown, implying either that this was the place where trade with the Europeans (or at least the Dutch) was carried on or that it was a signalling point. The latter is perhaps more plausible, given that in the nineteenth century the place where the Afro-European trade was carried on lay to the west of the Bouche du Roi, rather than to the east. However, this could also be explained by the changing position of the Bouche du Roi and/or the relocation of this settlement to the west of the opening, possibly as a defensive measure against the Hueda and the Fon.

The boundaries of the Hula kingdom were formed by the lagoons and the rivers. In 1879, Lawson reported that the 'Plah country' extended to the Gbaga ('Akraku river') in the west and the Bouche du Roi and Aho River/Lake Ahémé ('Peida river') in the east, covering a 20–mile/32–km stretch of coast.[115] However, he also indicated two exceptions. First, there was one Dahomean settlement inside this area, situated on the northern bank of the lagoon about a quarter of a mile/ 400 metres east of the Aho. This was a toll station, called 'Ahodenu' (evidently derived from the name of the river, with 'denu' meaning 'custom house' or 'toll station'), where tolls were received 'before entering Whydah territory proper.' According to him, 'this place originally belong[ed] to Plah. This is the only place on this side of the Peda river where the Dahomean power is acknowledged...'[116] Second, in his description of the Hula country he lists one settlement, 'Harqueng' (= Hakoué), which lay outside the area defined above, on the beach about a mile/1.6km east of the Bouche du Roi, implying that despite its location it belonged to the Hula kingdom.[117] This seems to be confirmed by Ellis, who (based on information from 1878) noted that Grand Popo extended from the Gbaga ('Akraku River') to roughly 3 miles/4.8km east of the village of Arlo (perhaps a mistake for 'Aho', with 'denu' gone after the toll station had ceased to exist), exagger-

---

[114] Cf. Barbot, *Barbot*, ii, 627–8, n. 10; Law, 'Earliest European Descriptions', 3.
[115] GNA: ADM 1/2/361, incl. in no. 26: Lawson 'Report'(1879), 56, 60–1, map. Cf. Pornain, 'Rapport de Monsieur Pornain', 46. 'Aho river' refers to the channel that links Lake Ahémé with the arm of the lagoon stretching along the coast and with the Bouche du Roi.
[116] GNA: ADM 1/2/361, incl. in no. 26: Lawson 'Report'(1879), 68: 'Ahor Denu'; map: 'Ahodenu'.
[117] *Ibid.*, 66. NB: The location of the present-day village of Hakoué does not correspond to that of the settlement referred to by Lawson. According to Rivallain, the old Hakoué was destroyed by the sea and subsequently relocated further east ('Le sel', 105).

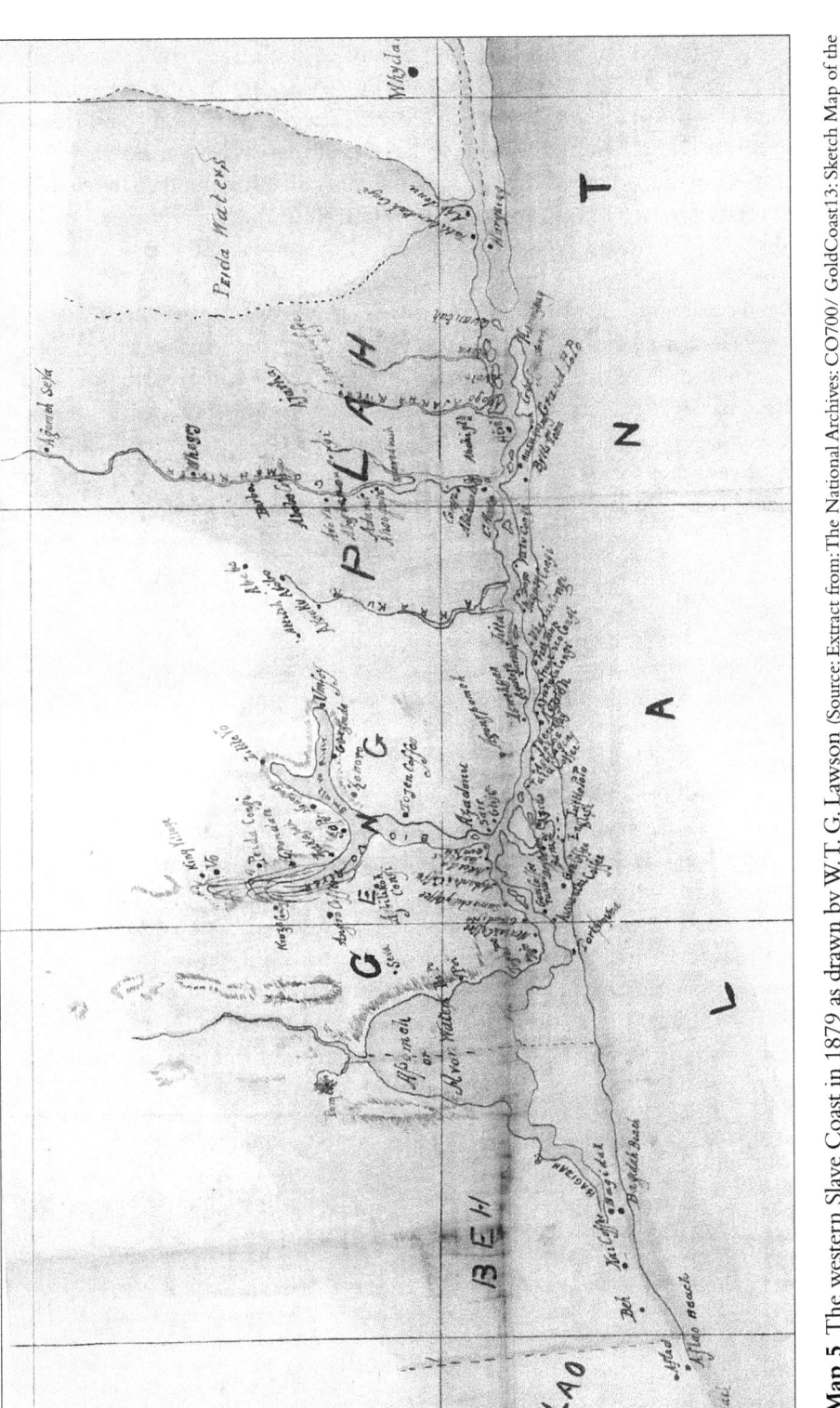

Map 5 The western Slave Coast in 1879 as drawn by W.T. G. Lawson (Source: Extract from: The National Archives: CO700/ GoldCoast13: Sketch Map of the Towns, Lagoons, Rivers, &c., of the Countries lying between the Volta and Peida Rivers, April 1879)

ating the distance.[118] The kingdom's extent to the interior is less certain. According to Lawson, it was some 13 miles/21km, but this is not reliable because it is based on second-hand information.[119] According to a French sketch from 1886, Grand Popo's northern boundary was 'unknown'.[120]

The waterways formed a natural defence against intruders, particularly to the east, where Grand Popo came repeatedly under pressure from its neighbours. This was noted by observers in the nineteenth century. With reference to the Bouche du Roi, Borghero observed that the people of Grand Popo 'take care to maintain this opening in order to prevent the king of Dahomey from covering the whole coast with his army.'[121] This was echoed by Lawson, who stated that the Aho ('Pedah') river was 'the greatest barrier in the way of Dahomey overrunning the whole of the Plah and Geng countries [= Grand Popo and Little Popo]. They made an attempt years ago [= in 1737?] but the river caused them much destruction of life.'[122]

Ewe and Aja settlers on the western Slave Coast

Besides the Hula, the western Slave Coast was also settled by other Gbe-speaking groups. In the west, the Hula ethnic and cultural space overlapped with that of the Ewe people, who were known pre-nineteenth century to the Europeans as 'Krepi'.[123] Strictly speaking, this was the name of one particular state in the interior, also called Peki, but it was commonly used for the group as a whole. According to Henrici, the name Ewe, which gained currency in the late nineteenth and early twentieth centuries, means 'country, homeland, and the interior as opposed to the coast', reflecting the fact that these people came to the coastal region from the interior.[124] They trace their origins to the town of Notsé in the interior of western Slave Coast some 55miles/ nearly 90km inland.[125] The date of their migration is not clear. Amenumey has suggested that the Ewe immigrants settled at Anlo on the coast around the mid-seventeenth

---

[118] Ellis, *Ewe-Speaking Peoples*, 6.
[119] GNA: ADM 1/2/361, incl. in no. 26: Lawson 'Report'(1879), 56, 61, 66, 68, map.
[120] ANB: 1E8.1–8, no. 204, Dossier K, Porto Novo [1886].
[121] Borghero, *Journal*, 122 (2 Feb. 1863). Cf. Bouche, *Sept ans*, 301.
[122] GNA: ADM 1/2/361, incl. in no. 26: Lawson, 'Report' (1879), 61.
[123] See Law, *Slave Coast*, 14–15.
[124] Henrici, *Lehrbuch*, 2–3.
[125] For Ewe traditions of origin and migration, see N.L. Gayibor, 'Agokoli et la dispersion de Notsé', in *Peuples du Golfe du Bénin*, 47–70; Gustav Härtter, 'Einige Bausteine zur Geschichte der Evhestämme (Togo)', I, *Beiträge zur Kolonialpolitik und Kolonialwirtschaft*, 3 (1901–1902), 432–48, pp. 432–40; C. Spiess, 'Ein Beitrag zur Geschichte des Evhe-Volkes in Togo: Seine Auswanderung aus Notsie', *MSOSB: Dritte Abteilung: Afrikanische Studien*, V (1902), 278–83; Spieth, *Die Ewe-Stämme*, 53–5; W.E.F. Ward, *A History of Ghana* (London, 1966), 133–6.

century, based on traditions.¹²⁶ However, Law argues that this event can probably be dated further back, as traditional genealogies and king lists recorded recently are simplified and foreshortened.¹²⁷

The Ewe did not form a unified state but comprised a number of political units or autonomous communities (*du*, pl. *duwo*), which acknowledged the ritual primacy of the ruler at Notsé.¹²⁸ In the early twentieth century, 'Eweland' comprised about 120 such units, of which Anlo, situated on the coast just east of the Volta, was the one best-known to the European traders.¹²⁹ On the western Slave Coast, they included Bé, lying to the east of Aflao and a couple of miles inland, and Togo, opposite Agbodrafo on the northern bank of the lagoon, just where it expands into Lake Togo. Togo is only documented in the nineteenth century.¹³⁰ Bé, however, was possibly already documented in 1682, in the form of 'Bequoe' (with '–quoe' perhaps representing the locative *axwé/ oxwé*, translated as 'home' or 'homestead').¹³¹ The immediate interior of Little Popo was settled by the Ouatchi. Their capital was at Notsé, first documented in the early nineteenth century, but apart from this there is hardly any information before the twentieth century, when they mainly occupied the region between the Zio and Mono rivers.¹³²

The region to the east of the Ewe was settled by Aja-speaking people, who centred on Tado. In the early twentieth century, they mainly occupied the territory between the Mono and Kouffo rivers, to the north of Grand Popo.¹³³ Although they are only documented in the nineteenth century, they had settled the country already by the 1680s and probably earlier.¹³⁴ The name of Glidji's original quarter, Adja Kpodji, indicates that their arrival in the region predates that of the Ga immigrants.¹³⁵ (See Chapter 2).

---

[126] See D.E.K. Amenumey, *The Ewe in Pre-Colonial Times* (Accra, 1986), 5–11.

[127] Law, *Slave Coast*, 31. Cf. Akyeampong, *Between the Sea*, 27.

[128] Law, *Slave Coast*, 14; Westermann, *Die Glidji-Ewe*, 166.

[129] Spieth, *Die Ewe-Stämme*, 34.

[130] UKHO: L7791, Struvé, 'West Coast of Africa': 'Tago'; Borghero, 'Lettre', xi-xxix incl. map: 'Toko'; GNA: ADM 1/2/361, incl. in no. 26: Lawson, 'Report' (1879), 42, map.

[131] Barbot, *Barbot*, ii, 619. For nineteenth-century references to Be, see WMMS: T.B. Freeman, 'West Africa', unpubl. ms, 488, 495 (19 April 1847); TNA: FO84/893, incl. in Hamilton, [London] 10 April 1852: Lieut. T. G. Forbes, 'Philomel', at Whydah, 5 Feb. 1852; GNA: ADM 1/2/361, incl. in no. 26: Lawson, 'Report' (1879), 26, map; Zöller, *Das Togoland*, 92–4. For the locative, see Westermann, *Wörterbuch*, 342 *s.v.* 'axwé' and derivations.

[132] Robertson, *Notes*, 236, 238 ('Oäche'); Westermann, *Die Glidyi-Ewe*, 7; Westermann, 749 *s.v.* watyí, map.

[133] Westermann, *Wörterbuch*, map. Cf. Law, *Slave Coast*, 15; Madeline Manoukian, *The Ewe-Speaking People of Togoland and the Gold Coast* (London, 1952), 11, map.

[134] For nineteenth-century references, see Bowdich, *Mission*, 222: 'Tadoo'; Sigismund Wilhelm Koelle, *Polyglotta Africana* (1854, new ed. Graz, 1963), 4: B.2: 'Anfue, in Sierra Leone called Adsa'; Robertson, *Notes*, 236: 'Zado'. Cf. Westermann, *Wörterbuch*, 85 *s.v.* adyá.

[135] Westermann, *Die Glidyi-Ewe*, 140. Iroko argues that the first settlers were Hula (*Les hula*, 71–2).

The local economy

As there is little information about the local economy of the region in the period before the 1840s, the following reconstruction depends largely on evidence from the nineteenth century. Wherever possible, this is complemented with evidence for the earlier period and for similar communities for which documentation exists, and oral traditions. However, it is clear that the situation in the nineteenth century was the result of a process of transformation connected with the development of the Afro-European trade from the seventeenth century. Among others, the external trade stimulated agricultural production and local commerce due to the demand both for provisions for Europeans and slaves on the coast and during the Middle Passage and, in the nineteenth century, for palm oil. The link between the internal and external economies is clearly reflected by the adoption of cowry shells, 'the money of the slave trade', as the local currency.[136]

The Hula were water people who were closely associated with the lagoon environment. Their economic life was based on the exploitation of the lagoons by fishing and salt-making. The produce of these activities was traded with the neighbouring people and those in the interior for agricultural products.[137]

Fishing. Fishing was perhaps the most important activity in Hula economic life. Fish, as noted in the nineteenth century, was the staple of the coastal people in the region. Crabs, shrimps and oysters were also caught or collected.[138] According to Duncan, 'large quantities' of fish were dried and 'send to the interior.'[139] This fish trade was already documented in the 1690s, when Bosman visited Grand Popo and reported that although the locals dabbled in the slave trade, 'their greatest Gain is by the Fish, which they catch in their River, and Trade with abroad.'[140] Although their name, Hula (or Pla), derives from the word for sea, they did not engage in sea-fishing. They lacked the incentive and technology to navigate the violent sea because the lagoons and rivers yielded a great abundance and variety of fish. This was observed by European visitors throughout the period of Afro-European trade. Bosman himself noted with regard to the lagoons at Ouidah, one of which 'runs by the two Popos [= Grand Popo and Little Popo]', that they were 'plentifully stored with Fish.'[141] According to

---

[136] Jan Hogendorn and Marion Johnson, *Shell Money of the Slave Trade* (Cambridge, 1986).
[137] For a discussion of the Hula economic life mainly in recent times, see Iroko, *Les hula*, 192–281.
[138] Burton, *Mission to Gelele*, i, 33; Bouche, *Sept ans*, 153; Duncan, *Travels*, i, 112; GNA: ADM 1/2/361, incl. in no. 26: Lawson, 'Report' (1879), 32; Klose, *Togo*, 82.
[139] Duncan, *Travels*, i, 171, also 96, 109. See also Westermann, 'Kindheitserinnerungen', 7.
[140] Bosman, *New and Accurate Description*, 337.
[141] *Ibid.*, 362a.

Adams 'From [Little] Popo to Old Calabar, the natives derive no advantage from the sea', but 'Fish abounds in most of the rivers, particularly mullet, of a large size and superior flavour'.[142] Sea-fishing was introduced into the region only in the nineteenth century.[143] Nevertheless, the locals profitted from the sea in the earlier period because (as discussed above) in certain seasons sea water entered the lagoons, which turned salty and harboured sea fish. Fishing was a seasonal activity, or at least its yield fluctuated according to the season.[144]

There is hardly any information about fishing methods and utensils for the period before the nineteenth century. The only exception dates from the 1790s, when an English trader at Little Popo sent home some souvenirs, including 'a small Canoe, Paddles & a Cast Net'. The latter was made of cotton (which grew wild in the region) and he regarded it as 'far superior' to the grass nets used by the Fante on the Gold Coast.[145] More information comes from the mid-nineteenth century. In the 1840s, Duncan and Struvé documented fishing weirs at various points on the lagoon, spanning its entire width with only a narrow passage for canoes. These weirs consisted of stakes driven into the lagoon bed and connected with wickerwork, leaving small spaces through which fish were led into traps. They were 'very firm and compact' and doubled for defence purposes and sometimes as toll stations.[146] Further, Duncan reported the use of wicker baskets as fish traps, 'on the same principle as that used on the rivers in Britain for catching eels.'[147] Observers from the early colonial period added various other methods, including the use of spears, trawling nets and fishing rods, or by hand.[148] Some of these methods may have been introduced by the immigrants from the Gold Coast or the Europeans, or evolved over time, but others had probably already been practised by the Hula in the early period.

Saltmaking. There is very little documentation of salt production by the Hula before the nineteenth century, and none of it refers to the western Slave Coast. This contrasts with the situation in the Volta region and at Ouidah, where the local salt industry is documented since the eighteenth century if

[142] Adams, *Remarks*, 189. He implies that the Anlo engaged in sea-fishing in this period, which however is mistaken. See also Duncan, *Travels*, i, 171.
[143] Akyeampong, *Between the Sea*, 38; Law, 'Between the Sea', 212–13.
[144] TNA: T70/1572, Searle to Miles, Popo Factory, 1 Feb. 179[4]; T70/1569, Searle to Miles [at Accra], Popo Factory, 23 Oct. 1794; GNA: ADM 1/2/361, incl. in no. 26: Lawson, 'Report' (1879), 55.
[145] TNA: T70/1484, Thomas Miles, Ship Iris [early 1794?].
[146] Duncan, *Travels*, i, 110; UKHO: OD 9A, Struvé, 'Report' (19 Dec. 1849). See also Zöller, *Das Togoland*, 101–2, 126; Klose, *Togo*, 84.
[147] Duncan, *Travels*, i, 158–59.
[148] Klose, *Togo*, 83, 102; H. Seidel, 'Der Fischfang in Togo', *Globus: Illustrierte Zeitschrift für Länder- und Völkerkunde* 82, 7 (21 Aug. 1902), 111–4, p. 112; Spieth, *Die Ewe-Stämme*, 33, Westermann, *Die Glidyi-Ewe*, 100. See also Grivot, 'La pêche', 106–28; Gustav Härtter, 'Der Fischfang in Evheland', *Zeitschrift für Ethnologie*, 1 & 2 (1906), 51–63; Manshard, 'Die Küsten- und Flußfischerei', 21–33.

not earlier and is consequently well studied. However, nineteenth-century documents, oral tradition and the existence of a salt industry in the Mono region in recent times indicate that the Hula people were major producers of salt, which they distributed to the interior. Among other indications, this is suggested by a Fon proverb which says that 'You can give salt even to a Hula', meaning that even a rich man can be given presents.[149] According to Pazzi, in the Mono valley salt was not called by its usual name, 'jè', but was known by the term 'xwlà-ko', meaning 'sand of the Xwla [= Hula]'.[150] Hula traditions as recorded by Mouléro (cited above) also recall that they produced salt and sold it to the interior.[151] In the 1840s, Duncan (who did not visit Grand Popo but only passed it on the lagoon) reported that a 'considerable quantity of salt' was produced at Little Popo and Agoué.[152] In 1852, the English naval officer T. G. Forbes noted that between Agoué and Agbanaken ('Grand Popoe') there were 'several Villages where trade is carried on in Salt making'.[153]

Some information about the pre-colonial Hula salt industry can also be gleaned from twentieth-century reports. In the 1940s, Grivot noted the revival of the indigenous salt industry in the district of Grand Popo due to the disruption of European salt imports during the war.[154] According to him, salt was produced in the villages of Allongo, Kouenta and Hakoué, situated on the banks of the lagoon around the Bouche du Roi, and in Atogbo and Kpétou on the banks of Lake Ahéme (although in the latter two villages this was probably by the Hueda who had established themselves there after the conquest of their country by Dahomey in the 1720s).[155] In the 1970s, salt production was documented in Hlihoué, situated on an island in the lagoon, Allongo and Avlo, lying on the beach to the south of the lagoon.[156] Presumably, these were settlements where salt had also been produced in former times.

The method of salt-making used by the Hula involved the boiling of water in pots. This method worked with both sea-water and lagoon-water (or, more precisely, leachate extracted from salty mud from the lagoons), but the fact that the surviving salt industry in the Grand Popo area is based on

[149] Pamphile Boco, *Proverbs de la sagesse fon (Sud-Bénin)*, 4 vols. (Cotonou, 2000), i, 98 n.515.
[150] Pazzi, 'Aperçu sur l'implantation', 16 n.16. Cf. Iroko, *Les hula*, 241.
[151] Mouléro, 'Histoires', 43. According to the version as recorded by Mouléro, the Hula learnt how to produce salt from the European traders but this is obviously an attempt to explain why salt was locally produced as well as imported from Europe. The name or title of the king was 'Djèken', i.e. Jakin, which is translated as 'he who sends or distributes salt.'
[152] Duncan, 'Note', 146.
[153] TNA: FO84/893, incl. in Hamilton, [London] 10 April 1852: Lieut. T. G. Forbes, HMS 'Philomel', at Whydah, 5 Feb. 1852.
[154] Grivot, 'L'industrie du sel', 23.
[155] According to Lawson, Allongo ('Alogo') and Kouenta ('Ouantah') were on islands in the lagoon (GNA: ADM 1/2/361, incl. in no. 26: W.T. G. Lawson 'Report', 66, map). For a discussion of the Hueda immigration and settlement, see Chapter 3.
[156] Rivallain, 'Le sel', 99–110.

the lagoon side indicates that lagoon water was used, which during the dry season had a higher salinity than seawater. This is corroborated by Duncan's account of this technique in the 1840s (although he refers to Ouidah).

> Near Whydah [= at the Bouche du Roi], the sea flows into the lagoon at high water, consequently it is very salt. During the ebb-tide the lagoon also ebbs, and the great heat of the sun causes such rapid evaporation, as to leave the salt on the surface, so as to resemble hoar-frost or a slight fall of snow. It is then scraped together, and frequently boiled, which cleanses and whitens it, but the natives generally use it in its original state.[157]

A century later Grivot gave a detailed description of this process, showing that it was more complex and that the boiling of the saltwater was not an extra but an intrinsic part of the process.[158] According to him, during the period when the lagoons' water level fell, salty earth was scraped from dried-up parts of the lagoon and stored in heaps. When the water level rose again this earth was taken to the villages, where it was stored and protected against the rains. In order to extract the salt, it was placed in special containers, measuring about 1m in diameter and 1.20m in height and made of wickerwork from mangroves, reinforced by clay. At the bottom of these containers was inserted a piece a bamboo, leading out from the centre. The salty earth was then drenched several times with lagoon water, dissolving the salt and running out through the bamboo pipe where it was collected into a vessel. A plug of coco fibres was used to stop the earth from entering the bamboo pipe. The filtrate was then poured into other vessels, which in Grivot's time were enamel cauldrons but (as he noted) had formerly probably been pottery, and put on special stoves for evaporation. The stoves were fired by mangrove branches and, for greater heat, by empty palm kernels. After the water had evaporated, a layer of salt remained at the bottom of the vessel. Grivot emphasised the extent to which this mid-twentieth-century salt industry relied on the means provided by the country: salty earth, mangroves, oil palms and bamboo. However, as he shows, some European tools had also been adopted by then, such as enamel cauldrons, which were more heat-resistant than the local pottery, and perhaps also the hoes used to scrape the salty earth, which had been adapted for this purpose by indigenous blacksmiths.[159]

Agriculture and animal husbandry. Grand Popo's natural environment was not well suited to agriculture and animal husbandry. As noted above, the

---

[157] Duncan, *Travels*, i, 190–1. Cf. Burton, *Mission*, i, 33n; Klose, *Togo*, 78–80.
[158] Grivot, 'L'industrie du sel', 23–4. For a description from the 1970s, see Rivallain, 'Le sel', 93–6.
[159] Grivot, 'L'industrie du sel', 23, 24. On the Gold Coast, the use of copper and brass cauldrons, imported from Europe, for salt-making is documented in the last decades of the seventeenth century. See Barbot, *Barbot*, 482, 488–89, n.1&2; Law, *English in West Africa*, part 3, no. 1000: John Browne, Agga, 15 Oct. 1695.

region was swampy and large parts of it were flooded during the rainy season. In the 1870s, Lawson stated that 'Supplies in this Country are very scarce [;] even common fowls are comparatively expensive and rare.'[160] Information from other fishing and salt producing communities on the Gold and Slave Coasts, such as at Accra, Ada and places on the eastern part of the Keta lagoon indicates that they tended not to engage in agriculture if the produce of these activities was sufficient to obtain other necessary provisions in exchange for it.[161]

However, the Ewe and Aja peoples were cultivators and the country west of the Gbaga was well suited for agriculture and animal husbandry, at least to the north of the lagoon.[162] Duncan, who visited the region in the 1840s, was positively impressed by the quality of the soil and the standard of cultivation there. According to him, to the north of Agoué the soil consisted of 'rich black loam and sand' and was 'partially cultivated for the growth of yams, cassada or manioc, cotton, and indigo.'[163] Further west, on the eastern banks of Lake Togo, 'the soil is of a light red, excellent for corn, maniocs, melons, gourds, and all sorts of vegetables', while a little further on, 'the soil is a black sandy loam, and produces excellent yams.'[164] Maize was the 'chief food' of the people of Little Popo, besides fish. It formed the basis for 'kankie', a kind of dumpling made from maize dough which had been fermented, wrapped in leaves and then baked or boiled.[165] Further, maize was used to brew beer.[166] Cassava, which was ground to flour ('farina', from Port. *farinha*), was also

[160] GNA: ADM 1/2/361, incl. in no. 26: Lawson 'Report'(1879), 55. Cf. Grivot, 'L'industrie du sel', 24.
[161] Grove/Johansen, 'Historical Geography', 1385, 1401–3; Isert, *Letters*, 111; Johannes Rask, *A Brief and Truthful Description of a Journey to and from Guinea*, transl. Selena Axelrod Winsnes (1754, Legon, 2008), 137–8; Rømer, *Reliable Account*, 224.
[162] Rask, *Brief and Truthful Description*, 84; Spieth, *Die Ewe-Stämme*, 28, 41–9. Cf. Westermann, *Die Glidyi-Ewe*, 75–8, 84–94, 96, 127. For a description of the 'working year' of the Ge, with its seasonal variations in cultivation, hunting, etc., see pp. 92–5. Westermann's informant, a member of the royal family at Glidji, referred to the Ouatchi as 'peasants' who spoke an Ewe dialect which he regarded as inferior, indicating the existence of a town-country dichotomy ('Kindheitserinnerungen', 10, n. 33). Cf. Law, *Ouidah*, 81, 87.
[163] Duncan, *Travels*, i, 97. Cf. Henrici, *Das deutsche Togogebiet*, 112–4.
[164] Duncan, *Travels*, i, 169.
[165] Duncan, *Travels*, i, 101. See also TNA: T70/1569, Account Current of Jacob P. Wrisberg with Thomas Miles, Prindsensteen, Quitta, 20 Oct. 1794: 'Canky'; Clapperton, *Hugh Clapperton*, 90: 'Kanky'. The term 'kankie' (= kenkey) was first documented on the Gold Coast in the 1600s but its origin are uncertain: see Pieter de Marees, *Description and Historical Account of the Gold Kingdom of Guinea* (1602), transl. and ed. Albert van Dantzig and Adam Jones (Oxford, 1987), 40–41 incl. n. 2. The Ewe term is *abólò* (*abló* in the Ge dialect) and derives from Akan ('Twi'), *abódòó*, via Ga, *aboló* (Westermann, *Wörterbuch*, 32 s.v. *abólò*). See also Henrici, *Das Deutsche Togogebiet*, 35; *Lehrbuch*, 180 s.v. ab'lò; Zöller, *Das Togoland*, 212-2.
[166] Duncan refers to this beer as 'peto' (= *pito*), another term from the Gold Coast whose origin is uncertain (de Marees, *Description*, 42 n. 5). In the early eighteenth century, Rask used 'ahaj' (= *aha*), the generic Ewe term for alcoholic drinks (Rask, *Brief and Truthful Description*, 83; Westermann, *Wörterbuch*, 293 s.v. *aha*). The Ewe term for beer, *liha*, derives from *li*, signifying millet, indicating that originally it was brewed from millet (Henrici, *Lehrbuch*, 207 s.v. *liha*; Westermann, *Wörterbuch*, 457 s.v. *liha*).

'much in use' as food both for the locals and for enslaved Africans bulked on the coast previous to shipment across the Atlantic.[167]

In the late eighteenth and nineteenth centuries, visitors documented a wide range of other vegetables and fruits that were grown in the region, besides those already mentioned, including sweet potatoes, plantains, bananas, calavance/ pulses, okra, shallots, cashew nuts, groundnuts, pumpkins, pineapples, limes and ginger.[168] Pepper and oil palms grew wild in the region and by the nineteenth century were also cultivated.[169] Coconut palms, which thrived on the sandspit between the sea and the lagoon, are documented from the early eighteenth century.[170]

Most of these crops originate from outside of Africa and were introduced during the era of the Atlantic slave trade, although it is not clear when exactly and by which routes they arrived in the western Slave Coast. The majority came from the Americas, such as maize, cassava, cashew nuts, groundnuts, pumpkins, pineapples and sweet potatoes. Bananas, plantains and coconuts are Asian crops, onions European. Citrus fruits, originally from Asia, arrived in West Africa via the Mediterranean and Madeira where they had been naturalised.[171] As noted above, the Hula traditions recorded by Mouléro recall that the Europeans introduced seeds which the local people began to grow. Spieth noted that formerly millet – of which a large variety is indigenous to West Africa – had been one of the most important crops of the coastal Ewe, but by the early twentieth century it had lost its importance and was used only for ritual purposes, having been replaced by maize.[172] This contrasted with the interior, where in the 1890s Klose observed the continuing importance of millet, with three different varieties being produced 'especially further away from the coast'.[173] Linguistic evidence suggests that maize may have entered the region from the Gold Coast, where it had arrived by the mid-sixteenth century and had become a staple

---

[167] Duncan, *Travels*, 101–2, 104. See also GNA: ADM 1/2/361, incl. in no. 26: Lawson 'Report'(1879), 23, 27, 55.

[168] Adams, *Remarks*, 173; Bouche, *Sept ans*, 56–7; Clapperton, *Hugh Clapperton*, 90; Duncan, *Travels*, i, 94, 101–2; GNA: ADM 1/2/361, incl. in no. 26: Lawson 'Report'(1879), 55; Strickrodt, 'Neglected Source', 300.

[169] Adams, *Remarks*, 174; Duncan, *Travels*, i, 94, 97; Zöller, *Das Togoland*, 119; Henrici, *Das Deutsche Togogebiet*, 120; Spieth, *Die Ewe-Stämme*, 56; Klose, *Togo*, 264.

[170] Van Dantzig, *Dutch and the Guinea Coast*, no.228, WIC 124, Minutes of Council Meeting, Elmina: 17 Feb. 1718: Oral report by Bookkeeper-General Ph. Eytzen; Duncan, *Travels*, i, 145; GNA: ADM 1/2/361, incl. in no. 26: Lawson 'Report'(1879), 29, 30; Henrici, *Das Deutsche Togogebiet*, 120.

[171] Stanley B. Alpern, 'The European Introduction of Crops into West Africa in Precolonial Times', *HiA*, 19 (1992), 13–43; Alpern, 'Exotic Plants of Western Africa: Where They Came from and when', *HiA*, 35 (2008), 63–102.

[172] Spieth, *Die Ewe-Stämme*, 28.

[173] Klose, *Togo*, 454, 553. He describes these varieties as white, yellowish and red millet, 'the latter generally known by the name of Guinea corn [= sorghum].' See also Harrison Church, *West Africa*, 97, 117–18; Morgan/Pugh, *West Africa*, 77–85.

by the beginning of the seventeenth century.[174] According to Westermann, the Ewe term for maize, *blí*, derives from the Twi (i.e. Akan) word *aburó* (meaning 'the European [corn]'), via Ga (*ablê*).[175] It is possible that maize arrived with the Gold Coast immigrants who settled at Little Popo from the mid-seventeenth century onwards. However, another explanation may be that the immigrants just brought the term and established it for the maize that was introduced by Europeans after the initiation of the slave trade in the region (see Chapter 2).

As early as 1683, when Afro-European trade started at Little Popo, it was noted that 'corne is always plenty' there.[176] It is not certain whether this refers to millet or maize, 'corn' being a generic term for cereals, but information from the early eighteenth century suggests the former. According to Rask, there were two different kinds of 'millie' on the Gold and Slave Coasts. The larger variety, evidently referring to maize, was cultivated on the Gold Coast, such as in Accra and Akwamu. The smaller variety, which from his description appears to be a kind of millet, was also produced at Accra but mainly east of the River Volta, by the Ewe ('Kræpees'), the 'Popos' and the people around Ouidah.[177] By the 1780s, when the provisioning of slave ships was an important part of Little Popo's trade with the Europeans, maize must have been established there (see Chapter 5). This is also indicated by Isert, who reported the sale of gruel made from 'Turkish corn', i.e. maize.[178] Robertson, whose activity in the region dated to the 1790s and 1800s, stated that 'Indian corn [= maize], yams, pulse, and a great variety of the leguminous species, are cultivated to a great extent' in the interior of the western Slave Coast.[179] The prevalence of two rainy seasons in the region made possible two or more annual harvests of maize, which is one factor that enabled the region to become a supplier of provisions during the period of the slave trade.[180]

As regards animal husbandry, accounts from the late eighteenth and nineteenth centuries document chicken, ducks, turkeys, goats, sheep, pigs and cattle in Little Popo and neighbouring Ewe regions.[181] With regard to

[174] Alpern, 'European Introduction', 25; de Marees, *Description*, 40.
[175] Westermann, *Wörterbuch*, 21, *s.v.* blí. Twi originally meant the language of the interior, as distinct from Fante, but by the late nineteenth century it had become adopted as the general name of the Twi-Fante group. It is in this sense that Westermann (and Christaller, see p.79, n.85) used it. In this study, I refer to this language complex as 'Akan', according to current scholarly convention.
[176] Law, *English in West Africa*, part 1, no. 495: Petly Wyborne, Guydah, 26 June 1683.
[177] Rask, *Brief and Truthful Description*, 138. For a similar distinction between large and small *millie* on the Gold Coast in the 1660s, see Wilhelm Johann Müller, 'Description of the Fetu Country', *German Sources for West African History 1599–1669*, ed. and transl. Adam Jones (Wiesbaden, 1983), 134–328, pp. 207–209; and in the 1740s, see Rømer, *Reliable Account*, 198.
[178] Isert, *Letters*, 124.
[179] Robertson, *Notes*, 234.
[180] Adams, *Remarks*, 164; Westermann, *Die Glidyi-Ewe*, 93, 98.
[181] TNA: T70/1573, George Lawson to Thomas Miles, Popoe, 21 Jan. 1796; Adams, *Remarks*, 186; Clapperton, *Hugh Clapperton*, 90; Duncan, *Travels*, i, 102, 108; GNA: ADM 1/2/361, incl. in no. 26: Lawson 'Report' (1879), 54–5; Henrici, *Das Deutsche Togogebiet*, 114–15; Klose, *Togo*, 72, 259–61.

the latter place, Robertson stated that 'horned cattle, sheep and other stock are numerous, and generally in good condition'.[182] In the 1820s, Monrad documented the existence of 'entire herds' of goats and sheep at (Little) Popo.[183] Some twenty years later, the British naval officer who compiled the sailing directions for the Bight of Benin listed Little Popo among the places where 'an abundance of stock' could be obtained for the provisioning of the vessels of the British navy's anti-slave trade squadron.[184] Cattle rearing was first documented at Little Popo in the 1840s, in the quarter of the family of Francisco Felix de Souza, a Brazilian slave trader based at Ouidah.[185] In the 1880s, Henrici reported that there was 'a good number' of cattle at Little Popo and further east, due to the demand for meat by Europeans.[186] However, few but the wealthiest Africans could afford to keep cows.[187] Henrici believed that cattle rearing was possible on the coast because there was no tsetse fly, but this seems doubtful as some tsetse species are especially associated with the riverine and lacustrine environments on the West African coast.[188] More plausibly, these cattle were of the kind that was relatively tolerant of trypanosome.[189]

It is impossible to say much about animal husbandry before the late eighteenth century, due to the lack of contemporary documentation. Evidently, the situation in the late eighteenth and nineteenth centuries had been shaped by the European demand for meat during the period of the slave trade, when the region was a supplier of livestock as well as agricultural produce. This demand resulted not only in the spread and intensification of animal husbandry, but also in the introduction of new breeds and species, such as pigs and turkeys.[190]

Crafts. Other economic activities noted by nineteenth-century visitors include the manufacture of pottery, bags, baskets, 'country mats', cotton cloth and hammocks, as well as blacksmithing, tannery and wood carving.[191]

---

[182] Robertson, *Notes*, 234–5. See also Adams, *Remarks*, 173.
[183] Monrad, *Description*, 176.
[184] UKHO: OD8, Denham, 'Remarks' (1846), 62, 66. The other places in this list are Woe ('Awey'), Keta, Elmina Chica, Ouidah and Badagry.
[185] Duncan, *Travels*, i, 103. In contrast, cattle breeding had a longer tradition in the Anlo region. A visitor in the early eighteenth century noted 'a multitude of cows and sheep' at Keta and on the route from Keta to Anloga counted 'not less than 13 herds of cows, each consisting of at least 100 animals' (van Dantzig, *Dutch and the Guinea Coast*, no.228, WIC 124, Minutes of Council Meeting, Elmina: 17 Feb. 1718: Oral report by Bookkeeper-General Ph. Eytzen).
[186] Henrici, *Das deutsche Togogebiet*, 114.
[187] Westerman, *Die Glidyi-Ewe*, 122 n. 2.
[188] Henrici, *Das deutsche Togogebiet*, 114.
[189] John Ford, *The Role of the Trypanosomiases in African Ecology: A Study of the Tsetse-Fly Problem* (Oxford, 1971), 44–7, 368–9, 381–4; Harrison Church, *West Africa*, 125–6.
[190] Harrison Church, *West Africa*, 133, 135; Duncan, *Travels*, i, 137.
[191] UKHO: OD 9A, Struvé, 'Report' (22 Aug. 1850); TNA: FO84/893, incl. in Hamilton, [London] 10 April 1852: Lieut. T. G. Forbes, HMS 'Philomel', at Whydah, 5 Feb. 1852; Duncan, *Travels*, i, 93–4; 101, 108; 146, Klose, *Togo*, 262–6; Zöller, *Das Togoland*, 136–7; van Zütphen, *Tagebuch*, 56.

The spinning and weaving of cotton cloth was already documented in the eighteenth century.[192] Its quality impressed European observers and was consequently much commented on. It was produced from local cotton, which grew wild in the region and by the mid-nineteenth century was also cultivated.[193] The cotton was spun, dyed in various colours and woven into strips of cloth four or five inches broad that were then sown together. Coloured thread from European cloth that had been unpicked for the purpose was also woven in, particularly of red colour which was not available locally.[194] According to Duncan, this cloth was 'very high in price' and 'much stronger and more durable than that manufactured in England.'[195] It may have been this kind of cloth, called 'Popo cloth', that is referred to when the ruler of Little Popo, Ashampo, was reported in 1744 to have sent the Danish Governor at Accra 'a negro *pantjes*' as part of a gift exchange.[196]

Markets, trade routes and toll stations. The salt and fish produced by the Hula were traded with neighbouring groups, such as the Ewe and Aja, for agricultural produce and other necessities. The place of exchange was the markets, of which there were three different kinds in the late nineteenth century: the great market, the market in the village and the market on the road. The great market was important for inter-regional trade. It was organised by groups of neighbouring settlements forming a market-cycle with markets being held at or near each place in rotation on successive days. On the western Slave Coast, several such market cycles had been set up already. Glidji and Little Popo participated in a cycle comprising five markets held successively in the following places: Agbanaken, Beta, Anyogboe, Vogan and Eklen.[197]

Agbanaken, on the northern bank of the Aného lagoon, was the place where the market for Glidji and neighbouring places was held.[198] It was

---

[192] Isert, *Letters*, 124–6.
[193] Duncan, *Travels*, i, 93, 101.
[194] Isert, *Letters*, 124–6; *PP* Colonies Africa 1842, p.117, Report from the Select Committee on the Coast of West Africa (Capt. H. Seward, 10 May 1842); Klose, *Togo*, 262. For a perceptive analysis of cotton weaving in pre-colonial West Africa, specifically the use of the narrow loom, see Gareth Austin, 'Resources, Techniques, and Strategies South of the Sahara: Revising the Factor Endowments Perspective on African Economic Development, 1500–2000', *Economic History Review*, 61/3 (2008), 587–624 (pp. 602–04).
[195] Duncan, 'Note', 144–5; *id.*, *Travels*, i, 106. For the name, see Jones/Sebald, *African Family Archive*, 1.250, F. Struve to G. L. Lawson Jr Esq., Brig *Ada Mary* off Whydah, Thursday, 14 Nov. 1850.
[196] Justesen, *Danish Sources*, XI.29: Opinions and votes of the members of the Secret Council in the matter of L. F. Römer's journey to Popo, 23–35 Sept. 1744 (L.F. Römer, Christiansborg, 25 Sept. 1744).
[197] Westermann, *Die Glidyi-Ewe*, 96–7. Cf. Manoukian, *The Ewe-Speaking People*, 19; Zöller, *Das Togoland*, 123. For the Slave Coast more generally, see Bouche, *Sept ans*, 196–7. Unless otherwise indicated, the following two paragraphs are based on Westermann. The traditional Ge week was based on this market cycle, with the five days named after the place where the market was held on the respective day. At Ouidah, the market was held every four days (Law, *Slave Coast*, 47; *Ouidah*, 82).
[198] N.B. This place is not to be confused with the royal capital of Grand Popo bearing the same name. It was a place near Glidji which was originally uninhabited but by the late nineteenth

documented by European visitors from the 1780s. Isert called this market 'the real breadbasket of [Little] Popo'. According to him, it was visited by the inhabitants of the coastal settlement of Little Popo, who came 'in crowds by way of the lagoon to fetch their victuals, which they would not be able to raise at [Little] Popo where the ground is so sandy.' Foodstuffs were so abundant that the traders 'not only supply the Popos, but they also handle substantial bulk cargoes, particularly salt, which are transported by canoe on an arm of the lagoon which stretches to Fida [= Ouidah] for sale there.'[199] The salt mentioned here possibly came from the Grand Popo area. Grand Popo's political status in this period is not clear, but it may have been a tributary to Little Popo, in which case (part of) the tribute may have been paid in salt (see chapter 5). In the 1840s, Duncan described this market as 'the principal market of commerce for all the neighbouring krooms and towns in the vicinity, either on the lagoon or inland', surpassed only by the market at Ouidah.[200] By the mid-1890s, it was dominated by the trade in palm oil and kernels but there was also a great trade in fish, 'the favourite and main food of the coastal people.'[201]

Beta lay near Togo, on the northern bank of the lagoon. This market was documented by Duncan, who listed its manufactures as 'cotton cloths, generally blue and white stripe, earthen pots, lime, indigo, country mats, and grass bags holding about a bushel'.[202] Anyogboe (or 'Seva Beach'), on the eastern banks of Lake Togo, was where the market for Seva was held. According to information from the 1880s, which can probably be extrapolated to earlier periods, this was where the Ouatchi bought fish from the people who fished in Lake Togo and other parts of the lagoon.[203] It was first documented by Duncan, who had missed the market which was held the day after his visit there.[204] Vogan ('Vo') was a market town at the end of the Zowla lagoon ('Vo lagoon'). This market also served the neighbouring town of Vo-Kutime ('Little Vo').[205] By the 1880s it functioned as a major entrepôt for the palm oil trade, being attended by 'several thousand and often up to 6,000 people.'[206] Finally, Eklen was the market for Agoué and Agouégan, among others.

(cont.) century had become occupied (Westermann, *Die Glidyi-Ewe*, 96). Europeans identified it as 'Glidji-Kpodji' or simply 'Glidji'. (See below, note 200).
[199] Isert, *Letters*, 122.
[200] Duncan, *Travels*, i, 106–8 ('Gregapojee'). See also UKHO: OD 9A, Struvé, 'Report' (19 Dec. 1849, 22 Aug. 1850); GNA: ADM 1/2/361, incl. in no. 26: Lawson, 'Report' (1879), 44; Henrici, *Das Deutsche Togogebiet*, iv-v ('Gridschibodschi').
[201] Klose, *Togo*, 82.
[202] Duncan, *Travels*, 146 ('Badaguay'). This place is marked on Lawson's map as 'Gbadigba' and in his report as Gbarugbe or GNA: ADM 1/2/361, incl. in no. 26: Lawson, 'Report' (1879), 42. See Map 5.
[203] Westermann, 'Kindheitserinnerungen', 7.
[204] Duncan, *Travels*, 150–2.
[205] GNA: ADM 1/2/361, incl. in no. 26: Lawson, 'Report' (1879), 47.
[206] Zöller, *Das Togoland*, 123–4. See also Klose, *Togo*, 70, 81, 83.

There were further interregional markets belonging to different market cycles. One was at Anfoin, at the end of the eastern branch of the Zowla lagoon, and fell on the same day as the market at Eklen.[207] It may have formed part of the same cycle as the market at Aklaku, on the Gbaga river, but information about this is lacking.[208] Further west, on the north-western bank of Lake Togo, there was 'a very large market place' near Gbome, first documented by Duncan in the 1840s. As in the case of the other markets mentioned here, all of which were situated on the lagoons or rivers, it had the advantage of 'convenient water-carriage'.[209]

Research on other coastal fishing and salt-producing communities in West and West Central Africa has shown that these communities were privileged to develop a strong middleman position in the Afro-European trade. The indigenous long-distance trade in salt and dried fish established the structures and routes that were subsequently used and expanded by the Afro-European trade.[210] The western Slave Coast's most important trade route to the interior was the Mono. According to information from the late nineteenth century, salt was traded up this river from Grand Popo to Atakpame, some 93 miles/150km inland. From there, it was taken overland through Kpessi to the Tchamba region and then distributed further into the interior.[211] Although this particular description refers to salt imported from France, which was traded especially during the rainy season when the supply of indigenous salt did not answer the demand, it can be assumed that the European salt was traded along established routes which had been used earlier by the Hula. This is also indicated by Klose who noted the importance of the rivers for the transport of salt both in his and former times.[212]

According to Isert, the King of Grand Popo called himself 'Master of the Lagoon', a title which reflects the control he exercised over the coastal waterways.[213] If this was largely a matter of ritual, he also drew real economic profit from it by means of tolls which he collected from canoes passing through his area.[214] There is no information about the toll stations in the period before 1800, but in the nineteenth century five such stations were documented at crucial points in the lagoon system. One was situated

---

[207] Westermann, *Die Glidyi-Ewe*, 96–7; GNA: ADM 1/2/361, incl. in no. 26: Lawson, 'Report' (1879), 49 ('Umfoy').
[208] GNA: ADM 1/2/361, incl. in no. 26: Lawson, 'Report' (1879), 49.
[209] Duncan, *Travels*, i, 152–4 ('Podefo'). See also GNA: ADM 1/2/361, incl. in no. 26: Lawson, 'Report', 27; Zöller, *Das Togoland*, 105; Klose, *Togo*, 91–2, 109.
[210] E.g. E. J. Alagoa, 'Long-Distance Trade and States in the Niger Delta', *JAH*, 11/3 (1970), 319–29; Austen/Derrick, *Middlemen*, 19–23; Lars Sundstrøm, *The Exchange Economy of Pre-Colonial Tropical Africa* (London, 1974), 123.
[211] Klose, *Togo*, 79, 454. See also Bouche, 'Notes', 94.
[212] Klose, *Togo*, 78–9.
[213] Isert, *Letters*, 127.
[214] TNA: FO84/893, incl. in Hamilton, [London], 10 April 1852: Lieut. T. G. Forbes, HMS 'Philomel', at Whydah, 5 Feb. 1852.

at the confluence of the Mono with the lagoon, just south of Agbanaken, and was designed to control both the passage along the coastal lagoons and the route along the Mono to the interior.[215] The collection of tolls there was already documented in 1803, when a British trader travelling along the lagoon from Ouidah to Little Popo was forced to make a detour to Agbanaken to pay duty.[216]

Another toll station, already noted above, was located at the eastern limits of Grand Popo, at Ahodenu, on the western bank of the Aho river close to its confluence with the lagoon. Lawson implies that it was a Dahomean station, reporting that tolls were collected there 'before entering the Whydah territory proper.'[217] Two toll stations were documented in the 1840s in Little Popo territory, at Glidji and Zalive. The latter was situated on the banks of the lagoon a short distance north-west of Glidji, where the Zowla lagoon branches off from the arm of the lagoon running along the coast towards Lake Togo. According to Duncan, these two stations, consisting of barriers thrown across the river, were only about one mile apart, their purpose being 'to catch all parties attending the markets of both the latter places, whether on descending or ascending the lagoon, each bar being respectively placed below and above both towns.'[218] Finally, in 1850 Struvé marked a 'toll house' to the west of Glidji, on the lagoon running from Little Popo to Lake Togo.[219] Its remains were documented by Zöller in the mid-1880s. By then, there were only two functioning 'toll fences' on the lagoon linking the towns between Grand Popo and Togo, one at Grand Popo and another at Agbanaken.[220] The question is of course whether these toll stations already existed in the earlier period. It seems likely that they were only established with the growth of the trade after the beginning of the Afro-European commercial enterprise, but due to the lack of information this is impossible to say with any certainty.

It is noteworthy that until the 1840s the tolls were paid in goods, that is cloth and liquor, rather than cowry shells, the local currency.[221] By 1859, however, they were paid in cowries, which may have been a result of the

[215] Ibid.
[216] M'Leod, Voyage, 137–8. For further references to this toll station, see Robertson, Notes, 237; Duncan, 'Note', 146 (mistakenly referring to the place as 'Little Popoe', while calling Little Popo simply 'Popoe'); id., Travels, i, 110–1; Fraser, 'Scraps from the daily memoranda', 7 Nov. 1851, in Fraser, Dahomey, 124–5; UKHO: L7791, Struvé, 'West Coast of Africa: Plan of the Coast Lagoon' (1849–50); WMMS: William West, Cape Coast, 6 June 1859; GNA: ADM 1/2/361, incl. in no. 26: Lawson 'Report' (1879), 65, map.
[217] Ibid., 68. See also Duncan, Travels, i, 182–3.
[218] Duncan, Travels, i, 145. According to Lawson, on the lagoon just north of Zalivé ('Save') lay 'Azedenu', which he described as an insignificant farming village. As noted above, 'denu' means toll station, suggesting perhaps that this was a defunct toll station (GNA: ADM 1/2/361, incl. in no. 26: Lawson, 'Report' [1879], 46, map).
[219] UKHO: L7791, Struvé, 'West Coast of Africa' (1849–50).
[220] Zöller, Das Togoland, 103.
[221] M'Leod, A Voyage, 138; Duncan, Travels, i, 111.

intensification of the use of money in consequence of the expansion of the palm oil trade.[222] (See Chapter 6). As noted above, the Hula traditions cited by Mouléro are a reminder that the Europeans introduced cowries (which originally come from the Maldive Islands) into the region.[223] The importation of cowries into Grand Popo in exchange for slaves was documented in the mid-seventeenth century.[224] In the early eighteenth century, Rask reported with reference to Grand Popo and Little Popo (among other places on the Slave Coast), that they 'much prefer, in trade and business, to receive payment in bussies [= cowries] rather than gold'.[225]

The more general transformations of the local economy through the interaction with the European trade will be discussed in detail in the following chapter.

[222] WMMS: West Africa Correspondence: Box 263: William West, Cape Coast, 6 June 1859. For a discussion of the link between the spread of the cowry currency and the palm-oil trade, see Robin Law, '"Legitimate" Trade and Gender Relations in Yorubaland and Dahomey', *From Slave Trade to 'Legitimate' Commerce*, ed. Law, 195–214 pp. 199–200.
[223] Mouléro, 'Histoire', 43.
[224] Jones, *West Africa*, 233.
[225] Rask, *Brief and Truthful Description*, 74.

2

The Atlantic connection
Little Popo & the rise of Afro-European trade on the western Slave Coast, c. 1600 to 1702

In the seventeenth century, the western Slave Coast was transformed by two interrelated developments; first, the development of European trade on this section of the coast and, second, the immigration and settlement of Gold Coast people in the region.

In 1471, the Portuguese arrived on the Gold Coast, which they called Costa da Mina, and started trading for gold there.[1] In the following year, they began charting the coast to the east of the Volta river. Initially, however, they showed little interest in exploring the commercial potential of the region that was to become the Slave Coast. Their focus was on the gold trade on the Costa da Mina and the commercial relations which they established elsewhere in West Africa were developed mainly in order to further this trade. Thus, slaves purchased in the kingdom of Benin (in today's Nigeria), where the Portuguese traded by the 1480s, were re-sold on the Costa da Mina in exchange for gold. Moreover, the forbidding conditions of the sea on the Slave Coast probably acted as a deterrent to any attempt to establish contacts with the people there. When they eventually did become interested in the Slave Coast, it was the outlets of the rivers and the lagoon into the sea which they explored. First they investigated the Lagos channel at the eastern end of the Slave Coast, which was evidently successful because through it they established contact with the kingdom of Ijebu. In 1530 their attention turned to the Volta on the western end of the Slave Coast, following reports that interlopers threatened the royal monopoly of the gold trade. This too was successful, and trade was established there soon afterwards, probably by 1536. The only other riverine outlet on the Slave Coast was the Bouche du Roi, which attracted the interest of the Portuguese in 1553, when a trade embargo with Benin prompted them to look

[1] For Portuguese activities on the coast, see also John Vogt, *The Portuguese Rule on the Gold Coast 1469–1682* (Athens, 1991).

elsewhere for alternative sources of slaves. However, the initial attempt to establish contact with the people on 'the river which is called the Papoues' was reported to have failed due to 'the bad management of those who went there'.[2] Nevertheless, commercial relations with Grand Popo were established soon afterwards, as indicated by a report from 1607 which includes 'Poupo' in a list of the West African trading sites frequented by the Portuguese. According to this document, the proceeds from trade at Popo equalled those from Benin and were half the size of those from Allada and twice as much as those from 'Faloim', which Law has identified with Ouidah (indigenous name, Glehué), the coastal port of the kingdom of Hueda.[3] Popo is also mentioned as a place of trade in Alonso de Sandoval's account from 1627, but it had a poor reputation, its ruler being allegedly 'a tyrant with those who arrive at his port.'[4]

The Portuguese organised their West African trade by dividing the coast into several administrative units, called 'capitanias', each of which had its own headquarters to take charge of the trade in the region. Thus, the 'Capitania da Mina' extended from Cape Palmas to the Volta and had its headquarters at Fort São Jorge da Mina, at Elmina. The 'Capitania de São Tomé', administered from Fort São Sebastião on the island of São Tomé, comprised the area from the Volta to the Congo river ('Rio Zaire') and included the region of the Slave Coast.[5] This pattern of trade changed in the first half of the seventeenth century, after the Dutch had replaced the Portuguese as the dominant European power on the West African coast. The Dutch trade on the Slave Coast was directed from the headquarters of the Dutch West India Company (WIC) at Elmina, from where they had ousted the Portuguese in 1637. Lodges for the slave trade were maintained at Allada between 1638 and 1643 and between about 1649 to 1653, while at other periods the trade was carried on by small yachts coasting between Elmina and Allada. The latter practice, which is first documented in 1645, appears to have been a Dutch innovation. In 1660 another lodge was established at Allada's port Offra, this time to be maintained for more than 30 years.[6]

The other European nations that joined the trade from the mid-seventeenth century also followed the Dutch pattern, establishing headquarters on the Gold Coast and trading on the Slave Coast either directly by vessel or through factories that were reportable to the headquarters.[7] Among them

[2] Brásio, *Monumenta*, 1st series, ii, no.97: Relatório de Jácome Leite a El-Rei, 8 Aug. 1553.
[3] Ibid., v, no.137: Relação da Costa da Guiné, 1607. The annual value of the Allada trade was estimated at 800 milreis, that of Popo and Benin at 400 milreis and that of 'Faloim' at 200 milreis. For identification of 'Faloim' with Ouidah, see Law, 'Problems', 349–51, Law, *Slave Coast*, 120.
[4] Sandoval, *Naturaleza*, 51, cited in Law, *Slave Coast*, 141–2.
[5] Brásio, *Monumenta*, 1st series, v, no.137: Relação da Costa da Guiné, 1607.
[6] Jones, *West Africa*, 2; Law, *Slave Coast*, 121–2.
[7] For the development of European trade on the West African Coast, see Law, *Slave Coast*, 116–36.

was the English Company of Royal Adventurers Trading into Africa, which in 1672 was replaced by the Royal African Company (RAC). In 1663 it established a factory at Allada and in 1665 its headquarters at Cape Coast Castle. The French, who had entered the trans-Atlantic slave trade with the formation of the Compagnie des Indes Occidentales in 1664, had no settlements on the Gold Coast in the period. They established a factory at Allada in 1670, which in 1671 was transferred to Ouidah. The Brandenburg African Company, which existed for a brief period from 1682 to 1716, had its headquarters at Gross-Friedrichsburg near Cape Three Points.[8] The Danish African Company was active on the Gold Coast from 1659 but (apart from a brief spell of interest in Allada in early 1660s) engaged in trade on the Slave Coast only after 1694.[9] Besides the chartered companies, interlopers, that is individuals trading in breach of the companies' monopoly of trade, were active on the coast.

The Dutch, who had become interested in the slave trade in the 1630s, were trading at Grand Popo by the mid-seventeenth century. A document from an anonymous manuscript written between 1642 and about 1655 notes with regard to Grand Popo, 'Here too one can obtain some slaves, if there have been no ships for 13–14 months.'[10] The merchandise recommended to enable traders to 'buy slaves quickly at Popo' included cowries, 'the more the better', various kinds of beads and cloths, iron bars and crystal rosaries.[11] In 1660, the WIC established a lodge at Grand Popo, which however appears to have functioned principally as a supplier of slaves for sale at Offra, Allada's main port, rather than as an independent point of embarkation.[12] This is indicated by the testimony of the French naval officer Delbée, who passed along the coast on his way to Allada in early 1670. Nevertheless, the local Dutch agent who communicated with Delbée offered him a cargo of slaves, wishing 'very much that one trades with him and that ships anchor in his road, to save the duty that he pays, this he said to us when we passed, by a man who came from him on board, and promised us 400 slaves in one month…'[13] In the following year, Henri Carolof established a factory for the French at Grand Popo, evidently in consequence of the disruption of the supply in slaves at Offra, due to local disturbances.[14] However, this venture presumably ended when the French transferred their factory from Offra to Ouidah in the same year. Another French trader, Jean

---

[8] Jones, *Brandenburg Sources*, 3; Law, *Slave Coast*, 132.
[9] Nørregård, *Danish Settlements*, 42–3; Law, *Slave Coast*, 124, 133.
[10] Jones, *West Africa*, 3, 197.
[11] Jones, *West Africa*, 233.
[12] Law, *Slave Coast*, 142, citing [NAN:] NBGK 81, Elmina Journal, 5 June 1660. According to van Dantzig, this lodge was established only in 1666 (*Les Hollandais*, 262).
[13] Delbée, 'Journal', 382. He used 'Tary' to refer to Grand Popo. See Law, 'Problems', 351–2.
[14] See Law, *Slave Coast*, 127–8, 143, citing TNA: ADM7/830: Jean Barbot, 'Description des Côtes d'Affrique, depuis le Cap Bojador jusques à celui de Lopo Gonzalves' [ms of 1688].

Barbot, visited Grand Popo in 1682. He reported that 'one manages to do a fairly considerable trade there for slaves (*captifs*), in exchange for cowries, iron, glass beads, linen (*toilles*), etc.'[15] He also mentions the existence of a Dutch lodge at Grand Popo, but this seems to be repeated from Delbée's account since the WIC's lodge had been destroyed by 'Lampi raiders', that is Adangme bandits, in 1680.[16] In July 1682, the WIC sent out an agent to Allada with instructions to investigate the advisability of re-establishing this lodge (as well as that at Ouidah) 'for the furtherance of the slave trade', but this did not materialise until 1688.[17]

In this period, Grand Popo played a role of secondary importance for the European slave traders, whose interest focused on Allada and, from the 1670s, on Ouidah. This was due to the comparatively small number of slaves that the kingdom was able to supply, which can probably be explained at least partly by Grand Popo's subjection to Allada. Slaves for export were sent there rather than being sold directly to Europeans traders.

The immigration of Gold Coast canoemen

Besides the coasting trade, the Dutch also appear to have initiated the practice of recruiting Gold Coast canoemen for service on the Slave Coast. As discussed in the previous chapter, the difficult conditions on the Slave Coast made landing impossible for European vessels or their boats and the local people lacked the skill and technology for maritime navigation. Therefore, the Europeans were dependent on canoemen and canoes from the Gold Coast for managing the passage of goods and people from ship to shore and back through the surf.

The practice of taking canoemen and canoes to the Slave Coast, which was followed throughout the period of the slave trade until the mid-nineteenth century, is first documented in an anonymous Dutch manuscript from the mid-seventeenth century, in a document giving instructions for trade at Grand Popo ('Popo'): 'If you wish to trade here, you must bring a new strong canoe with you from the Gold Coast with oarsmen, because one cannot get through the surf in any boat.'[18] Instructions prepared in 1670 by Carolof for the use of French captains trading at Allada also say that canoes

---

[15] Barbot, *Barbot*, 620 (author's/editor's italics). A Danish document from 1680, citing a Dutch source, gives similar information about the trade goods demanded at Grand Popo but adds brandy, knives, guns and gunpowder: Justesen, *Danish Sources*, I.22.,V.-g.K.; 77, List of the kinds of goods in demand in Guinea, undated [1680].

[16] Law, *Slave Coast*, 243; Barbot, *Barbot*, 629 n.15, citing R. A. Kea, 'I am here to plunder on the general road': Bandits and Banditry in the Pre-Nineteenth-Century Gold Coast', *Banditry, Rebellion and Social Protest in Africa*, ed. D. Crummey (London, 1986), 109–32, p.130 n.57; [NAN:] WIC 1024, unsigned letter, Offra, 29.12.1680.

[17] Van Dantzig, *Dutch and the Guinea Coast*, no. 14: Instructions for Martin Witte, 3 July 168[2].

[18] Jones, *West Africa*, 197.

were to be brought from the Gold Coast. The captains were required to stop on the Gold Coast at Takoradi (east of Cape Three Points), in order to buy a canoe from Ahanta ('Ante'), these being 'light and the most suitable for use at Ardres [= Allada]'.[19] Barbot also refers to this practice when noting that 'The men of Mina are the best at manoeuvring [the large bar] canoes over the breakers without an upset, at least more often than not without one, and you could hardly manage with any other men at Juda and Offra, where the breakers are more dangerous than anywhere else in Guinea.'[20]

There is little information about this practice for the mid-seventeenth century, but documents from the 1680s and 1690s give much detail which can probably be extrapolated to the earlier period. According to them, canoes for use on the Slave Coast were usually bought in the neighbourhood of Cape Three Points, where there was forest that provided the timber for their construction.[21] Sometimes canoes were also purchased second-hand at other places, as recorded by the English ship's captain Thomas Phillips, who in 1694 bought a second-hand canoe at Accra.[22] The canoes were then adapted by the European traders to the boisterous conditions on the Slave Coast by fitting weatherboards, 'to keep the sea out, they plunging very deep when they go against a sea'.[23]

The canoemen were Akan-speaking people from the coastal area west of the Sakumo/Densu river, who were normally recruited by the European traders at the places where their respective nations had settlements. Thus, the Dutch mainly hired people from Elmina, the seat of their headquarters, although they also had a number of other settlements on the Gold Coast. Elmina canoemen were credited with outstanding skills in negotiating the crossing on the Slave Coast, as documented among others by Barbot, quoted above.[24] The French and the Portuguese, who did not have settlements on the Gold Coast, also seem to have recruited Elminans.[25] The

---

[19] Cf. Law, 'Between the Sea', 225, quoting Delbée, 'Journal', 482–4.
[20] Barbot 1732, p. 84, in Barbot, *Barbot*, ii, 529. Cf. Law, 'Between the Sea', 225.
[21] Barbot, *Barbot*, ii, 528–9; Jones, *Brandenburg Sources*, 187 n.24.
[22] Thomas Phillips, 'A Journal of a Voyage made in the Hannibal of London, Ann. 1693, 1694, From England to Cape Monseradoe, in Africa; And then along the Coast of Guiney to Whidaw, the Island of St. Thomas, and so forward to Barbadoes', *A Collection of Voyages and Travels, some now first printed from original manuscripts, others now first published in English*, comp. A. and J. Churchill (1732, repr. London, 1746), 227. Cf. Law, 'Between the Sea', 225–6.
[23] Phillips, 'Journal', 244. See also *ibid.*, 226; Law, *English in West Africa*, part 2, no.807, Marcus Bed: Whiting, James Fort, Accra, 4 April 1688. Cf. Law, 'Between the Sea', 227.
[24] Barbot 1732, p. 84, in Barbot, *Barbot*, ii, 529. Already in the 1620s it was noted that the 'Mina' were 'skilful fishermen, greatly outnumbering all their neighbours both in canoes and in people' ('1629 map' cited in Barbot, *Barbot*, ii, 388 ed.'s n.30).
[25] As regards the French, this is implied by Barbot (see above). The correspondence from the RAC factor at Ouidah in the 1680s also mentions a French captain who had brought a 'Mina cano', i.e. a crew of canoemen from Elmina, to Ouidah (Law, *English in West Africa*, part 2, no.817, John Carter, Whiddah, 7 June 1686). The Portuguese trade on the Slave Coast revived from the 1680s. From 1689 the Portuguese vessels on their way to the Slave Coast were obliged to stop at Elmina to pay a tax on their cargoes, and presumably also hired canoemen there (Law, *Slave Coast*, 135).

English mainly recruited canoemen from Cape Coast, the seat of their headquarters, but also from other settlements such as Anomabo.[26] The Brandenburgers are documented to have taken canoemen at Anomabo, but presumably also hired them at other (English?) settlements.[27] At the last port of call on the Slave Coast the canoemen would be released to make their own way back to the Gold Coast, while the European ships made their way back to the Gold Coast, Europe or the Americas along the usual route via the Gabon. According to Phillips, the canoemen received half their pay (in gold) in advance on the Gold Coast and the other half (in goods) when discharged on the Slave Coast, and were normally given a canoe to return in.[28]

With the establishment of permanent trade posts on the Slave Coast, the Europeans came to rely on Gold Coast canoemen for yet another kind of service: as messengers between the factories on the Slave Coast and the headquarters on the Gold Coast. The correspondence of the RAC chief factor at Ouidah in the 1680s, John Carter, shows that his communication with his superiors at Cape Coast Castle was normally conducted via canoemen who were returning to the Gold Coast after having been engaged on the Slave Coast.[29] The same was the case for the Dutch, who between 1660 and 1692 had a factory at Offra, although in the 1680s the WIC also employed a small yacht for communication between the Elmina and Slave Coast.[30] The canoemen's services were particularly important for communications from the outforts to the headquarters on the Gold Coast, due to the prevailing currents which made it difficult for European vessels to sail from east to west. Nevertheless, sometimes canoemen were also used to convey messages from the headquarters to the outforts, especially if there were no European vessels by which they could be forwarded.[31]

While many of the canoemen employed by the Europeans on the Slave Coast returned to the Gold Coast once their term of employment was finished, some also came to settle on the Slave Coast, where they offered their services to the European factors and traders. At Allada, this appears to have been happening already by the early 1650s, as implied by the anonymous Dutch manuscript which mentions a 'Captain Honga' among the king's noblemen, i.e. a local official who was the 'captain of [the] boat which

---

[26] See, for example, Law, *English in West Africa*, part 2, no.814, John Carter, Whidah, 1 March 1686; no.822, John Carter, Whiddah, 6 Jan. 1686/7; no.824, John Carter, Whidah, 16 March 1687.

[27] Jones, *Brandenburg Sources*, no.79: Johann Peter Oettinger's Account of his Voyage to Guinea (1692–3), 180–98, p.188.

[28] Phillips, 'Journal', 245. See also Law, *English in West Africa*, part 2, no.814, John Carter, Whidah, 1 March 1686. This practice continued into the nineteenth century: see e.g. van Zütphen, *Tagebuch*, 36.

[29] See Law, *English in West Africa*, part 2, nos.814–826, John Carter, Ouidah, 1686–7.

[30] *Ibid.*, no.822, John Carter, Whiddah, 6 Jan. 1686/7; no.826, John Carter, Whiddah, 29 Aug. 1687.

[31] *Ibid.*, no.814, John Carter, Whidah, 1 March 1686.

goes in and out.'³² Carolof's 'Instruction' from 1670 seems to confirm this because it requests only canoes to be brought from the Gold Coast, while the canoemen who conveyed them ashore were 'local Blacks'.³³ Since the local people were not skilled in maritime navigation, these local canoemen must have been immigrant Gold Coast canoemen who had settled there. By the 1690s Ouidah too boasted a community of canoemen from Elmina. According to Phillips, who visited the place in 1694, 'About half a mile from [the English] factory is a croom of negroes, which call themselves *Mine-men*, and assist the *Dutch* ships that come here in their business…'³⁴

The Dutch coasting trade and the practice of employing Gold Coast canoemen on the Slave Coast apparently inspired the development of an African coasting trade between the Gold Coast and the Slave Coast.³⁵ It is first documented in 1659, when it was reported that 'for some years' the trade in 'akori' beads, which had earlier been purchased by the Europeans from Allada and Benin for re-sale on the Gold Coast in exchange for gold, had been monopolised by African traders from the Gold Coast, who were going in canoes to 'Lay [= La or Labadi, in the kingdom of Ladoku, west of Accra], Great and Little Popo and as far as Ardra [Allada] to buy them.'³⁶ In the 1680s, Barbot noted that Gold Coast 'cargo canoes' travelled 'from Gold Coast to all parts of the Gulf of Ethiopia, and beyond that to Angola', but it is not clear whether he meant that they were taken there by Africans from the Gold Coast themselves or by European vessels.³⁷ Barbot further reported that ivory for local use was imported from the Congo, while another French observer noted in 1688 that Gold Coast traders had tapped the trade in cloth at Ouidah: 'the Negroes even come with canoes to trade them, and carry them off ceaselessly.'³⁸

---

³² Hun-gan means 'boat-chief' in Fon. See Jones, *West Africa*, 41, 199 incl. n.2.
³³ Delbée, 'Journal', 484.
³⁴ Phillips, 'Journal', 244 (author's *italics*). See also van Dantzig, *Dutch and the Guinea Coast*, no.228, WIC 124: Minutes of Council-meeting, Elmina, 17 Feb. 1718: Oral report by Bookkeeper-General Ph. Eytzen.
³⁵ See Law, 'West Africa's Discovery', 8–9; Law, 'Between the Sea', 224–9; Law, *Slave Coast*, 148–9. It has been argued that a commercial connection between the Gold Coast and the Slave Coast had existed before the Europeans arrived on the West African coast (e.g. J. D. Fage, 'Some Remarks on Beads and Trade in Lower Guinea in the Sixteenth & Seventeenth Centuries', *JAH* 3, 2 [1962], 343–7, pp.343–4). However, due to lack of documentation this remains speculation.
³⁶ Report by J. Valkenburgh, Elmina, Sept. 1659, cited in Law, 'Between the Sea', 231. Cf. Law, *Slave Coast*, 149. Kea also cites this document but includes 'Afraa' in the list of places mentioned, which seems to be a mistake (222). Earlier attempts by African traders to establish trade relations between the Gold Coast and the area to the east are documented, but they were apparently fruitless and it is not clear whether they involved a coasting trade or overland connections. See Law, 'Between the Sea', 230.
³⁷ Barbot, *Barbot*, ii, 529. Cf. Law, 'Between the Sea', 231.
³⁸ Barbot, 'Description', iii, 135; J.-B. Ducasse, 'Relation du voyage fait en 1687 sur la frégate "La Tempeste" par le Sieur du Casse', in P. Roussier (ed.), *L'Établissement d'Issigny 1687–1702* (Paris, 1935), 1–47, p.15; both cited in Law, 'Between the Sea', 231.

The foundation of Aneho

Today there are a number of communities on the West African coast which trace their origins to immigrant canoemen and traders from the western Gold Coast. At Ouidah, there are three families whose ancestors are said to have been Gold Coast canoemen in the service of European traders: the Cotia, Kocou and Agbessikpé.[39] Accra is another example. It experienced a large immigration of Akan-speaking people who are credited with having introduced maritime navigation and sea-fishing to the local people.[40] Notably, one of Osu's (formerly Danish Accra) quarters is called Aneho, like the settlement on the western Slave Coast. Although its origins are obscure, the name suggests a connection between the two, and it seems likely that like the latter, the quarter at Accra had been founded by Akan-speaking canoemen and traders.[41]

At Aneho, the former Little Popo, the people of the Adjigo clan trace their origins to Gold Coast canoemen or traders. Their ancestors are regarded as the founders of the Aneho quarter, that is the settlement on the beach (rather than Aneho in the modern sense, which comprises Degbenu, Badji and Adjido as well as the original Aneho quarter). Their original settlement can probably be identified with modern Fantekome ('quarter of the Fante'), although in the late nineteenth century, when the name 'Aneho' was first documented, it was used to refer to the whole settlement on the beach which by then also comprised quarters founded by immigrants who had arrived later.[42] According to Bouche, who visited the region in the 1870s,

> ... the town has three distinct quarters, which have their own existence and interests. One of these quarters has the name Anéjo (houses of the Anès). It is there that the Mina blacks of the Anès tribe established themselves, who, coming from the Gold Coast, were thrown on the beach

[39] Law, *Ouidah*, 74–75.
[40] John Parker, *Making the Town: Ga State and Society in Early Colonial Africa* (Portsmouth, NH, 2000), 4–5, 16. Maritime navigation at Accra is documented in the 1590s, i.e. by this time the immigration of Akan-speaking people from the west had begun (de Marees, *Description*, 85). By the 1690s, when Bosman visited the coast, a large number of immigrants had settled there and the coastal economy thrived on sea-fishing, salt-making and trade with the Europeans (*New and Accurate Description*, 70). Parker dates the Fante immigration to the mid-eighteenth century (4–5).
[41] The earliest reference to the Aneho quarter at Osu (so far located) dates from 1814. However, the quarter was probably much older (O. Justesen, p.c., 22 April 2001). Another place that may have been settled by Gold Coast canoemen is Elmina Chica (to the east of Keta), as suggested by its name. It was first documented in 1852, as 'Adiner [= 'Edina', the indigenous name of Elmina] Cooma, or Elmina Chica' (TNA: FO84/893, incl. in Hamilton, [London] 10 April 1852: T. G. Forbes, 'Philomel', at Whydah, 5 Feb. 1852).
[42] Lawson 'Report', 35; Bouche, 'Notes', 99; Henrici, *Das Deutsche Togogebiet*, 'Erläuterungen zur Karte', IV-V.

by the storm. Their establishment at this place gave birth to the quarter which carries their name, but not to the town; Little Popo had already existed for a number of years [i.e. the original Hula town].[43]

In the 1880s, Henrici gave further detail regarding the origin and occupation of the immigrants. They were said to be traders from Elmina who travelled in their boats along the coast to Lagos:

> People from Elmina (the correct name of Elmina is Edina), that is Fanti, who made trade voyages in their boats from Elmina to Lagos, founded [...] on the Gridyi-beach, that is where today Anecho is, a resting place; they had seen smoke rising there from fishermen's [= Hula] camps and hoped that there would be good drinking water; the first tents, according to tradition, stood on the place where there is now the factory of the black Cole.[44]

Versions recorded in the twentieth century identify the ancestor of the Adjigo people as Quam Desu (Quam, i.e. Kwame, being the Akan name given to boys born on a Saturday), who is said to have been the leader of the immigrants from Elmina and who subsequently became the chief of the beach and collector of taxes from the European traders on behalf of the king at Glidji.[45] According to these traditions, the arrival of the Gold Coast canoemen or traders and the foundation of Aneho occurred later than the arrival of the Ga immigrants from Accra, who founded Glidji, the royal capital of Little Popo, in the 1680s. Contemporary documentation, however, shows that this is not correct but that the canoemen arrived before the Ga. The traditions can therefore be interpreted as an attempt to rationalise the political seniority of the Ga, who became the rulers of the place.

Little Popo ('Kleyn Popo') is first documented in 1659, more than 20 years before the arrival of the Ga, in Valkenburgh's report, already quoted above (note 36). Law has argued that it is significant that the earliest reference to it occurs in the context of the African coasting trade and that its purpose probably was to facilitate this trade.[46] This is supported by evidence from the 1680s, showing that Little Popo played an important

---

[43] Bouche, *Sept ans*, 305.
[44] Henrici, *Lehrbuch*, 4. As his source of information, Henrici gives 'the old lord ['Fürst'] Pedro Kwadjovi of Anecho, who died in the mid-[18]80s at the age of 90; he was born about 1794 and his great-grandparents belonged as children to the first settlers' (5). It is not clear whom he is referring to here, Pedro Kodjo/Quadjo or Kodjovi/Quadjovi aka Jehowey, both of whom were members of the Adjigo clan. According to a sketch of Little Popo from 1884, S.B. Cole's factory did indeed lie in Aplaviho, the former Hula settlement (Jones/Sebald, *African Familiy Archive*, map 2: [W. Stubenrauch, S.M.S. Sophie], 'Little Popo in February 1884').
[45] Agbanon II, *Histoire*, 36–7, 119, 137; n.a., *Adjigovi* (n.p., 1933), 4–5; Gaba, 'History', 36–9.
[46] Law, 'Between the Sea', 232. Cf. Law, *Slave Coast*, 149–50.

role in the lateral movement of canoemen along the coast. It served as a place of trans-shipment of the canoes from the lagoon to the sea as well as a way-station where the canoemen waited for the right season to proceed to the Gold Coast and where they supplied themselves with provisions. Carter's correspondence from the 1680s shows that canoemen returning from service at Allada or Ouidah made the first leg of the voyage, to Little Popo, by the lagoon. At Little Popo the canoes where hauled across the sandspit which separates the sea and the lagoon, continuing their voyage to the Gold Coast by sea. Carter explained that the canoes 'doe nott goe of from hence [Ouidah] but from Pickaninee Popo.'[47] It can be assumed that a similar practice was followed in the earlier period, and that Little Popo owed much of its initial importance to this function as the point of trans-shipment of canoes from the lagoon.[48]

The choice of Little Popo as the point of trans-shipment was probably due to its position towards the western end of the navigable lagoon-system and the closeness of an arm of the lagoon to the sea.[49] Another advantage must have been the existence of a Hula settlement which facilitated the supply of provisions and water. This is recalled in the traditions recorded by Henrici, quoted above, which note that it was particularly the availability of fresh water which attracted the attention of the immigrants. The abundance of corn (presumably supplied by Ewe and Aja cultivators north of the lagoon) also played a role. This was documented by Carter, who explained the canoemen's delays at Little Popo with the opportunity of 'victualling cheap', 'corne being more plenty there then [sic] here.'[50]

Carter further noted that the delays of the canoemen at Little Popo were due to the seasonal changes, particularly the canoemen's unwillingness 'to goe up at any other time than about the hermitan time…'[51] The harmattan season prevailed from about December to February, when the currents flowed from east to west, contrary to their normal direction. It coincided with the season when the Volta river ran low and its outlet was easy to pass, which according to eighteenth-century sources was from December or January to May.[52] Outside this period the river's outlet was difficult if not impossible to pass, due to the river's 'extraordinary rapid Discharge into the Sea'.[53] According to Bosman, 'one cannot convince any Negro to get past

---

[47] Law, *English in West Africa*, part 2, no.814, John Carter, Whidah, 1 Mar. 1686. See also Law, nos.820, 821, 824, John Carter, Whiddah, 6 Dec. 1686; 20 Dec. 1686; 16 March 1687.
[48] Law, 'Between the Sea', 232.
[49] Cf. *ibid*.
[50] Law, *English in West Africa*, part 2, no.820, John Carter, Whiddah, 6 Dec. 1686. See also no.824, Law, Whiddah, 16 March 1687.
[51] *Ibid.*, nos.814, 824, John Carter, Whidah, 1 Mar. 1686; 16 Mar. 1687.
[52] Rømer, *Reliable Account*, 207; Isert, *Letters*, 79.
[53] Van Dantzig, 'English Bosman', 273 (cf. Bosman, *New and Accurate Description*, 328). According to Bosman, 'one can pass it with a canoe only twice per year, mostly before April and before November.'

it, as they always stick to their habit of sailing close to the shore, which they cannot do here because of the aforesaid surf.'[54]

The traditions of the Adjigo people of Aného implicitly acknowledge the overlordship of the king of Grand Popo over the area settled by them. Some versions do so by recalling that a Hula settlement already existed there when the immigrants arrived, others by noting that the immigrants were granted the permission to settle by the king of Grand Popo.[55] This is quite plausible, given that the canoes from Offra and Ouidah to Little Popo must have passed along the lagoon through the territory of Grand Popo, for which they presumably acquired the king's permission and paid a tax or fee, as is recorded for the nineteenth century.[56] Moreover, evidence from the eighteenth century indicates that the canoemen acknowledged Grand Popo's overlordship. In the 1780s, Isert noted that the people of Little Popo recognised the religious authority of the king of Grand Popo, who (as noted before) called himself 'Master of the Lagoon' and visited Little Popo 'at different times of the year' to collect tribute from the locals and the European traders. The king's ritual authority over the canoemen was not restricted to the lagoons but also extended over the passage from ship to shore. He had the power to prevent the canoemen from launching their canoes into the sea by placing a 'fetish' on the beach.[57]

Ga-Adangme immigration into the western Slave Coast

In the late seventeenth and early eighteenth centuries, the western Slave Coast experienced another kind of immigration from the Gold Coast, by refugees from the kingdoms of Accra and Ladoku. This was due to the expansion of the Akwamu empire, in the interior of the eastern Gold Coast, which in this period conquered these two kingdoms, causing large numbers of the people to seek refuge to the east of the Volta.

The Ga kingdom of Accra had been the dominant middleman state on the eastern Gold Coast, controlling the trade in gold and slaves from the interior for the goods imported from the Europeans.[58] It occupied the stretch of coast between the Sakumo lagoon and Tema, with its royal capital, Great Accra, lying some fifteen kilometres in the interior. By the time of the

---

[54] Van Dantzig, 'English Bosman', 273 (cf. Bosman, *New and Accurate*, 328).
[55] Bouche, *Sept ans*, 305, Henrici, *Lehrbuch*, 4; n.a., *Adjigovi* (1933), 5; Gaba, 'History', 39.
[56] TNA: FO84/893, incl. in Hamilton, [London] Admiralty, 10 April 1852: T. G. Forbes, 'Philomel', Whydah, 5 Feb. 1852.
[57] Isert, *Letters*, 95. See also GK 156, I. [sic, should be J.A.] Kiøge, N. H. Weile, Little Popo, 25 Aug. 1774, cited by Gayibor, *Le Genyi*, 136 n. 3; Bjørn, 'Beretning 1788', 227, showing that in the 1770s and 1780s the king of Grand Popo received a fee for the Danish lodge at Little Popo.
[58] Ivor Wilks, 'The Rise of the Akwamu Empire, 1650–1710', *THSG* 3, 2 (1959), 99–136, pp. 104, 106, Parker, *Making the Town*, 2, 9–10; Barbot, *Barbot*, ii, 441 editor's n.1. See also Daaku, *Trade*; Kea, *Settlements*.

Akwamu conquest of Accra, there were three European forts on the Accra coast, the Dutch fort Crèvecoeur at Little Accra (Aprag), the Danish fort Christiansborg at Osu and the English James Fort at Soko, all lying within four kilometres of each other. The Danes had supplanted the Swedes, who had traded at Osu in the 1650s, and were themselves eclipsed for a brief period by the Portuguese, who between 1679 and 1683 occupied Christiansborg.

The Adangme kingdom of Ladoku (known to the Europeans as 'Lampi' or 'Alampo') was situated to the east of Accra.[59] It stretched from east of Tema to the area settled by the Agave people just west of the Volta, comprising the modern areas of Ada, Kpone, Osudoku, Ningo, Prampram and Shai. The capital, Ladoku, was situated a few kilometres inland, while Ningo and La (modern Lepunguno) were important port towns where the Europeans traded for gold and slaves.

The chronology of the Akwamu conquest of these kingdoms is not very clear. It has been discussed in an article by Wilks which is often cited in the scholarly literature but who uses very few strictly contemporary sources, presumably because few were available at the time.[60] According to him, Akwamu's conquest of Accra began with a successful attack of the capital, Great Accra, in 1677. The capital was destroyed and the king, Okai Koi, and his eldest son were executed. The people who survived this attack fled to the coastal towns, seeking protection under the cannons of the European forts. Among them was a younger son of Okai Koi, Ofori, who became the successor to his father, and his mother. This is corroborated by contemporary Danish sources.[61] They settled at Little Accra, near the Dutch fort, which is where Barbot met them during his visit in early 1679. According to him, 'King Fourri' was 'a young man of 22–23', 'of short stature and also plump.'[62]

The Ga refugees in the coastal towns held out against Akwamu for several years, with the help of the Europeans in the forts. Akwamu launched a number of attacks that were eventually successful, partly because the English changed their alliance from Accra to Akwamu.[63] Many of the survivors of these attacks fled across the Volta, while king Ofori sought refuge with the king of Fetu, to the west, who was 'a near relative'. The precise date of the conquest of the coastal towns is not clear but it had occurred by early 1682, when Barbot returned to Accra and found that Ofori had gone to Fetu.[64] In his account written between 1683 and 1688, Barbot at different points gives 1680 and 1681 as the dates of the conquest, making it look as if one of

[59] Wilks, 'Rise', 112–3.
[60] Ibid., 105–17; Daaku, *Trade*, 154; Greene, *Gender*, 24–5; Parker, *Making*, 9–10.
[61] Justesen, *Danish Sources*, no.II.2, V.-g.K. 78: Prange, Frederiksborg, 7 April 1681.
[62] Barbot, *Barbot*, ii, 430, 440–2 editors' n.1 and 3, 593–4.
[63] Daaku, *Trade*, 154–5; Wilks, 'Rise of the Akwamu Empire', 108–11.
[64] Ibid.; Barbot, *Barbot*, ii, 430, 440–2 n.1 and 3. According to the editors of Barbot's account, Ofori is documented at Fetu in 1681, although no precise source is given (*ibid.*, ii, 442 n.3).

them is a slip.⁶⁵ However, in the published version from 1732 he gives the impression that the conquest took place over a prolonged period of time or consisted of several attacks.⁶⁶

The chronology of the Akwamu conquest of Ladoku is even less clear. According to Wilks, Akwamu's initial attack of Ladoku was carried out in 1679, which however is based on an account from the late eighteenth century.⁶⁷ There is no contemporary documentation of an attack at this date; the first invasion documented in the sources dates from 1682. However, it is possible that there had been an earlier attack which was not documented or for which documentation has been lost or not yet been found.⁶⁸ In May 1682, the English factor at Accra reported that an Akwamu army 'hath routed all the people from Ningo to the River Volta and all the Allampas [= Adangme people] are fled to a place about 4 leages leward [sic] of the River Volta to a place called Quitto [= Keta]'.⁶⁹ Another attack was reported on 10 March 1683, which again caused the Adangme people seek refuge to the east of the Volta.⁷⁰ In January 1688 the threat of another Akwamu attack again prompted the Adangme people to flee east across the Volta.⁷¹ A Danish report from October of that year identifies the refugees as 'the *Poniese*, the *Prampramse* and the *Laddacoese*', that is people from Kpone, Prampram and Ladoku (the latter probably referring to the port of La rather than the kingdom), who this time were joined by the Agave people ('the *Crophijse*') who occupied the banks of the Volta.⁷² According to this report, the refugees had wished to settle east of the river 'but a hundred of them have now been beheaded and fifty sold as slaves'. The wording is not clear but possibly the ill-usage of the refugees refers specifically to the Agave, who previously had been allies of Akwamu. According to Wilks, 1702 was the date when Akwamu finally destroyed Ladoku, causing yet another wave of refugees to pour across the Volta and into the western Slave Coast.⁷³ This time the Akwamu force crossed

---

⁶⁵ *Ibid.*, ii, 431, 605. Daaku cites English reports indicating that 1680 (but presumably Old Style, so possibly early 1681) was the date of conquest, but the document references are wrong and I have been unable to find any evidence (*Trade*, 155 n.1). In English documents before 1752, the dates are usually given in Old Style, with the legal year beginning on 25 March rather than 1 January. In some source editions, this is made clear by using double dates (e.g. 1680/1681) for the period between 1 January and 25 March (see e.g. below, notes 70 and 71).
⁶⁶ *Ibid.*, ii, 436.
⁶⁷ Wilks, 'Rise', 113–4, quoting Bjørn, 'Beretning 1788', 223–4.
⁶⁸ Cf. Law, 'Earliest European Descriptions', 4.
⁶⁹ Law, *English in West Africa*, part 1, no.431: Ralph Hassell, James Fort, Accra, 22 May 1682.
⁷⁰ *Ibid.*, no.451, Ralph Hassell, James Fort, Accra, 14 March 1682/3. For the date of this attack, see *ibid.*, no.452, Ralph Hassell, James Fort, Accra, 22 March 1682/3.
⁷¹ *Ibid.*, part 2, no.796, Marcus Bed. Whiting, James Fort, Accra, 25 Jan. 1687/8; no.803, Marcus Bed: Whiting, James Fort, Accra, 4 March 1687/8. Cf. Wilks, 'Rise', 116; Law, *Slave Coast*, 243.
⁷² Justesen, *Danish Sources*, no.II.17: Nicolay Fensman, Daybook, Christiansborg, 19 Oct. 1688 (editor's italics).
⁷³ Wilks, 'Rise', 116, citing [NAN?] VGK: Dag-Journal 1699–1703, entries for March 1702. For a discussion of the 1702 campaign, see *ibid.*, 124; Law, *Slave Coast*, 250.

the river and the Adangme ('Ladoku') refugees are said to have fled to Little Popo. However, it is not perfectly clear what happened on this occasion. The refugees referred to here may have been the Adangme who had settled in the Anlo region after the previous Akwamu campaigns, rather than those who had remained in Ladoku, because this Akwamu campaign was directed against the region east of the Volta (see Chapter 3). This would also explain the presence of Anlo settlers at Little Popo, as noted by Agbanon II.[74]

The foundation of Glidji

The traditions of the royal clan at Little Popo as recorded in the 1930s claim that the capital of the kingdom, Glidji, was founded by a prince of the Accra royal family, called Foli Bebe, who had fled from the Akwamu conquerers.[75] ('Foli' is the local version of the Ga name 'Ofori'.) This movement can be dated fairly precisely, to between 1683 and 1687.[76] According to Wilks, Ofori remained at Fetu until at least February 1683, which is the date when the Danes were able re-occupy their Fort Christiansborg at Accra after a spell of Portuguese rule there. During their exile at Fetu, Ofori and the Danes had allied against the Akwamu, which however ended with the Danish re-occupation of Christiansborg. It was only then that Ofori gave up his kingdom as lost and joined the exodus to Little Popo.[77] By May 1687, when John Carter, the RAC chief factor at Ouidah, visited Little Popo, 'Offerry Grandy [= Great Ofori], the king of Accraa' was already established there.[78] In fact, as noted by Law, 1683 is a plausible date for the settlement of the Accra immigrants at Little Popo because this was when direct commercial contact with the Europeans was initiated.[79] The Accras were experienced traders and it is likely that it was they who established the Afro-European trade after their arrival there. Moreover, the disorder associated with their immigration presumably generated slaves who could be offered for sale.

According to Law, Carter's account shows that the traditions of Glidji's foundation by Foli Bebe represent 'a simplified, telescoped version of events, in which the deeds of more than one person have been conflated into a single figure.'[80] Carter records meeting two persons called Ofori at

[74] Agbanon II, *Histoire*, 44, 50.
[75] Ibid., 11–18. Cf. Westermann, *Die Glidyi-Ewe*, V, 245.
[76] Law, 'Earliest European Descriptions', 4; Law, *Slave Coast*, 244–5.
[77] Wilks, 'Rise', 111. According to Nørregård, the Danes reoccupied Christiansborg on 26 February 1683 (*Danish Settlements*, 46).
[78] Law, *English in West Africa*, part 2, no.825, John Carter, Whiddah, 10 May 1687.
[79] Law, *Slave Coast*, 144–5, 244–5.
[80] Law, 'Earliest European Descriptions', 4. Cf. Law, *Slave Coast*, 244–5, 248; Gayibor, *Le Genyi*, 56–74; Gayibor, 'Les Rois de Glidji: Une chronologie revisee', *HiA*, 22 (1995), 197–222, pp. 198–205. For the telescoping of traditions, see David P. Henige, *The Chronology of Oral Tradition: Quest for a chimera* (Oxford, 1974), 27–38.

Little Popo, who were established at two different settlements: first, Great Ofori ('Offerry Grandy'), the displaced king of Accra, and secondly, Little Ofori or Safori ('Soffery or Ofori Occammyes', generally called 'Sofferry Pickaninnee', Pickaninnee being a corruption of *pequeneno*, Portuguese for 'little' or 'small'), 'the Generall of the Accraes.' According to Carter, the latter 'shews a respect to the king of Accraa, but the king is nothing without him and they are as brothers.' Contemporary documentation indicates that by the early 1690s 'Little Ofori', the general, had succeeded 'Great Ofori' as king. On his death in late 1693 he was in turn succeeded by his brother, called 'Offerry Bembeneen', and it is presumably the latter who is to be identified with the 'Foli Bebe' of tradition.[81] According to another version of the traditions, recorded in the mid-eighteenth century, it was the sister of the king of Accra who is remembered as the ancestress of the kings of Little Popo.[82] Contemporary evidence also suggests roles of political importance for female relatives of the king. According to Barbot, both Ofori's mother and his favourite wife were present at his reception by the king at Dutch Accra in 1679, the former sitting on Ofori's right side and the latter on his left.[83]

The link between the kingdoms of Accra on the Gold Coast and Little Popo on the western Slave Coast is also evident from their indigenous names, which are the same although different spellings have become established, Ga (Gã) and Ge (Gen/Guin) respectively, pronounced with 'a short, low toned, nasal a'.[84] Ga is the indigenous name for Accra and the people belonging to it.[85] The names 'Ge' and 'Genyi', referring both to the kingdom and the people,[86] were explained by Westermann. According to him, 'Ge' is the term used by the people themselves for their country, while 'Genyi' ('lower Ge') was used by their Ewe neighbours, to the west, in distinction

[81] Law, *English in West Africa*, no. 1352, Josiah Person, Whydah, 8 Apr. 1695. This document shows that the king of Little Popo who died in late 1693 was 'Offery Pinccaniny'. See also Bosman, *New and Accurate Description*, 332–3. Cf. Law, *Slave Coast*, 245 n.72.
[82] Rømer, *Reliable Account*, 118. Cf. Spieth, *Die Ewe-Stämme*, 38. It is not clear where Rømer received this information, whether at Accra, where he was based as a trader, or at Little Popo, which he visited in 1744. According to Agbanon II, Foli Bebe arrived at Little Popo in the company of an elder sister of his father, the deceased king of Accra, as well as a brother (*Histoire*, 13). Other versions of the traditions identify the founder of Glidji with other important personages from Ge history, illustrating how such traditions tend to conflate events and persons (Reindorf, *History*, 36–7; Henrici, *Lehrbuch*, 4).
[83] Barbot, *Barbot*, ii, 593–4, also 598 n.6.
[84] J. G. Christaller et. al., *A Dictionary, English, Tshi (Asante), Akra; Tshi (Chwee) comprising as Dialects: Akán (Asànté, Akán, Akuapém &c) and Fànté; Akra (Accra) connected with Adangme; Gold Coast, W. Africa* (Basel, 1874), XII.
[85] According to Christaller, 'Accra' is a European corruption of the term used by the Akan ('Twi')-speaking people to the west to designate the place and the people, 'Nkran' (*Dictionary, English*, XII; cf. Henrici, *Lehrbuch*, 4; Parker, *Making the Town*, 6).
[86] However, according to Westermann, 'Genyi' is used mainly with reference to the country or region (*Die Glidyi-Ewe*, 167). His is the earliest reference to this term that I have been able to find, while 'Ge' ('Geng') is documented in Lawson's account from 1879 (GNA: Lawson, 'Report').

to 'Gedzi' ('upper Ge') which designated the Ga area to the west of the Volta river.[87] The Ge kingdom is further referred to as 'Glidji', after its royal capital. When used with reference to the people, however, this term strictly speaking designates the royal clan, that is the descendants of Foli Bebe who, as discussed above, is credited with its foundation.[88]

The Ga people at Accra used the name 'Ton' to refer to the Ge kingdom, as was recorded by Christaller and Reindorf in the late nineteenth century.[89] This term also appears in the traditions of Little Popo, as 'Tonu'.[90] It has been interpreted by modern scholars, including the editor of Agbanon II's account, as referring to a particular place on the western Slave Coast where the immigrants settled before the foundation of Glidji, and its identification has been subject to some speculation.[91] The discussion has been fuelled by the fact that in the local languages, 'tonu' means 'at the mouth of the water' and forms part of place names (such as in 'Cotonou' and, on the western Slave Coast, Gun Kope Tonu).[92] However, in Agbanon II's account it clearly is the country generally rather than a particular place which is referred to as 'Tonu'.

The traditions also give some information about the immigration of the Ga refugees into the western Slave Coast, although this is not verifiable due to the lack of contemporary sources. According to some versions, the passage of the Ga immigrants was opposed by the inhabitants of Bé, which (as noted in the previous chapter) was an Ewe settlement and first documented in 1682.[93] This led to a fight between the two parties, ending in the defeat of the Bé. According to the version recorded by Westermann, the Ga had enlisted assistance from the Anlo – possibly referring to Ga and Adangme immigrants who had settled there – and together with them forced their passage. According to Spieth, the Bé were expelled. The proverbial grain of truth may be that from the point of view of the local people the Ga refugees were invaders who settled the region by force. This also explains the differences which exist with regard to the identity of the overlord from whom the Ga immigrants received permission to settle at Glidji. Hula traditions state that it was the king of Grand Popo who gave

[87] Westermann, *Die Glidyi-Ewe*, V. Cf. ibid., 167; Spieth, *Die Ewe-Stämme*, 38.
[88] Westermann, *Die Glidyi-Ewe*, 134.
[89] J. G. Christaller, *Dictionary of the Asante and Fante Language* (Basel, 1881), 651. See also Reindorf, *History*, 44.
[90] Agbanon II, *Histoire*, 13–4, 33. Agbanon used Reindorf as a source of information and it seems likely that he borrowed the term from there.
[91] Agbanon II, *Histoire*, 13, editor's n.16; Albert van Dantzig, 'Some Late Seventeenth-Century British Views on the Slave Coast', *Peuples du Golfe du Bénin*, ed. Medeiros, 71–85, p.83; Nicoué Lodjou Gayibor, 'Toponymie et toponymes anciens de la Côte des Esclaves', *Toponymie historique*, ed. Gayibor, 25–42, p.29; Gayibor., *Le Genyi*, 45; Gayibor., 'Les villes', 39; Law, 'Earliest European Descriptions', 8.
[92] See Lawson 'Report' (1879), map. (See Map 5).
[93] Barbot, *Barbot*, 619; Spieth, *Die Ewe-Stämme*, 38; Reindorf, *History*, 36; Westermann, *Die Glidyi-Ewe*, 248–9. The latter cites Anlo and Glidji traditions.

this permission, implying that the immigrants acknowledged his political seniority.[94] However, this is categorically rejected by the Ge, who insist that the immigrants received the permission to settle from the king of Tado, thus implying their independence from Grand Popo.[95] As noted above, the Akan-speaking canoemen and traders who had settled at Aneho by the mid-seventeenth century acknowledged the seniority of the king of Grand Popo. The Ga warriors, however, took possession of the land by conquest. This is also suggested by Carter's report of his visit to Little Popo in 1687, stating that the Ga general, Little Ofori, had 'allways a good strength of soldiers at his command' and consequently was 'more than all the people in those parts and can do as he pleases.'[96]

The place where the Ga immigrants founded Glidji had been settled prior to their arrival. According to Westermann, one of Glidji's quarters was called Adja Kpodji ('Adyakpódyi'), meaning 'on the Aja hillock', Aja referring to the previous settlers.[97] Ge traditions recall that there had been a hut which had been constructed by 'a hunter called Adikpi, from Watchikope', implying that the previous settlers were Ouatchi, that is Ewe people. Adikpi was subsequently executed by the Ga immigrants, indicating the violence which accompanied their settlement in the country.[98] Glidji's position near the confluence of several lagoon arms was strategically advantageous, giving the Ga control over the trade and communications both along the coast and into the interior. Further, it lay just a few kilometres north of the Mina settlement, with which it was connected by convenient lagoon transport and which subsequently became the kingdom's main coastal outlet. The location on the northern bank of the lagoon meant that there was the fertile agricultural land.

Some Ga refugees from the Gold Coast probably settled at other places besides Glidji. This is suggested by the traditions of the Vifeme clan at Anlo, according to which the clan's founders included people from the Ga-speaking area of Legon.[99] It is possible that Ga immigrants also settled other places on the western Slave Coast, but their identification is difficult because in the eighteenth century the Ge at Little Popo expanded their influence over the region, making it impossible to say whether Ga settlers elsewhere date from the time of the original immigration or the later period.[100]

[94] Gayibor, *Le Genyi*, 48–50.
[95] Agbanon II, *Histoire*, 14.
[96] Law, *English in West Africa*, part 2, no.825, John Carter, Whiddah, 10 May 1687.
[97] Westermann, *Die Glidyi-Ewe*, 140.
[98] Agbanon II, *Histoire*, 14, 31.
[99] Sandra E. Greene, 'Land, Lineage and Clan in Early Anlo', *Africa*, 51/1 (1981), 451–64, p.458, citing M. E. K. Dakubu, *Ga-English Dictionary* (Legon, 1973), 145; Greene, *Gender*, 26 n.14.
[100] E.g., a Ga presence was documented at Keta in the 1730s, but this may have been a recent development, comprising traders (van Dantzig, *Dutch*, no.326, NBKG 98: Elmina Journal, 8 Jan. 1732, citing a letter by Hoeth, Little Popo, 15 Dec. 1731; *ibid*., no.393: Declaration of Johan Joost Steirmark, Elmina, 4 Dec. 1737).

Adangme settlements on the western Slave Coast

There are today a number of Adangme communities on the western Slave Coast and in neighbouring regions which trace their origins to the immigration of refugees following the Akwamu invasions of the Adangme homeland. In Anlo, traditions recorded in the twentieth century recall that several clans ('hlo') there were founded by Adangme immigrants.[101] First, the clan of the 'Vifeawo, Vifemeawo', 'the people from the compound of Vi', regard themselves as descendants of Le, who is said to have immigrated from Adangmeland (as also indicated by his name) and been received in Anlo by a woman called Vi. Information concerning his exact place of origin varies with the different versions of the traditions.[102] According to Westermann, the members of this clan were regarded as part of the royal family in Anlo.[103] Second, the members of the clan of the 'Dzevíawo', 'salt children', trace their origins to Aduaduí, who is credited with having introduced the knowledge of how to produce salt and the worship of the clan divinity, Nyigbla, from the Gold Coast.[104] Thirdly, the members of the Blu clan also trace their origins to the 'Ga-Adangbes'.[105]

This information is supported by contemporary evidence, which shows that large numbers of Adangme refugees settled in Anlo. An Adangme presence was noted there already in 1680s, when a group of 'Lampi Blacks' engaged in banditry on the western Slave Coast. However, it is not clear whether this was connected with the Akwamu expansion on the eastern Gold Coast or whether it was an independent development.[106] Traders who visited the region in the 1690s also noted the influence of the Adangme there. Bosman, who called the country 'Coto [= Keta]' after its most important port, observed that it was 'by most called the Land of the Lampi' due to the Adangme influence, its inhabitants 'very nearly' resembling the Gold Coast people in 'Politicks, Religion and Oeconomicks'.[107] According to him, the language of the Anlo people was 'mostly that of Acra [sic], with

[101] Greene, 'Land', 455–9; Westermann, *Die Glidyi-Ewe*, 147–8.
[102] Gustav Härtter, 'Einige Bausteine zur Geschichte der Evhestämme (Togo)', II, *Beiträge zur Kolonialpolitik und Kolonialwirtschaft*, 3 (1901–02), 464–80, p. 476; Westermann, *Die Glidyi-Ewe*, 148; Greene, 'Land', 458, citing Dakubu, *Ga-English Dictionary*, 145; Greene, *Gender*, 26 n.14.
[103] Westermann, *Die Glidyi-Ewe*, 169.
[104] Greene, 'Land', 457; Härtter, 'Einige Bausteine', II, 476; Westermann, *Die Glidyi-Ewe*, 147. Another clan in Anlo whose origin may reach back to this time is that of the 'Agaveawo', which is said to have been founded by an Agave immigrant. This clan's responsibilities in Anlo comprise mainly functions in state and warfare; its members are credited with having taught the Anlo the skill of fighting (Härtter, 'Einige Bausteine', II, 475–76). As discussed, contemporary information indicates that Agave people joined the Adangme refugees who crossed the River Volta in 1688.
[105] Greene, *Gender*, 66, also 2, 4, 17–8.
[106] See Law, *Slave Coast*, 243; Law, 'Earliest European', 4.
[107] Bosman, *New and Accurate*, 329. Cf. Phillips, *Journal*, 230.

a very small alteration', evidently referring to the Adangme language which is closely related to the Ga language spoken at Accra.[108]

Aflao also received Adangme refugees. According to a report by the Danish trader Biørn from the 1780s, a party of Adangme people, 'proper Adampe of Lathe formerly situated between Crobbo and Aquapim', settled there in consequence of the Akwamu expansion.[109] 'Lathe' can be identified with the small state of Latebi (the modern Larteh Division of Akuapem), to the north of Ladoku, which by 1646 had been claimed by Akwamu, and more specifically perhaps with the market town of Late Amanfro ('Latabij') belonging to this kingdom.[110] Biørn's evidence is supported by information from the Dutch trader Eytzen, who in 1717 visited 'Offra Lade', which from its location and name can be identified with Aflao. The first part of the name, 'Offra', is evidently a variant of Afla/Aphla, indicating that this was a Hula settlement, while the latter part, 'Lade', suggests an Adangme connection. According to Biørn, the Adangme immigrants at Aflao subsequently relocated to 'Akotim', that is Agotime, a region on the modern Ghana-Togo border, to the south of Kpalime. However, in the 1810s Bowdich noted that 'a mixture of Adampë and Kerrapay [= Krepi, i.e. Ewe]' was spoken at 'Afflou or Afflahoo', due to 'the emigration of a large body of [Adampë] people', indicating that there still was an Adangme element in the early nineteenth century.[111]

At Little Popo, the Adangme presence can be traced through the names and traditions of some of the clans and some of the coastal settlement's quarters.[112] The name of the Nugo/ Nungo clan indicates a link with Ningo, that of the Gbuglan/ Gnigblenvi clan with Prampram and that of the Ela clan with La, or more generally with the kingdom of Ladoku.[113] The members of the Ela clan inhabited a quarter of the same name, situated in the coastal settlement to the east of Fantekome. There is also a quarter called 'Lagbonu', which translates as 'public space/market of the La'.[114] Agbanon II calls all these clans 'sub-clans' of the Tugban clan, that is the royal clan of the Ge at Glidji which traces its origin to Foli Bebe, indicating that the Adangme immigrants closely associated with the Ga immigrants while

---

[108] *Ibid.*, 331. According to Christaller *et al.*, the Ga and the Adangme languages are cognate and mutually understandable, although the difference between them is greater than that between the various Akan languages (*Dictionary, English*, XI-XII).
[109] Bjørn, 'Beretning 1788', 224.
[110] Kea, *Settlements*, 25, 71; Wilks, 'Rise', 101.
[111] Bowdich, *Mission*, 221.
[112] Agbanon II, *Histoire*, 134–5; Gaba, 'History', 60.
[113] Greene implies that Gugbla is or was an alternative name for Prampram (*Gender*, 25). Agbanon II explains the name 'Gnigblenvi' with the name of the clan divinity, 'Nyigblin', that is Nyigbla (*Histoire*, 134). For the Ela clan, see *ibid.*, 133–5.
[114] Agbanon II, *Histoire*, 134; Gayibor, *Le Genyi*, 125 n. 1. The names of these quarters were first documented in the 1880s: see Jones/ Sebald, *African Family Archive* (index): 'Alah'/'Alar', 'Lagbanu'; Henrici, *Das Deutsche Togogebiet*, V, 'Erläuterungen zur Karte': 'Elá', 'Legbano'.

acknowledging their primacy.[115] The existence of an Adangme community at Little Popo in the late eighteenth century is suggested by Biørn, who lists, among others, 'Great Ogie Koram over Labodee' as one of the main caboceers at Little Popo.[116]

Further, there are a number of Adangme communities in the hinterland of the western Slave Coast, such as in Agotime and on the Haho river. According to versions of the local traditions recorded by Sprigge in Agotime in the 1960s, the settlement of Afegame, which is regarded by the Adangme settlements on the Ghanaian side as the most senior settlement chronologically, was founded by a group of ancestors coming from 'Lekpo'.[117] This was interpreted as referring to modern Lekponguno ('Lay' in the contemporary documents, i.e. La), and representatives of the Ghanaian part of Agotime still attended customary activities in Lekponguno and other Adangme places in the 1960s. Earlier versions of the traditions as recorded by Biørn and Westermann hold that the settlements in Agotime were founded by Adangme people who had first settled at other places, identified as Aflao and Augoja (east of Keta) respectively, but had been driven away by warfare.[118] Sprigge notes that members 'of all or most' of the 32 communities comprising Agotime were called 'Le-persons' and in some of these communities Adangme was still spoken at the time when he did his research.[119]

On the Haho, there was another group of settlements which traced their origins to Adangme refugees. The most important of them was the town of Adangbe, ten of whose thirteen divisions are said to have been founded by immigrants from 'Lekpo' who had left their homeland due to war.[120] It is recalled that the place had been settled before, by Ewe-speaking people who were subsequently driven away by the newcomers. Adangme was not spoken in these settlements any more in the 1960s, but according to Henrici it still was in the mid-1880s.[121] During his visit to Dekpo (on Lake Togo) in 1884, Zöller heard reports 'of an important place further north which was called Adangbe' and whose inhabitants 'had immigrated and were not related to their neighbours.'[122] In the environs of Adangbe there were four villages, Essé Godjémé, Essé Godjin, Essé Zogbedji and Essé

[115] Agbanon II, *Histoire*, 133–5.

[116] Bjørn, 'Beretning 1788', 226. According to Gayibor, Biørn also gives a list of the five most important settlements in the kingdom, Little Popo, Greghi (Glidji), Popo Labodi, Popo Adannepugie and Popo Adannepragu (*Le Genyi*, 125). The names of the latter three show Adangme influence, Labade being an Adangme port on the Gold Coast. However, I am unable to find this in Biørn's report.

[117] R. G. S. Sprigge, 'Eweland's Adangbe: An Enquiry into an Oral Tradition', *THSG* 10 (1969), 87–128, pp.91–5. Cf. Greene, 'Land', 457.

[118] Bjørn, 'Beretning', 224; Westermann, *Die Glidyi-Ewe*, 147.

[119] For Adangme being spoken in Agotime, see Robert Cornevin, *Histoire du Togo* (Paris, 1959), 61, 89; Henrici, *Lehrbuch*, VII, 5; Spieth, *Die Ewe-Stämme*, 41.

[120] Bjørn, 'Beretning 1788', 224; Sprigge, 'Eweland's Adangbe', 100–8. Cf. Greene, 'Land', 457.

[121] Henrici, *Lehrbuch*, VII, 5.

[122] Zöller, *Das Togoland*, 141.

Nadjé, which according to local traditions had been founded by Adangme immigrants from Dodowa, the capital of Shai, an Adangme state situated to the north of Ladoku.[123] This connection is also suggested by the prefix in the names of all these places, 'Essé', which is a variant spelling for 'Shai'.[124] Adangbe was still spoken in these places in the 1960s. Another village, Gati, about 2.5 miles/4km south-east of Adangbe, is said to have been founded by immigrants from Ada, the coastal settlement immediately west of the Volta.[125]

Finally, Bjørn's 1788 report mentions two more Adangme settlements in the interior of the western Slave Coast, for which however neither contemporary nor recent information is available.[126] First, an Adangme settlement is said to have existed at Tetetu, which can probably be identified with modern Tététou, to the north-east of Adangbe near the Mono river, first documented in the early nineteenth century by Bowdich ('Tettaytokoo').[127] Second, there is said to have been an Adangme settlement at a place in 'the high mountains about 20 [Danish] miles [= about 93 miles/150km] from the sea, which for the present time is called Augo, and consists of 19 towns situated in the mountainous parts, with one town in the valley'. This can probably be identified with the region around Mount Agou, a short distance to the northeast of Agotime.

Little Popo: a plural community

The settlement of the various groups of immigrants resulted in the formation of a plural community in Little Popo, particularly at its the coastal settlement, where Hula, Ewe, 'Fante', Ga and Adangme people (and other groups that subsequently joined them, such as slaves from the interior) lived together, if in separate settlements. The fact that Little Popo was not one unified settlement but rather 'a group of villages' was observed by visitors in the late eighteenth and nineteenth centuries.[128] It had already been noted by the RAC factor, John Carter, in 1687, who described three separate settlements.[129] According to him, there was the place of the canoemen, called Attome, 'being a few houses (or rather beehives only larger) standing

---

[123] Sprigge, 'Eweland's Adangbe', 96–9. In the 1780s, Biørn also noted that the region ('Great and Little Schay, Tetetu, or one and all Adampe-Land') had been settled by refugees from 'Schay' ('Beretning 1788', 224).
[124] The modern map shows another settlement which bears this prefix, 'Esse Ana'. It lies in the area of Essé Godjemé and Essé Godjin, close to the Mono.
[125] Sprigge, 'Eweland's Adangbe', 99–100.
[126] Bjørn, 'Beretning 1788', 224, Sprigge, 'Eweland's Adangbe', 122. Cf. Greene, 'Land', 457.
[127] Bowdich, *Mission*, 221.
[128] N.a., *Report of the Wesleyan-Methodist Missionary Society for the Year ending April, 1855*, 61.
[129] Law, *English in West Africa*, part 2, no.825, John Carter, Whiddah, 10 May 1687. Cf. Law, 'Earliest European Descriptions', 3, 4; van Dantzig, 'Some Late', 81–3.

on the sand by the sea side', that is on the beach south of the lagoon. It can probably be identified with Aneho (as defined by W.T.G. Lawson in 1879, i.e. the part of modern Aného which lies to the south of the lagoon), or part thereof, possibly Fantekome.[130] Second, there was the settlement of Great Ofori, 'the king of Accraa', which lay 'halfe a myle' from Attome and evidently on the opposite bank of the lagoon, as Carter went there by canoe. Therefore, it seems legitimate to identify it with Glidji, although it may not have been in exactly the same place as the modern town. Thirdly, there was the settlement of Little Ofori, 'the Generall of the Accraes', who was said to live 'in much more grandeuir than the king.' His settlement lay 'about 2 or 3 myles [= 4.8km] more windward' from that of the king, 'the river [= the lagoon] comes up to his croom, having 5 times the houses that is att the towne of Attome, and [he] lives in the midway betweene the sea and the river, and the sea is about a quarter of a myle [away].' There has been some speculation concerning the identity of this place, but in the absence of more specific information this seems unfruitful.[131]

A century later, in the 1780s, Isert described the coastal settlement as 'a considerable Black settlement formed of five separate towns, each of which has its own kabossie', i.e. chief.

> One of these towns is composed wholly of Krepees, the original inhabitants of the land. However, the other towns have been peopled by Akras who, in the last century, when their king had been defeated by the Aquambos, sought refuge here; and who, since they understood the use of weapons better than the simple Krepees, made themselves masters over the latter, a position they still hold today. Through the middle of the united towns, and stretching far inland, runs an arm of a fresh-water lagoon...[132]

Isert's division of the inhabitants as 'Krepees' and 'Akras' clearly represents a simplified version of the reality. 'Akras' can probably be understood to mean the Gold Coast immigrants more generally, including 'Fante' and Adangme as well as Ga, while 'Krepees', which is used for the original inhabitants, presumably refers to both the Hula and the Ewe.[133] Any identification of these 'towns' remains speculative due to the lack of further detail, although it can probably be assumed that Aplaviho (settled by the Hula), the canoemen's place, i.e. Carter's 'Attomé' (present-day Fantekome?), and a town settled by the Adangme immigrants (present-day Ela and Lagbonu) were among them.

[130] Lawson 'Report', 35–9; Agbanon, *Histoire*, 39, 43.
[131] Gayibor, 'Toponymie', 30.
[132] Isert, *Letters*, 89.
[133] For a description from the early twentieth century which makes a similar distinction between the descendants of the original inhabitants ('Kplas', i.e. Pla/ Hula) and the immigrants ('Minas'), see ANB: 1E12.8, no.28, Rapport de l'administrateur de Grand Popo, Grand-Popo, 4 Jan. 1910.

Another century later, in 1879, Little Popo was described as consisting of four 'Townships', 'Anehor, Barsaji [= Badji], Degbenu and Ajido'.[134] 'Anehor' was situated 'on a strip of land along the beach about ¾ of a mile in length and 100 yards wide from Lagoon to sea'. Badji was 'separated from Anehor by an arm of the Lagoon' and had been founded in the early nineteenth century. On the banks of the lagoon to the north of Badji lay Degbenu, 'an old native village'. Adjido, which had been founded in the late eighteenth or early nineteenth century by Francisco Felix de Souza, was 'separated from Anehor by another arm of the lagoon', lying to the north of it on a peninsula (see Chapter 5).

According to Henrici, who visited the place in the 1880s, Aneho, i.e. the 'township' on the beach rather than the modern town, comprised fifteen parts, which were, from west to east: 'Djóssi, Degbenú (not to be confused with Degbenú west of Badji), Inglés [= English ('Nlesi')], Dschalmadschi [= Djamadji], Elá, Bokótikun, Flamani, Legbano, Fantikome, Sosime, Mann[h]á, Agbodschi, Akplovihó Konn[h]i (Ewénmedi), Akponugbá.'[135] Further, he mentions 'Adschidó [= Adjido]' and 'Lanó [= Landjo]', the latter of which lay to the west of Adjido on the peninsula to the north of Aneho. According to the traditions of the da Silveira family of Little Popo, descendants of Pedro Kodjo, Landjo was given to Pedro Kodjo by the de Souza family and settled by his slaves.[136]

According to Agbanon II, Degbenu, i.e. the village to the north of Badji, had been founded by immigrants from Anlo – possibly to be interpreted as a reference to Ewe people more generally – who were subsequently joined by Ga people. He uses the metaphor of a marriage between the daughter of the Anlo man and a Ga man.[137] Another quarter which is said to have been settled by the Ga is Djossi.[138]

Information regarding the various cults introduced by the immigrants from the Gold Coast also throws light on their settlement patterns. According to Agbanon, the Ga immigrants from Accra brought with them their principal cults Sakumo ('Sakuma') and Korle ('Kole'), the lagoon divinities, as well as Mama Nyagan, the divinity of pregnant women.[139] Sakumo was installed at Glidji-Kpodji, Kole at Glidji-Kpodji and Degbenu, and Mama-Nyagan at Degbenu. The people of the Nugo clan placed their cult 'Djobu' at Glidji-Kpodji and the Ela people their 'great fetish' Lakpan (cf. Lekpo/Lagbonu)

[134] Lawson, 'Report', 35–7.
[135] Henrici, *Das Deutsche*, IV-V, 'Erläuterungen zur Karte'. A local map from 1982 shows Agbodji lying east of 'Aplayiwo' (A. A. Akolly, *Renovations urbaine & économique Aného: evolution spatiale*, Lomé, June 1982).
[136] León da Silveira, p.c., Aného/Togo, 2 Aug. 2000.
[137] Agbanon II, *Histoire*, 36, 44–5, 134.
[138] Ibid., 134.
[139] Ibid., 44–5; Westermann, *Die Glidyi-Ewe*, 94–5. Agbanon II also lists Lakpan, but this seems to be a slip as elsewhere he describes it as 'the great fetish of the Ela', i.e. Adangme immigrants (45, 134). For the Sakumo and Korle cults at Accra, see Parker, *Making the Town*, 21.

at Djamadji. There is no information regarding Hula cults. According to Agbanon II, the Hula left the place 'to return home' when fishing became less productive.[140] However, more plausible seems the explanation that they became assimilated with the immigrants.

Regarding the cultural identities of these various immigrant groups at Little Popo, two contrary tendencies were at play: on the one hand, a tendency to preserve their separate cultural identities and, on the other hand, a tendency to acculturation. The former was promoted by the strong links which the various immigrant groups maintained with their homelands. This is especially well-documented in the case of the Ga immigrants, who remained connected with Accra by religious, cultural, family and trade links into the twentieth century. In the 1720s, the Danish governor at Christiansborg noted that the majority of the Ga were living at Little Popo with the 'expelled *Acraiske* King' rather than at Accra: 'They seek their refuge there when they are in trouble'.[141] In the 1790s, more than a century after the original Ga immigration into the western Slave Coast, the people of the two places were still so close that a European trader described them as 'one and the same people.'[142] Until at least the early twentieth century the priests of the Sakumo cult at Accra and Little Popo maintained contact, with the former sending the latter instructions such as regarding the date of the beginning of the new year.[143] Another indication of the preservation of the various cultural identities was the use of the respective languages. For example, Fante was still spoken by some of the canoemen's descendants in the mid-nineteenth century, such as the chief of Agoué.[144] The 'Mina' or 'Fante' identity was further reinforced by the continued employment of canoemen from the Gold Coast by Europeans until at least the 1860s.

The tendency to acculturation was promoted by local mixing and intermarriage. The Ga warriors married local women, and so presumably did the other immigrants.[145] Furthermore, the Ga-Adangme- and Akan-speaking immigrants (and probably also the other groups) married among each other, as shown by the family trees of the leading families of Aného.[146] Ga individuals moved from Glidji to the port town to engage in trade, as documented in the case of prominent traders such as Akue and Lattie (see Chapter 5). As noted above, according to Agbanon the Hula left the place, but it is much more likely that they became culturally and linguistically absorbed. An indication for this tendency of acculturation is again the way

---

[140] Agbanon II, *Histoire*, 39, 51.
[141] Justesen, *Danish Sources*, no. VIII.20,V.-g.K. 122:Von Suhm, Christiansborg, 8 and 18 Feb. 1725.
[142] TNA: T70/1565, William Roberts to A.R. Bjørn, James Fort, Accra, 10 April 1792.
[143] According to Westermann, the Sakumo priests of Accra sent their instructions in the form of stones, which the priests at Little Popo knew how to 'read' (*Die Glidyi-Ewe*,VI, 95).
[144] WMMS: West Africa Correspondence: Box 263: William West, Cape Coast, 6 June 1859.
[145] Westermann, *Die Glidyi-Ewe*,VI.
[146] Agbanon II, *Histoire*, 46–7, 191–3.

in which the various languages developed. By the late nineteenth, early twentieth centuries they had been amalgamated into one language, which contemporary linguists called the Aneho dialect of Ewe and the people themselves called Ge, that is the Gbe language, and which is not mutually intelligible with Ga anymore.[147] In French, the term 'Mina' is also used to refer to the people and their language and culture.

Political developments on the western Slave Coast, c.1680 to 1702

Delbée's report from 1670 suggests that Grand Popo was under Allada's control in the period.[148] However, by 1682, when Barbot visited the place, it had regained its independence. According to Barbot, in 1682 'the king of Popo was at war with those of Monte and of Juda [= Hueda], who forced him to make peace with the latter when he was on the point of losing his territories, and the two came to an understanding and made an alliance against the king of Monte.'[149] 'Monte' can probably be identified with the headland of Cape Monte (Portuguese 'Cabo de Monte'), which maps from the sixteenth and seventeenth century show in the vicinity of Kpeme, just west of Little Popo, but which is now lost through coastal erosion.[150] Law suggests that the term here refers to a party of 'Lampi Blacks', that is Adangme raiders from west of the Volta river who engaged in banditry. Their first incursion into the western Slave Coast dates to 1680, when they also raided Grand Popo and destroyed the Dutch lodge there. Another attack against Grand Popo was reported in 1682, prompting the latter to seek assistance from Hueda. This was evidently the war referred to by Barbot.[151]

According to Bosman, who visited the region in the late 1690s, Grand Popo's alliance with Hueda led to its subjugation and the installation of a puppet ruler by the Hueda king.[152] However, the new king subsequently rebelled against his Hueda overlord, which prompted the latter to organise

---

[147] Henrici, *Lehrbuch*, 3–5; Westermann, 'Kindheitserinnerungen', 3. Henrici noted that by the 1890s Ga had become extinct as a familiar language in Little Popo. However, according to Christaller the descendants of the Ga immigrants at Little Popo still used 'their own language besides speaking Ewe' in the early 1880s, although this may not be based on first-hand information (*Dictionary of the Asante*, 651). It was still used by the priests of the Sakumo cult at Glidji in the early twentieth century, as a 'secret language' (Westermann, *Die Glidyi-Ewe*, VI, 95).
[148] Delbée, 'Journal', 382. See Law, *Slave Coast*, 242–52. For the political situation on the Slave Coast more generally, see also van Dantzig, *Les Hollandais*, 66–76.
[149] Barbot, *Barbot*, 620.
[150] Law, 'Problems', 339.
[151] Law, *Slave Coast*, 243, citing [NAN:] TWIC.1024, unsigned letter, Offra, 29 Dec. 1680 and J. Bruyningh, Offra, 14 March 1682. See also Kea, 'I am here', 119.
[152] For Bosman's account of the relations between Grand Popo and Whydah, see *New and Accurate Description*, 335–6; van Dantzig, 'English Bosman', 275.

a punitive expedition in which the French reportedly also played a role. The attack failed, due partly to Grand Popo's amphibious environment which facilitated the settlement's defence.[153] The French involvement in this war can be explained with the situation at Ouidah in the period, where the French sided with the Hueda while the English (with whom the French were at war in the period) corresponded with the latter's other enemies, the Ga at Little Popo. Following the failure of his punitive expedition, the Hueda king tried to hire mercenaries to re-subjugate Grand Popo, 'even to the present times', but without success. However, the situation at Grand Popo remained difficult since a blockade by the Hueda king left the Grand Popo people unable to cultivate their fields, causing a shortage of foodstuffs. Therefore, provisions had to be imported. They were mainly supplied by Hueda people, despite their king's prohibition, 'because of the profits the Popo people are giving them.'[154]

These events can be dated with the help of contemporary European information. According to a visitor at Ouidah, in 1688 the king of Hueda received tribute from the neighbouring rulers of 'Papo [= Grand Popo]' and 'Anfro', suggesting that this was before the war.[155] Five years later, in March 1693, another visitor noted that the 'greatest enemies [of the Hueda king] are the kings and chiefs of the Great Popo country, to fight whom he can muster two hundred warriors fit for battle within 24 hours.'[156] This means that by this date the rebellion of Grand Popo's puppet ruler against Hueda, as reported by Bosman, had taken place. According to the RAC factor at Ouidah, in the same year the Hueda unsuccessfully attempted to re-subject Grand Popo with assistance of the Adangme (who had just defeated Little Popo, see below), 'but all to noe purpose they being forced to returne after they had besieged the Popoe upwards of a Month.'[157] Subsequently, the Hueda king abstained from direct attacks but the situation between the two countries remained tense.

The Ga immigrants at Little Popo represented a new factor in the political and military life of the western and central Slave Coast. They were a considerable military force, as was noted by European observers. According to Bosman, they were 'not very populous; but on the other hand are very War-like. Not many Years since they had a brave Soldier for their King, whose name was *Aforri*, Brother to the present King. This Prince

[153] Ibid., 336; van Dantzig, 'English Bosman', 275.
[154] Bosman, *New and Accurate Description*, 335–6; van Dantzig, 'English Bosman', 275–6.
[155] Père Gonzales, 'Relation abregée du voyages des Pères de l'Ordre des Frères Prêcheurs, missionaires en Afrique et en Guinée', *L'Année dominicaine*, 14 (1702; new ed., Lyon, 1900), 462–75, p.473, cited in Law, *Slave Coast*, 244. Law interprets 'Anfro' as a reference to Aflao, which however seems unlikely. Aflao was originally a Hula settlement, but by the 1680s this area was dominated by the Ga and Adangme immigrants. Nor is it in the neighbourhood of Grand Popo.
[156] Jones, *Brandenburg Sources*, no.79: Oettinger's Account (1692–93), pp.194–5.
[157] Law, *English in West Africa*, part 3, no.1349, Josiah Pearson, Whydah Factory, 3 April 1694. Cf. Law, *Slave Coast*, 249.

on account of his Valour was very much feared and respected…'[158] This Ofori, who in another contemporary source is also referred to as 'Offerry Pincaniny', i.e. 'Little Ofori', can be identified as the general 'Little Ofori' whom Carter had met at Little Popo in 1687 and who had subsequently succeeded to kingship. At Little Popo, the Ga soon began to hire out their services as mercenaries. Already in May 1687 Little Ofori was reported to be in correspondence with Isaac van Hoolwerff, the Dutch factor at Offra, Allada's rebellious main port.[159] Later that year, Hoolwerff was reported to have employed a large party of 'Accra and Myna Negroes' to impose peace at Offra.[160] Given Hoolwerff's earlier correspondence with Little Ofori as well as the combination of Ga and Mina on this occasion, it seems likely that this was actually a force from Little Popo. As noted by Law, this would be the first time that the employment of mercenary forces is documented in the region.[161]

In 1692, the Ga at Little Popo became involved in the conflict between Allada on the one hand and Offra and Hueda on the other hand.[162] This time they lent their services to the king of Allada for an attack on Offra.[163] The campaign took place in January 1692, when the town was devastated and the Dutch factory burnt, prompting the local governor, his chiefs and the Dutch factor to flee to Ouidah. According to Bosman, Ofori then turned to invade Hueda, stationing his army on Hueda's borders.[164] Law argues that it is likely that an attack against Hueda had been part of Allada's plan from the beginning, presumably because Hueda had been allied with Offra.[165] According to the RAC factor at Ouidah, John Wortley, Ofori himself harboured a grudge against the Hueda because they had ambushed some of his soldiers on their return from the Offra.[166] In the event, however, this attack did not materialise until the end of the year (although throughout the year there were threats that it was imminent).

Meanwhile, Wortley was corresponding with Ofori in an attempt to strengthen the English position at Ouidah against his European rivals, especially the Dutch and the French. Already in January 1692, when he was engaged in a quarrel with the Dutch over the late Petley Wyborne's

[158] Bosman, *New and Accurate Description*, 332. See also Law, *English in West Africa*, part 2, no.825, John Carter, Whiddah, 10 May 1687 (quoted above, p. 81, n.96).
[159] Law, *ibid.*
[160] Law, *Slave Coast*, 245; Van Dantzig, *Les Hollandais*, 71–2.
[161] Law, *Slave Coast*, 245.
[162] See *ibid.*, 245–7; Van Dantzig, *Les Hollandais*, 73–4.
[163] Van Dantzig, *Dutch and the Guinea Coast*, no.72: WIC 124, Minutes of Council, Elmina, 18 Feb. 1692, no.74: 31 May 1692, no.75: 16 Sept. 1692. See also Bosman, *New and Accurate Description*, 332.
[164] Bosman, *New and Accurate Description*, 332; van Dantzig, 'English Bosman', 274.
[165] Law, *Slave Coast*, 246; Law (ed.), *Correspondence from the Royal African Company's Factories at Offra and Whydah on the Slave Coast of West Africa, in the Public Record Office, London, 1678–93* (Edinburgh, 1990), no.41, Joshua Platt, *et al.*, Cabo Corso Castle, 6 April 1692, n.1.
[166] Law, *English in West Africa*, part 3, no.1343, John Wortley, Whydah Factory, 17 Jan. 1692.

house, he reported that he had engaged 'a Black that is one of Offrys great Cabboosheers, an Accra man, into it and to pay him 4 ac[kies] per month to stand by me on all occasions or pallaveroes'.[167] In April, the Hueda king seized and subsequently exiled Wortley, explaining that the latter 'had correspondence with Offree, his enimie, and threatned him that Offree should come and take his country'.[168]

Ofori for his part was negotiating for support from Akwamu for his campaign against Hueda, which was possibly the reason for its delay. In May there had already been reports that he had been successful and that 'part of the Quambures' were going to join him in the battle.[169] However, another report from October states that Ofori and the Hueda king were competing for Akwamu's support, both having sent 'a wast [= vast] sum' in presents, and consequently the Akwamu were 'divided one part for Offree and the other part for the King of Whydah.'[170] In the end, it was Ofori who gained their support. The combined Ga and Akwamu forces invaded Hueda in late October or early November, laying 'waste great part of this country especially this place [= Ouidah]'. According to the local RAC factor, they occupied Ouidah for 'about 25 days'.[171] In late November, the army proceeded to Offra and from there 'up the country to gett people to help him'. This has been interpreted as a reference to Allada. Another possibility is that these were Fon from the interior, since the report describes the new allies as 'men eaters' and the Fon were believed to be cannibals.[172] Strengthened by these additional forces, Ofori returned to Hueda, taking the country 'within a mille of the Kings town', that is Savi.[173] At this point the documentation stops, but Bosman later noted that Ofori abandoned the campaign for lack of ammunition.[174]

Having returned from this campaign, Ofori and his army proceeded to attack the Adangme in the Keta region, who had planned to assist the Hueda.[175] It is in fact possible that Ofori had been informed of this threat while still engaged in the Hueda campaign and that this was why he had abandoned the attack on Savi. However, the Adangme campaign ended in disastrous failure for the Ga forces; they were completely routed and Ofori himself was killed. According to the RAC factor at Ouidah, this happened on 29 December 1693 (8 Jan. 1694 according to New Style). The Adangme

[167] *Ibid.*, no.1342, John Wortley, Whydah, 5 Jan. 1691/2.
[168] *Ibid.*, no.1344, Edward Jackline, Widah, 10 May 1692; no.1207, John Bloome, Accra, 9 June 1692.
[169] *Ibid.*, nos.1205 and 1211, John Bloome, Accra, 3 May 1692, 30 Aug. 1692; Van Dantzig, *Dutch and the Guinea Coast*, no.75, WIC 124: Minutes of the Council, Elmina, 16 Sept. 1692.
[170] Law, *English in West Africa*, part 3, no.1345, Edward Jackline, Whydah, 13 Oct. 1692.
[171] *Ibid.*, no. 1346, Edward Jackline, Whydah, 25 Dec. 1692.
[172] Law, *Slave Coast*, 246–7.
[173] Law, *English in West Africa*, part 3, no.1345, Edward Jackline, Whydah, 25 Dec. 1692.
[174] Bosman, *New and Accurate Description*, 332–3.
[175] *Ibid.*, 333.

followed up their victory by invading Little Popo and destroying Ofori's town, forcing the Ga at Little Popo to take refuge in Allada. The Adangme then proceeded to besiege Grand Popo, in support of the Hueda king, as discussed above.[176]

The relationship between the Hula at Grand Popo and the Ga at Little Popo in this period is not documented. However, since they shared common enemies, Hueda to the east and the Adangme to the west, it seems plausible that they formed some sort of alliance. This also makes sense as Little Popo's forces had to proceed through the Hula territory to carry out their attacks against the Hueda. Grand Popo's situation must have been rather uncomfortable, sandwiched as it was between the increasingly powerful Hueda to the east and the militarily experienced Ga and Adangme immigrants to the west. An alliance with one of its neighbours would have been advantageous, and given their enmity with the Hueda and the Adangme, the Ga seem the most likely candidates.

The Ga returned to Little Popo after about a year, by mid-February 1695. They had been rallied by their new king, 'Offery Bembeneen', or Foli Bebe, who as noted above is remembered in the local traditions as the founder of Glidji. According to Bosman, he was 'more Peaceable and Mild' than his predecessor.[177] Nevertheless, his campaign against the Adangme, in December 1694 or January 1695, was successful, ending with their conquest and an abundance of prisoners.[178]

The Ga-Adangme wars of 1694 and 1695 were but the beginning of a conflict which lasted for most of the eighteenth century and in which Akwamu was to take active interest.[179] Information about this conflict comes from Bosman, drawing on his visit to the region in 1698. According to him, Keta's strength, which was 'very inconsiderable' anyway, 'abates daily by its Wars with *Popo*; that have continued for some Years successively; and they being pretty even in Force, their dispute is not like to be ended before one of them engages some other Country to their assistance.' Akwamu indirectly controlled the politics of the region, taking care 'that neither be destroyed, by sending assistance of Forces to the weakest side.' Akwamu had two rulers in the period, one of whom, Basua ('the Old'), is reported to have supported Little Popo while the other, 'Ado' ('the Young'), supported Keta.[180] This division of power at Akwamu apparently resulted from the succession to the throne of a minor, Ado, after Ansa Sasraku's death in 1689.[181] It lasted until

---

[176] Law, *English in West Africa*, part 3, no.1349, Josiah Pearson, Whydah Factory, 3 April 1694. Cf. Law, *The Slave Coast*, 248; van Dantzig, *Les Hollandais*, 274.
[177] Bosman, *New and Accurate Description*, 333.
[178] Law, *English in West Africa*, part 3, no.1352, Josiah Pearson, Whydah, 8 April 1695.
[179] For a history of this conflict in Anlo traditions (recorded in the late nineteenth century), see Härtter, 'Einige Bausteine', II, 477–80.
[180] Bosman, *New and Accurate Description*, 329.
[181] See Wilks, 'Rise', 119–23; Wilks, *Akwamu 1640–1750*, 22–26.

the death of Basua, who had originally been enstooled until Ado's coming of age but clung on to power. Wilks suggests that Ado succeeded in establishing 'some sort of control' over the Keta area, and Basua, fearing the growth of Ado's power, responded by giving assistance to Little Popo. This may also explain Akwamu's cooperation with Little Popo in the 1692 attack on Hueda.

Basua died in 1699, leaving Ado, Keta's champion, in control of Akwamu. However, at this moment Ado's attention was distracted from the region east of the Volta by a series of attacks on Akwamu by Akyem. In the following year, the Ga at Little Popo used this opportunity to inflict a defeat on the Adangme and dislodge them.[182] However, Bosman predicted that Akwamu would soon intervene and 'clap a Bridle into the Mouth of the *Popoeans*'. Subsequent events proved him right and in 1702 Akwamu invaded Little Popo.

The development of Afro-European trade, c. 1680 to 1702

Grand Popo had participated in the Afro-European trade since the late sixteenth century. However, the region to the west, between the Mono and Volta rivers, was not directly engaged in the trade until the 1680s. It was the Gold Coast immigrants, the Ga at Little Popo and the Adangme at Keta, who initiated the Afro-European trade in the region. They brought with them expertise both in the trade and in the warfare which generated the slaves who could be sold to the Europeans. Indirectly, however, the area had been linked with the trans-Atlantic system before. Slaves from the region had been fed into the system via the lagoons and had been exported from ports to the west, such as Grand Popo and Ouidah. This is suggested by information from a list of slaves on a sugar estate in French Guyana in 1690, which gives details of the origins of many African-born slaves. Among them are five slaves who are described as coming from 'Popo', including two from Little Popo. One is described as coming from 'Coécoé [?], near Petit-Popo' and the other 'from Grand-Popo, from a village called Aboré', the latter being a name used in other contemporary sources for Little Popo. The former slave had been bought before the Franco-Dutch war of 1672, while the latter had come on the ship 'La Perle', one of the ships in Barbot's squadron in 1682.[183] This slave, at least, had probably been purchased at Grand Popo, where Barbot did some trade. Further evidence

---

[182] Bosman, *New and Accurate Description*, 330. He notes that during his visit to 'Coto' in 1698, the king had resided at 'the Village *Coto* or *Verhou*', which can be identified with Keta (often given as 'Quitto' in contemporary sources), but implies that since then he had moved, due evidently to Little Popo's invasion of the country (329). In recent times, the capital of Anlo has been at Anloga.
[183] Law, 'Earliest European Descriptions', 3, citing G. Debien & J. Houdaille, 'Les origines des esclaves aux Antilles, no.32: Sur une sucrérie da la Guyane en 1690', *Bulletin de l'IFAN*, series B, 26 (1964), 166–94, pp.168, 177. For the identification of 'Abree', see *ibid.*, appendix 1.

is given by the interloper Petley Wyborne, who had established a factory at Ouidah in December 1681.[184] In June 1683 he reported that he maintained trade relations with the people at 'Abree', lying 'about 8 leagues [= 24 miles/38.4km]' west of Grand Popo, 'I send from Guydah to this place by river [= lagoon].'[185]

The first suggestion of European trade in the region between the rivers Mono and Volta dates from May 1682 and is directly linked with the population displacements caused by the Akwamu expansion.[186] The RAC factor at Accra noted that 'all the Allampas [= Adangme] are fled to a place about 4 leages [sic] leward of the River Volta to a place called Quitto [= Keta], att which place I beleeve there is good tradeing'.[187] In the following year, in April or May 1683, an RAC ship which had originally intended to take in slaves at Ouidah bought them at Keta instead.[188] Shortly afterwards, in May 1683, another RAC vessel at Ouidah is documented to have sent two boats 'to windward' in order to purchase 'what slaves they could' there, due to difficulties which it experienced in the trade at Ouidah. The boats were captured by the French pirate Jean Hamlyn to the west of 'Little Pawpaw', which suggests that they had been on their way to trade at Keta.[189] Hamlyn is further reported to have taken another English ship, belonging to the interloper captain Booth, at 'Little Pawpaw', which (as Law has noted) is the earliest explicit record of any European trade at that place.[190] According to the RAC factor at Ouidah, Booth had been supplied with slaves by Wybourne, who had purchased them during a six-week visit to 'a place called Abree, about 16 leagues [= 48 miles/76.8km] to windward of Guydah'. The factor's impression was that 'itt is a good place for slaves [...] The cheife goods they covett are booges, topsells, allejars and pintado's', that is cowry shells and various kinds of cloth.[191] He believed that Wybourne intended to settle an agent there, which he proposed to pre-empt by establishing a RAC lodge there. Wybourne however wrote to the RAC himself, offering them the place, 'I know itt is a place that in a short time would be verry convenient for the Company, being well managed, there is noe gold but there is aggree [= beads] and slaves, corne is always plenty'.[192] In

[184] Law, *Slave Coast*, 128.
[185] Law, *English in West Africa*, part 1, no.495, Petly Wyborne, Guydah, 26 June 1683.
[186] In this reconstruction of the development of Afro-European trade I am following Law, 'Earliest European Descriptions', 4–6. Cf. Law, *Slave Coast*, 141–8.
[187] Law, *English in West Africa*, part 1, no.431, Ralph Hassell, James Fort, Accra, 22 May 1682.
[188] *Ibid.*, no.636, John Waugh, St Thoma, 5 June 1683; no.494, John Winder, Guydah, 24 June 1683.
[189] Law, *English in West Africa*, part 1, no.632, William Williford, [Guydah], 9 June 1683; TNA: CO1/93, Narrative of Thomas Phipps concerning Pyracies Committed by the Pyrate Jean Hamlyn upon the Coast of Africa, 24 Oct. 1683, cited in Law, 'Earliest European Descriptions', 11 no.12. According to Phipps, another long boat, sent by another English captain at Ouidah, was also captured west of Little Popo.
[190] *Ibid.*
[191] Law, *English in West Africa*, part 1, no.494, John Winder, Guydah, 24 June 1683.
[192] *Ibid.*, no.495, Petly Wyborne, Guydah, 26 June 1683.

the end nothing became of this project due to the lack of personnel and supplies.[193] However, the RAC continued to be interested in the region and traded there 'under sail'. In August 1683 a vessel was dispatched from the company's headquarters at Cape Coast to Keta for 'Quitto Negroes.'[194] In September of the same year, another vessel was dispatched to the western Slave Coast to purchase the slaves that the company had been unable to supply on the Gold Coast. The captain was to visit 'Quitto Abrow & wt other places of Trade to Leeward of the River Volta there to Purchase his Complemt of Slaves but if he should not be Successfull at those places he is to proceed to Quidah there to Compleate the rest'.[195] In 1684 the Agent-General at Cape Coast Castle requested the RAC in London to instruct vessels to call at Keta.[196] There is a gap in the documentation between 1684–5, but when it resumes in 1685 a RAC captain, Sylvanus Paine, is reported to have purchased 150 slaves at 'Kitto' in November 1685. Another RAC vessel called there at the same time but finding only 'small trade' went to trade at Ouidah instead.[197] A third RAC vessel called at Little Popo and purchased 14 slaves (compared to 54 taken previously at Cape Coast and 211 subsequently at Ouidah), while a RAC sloop was at Grand Popo.[198]

However, the conditions on the western Slave Coast proved problematic for the European traders, due to inadequate supplies of slaves and disturbances in the region. At Keta, Paine and a number of his crew were killed following a quarrel with the local people.[199] At Grand Popo, the RAC sloop was taken over in a slave rebellion and wrecked.[200] According to a report from the RAC factor at Ouidah, this rebellion was supported by the Keta people who had killed Paine, who also 'killd the [sloop's] Commander and all they could and took all the gold and slaves.'[201] It is not clear how reliable this is, being based on hearsay. Following these disturbances, the factor at Ouidah requested his superiors at Cape Coast that vessels should be

---

[193] Law, *Correspondence*, no.12, John Winder, Guydah, 14 October 1683.

[194] TNA: T70/11, Agent-General & Council, Cape Coast Castle, 30 Aug. 1683. Cf. Law, 'Earliest European Descriptions', 11 no.9.

[195] TNA: T70/16, Agent-General & Council, Cape Coast Castle, 13 Sept. 1683. Cf. Law, 'Earliest European Descriptions', 11 no.10.

[196] TNA: T70/11, Agent-General & Council, Cape Coast Castle, 3 April 1684. Cf. Law, 'Earliest European Descriptions', 11 no.13.

[197] Law, *English in West Africa*, part 2, no.903, John Collins, [no place] 6 Feb. 1686.

[198] Ibid., no.900, Robert Elwes, [Cape Lopez], 31 Jan. 1686.

[199] Law, *Correspondence*, no.23, John Carter, Guidah, 28 Dec. 1685; Law, *English in West Africa*, part 2, no.707, Mark Bedford Whiting, Accra, 15 Jan. 168[6]; no.900, Robert Elwes, [Cape Lopez], 31 Jan. 1686; no.710, Mark Bedford Whiting, Accra, 2 Feb. 1686; no.903, John Collins, [no place] 6 Feb. 1686; no.46, John Carter, Guidah, 11 Nov. 1686.

[200] Ibid., no.708, Mark Bedford Whiting, Accra, 24 Jan. 1686; no.900, Robert Elwes, [Cape Lopez], 31 Jan. 1686.

[201] Ibid., no.819, John Carter, Whiddah, 22 Nov. 1686. In another letter, Carter implicates the Mina people at Attome, the coastal village at Little Popo, in this event: no.825, John Carter, Whiddah, 10 May 1687.

instructed not to call at the ports between the Volta and Ouidah anymore, 'for it doth but encourage a parcell of runaway rouges that harbour there at Kitto.'[202] Nevertheless, trade in the region continued even if the English may have given it a break. By May 1687 there was a factory of the Brandenburg African Company at Little Popo. The local factor was reported to have recently dispatched two vessels (with slaves), but due to his involvement in a local quarrel was not expected to be able to continue his trade.[203] However, a few months later, in December 1687 or January 1688, a Brandenburg ship was reported to have been captured by the Dutch off Little Popo or Grand Popo, indicating that the Brandenburgers continued to be active in the region.[204] In mid-1687, a RAC vessel called at Little Popo ('Little Paw Paw') and bought fifty slaves there, after which the captain found that he 'could Purchase noe more' although only five slaves were missing to make up his complement. He went to Ouidah to complete it.[205] In early 1688, a French ship setting out from Accra was expected to purchase slaves 'if possible to windward of Whydah, if not to proceed further [to Whydah]', but there is no information as to where it took the slaves.[206]

There was also renewed activity at Grand Popo in this period. In February 1688 the Dutch factor at Offra decided to re-establish the WIC's lodge there, due to the difficulties he was experiencing in his trade at Offra, and requested the company to instruct ships to call there.[207] In June, he informed his superiors that the lodge 'becomes quite effective' and credited it with having enabled him to speedily dispatch the ship 'de Goude Leeuw'.[208]

In the same year, the RAC established a factory at Little Popo. This was on Wybourne's initiative, the former interloper at Ouidah who had initiated trade with Little Popo in 1683. In early 1688 he had returned to Ouidah, this time in the capacity of the RAC's local factor at Ouidah.[209] Shortly afterwards, he reported having settled a factory at 'Papea' and requested the RAC in London to instruct ships to call there.[210] Later that year he

[202] *Ibid.*, no.819, John Carter, Whiddah, 22 Nov. 1686.
[203] *Ibid.*, no.825, John Carter, Whiddah, 10 May 1687. The factor, Johan Poeselwit, had left his post on the Gold Coast in October 1685 together with Petley Wyborne, suggesting that Wyborne may have facilitated the Brandenburgers' establishment at Little Popo (Jones, *Brandenburg Sources*, no.42, Accounts of Akwida, end of Oct. 1685; no.33, Accounts of Gross-Friedrichsburg, end of Aug.1685; p.127 n.7). According to Westergaard, five Brandenburg slave vessels were sent to West Africa in 1686 (*The Danish West Indies under Company Rule [1671–1754]* [New York, 1917], 79).
[204] Van Dantzig, *Dutch and the Guinea Coast*, no.21, WIC 180, Isaac Van Hoolwerff, [Offra] 26 Jan. 1688; Law, *English in West Africa*, part 2, no.827, Petley Wybourne, Whiddah, 18 Feb. 1688.
[205] Law, *English in West Africa*, part 2, no.943, Joseph Blyth, from on board the George Sloope, Whidah, 7 Aug. 1687.
[206] *Ibid.*, no.804, Mark Bed: Whiting, Accra, 20 March 1688.
[207] Van Dantzig, *Dutch and the Guinea Coast*, no.22, WIC 180, Isaac Van Hoolwerff, [Offra] 10 Feb. 1688; no.23, WIC 180, Isaac Van Hoolwerff, [Offra] 10 Feb. 1688.
[208] *Ibid.*, no.24, WIC 180, Isaac Van Hoolwerff, [Offra] 15 June 1688.
[209] Law, 'Earliest European Descriptions', 5–6.
[210] Law, *Correspondence*, no.27, Petley Wyburne, Whida, 2 April 1688.

complained that he had collected 500 slaves at 'Poccahonna' (probably a corruption of Popo Pequeno/Pequeneno, that is Little Popo) but due to the refusal of two English captains at Ouidah to go there, had been forced to sell them to a Portuguese vessel.[211] In early 1689, the RAC responded to Wybourne's request by ordering a vessel to call 'to the windward of Papa', that is west of (Grand) Popo, referring evidently to Little Popo, to take any slaves which Wyborne may have collected there, but it is not recorded whether this actually happened.[212]

In 1688, a Brandenburg ship trading at 'Laij [= La], Lampe [= Adangme, possibly referring to Keta] and Popou' found slaves were 'very scarce and few were to be obtained'. It managed to buy only 27 at these three ports together.[213] In the case of 'Popou', this may have been due partly to competition from the Dutch factory (at Grand Popo) or the English factory (at Little Popo). Nevertheless, it shows that the places on the western Slave Coast were unable to compete with Ouidah, where despite the competition of two other European factories the local RAC factor was able to provide a vessel with 545 slaves within three months.[214] This is also supported by the report of a French captain from 1688, estimating that Grand Popo and Little Popo together supplied (only) 300 slaves a year.[215]

For the period between 1688 and 1691, detailed documentation of the English trade in the region is lacking through another gap in the records. In February 1690 Wybourne died at Ouidah and his factory at Little Popo was evidently abandoned.[216] The Dutch factory at Grand Popo suffered a similar fate. It is still documented in early 1690 but had evidently been abandoned by early 1692, when the Dutch briefly considered whether it should be re-established as a substitute for the lodge at Offra, which had been destroyed in local political disturbances.[217] In the end, however, nothing came of it. According to Bosman, this was due to 'the Declension of Trade, since the Enmity betwixt *Fida* and *Popo*'.[218] Although Bosman added that 'since that time we have not traded with them', the Dutch continued to trade with the region (if not at Grand Popo) at least occasionally, when there were problems with the supply of slaves elsewhere. In early 1692, for example, a Dutch ship was sent to the

---

[211] *Ibid.*, no.30, Petley Wyburne, Whidah, 16 Nov. 1688. For a discussion of 'Poccahonna'/'Paccahenny', see Law, 'Earliest European Descriptions', appendix 1.
[212] Law, *Correspondence*, no.31, RAC, 8 Jan. 1688/9.
[213] Jones, *Brandenburg Sources*, no.68, Hoofman Friedson, Whydah, 21 June 1688. Cf. Law, *Slave Coast*, 145.
[214] Jones, *Brandenburg Sources*, no.68, Hoofman Friedson, Whydah, 21 June 1688.
[215] Ducasse, 'Relation', 14, cited in Law, *Slave Coast*, 145.
[216] Law, 'Earliest European Descriptions', 6. For Wybourne's death, see Law, *Correspondence*, no.33, Samuel Humfreys *et al.*, Cabo Corso Castle, 8 May 1690.
[217] Van Dantzig, *Dutch and the Guinea Coast*, no.68, WIC 124, Resolutions of the Council, Elmina, 11 April 1690; no.72, 18 Feb. 1692. For the destruction of the Dutch factory at Offra, see Law, *Slave Coast*, 241.
[218] Bosman, *New and Accurate Description*, 337.

coast between Accra and Ouidah to purchase slaves, evidently in search of an alternative source of slaves after the destruction of the lodge at Offra.[219] It is not reported where it took its cargo, but in May of that year the RAC factor at Ouidah reported that Ofori of Little Popo 'has gott a great dale [of] amunition out of a Dutchman' for the purpose of attacking Ouidah, which suggests that the vessel had traded at Little Popo.[220]

In April/May 1692, a RAC ship took its cargo of slaves at Little Popo ('Paokahnee') rather than proceeding to Ouidah where four vessels were reported to be trading already. According to the ship's captain, 'our incouragment by Offree [= Ofori] here being very great, for he told he would dispatch us in a week or 10 dayes and I believe in a fortnight [we] had been dispatched had we had good weather'.[221] In the end, the vessel was kept there for a month and still left without a full complement.[222] In June/July 1692, another RAC ship went to trade for slaves at 'Little Po Po' and experienced similar delays (before being lost to the French, who let her run ashore after plundering her). The factor at Ouidah reported, 'Offree put tricks on all of them, for when Captain Bell came to anchor he promised to slave him in 10 days, but after Offree had got some goods and white men ashore he lay there 3 weeks without getting one slave'.[223] According to Bosman, this was a common practice at Little Popo which continued after the death of Little Ofori and was much resented by European traders.[224] In October 1692, the RAC factor at Ouidah noted that due to the troubles experienced by the English at Ouidah at the time, their vessels avoided Ouidah, 'all staying at Po Po' instead.[225] In August 1693, a Brandenburg ship went to Little Popo ('Offere's') for slaves but 'could not git any, lying there four days without purchasing a slave'. It subsequently went to Ouidah, where it was reported to have purchased 729 slaves in 26 days.[226]

As discussed above, in late 1693 the Ga of Little Popo were defeated by the Adangme at Keta. The king, Little Ofori, was killed and the people were forced to flee their country, which resulted in the disruption of the trade at Little Popo. It was resumed in early 1695, after the Ga had defeated the Adangme. An 'abondance [sic] of prisoners' was taken in this campaign, who were subsequently sold to a RAC vessel that arrived at 'Paccaheny' shortly afterwards, enabling the captain to complete his complement within four weeks. This was good news to the RAC factor at Ouidah, who hoped that

[219] Van Dantzig, *The Dutch*, no.73, WIC 124, 18 Feb. 1692.
[220] Law, *English in West Africa*, part 3, no.1344, Edward Jackline, Widah, 10 May 1692.
[221] *Ibid.*, no.1386, Francis Buttram, Ship Fauconburgh, Paokahnee, 14 May 1692.
[222] *Ibid.*, no.1344, Edward Jackline, Widah, 10 May 1692; no.1386, Francis Butteram, Ship Fauconburgh, Paokahnee, 14 May 1692; no.1345, Edward Jacklin, Whydah, 13 Oct. 1692.
[223] *Ibid.*
[224] Bosman, *New and Accurate Description*, 334.
[225] Law, *English in West Africa*, no.1345, Edward Jacklin, Whydah, 13 Oct. 1692.
[226] *Ibid.*, no.1347, Francis Smith, Whydah Factory, 20 Sept. 1693; Jones, *Brandenburg Sources*, no.82, Memorandum of the Slaves delivered by Three Brandenburg Ships to St. Thomas, 11 June 1696.

Little Popo would be 'a good place to slave a single ship att some times', if the Ga managed to keep their country. He added, 'I doe hear a verry good caracter of Offery Bembeneen, the successor of Offerry Pincaniny, that he is a fair trader and mightily ambitious of a correspondence with whitemen, but more especially with the English…'[227]

However, Little Popo's trade did not improve and supplies of slaves remained fitful and inadequate. Bosman reported that during a visit to Little Popo in 1697 he could purchase only three slaves there. Ofori promised him that he would get 'one or two hundred' in three day's time, but not trusting him he left for Ouidah. There he was informed that the Ga 'returned with above two Hundred Slaves: which, for want of other Ships, they were obliged to sell to the *Portuguese*.' This gives an indication of the sources of the slaves sold at Little Popo. They were taken in local warfare, which also explains the lack of adequate and regular supplies. According to Bosman,

> The Inhabitants of *Popo*, as well as those of *Coto*, depend on Plunder and the Slave Trade; in both of which they very much exceed the latter; for being endowed with a much larger share of Courage, they rob more successively, and consequently by that means encrease their Trade: Notwithstanding all which, to fraight a Ship with Slaves, here would require several Months Attendance.[228]

Bosman's contempt for the Portuguese traders was based on their 'sorry goods'. According to him, they were cheated by the people of Little Popo more than others, but they had no choice as they were unable to compete for slaves at other places.[229] This was before the discovery of Brazilian gold in the early eighteenth century and the increasing demand for tobacco, which radically changed the Portuguese position on the coast. Bosman also reported that in 1698 he found a Danish vessel at Little Popo, 'which was obliged to wait a longer time to deal for five Hundred Slaves, than I spent in trading for two Thousand at *Fida*.'[230] This vessel was the 'Københavns Børs', which traded at Little Popo from mid-March 1698 and left the coast with 506 slaves (some of whom had been bought previously at Accra). The agent in charge of the ship's trade, Erich Tilleman, reported from Little Popo that he had negotiated with 'King *Affore* and his *cabusseers* here at Little Popo to get the rest of our slaves within two months', which probably was successful.[231] In his account from 1697, Tilleman listed Popo, evidently

---

[227] Law, *English in West Africa*, no.1345, Josiah Pearson, Whidah Factory, 8 April 1695.
[228] Bosman, *New and Accurate Description*, 333; van Dantzig, 'English Bosman', 275.
[229] Bosman, *New and Accurate Description*, 334.
[230] *Ibid*.
[231] Justesen, *Danish Sources*, II.25, Erich Tilleman, Little Popo, 30 April 1698; Nørregård, *Danish Settlements*, 61. Tilleman was reported to have purchased about ninety slaves at Accra, who were probably included in the 'København Børs' cargo (Justesen, *Danish Sources*, II.24, Erich Olsen

referring to Little Popo, as one of the 'three true slave places', besides Allada ('Arder') and Ouidah ('Fida').[232]

As regards Grand Popo, Bosman indicates that although the Dutch had not traded there since the abandonment of their lodge in the early 1690s, the locals continued to engage in the slave trade, if only on a small scale, selling their slaves to Little Popo if there were no ships. However, their main business was fishing and the fish trade.[233]

As is clear from the above account, in the 1680s and 1690s the western Slave Coast attracted mainly the smaller players, the Portuguese, Brandenburgers and Danes, who were unable to compete with the Dutch, English and French at the central places of the slave trade, that is Offra and Ouidah. The Dutch and the English showed interest in the western Slave Coast mainly as a substitute when there were problems with the supply of slaves elsewhere. The problem on the western Slave Coast was the intermittent and unreliable supply of slaves and the comparatively small numbers it was able to furnish. This can be explained by the fact (noted by Bosman) that the slaves were taken in local warfare, in which especially 'Little Ofori' engaged extensively, rather than being supplied via trade links from the interior, as was the case at Offra and Ouidah.[234] The explanation for this involves two issues. First, the absence of a large expansionist state in the immediate interior that could supply abundant slaves, as Dahomey did for Ouidah. Second, the limitation of Little Popo's hinterland by the Togo-Attacora mountains, which precluded the establishment of trade links with the remote interior, such as existed between Oyo and Porto Novo. This problem persisted in the later period, as will be shown in the following chapters.

(cont.) Lygaard, 30 March 1698). For the number of slaves, see Westergaard, *Danish West Indies*, 146, 320; Per O. Hernaes, *Slaves, Danes and African Coast Society* (University of Trondheim, Dept. of History, 1998), 251.
[232] Tilleman, *Short and Simple Account*, 34, 35.
[233] Bosman, *New and Accurate Description*, 336–7.
[234] Cf. Law, *Slave Coast*, 148.

3

The era of the warrior kings 1702 to 1772

The period between 1702 and 1772 was defined by the intrusions of Akwamu and Dahomey into the Slave Coast, resulting in the dislocation of communities and the spread of warfare and banditry in the region. Little Popo played an active role in this warfare, consolidating its position in the region vis-à-vis its rivals Anlo and Dahomey. This was the era of the warrior kings, epitomized by Ashampo (c.1737–1767) who was a very successful warrior. However, the relationship between Ashampo and the European traders was often problematic, illustrating the complex relationship between warfare and the Atlantic slave trade.

Akwamu power east of the Volta

1702 marks the beginning of major involvement by Akwamu in the politics of the western Slave Coast. As discussed above, in 1700 Little Popo had used the opportunity of Akyem attacks against Akwamu to drive the Adangme out of Keta. However, in the same year the Akwamu ruler, Ado, succeeded in appeasing Akyem with a handsome payment and soon afterwards his attention returned to the region east of the Volta river.[1] According to Wilks, this was part of Ado's imperialistic projects of territorial expansion to the east. In mid-February 1702 he launched a major military campaign, in the course of which Akwamu control was re-established in the Keta area and, in mid-April, Little Popo was overrun.[2] The king of Little Popo, his subjects

---

[1] See Wilks, 'Rise', 124–6, 128–9; Law, *Slave Coast*, 250–2.
[2] According to Danish documents, the attack against Little Popo was prompted by its refusal to hand over Adangme refugees who had fled there, due to the existing enmity between Little Popo and the Akwamu ruler (Justesen, *Danish Sources*, no.III.21, V.-g.K.; 884, Journal kept at Christiansborg, 23 Dec. 1698–1 Sept. 1703: 1 April, 10 April 1702). However, this seems incongruous given that the Little Popo people had expelled the Adangme from Keta in 1700.

and the Adangme fled to Allada. The Akwamu forces then continued to Hueda, with whom they were believed 'to have common cause.'[3] They remained there until a threat from Denkyira against their homeland prompted their return west of the Volta at the end of June.[4] However, it appears that Akwamu stationed or soon afterwards sent an occupying force east of the river. In April 1705 it was reported that an army of 'already 8 to 9,000 men' under a commander named Dondo was established near Keta.[5] By then, the Ge had evidently recovered from the 1702 attack, since they were reported to have faced up to Dondo's marauding soldiers, prompting Ado's successor, Akwonno, to pay another visit to the region in 1707 in order to settle 'disputes between the Accras [= Ge] and Dondo's people'.[6] This visit formed part of another Akwamu campaign east of the river, which was mainly directed into the interior, where Akwamu control was extended over the Ewe districts of Peki, Ho and Kpandu.[7]

The consequences of these Akwamu campaigns for the western Slave Coast are difficult to assess due to the limited documentation. According to Wilks, the 1702 campaign established Akwamu supremacy as far east as Hueda, that is including the western Slave Coast. However, it is not clear how 'real' this was and what exactly it meant for Little Popo. Akwamu certainly had become a major factor in the politics of the region and Little Popo had to reckon with it. However, Akwamu influence appears to have been indirect rather than direct. There was no direct military intervention by Akwamu after 1707 until 1727. The indirect influence was by way of potential Akwamu support for Little Popo's rivals, Keta/Anlo and Hueda. The latter continued to cultivate Akwamu support after 1702, hiring Akwamu forces as mercenaries.[8] In 1717 Little Popo gave mercenary assistance to Hueda, which possibly indicates a more friendly approach to Hueda than before the Akwamu campaigns. However, alternatively perhaps this was influenced purely by financial considerations, Little Popo hiring out its forces to anybody, irrespective of former political allegiances or conflicts.

In a regional perspective, however, Akwamu control – if it existed – seems to have mattered little to Little Popo. After its 1702 defeat it was soon able to re-establish itself both as an independent state and the major power in the region.[9] By 1709 'Caboceer Auferri of Little Popo', that is king Foli Bebe, was again able to hire out mercenary forces to third parties.

[3] *Ibid.*, 16 April, 18 April 1702.
[4] *Ibid.*, 5 May, 26 May, 29 June 1702.
[5] Van Dantzig, *Dutch and the Guinea Coast*, no.119, NBKG 1: Report by W. de la Palma on his Voyage to the Kingdom of Fida, 19 Feb. – 6 April 1705.
[6] Van Dantzig, *Les Hollandais*, 215. Cf. Law, *Slave Coast*, 251.
[7] Wilks, 'Rise', 129; Law, *Slave Coast*, 250–2.
[8] For a discussion of the Akwamu-Hueda relationship after 1702, see Wilks, 'Rise', 125; Law, *Slave Coast*, 251.
[9] Cf. Law, *Slave Coast*, 251.

In November of this year, the WIC's factor at Ouidah, who at this time had trouble with the French at the place, reported that Ofori had 'offered to help us with armed men in time of emergency...'[10] By 1717, Ofori was again claiming authority over Keta, as indicated by a report which describes him as 'Offori the King of the Accraes and commander of both Popo and Quitta'.[11] In 1718, Ofori kidnapped passing messengers from the Akwamu king to Hueda, which suggests a lack of both respect for Akwamu authority and concern about reprisals.[12]

In April 1717, Little Popo's mercenary forces, engaged by Hueda, attacked Jakin, but this time were defeated. The Hueda forces took flight, leaving the Popo forces to fight alone. Most of the Popo commanders were killed, as well as a large number of Hueda soldiers.[13]

Philip Eytzen's journey across the western Slave Coast, December 1717

In late 1717 the Dutch official Philip Eytzen made an overland trip from Ouidah to Accra, crossing the western Slave Coast. His report of this journey gives a rare insight into the conditions in the region in the period and is therefore discussed in detail.[14] The first settlement Eytzen visited west of Ouidah was Grand Popo, although unfortunately he does not make clear whether this refers to the coastal settlement or the royal capital, Agbanaken. He reported, 'The village is rather large, and the Negroes [...] are polite and friendly. But they are poor, and are being impeded in their trade by the Fidase [= Hueda] who have been oppressive to them for a long time.' This shows that the hostility between the two countries which had been noted by Bosman in the late 1690s still continued. The local ruler was eager for the establishment of a factory. Eytzen promised to look into this, noting that although the WIC factor at Ouidah was responsible for trade in neighbouring places, the bad state of Ouidah's trade prompted the WIC to consider alternatives such as Grand Popo.

Next, Eytzen came to Little Popo, where he stayed on 19 and 20 December. He describes it as a village 'inhabited by Mynse [= Mina] Negroes who have from time to time repaired to this place', evidently referring to the settlement of canoemen which Carter had called 'Attome' in the 1680s. At this place he mediated in a dispute between 'Caboceer Crakou' (perhaps a

---

[10] Van Dantzig, *Dutch and the Guinea Coast*, no.170, NBKG 81: Elmina Journal, 29 Nov. 1709, citing Engelgraaf, Whydah, 8 Nov. 1709.
[11] TNA:T70/1475, William Baillie, Whydah, 21 Mar. 1717. Cf. Law, *Slave Coast*, 252.
[12] Law, *Slave Coast*, 260.
[13] See *ibid.*, 252, 257–8, 260.
[14] Van Dantzig, *Dutch and the Guinea Coast*, no.228, WIC 124, Minutes of Council Meeting, Elmina: 17 Feb. 1718: Oral report by Bookkeeper-General Ph. Eytzen.

corruption of the Akan name Kwaku) and the Mina canoemen at Ouidah. Indeed, resolution of this conflict had been one of the reasons for his journey, 'in order to preserve the free passage of letter-carriers between Fida and Mina [= Elmina]', indicating the important role that Little Popo continued to play in communication along the coast. Eytzen also met 'Cabocceer Offori', that is Foli Bebe, who came to see him at the coastal settlement. The people requested the establishment of a Dutch lodge, 'promising that they would no longer allow the Englishman to reside here' if this was done. This Englishman was a RAC agent who been installed earlier in 1717 by the RAC chief factor at Ouidah due to the problems in the trade there.[15] Eytzen also gives some information regarding the immediate neighbourhood of Little Popo. 'Good villages' were said to lie on the arm of the lagoon leading to the interior, that is the arms of the Aného and Zowla lagoons to the north of present-day Aného. A short distance ('about a two-pounder shot') inland from Little Popo lay a village that was 'nicely planted with trees', possibly a reference to Degbenu.

Continuing his march westwards for seventeen hours, Eytzen arrived at 'Offra Lade', which (as noted in Chapter 2) can probably be identified with Aflao. He describes it as 'very impoverished'. Eytzen found himself unable to communicate with the locals 'as there was nobody among us who could speak properly with them', suggesting perhaps that commercial contact with Europeans had not yet been established there. From Offra Lade, Eytzen continued westwards to the Volta, passing through 'Abodja' or 'Abjotta' (= possibly Augoja), Keta and 'Awouna' (= Anloga). Although these places lay outside the western Slave Coast as defined in this study, there is nevertheless some relevant information concerning trade in this region. First, Eytzen shows that Keta had established itself as an outlet of the slave and ivory trade, which explains the interest of the Ge in this place. Second, there were 'plenty of slaves and ivory' in the settlements along the Volta and its tributaries, which 'as no trade is being carried on […] are taken away by the Aquamboese [= Akwamu], and on the other side by the Quahoese [= Kwahu], and thence they are carried to the side of Ardra and Fida.'

Consequences of the Akwamu and Dahomey expansion

In the late 1720s the western Slave Coast suffered from political disorder connected with the Dahomean conquest of the Hueda kingdom in 1727, compounded by an Akwamu incursion in the same year. The latter was carried out by an Akwamu army assisted by 'Crepees', that is Ewe people north of Anlo, who had fallen under Akwamu control in 1707. In September 1727, this Akwamu-Krepi force overran Keta and Aflao, putting the inhab-

[15] TNA: T70/1475, William Baillie, Whydah, 21 May 1717. Law, *Slave Coast*, 147.

itants to flight, and plundered the WIC lodge at Keta and the RAC lodge at Aflao.[16] The Akwamu apparently left behind an occupying force, presumably in the Keta region. This is indicated by a report from February 1728, which states that the overland passage between Little Popo and Accra was blocked by 'the King of Quamboes Couzin'.[17] The object of this Akwamu campaign is not clear; possibly to curb Little Popo's influence in the region. Little Popo presumably lost control over the area to the west of Aflao on this occasion. However, by this time Akwamu itself was in a weak position at home, where it was threatened by Akyem. It was defeated by the latter in 1730 and forced to relocate east of the Volta, where a new Akwamu state was founded in the Peki ('Krepi') country, to the north of Anlo. Akyem invaded the Anlo region in November 1731 and again in 1735 in pursuit of Akwamu refugees and occupied Keta on both occasions.[18] Little Popo appears to have used this moment of Akwamu weakness to forge an alliance with Akyem and regain its hold over Keta. This is suggested by a report by the RAC factor at Keta, from mid-May 1731, of an anticipated attack by Little Popo ('the Accras'), which prompted him to send messengers to 'J'ee [or 'G'ee'?] & Aufferre Cabb[ocee] rs of Popo for advice'.[19] The invasion in November 1731 was carried out under the leadership of two generals, Amu ('Amoe'), the chief broker for the Dutch settlements on the Gold Coast and former Akwamu governor of Accra, and Ofori ('Affoery').[20] The identification of the latter is not clear as Ofori was a common name on the coast and not exclusive to the royal family at Glidji. While it is possible that this was the king of Little Popo (particularly in the light of the RAC factor's letter earlier this year), it may also have been an Akyem general.[21] The 1735 invasion was led by the Akyem ruler Owosu ('Ursue'). Intriguingly, a Danish letter reported that Owosu's object was to 'go to Quitta and help the King down there, by the name of Ofolie, to attack certain towns', probably referring to the king of Little Popo.[22] As Foli Bebe is reported to have died in late October or early November 1727, this

---

[16] Law, *Ms. Francklin*, no.5, Abraham Duport, William's Fort Whydah, 12 Nov. 1727; Justesen, *Danish Sources*, no.VIII.39, V.-g.K. 122: Pahl et al., Christiansborg, 10 Sept. 1727 (giving Aflao as the location of the WIC lodge, which is probably a mistake); VIII.47, V.-g.K. 880: Sekret [sic] Council minutes, 4 Feb. 1728.
[17] Law, *Ms. Francklin*, no.29: Charles Guyon, Little Popo Factory, 26 Feb. 1727/8.
[18] Law, *Slave Coast*, 315–6.
[19] TNA: T70/1466, Quittah Diary, 17 May 1731.
[20] Van Dantzig, *Dutch and the Guinea Coast*, no.326, NBKG 98: Elmina Journal, 8 Jan. 1732, citing Hoeth, Little Popo, 14 Dec. 1731 and Capts. J. de Rhee and Van der Cruyssen, off Little Popo, 15 Dec. 1731; no.327, 11 Jan. 1732. For Amu, see Ivor Wilks, 'Akwamu and Otublohum: An Eighteenth-century Akan Marriage Arrangement', *Africa*, 29/4 (1959), 391–404, pp.393–98. According to Wilks, Amu's forces were fighting in Little Popo in 1733, but he does not give any sources for this (397).
[21] For the latter interpretation, see Law, *Slave Coast*, 316.
[22] Justen, *Danish Sources*, X.4, V.-g.K. 887: P.N. Jørgensen, Ada, 4 Dec. 1735. See also *ibid.*, no.X.3, J.C. Grøen and T. Wendelboe, off Keta, 23 Oct. 1735.

Ofori was presumably his successor.²³ If the reference is indeed to the king of Little Popo, it would imply that Little Popo had re-established its authority over Keta already by 1735 and not, as is argued in the literature, only in 1741.²⁴ This is also supported by a letter from a Dutch agent at Keta in 1735, reporting his hopes that a 'caboceer Adwoma' from Little Popo would be useful for the promotion of the Dutch trade at Keta.²⁵

Of more serious consequence for the region than the Akwamu incursion was the expansion of the inland kingdom of Dahomey, to the east. In 1724 Dahomey conquered the kingdom of Allada and in 1727 the Hueda kingdom, thus gaining direct access to the sea and the Afro-European trade. For the western Slave Coast, these events had two major immediate consequences; first, the relocation of the Hueda kingdom to the west of Aho river/Lake Ahéme, that is into Grand Popo territory, and secondly, the spread of banditry and strife in the region, in which the Ge at Little Popo played an active part.

Dahomey attacked and conquered the Hueda kingdom in early March 1727.²⁶ The Hueda king, Hufon, and a large number of his followers fled for safety across the lagoon into Grand Popo territory. Soon afterwards, by mid-March 1727, they were reported to have taken refuge 'on an island between Fida and Popo'.²⁷ References to 'islands' in contemporary accounts should be treated with reserve because the term is often used to describe places only partially surrounded by water, of which there were many in Grand Popo. However, there are some real islands in the lagoon east of Hévé, and it is possible that at some stage the Hueda refugees retreated there. In early May 1728, the place where Hufon is reported to reside is named as 'Topoy', which, as Law has noted, may represent 'Tokpa', a generic toponym meaning 'on the waterside'.²⁸ This place however was attacked and destroyed by the Dahomeans soon afterwards, forcing Hufon to remove elsewhere. A few months later, in mid-July 1728, the RAC factor at Ouidah reported that Hufon 'with all his caboceers and a great many thousands of people' was on an island 'a little below' (i.e. east of?) Grand Popo and the Dahomeans were unable to reach them because this 'island is in the middle

---

²³ Law, *Ms. Francklin*, no.26: Charles Guyon, Little Popo Factory, 20 Nov. 1727. Rømer confirms that 'Afolli' (Ofori/Foli) preceded Ashampo, who ruled by the early 1740s (*Reliable Account*, 186). Local traditions omit this king Ofori, giving a telescoped genealogy, and state that Ashampo was the son and successor of Foli Bebe (Agbanon II, *Histoire*, 15, 26). Cf. Gayibor, 'Les Rois de Glidji', 205–6.
²⁴ Gayibor, *Le Genyi*, 119–20; Greene, *Gender*, 56, 82; Kea, 'Akwamu-Anlo Relations', pp. 37–8. None of these authors uses strictly contemporary sources in their discussion of this episode.
²⁵ Van Dantzig, *Dutch and the Guinea Coast*, no. 382, WIC 110: From, Quita, 18 Mar 1735.
²⁶ See Akinjogbin, *Dahomey*, 64–100; Law, *The Slave Coast*, 282–87; Law, *Ouidah*, 50–59.
²⁷ Van Dantzig, *Dutch and the Guinea Coast*, no.252, NBKG 94: Elmina Journal, Hertogh, Jakin, 18 March 1727. Cf. William Snelgrave, *A New Account of Some Parts of Guinea, and the Slave-Trade* (1734), 14–5.
²⁸ Law, *Ouidah*, 52, citing ANF: C.6/25, unsigned letter [Dupetitval], Ouidah, 20 May 1728.

of the River, and their [sic] is no coming to them but by canoes which they don't know the use of.'[29] In early 1729 the English trader Snelgrave visited Grand Popo and was informed that the Hueda king, together with one of his senior chiefs, Assou, was 'near that place [...] on two barren Islands, with many other People.'[30] Snelgrave's first mate visited the exiles and received the following account of their situation.

> That the King and Captain *Ossue*, had with them many Thousands of People, who lived in a miserable manner, the Islands they were on being so barren, that they produced nothing: But by means of the River which separated them from the Continent, they were very well secured from the *Dahomes* Power; who not understanding the Management of *Cannoes* [sic] could not invade them. Moreover, they had planted several great Guns, which secured the Passes, so that they were in no fear of the Enemies. But then, on the other hand, they could not sow Corn, or other Pulse in that barren place, but were supplied with what they wanted by their Neighbours of *Great* and *Little Popo*. However, this constantly decreased their Numbers, they being obliged to sell their Wives, Children, and Servants for Provisions and other necessaries, because they had no Money left.[31]

For several years after the Dahomean conquest, the exiled Hueda attempted to repossess their country by attacking Dahomey, sometimes with the assistance of Grand Popo forces, but without success.[32] According to Snelgrave, Grand Popo's support for the Huedas' cause derived partly from their desire for the revival of the trade, 'they now assisted the *Whidaws* out of Policy; thinking, if they were reinstated in their Country, Trade would soon revive, which had been so long interrupted on account of the War.'[33] By mid-1731 Hufon had given up hope of being able to regain his kingdom and became increasingly desperate. In August of that year he raided the European tents on the Ouidah beach, killing six Europeans and mutilating their bodies, in retribution for their lack of support for his cause.[34] At the same time, relations between the Hueda and their Hula hosts at Grand Popo deteriorated. In mid-1731 it was reported that the paths to the west of Ouidah were closed because 'the Fidase and the Popose are at war with each other.'[35] In 1733 the paths were still or again blocked, prompting the French factor at Ouidah to visit the exiled Hueda to negotiate free passage for goods coming to Ouidah. The conflict between the Hueda and the Hula culmi-

[29] Law, *Ms. Francklin 1055/1*, no.22, Thomas Wilson, William's Fort Whydah, 12 July 1728.
[30] Snelgrave, *New Account*, 112. Cf. TNA: T70/1466, Diary of RAC Whydah Fort, 30 Dec. 1729.
[31] Snelgrave, *New Account*, 112–13 (author's italics).
[32] See Law, *Slave Coast*, 287–95, 298–300; Law, *Ouidah*, 52–9.
[33] Snelgrave, *New Account*, 124 (author's italics).
[34] Van Dantzig, *Dutch and the Guinea Coast*, no.305, WIC 138: Hertogh, [Jakin] 2 Aug. 1731.
[35] *Ibid.*, no.303, WIC 138: Hertogh, [Jakin] 26 June 1731.

nated in June 1733, when the Hueda attempted to seize control of Grand Popo, burning 'the western half of the island', probably referring to the royal capital at Agbanaken, before being defeated and forced to retreat with some casualties.[36] The cause of this conflict, although not stated, may reasonably be conjectured. As Snelgrave's report indicates, the Hueda's situation was desperate already in 1729 and can only have deteriorated with the passage of time. Furthermore, they were numerous and well-armed. The attack was probably prompted by the realisation that they were unable to regain their old kingdom. An obvious solution to their problems would have been to gain control of another kingdom, and ideally a coastal one which would allow them to continue the trade by which they had previously earned their living. Grand Popo fitted this description perfectly.

Soon after their failed attack on Grand Popo, the leaders of the Hueda resistance, King Hufon and Captain Assou, died. Hufon's succession was contested by two of his sons, one of whom gained the support of the Dahomeans. The latter then invaded Grand Popo territory and besieged their candidate's rival and his followers, eventually capturing and executing him. The successful candidate returned with his followers to Savi, the capital of Hueda, where he was installed as a puppet king. The Hueda who stayed behind in exile eventually settled a few miles inland, on the western shore of Lake Ahéme, where they founded a successor kingdom, Hueda-Henji, with its capital at Houéyogbe. They halted their attacks against Dahomey until the 1740s, when they resumed them, this time in alliance with Little Popo.[37]

The overthrow of the Hueda kingdom by Dahomey also led to a more general spread of banditry. This resulted in the closure of paths, to the detriment of trade in the region. The Ge at Little Popo appear to have played an active role in this development. This is indicated, among other things, by a report from the RAC factor at Ouidah, that he was forced to discontinue the factory at Little Popo because its supplies were 'Continually Panyard for [= seized] since the Whydah Country is destroyed those Rob[b]ers the Accras makes all free prizes that comes from this place Even though it belongs to the whites…'[38] These 'Rob[b]ers the Accras' were probably bandit gangs from Little Popo. Another incident occurred in July 1728, when the RAC factor at Ouidah reported that the temporary retreat of the Dahomean occupation force was followed by the approach of another army, comprising 'Acras Crepees and other Countrys as High as allampo' and numbering 'about 30000 [sic!]' men: 'these Robbers designe to plunder both Blacks and whites Believing themselves to be Stronger than Either the Whydahs or the Dahomys, so that they come to help neither but Rob both'.[39] A French report

---

[36] ANF: C.6/25, Levet, Juda, 26 Aug. 1733 ('lettre de nouvelles').
[37] See Law, *Slave Coast*, 299–300; Law, *Ouidah*, 58–59.
[38] Law, *Ms. Francklin*, no.22: Thomas Wilson, William's Fort Whydah, 12 July 1728.
[39] Ibid.

describes this army as 'the Minois of Little Popo' and dates its arrival to 13 July 1728. It retreated after three weeks when it was threatened by the approach of a Dahomean army of 12,000 to 15,000 men, taking with them 'as many as they could of the people of Judah [= Hueda]'.[40]

In August 1733, it was reported that the lagoon between Grand Popo and Little Popo was not safe to travel due to the encampment there, half-way between the two places on the banks of the lagoon, of an army of 300 to 400 people led by 'a Mina black called Assina who the other blacks call the robber ["le Forban"]', who were robbing travellers on the lagoon.[41] It seems likely that this is again a reference to bandits from Little Popo. The location of their camp is not identified but half-way between Grand and Little Popo, on the northern bank of the lagoon, lies Agoué (modern Agouégan) and it is possible that this is the place referred to.

Afro-European trade c.1700 to 1736

Despite these disturbances, European commercial interest in the western Slave Coast occasionally revived during the early eighteenth century, due mainly to problems elsewhere.[42] In the early 1700s, the Dutch WIC considered re-establishing its lodge at Grand Popo as well as at Offra because of disruptions of trade on the Gold Coast caused by Akwamu's expansion. In 1703 an agent was sent to Grand Popo to reconnoitre.[43] At the same time, the king of Grand Popo (jointly with the king of Allada) sent an embassy to the WIC's headquarters at Elmina, 'with the urgent request' for the establishment of a lodge at his place.[44] Despite these favourable conditions nothing came of these efforts, due to lack of personnel.[45] Nevertheless, it is noteworthy that due to the problems which the Dutch experienced in their slave trade in the period, the WIC's agent sent to the Slave Coast was also instructed to gather information about other commodities, specifically indigo, which the locals used to dye cloth, the manner of working leather and 'all rare animals, birds, fishes and quadrupeds', of which samples were to be bought.

The Danes also looked to the Slave Coast, particularly Little Popo and Ouidah, when the Akwamu campaigns spoilt the trade on the eastern Gold

[40] ANF: C.6/25, Dupetitval, Whydah, 8 Oct. 1728, cited in Law, *Slave Coast*, 290; Law, *Ms. Francklin*, 52, n.104. Cf. Akinjogbin, *Dahomey*, 85, 90. The fact that the bandit army was frightened by a Dahomean army of 12,000 to 15,000 men suggests that the number given by the RAC factor is too high, perhaps including a surplus zero due to miscopying.
[41] ANF: C.6/25, Levet, Juda, 26 Aug. 1733 ('lettre de nouvelles').
[42] See Law, *Slave Coast*, 146–8.
[43] Van Dantzig, *Dutch and the Guinea Coast*, no.101, WIC 98: W. de la Palma, 10 Oct. 1703; no.103, incl. in W. de la Palma, 10 Oct. 1703: Provisional Instruction for Ja.Van den Broucke, 2 April 1703
[44] *Ibid.*, no.101, WIC 98: W. de la Palma, 10 Oct. 1703.
[45] *Ibid.*, nos.111 and 115, WIC 98: W. de la Palma, 31 Aug. 1704 and 12 Feb. 1705.

Coast, their main region of interest (which they called 'the Little Slave Coast').[46] For them, a major attraction of the western Slave Coast was the lack of competition from other European nations. In March 1702, the Danish governor hoped to complement the slave cargo for the company ship 'Christianus Quintus' 'at Poe Poe or thereabouts', noting that English ships avoided the place because they feared reprisals after English interlopers had abducted free Africans there.[47] Nothing came of these plans, but when the ship returned to the coast in 1704 some slaves were purchased at Little Popo before it went to Ouidah to complete its trade.[48] In 1707 an agent, Johan Daniel Richelieu, was sent to Little Popo to buy slaves for another of the 'Christianus Quintus' voyages.[49] He appears to have travelled from Christiansborg overland, arriving on 26 March 1707 at a place called 'Bonesee', lying 1 ½ Danish mile (about 7 English miles/11km) from (= west of) Little Popo and evidently on the lagoon. From there he was fetched by canoe by 'Caboceer Ando' of Little Popo. At Little Popo, Richelieu discussed the trade with king Ofori, i.e. Foli Bebe, who assured him that the slaves for the 'Christianus Quintus' would be delivered shortly after the ship's arrival, 'and if there were three more ships, they would be ready in a short while and could get enough slaves.' However, despite his repeated requests, Richelieu was not shown any slaves,

> for the king says that when the slaves find out they are to be sold, then they run away; for they walk freely around all the towns, as they are free slaves. But because they will not serve the king as he wishes, he will catch them and sell them as soon as the ship comes.

This suggests that the slaves to be sold were domestic slaves who were not usually destined for export. Richelieu's report is interesting also because it gives a rare glimpse of the commercial organisation at Little Popo and the king's role in the trade. According to Richelieu, the king demanded 36 rigsdaler for a 'good man' and 32 rigsdaler for a 'good woman' but 'he wishes to arrange it so the others' slaves can be had as cheaply as can be agreed.' This shows that although the king controlled (or tried to control) the trade, which presumably only started after he had sold his slaves at the high price which he demanded, he did not monopolise it and there were other people besides him who sold slaves to the Europeans. Ivory was also reported to be available. The king and the caboceers requested the establishment of a Danish lodge.[50] The

---

[46] Justesen, *Danish Sources*, no. IV.4, V.-g.K. 120: Sevdrup et al., Ouidah, 3 Feb. 1704; no. IV.6. Svedrup, Christiansborg, 14 May 1704.
[47] *Ibid.*, no. III.14, V.-g.K. 121: Thrane, Christiansborg, 27 Mar. 1702.
[48] *Ibid.*, no. IV.3, V.-g.K. 120: Meyer, Christiansborg, 1 Feb. 1704; no. IV.4, V.g.-K. 120: Sevdrup et al., Ouidah, 3 Feb. 1704; IV.6. Svedrup, Christiansborg, 14 May 1704.
[49] *Ibid.*, no. V.9, V.-g.K. 121: J. D. Richelieu, Little Popo, 29 Mar. 1707.
[50] *Ibid.*

'Christianus Quintus' was sent to Little Popo on 12 April 1707.[51] However, of the 447 slaves taken off the coast by her, only 72 were purchased at Little Popo, compared to 236 on the Gold Coast and 139 at Ouidah.[52] This was despite the stiff competition at Ouidah, where there were three vessels at the time and five more had sailed a month earlier, clearly illustrating Little Popo's inferiority as a slave port as compared to Ouidah.[53] In 1709, the 'Christianus Quintus' was again sent to Ouidah, with the order to purchase 120 slaves on its way, between Christiansborg and Little Popo. However, it managed only half this number, some or all of them at Little Popo, because the ship's canoe was wrecked at Little Popo and the ship then went to Ouidah to complete its trade.[54]

In 1719, both the Danes and the Dutch established lodges at Keta. The Danes, who had hoped to have the place to themselves, were irritated by the Dutch presence and vainly tried to prevent the latter's settlement with presents 'both to the king [of Little Popo, probably] and the caboceer'.[55] They were themselves forced to abandon Keta after their lodge was destroyed on 25 June 1723 by a Little Popo force 'of more than 400 Akras'. This was in revenge for disturbances at Accra, where the Danes had allied with Akwamu against the English and Dutch towns.[56] These differences between the Danes and Little Popo appear to have been settled by March 1726, when a Danish vessel traded at Keta and Little Popo.[57] The Dutch lodge at Keta seems to have been maintained until at least 1727, when it was plundered by Akwamu.[58]

The French and the English began to take increasing interest in the western Slave Coast from the mid-1710s, due to difficulties in their trade at Ouidah. In 1717, the RAC factor at Ouidah established a lodge at Little Popo. He had negotiated the agreement concerning this lodge, and a projected one at Keta, with the Ge king, who had promised his son as a pawn for the security of these lodges.[59] This was the establishment Eytzen

[51] Ibid., no.V.11, V.-g.K. 121: Lygaard, Christiansborg, 16 Apr. 1707.
[52] 'Voyages: The Trans-Atlantic Slave Trade Database' (2009): http://www.slavevoyages.org/tast/database/search.faces (accessed 25 Nov. 2011), voyage 35061: Christianus Quintus (a) Christian V (1707).
[53] Justesen, *Danish Sources*, no.V.9, V.-g.K. 121: Johan Daniel Richelieu, Little Popo, 29 March 1707.
[54] Ibid., nos.V.20, V.21, V.23, V.-g.K. 121: Lygaard, Christiansborg, 19 Aug., 29 Aug., 5 Oct. 1709.
[55] Ibid., no.VII.9, V.-g.K. 121: Rost, Christiansborg, 15 June 1719.
[56] Ibid., no. VIII.9, V.-g.K. 880: Sekret Council Minutes, citing H.H. Sparre and J. Carl, Christiansborg, 29 July 1723.
[57] Ibid., no. VIII.29, V.-g.K. 122: von Suhm, Christiansborg, 28 Sept. 1726; cf. 'Voyages: The Trans-Atlantic Slave Trade Database' (2009): http://www.slavevoyages.org/tast/database/search.faces (accessed 25 Nov. 2011), voyage 35095: Unge Jomfrue (a) Vergo Juvenis (1728).
[58] Ibid., no. VIII.39, V.-g.K. 122: Pahl et al., Christiansborg, 10 Sept. 1727 (giving Aflao as the location of this lodge, probably mistakenly); no.VIII.47, V.-g.K. 880: Sekret Council Minutes, 4 Feb. 1728. As noted above (n. 15).
[59] TNA: T70/1475, William Baillie, Whydah, 21 May 1717. Cf. Law, *Slave Coast*, 147.

noted when he visited the place in late 1717. It appears to have been active until 1722, although in 1718 the factor wanted to abandon it as a failure, implying that it was not very profitable.[60] By January 1722 the RAC had also established a lodge at Grand Popo and by July 1723 another one at Keta. The lodge at Grand Popo is documented until 1725.[61] In this year, the RAC established a lodge at Aflao, which was maintained until 1727 when it was destroyed during the Akwamu incursion discussed above.[62] In 1726, the lodge at Little Popo was revived, and this time maintained until 1728 when it was discontinued due the problems of supplying it amidst the spread of local banditry.[63]

The purpose of these lodges on the western Slave Coast was to supplement the trade at Ouidah, the slaves purchased there being sent to the Ouidah for embarkation onto ships. Further, in the case of the English, they served to facilitate communication with the Gold Coast. A French report about the state of the trade at Ouidah from 1722 noted the advantages which the English and the Dutch enjoyed in their trade because of these lodges.[64] The writer of the report, probably an official at the French fort at Ouidah, proposed to follow the English example and establish factories at all three places, 'it needs but a little house', with one local agent each at Grand and Little Popo and two at Keta, in order to collect slaves for embarkation at Ouidah.

In the following year, the French director at Ouidah went to Grand Popo to investigate the possibilities for a French establishment there and was impressed.[65] In his report, he gave a list of Grand Popo's advantages. First, the coastal bar was not as bad as at Ouidah and therefore the beach was more easily approachable for Europeans. Second, an establishment could be settled without the permission of the king, indicating a high degree of independence in the coastal settlement. Third, there was an abundance of building material to construct a lodge, wood as well as clay for making bricks. Fourth, there was an abundance of fresh water. Fifth and sixth, porterage costs and customs duties were low, the former due to the easy transport afforded by the lagoon. All of these points compared favourably

---

[60] TNA: C113/276, William Baillie, 18 Jan. 1718; T70/885–6, Ledgers, William's Fort, Whydah, 1718–1721 (includes Jan.1722). Cf. Law, *Slave Coast*, 147.
[61] TNA: T70/886–87, 890, Ledgers, William's Fort, Whydah, 1721, 1724, 1725.
[62] TNA: T70/7, Tinker & Humfreys, Whydah, 25 Feb. 1725; T70/889–91, Ledgers, William's Fort, Whydah, 1725–26; Law, *Ms. Francklin*, no. 5, Abraham Duport, William's Fort, Whydah, 12 Nov. 1727; no.22. Cf. Law, *Slave Coast*, 147–8.
[63] Justesen, *Danish Sources*, no.VIII.47, V.-g.K., 880: Sekret Council Minutes, Christiansborg, 4 Feb. 1728; Law, *Correspondence of the RAC's Chief Merchants at Cabo Corso Castle with William's Fort, Whydah, and the Little Popo Factory, 1727–28: An Annotated Transcription of MS. Francklin 1055/1 in the Bedfordshire County Office* (African Studies Program, University of Madison-Wisconsin, 1991), no.22, Thomas Wilson, Whydah, 12 July 1728. Cf. Law, *Slave Coast*, 148, 315.
[64] ANF: C.6/25, 'Mémoire concernant la Colonie de Juda, Côte de Guinée', 1722.
[65] Ibid., Levesque, Juda, 30 Jan. 1723. Cf. Law, *Slave Coast*, 148.

with conditions at Ouidah, where the Europeans experienced difficulties in their trade in this period, particularly high prices and the lack of slaves, 'this country of Ouidah being almost lost'. Therefore, the agent proposed to abandon Ouidah for Grand Popo. It is noteworthy how Grand Popo shifts during 1722–3 from being a supplement to the Ouidah factory to being a replacement for it.

A French lodge was established at Grand Popo by early 1725, manned by two French agents and several African servants and subordinated to the fort at Ouidah.[66] It did not last very long, probably not much beyond 1728 when it was judged to be 'quite useless' due to the lack of slaves.[67] French trade at Grand Popo continued under sail, as indicated by a report which noted that in 1730 three French vessels traded there.[68] Further, there is information that Grand Popo provided slaves for French vessels at Ouidah, probably by the lagoon.[69]

The RAC lodge at Little Popo, 1726 to 1728

The RAC lodge at Little Popo from 1726 to 1728 is unusually well-documented and will be discussed in more detail, in order to give an impression of the nature and volume of the trade at Little Popo. The records of this lodge clearly demonstrate that the value of its trade was comparatively small, at least as regards slaves.[70] Only 12 slaves were purchased during the 15-month period of the lodge's existence and they were bartered away for French brandy, Portuguese tobacco and cloth, which were then used to purchase gold and ivory. Ivory became a major item of export from the western Slave Coast in this period and continued to be so until the early nineteenth century. According to the RAC local agent, it was abundantly available at Little Popo but his trade was hampered by the lack of goods.[71] There is very little information concerning its source. During his visit to the Keta region, Eytzen had noted that ivory was brought from the interior down the Volta. The ivory sold at Little Popo presumably also came from the interior, by transport along the rivers and the lagoons as well as by porterage. In 1731, it was

[66] BNP: Fonds français: 24223: 'Journal du voiage de Guinée et Cayenne, par le Chevalier Des Marchais Capitaine comandant la fregatte de la Compagnie des Indes, l'Expédition, pendant les Années 1724, 1725 et 1726', 47; Labat, *Voyage*, 6. Cf. Law, *Slave Coast*, 148.
[67] ANF: C.6/25, unsigned (draft) letter, Whydah, 28 May 1728, cited in Law, *Slave Coast*, 148 n.153.
[68] Van Dantzig, *Dutch and the Guinea Coast*, no.291, WIC 138: Hertogh [Jakin], 12 June 1730.
[69] Jean Mettas, *Répertoire des éxpeditions négrières françaises au XVIIIe siècle*, vol. 2: *Ports autres que Nantes* (ed. Serge et Michèle Daget) (Paris, 1984), voyage no. 2055.
[70] For the accounts of this lodge, see TNA: T70/391 and T70/392. For the local agent's correspondence, see Law, *Ms. Francklin*, nos.25–29.
[71] Law, *Ms. Francklin*, no.26: Charles Guyon, Little Popo Factory, 20 Nov. 1727.

reported that the Ge at Little Popo do their 'best to bring the ivory trade of Lampi [= Adangme] and Quahoe [= Kwahu] to this side', suggesting the source was somewhere west of the Volta.[72]

The gold purchased by this lodge was Brazilian gold which had been imported by the Portuguese. The Portuguese position in the West African trade changed radically in the early eighteenth century from being despised for their 'sorry goods', as had been noted by Bosman, to having the choice of the best slaves. This was due to the discovery of gold in Brazil, which they began to import into West Africa, and to increasing African demand for tobacco. In this period, the RAC as well as the other European companies were interested as much in purchasing Brazilian gold as slaves as the companies were trying to adapt to the loss of their monopoly and investigating alternatives or supplements to the slave trade. The gold was purchased either directly from the Portuguese, for slaves, or from the locals who had imported it from the Portuguese. There was a hiatus in the gold trade of the RAC lodge between 30 September 1727 and 1 March 1728, which reflects the general situation on the Slave Coast in this period, with traders complaining of the lack of gold due to the great Dahomean demand for it.[73]

Apart from the information concerning the lodge's trade, the accounts also give some detail regarding its operation. The factory paid a monthly ground rent (in guns, cloth, iron and copper bars) to 'the King of Little Popo' as well as various trading charges to 'the King & Sundry other Cabb[ocee]rs Traders and Black Visitors', mainly in rum. The king referred to here is probably the Ge king at Glidji, who initially was still Foli Bebe and then, after his death in late 1727, another Ofori (as noted before).[74] Only one local trader is named in the lodge's records, 'Aumane', who sold one slave to the factory.

The WIC lodge at Little Popo, 1731 to 1732

A temporary Dutch lodge was established at Little Popo in November 1731 as a substitute for the WIC's factory at Keta, which had been abandoned due to the Akyem invasion of the Anlo region in late 1730, discussed above. The Dutch factor, Hoeth, first fled to Jakin but from there was sent to Little Popo to make up the complement of slaves for the vessel 'Goude Put',

[72] Van Dantzig, *Dutch and the Guinea Coast*, no.326, Elmina Journal, 8 January 1732, citing Hoeth, Little Popo, 14 Dec. 1731.
[73] See Robin Law, 'The Gold Trade of Whydah in the Seventeenth and Eighteenth Centuries', *West African Economic and Social History: Studies in Memory of Marion Johnson*, ed. David Henige and T.C. McCaskie (African Studies Program, University of Wisconsin, Madison, 1990), 105–18, pp.106–10.
[74] Law, *Ms. Francklin*, no.26: Charles Guyon, Little Popo Factory, 20 Nov. 1727.

which was expected to take at least two months.[75] The documents give no details about this trade, but Hoeth must have been successful because he was still there four months later, proposing the establishment of a permanent lodge. However, amid fears of the warfare spreading to Little Popo, the WIC decided to recall him.[76]

Hoeth's letters from Little Popo also give some insight into the local operation of the trade, mentioning two local notables by title or name. First, there was a 'Caboceer Fiterre', who accommodated Hoeth in his house.[77] Further detail about this person is given in reports of other visitors. In late 1729, an RAC agent who passed through Little Popo on his way to Ouidah reported that 'Capt. Fettera Cabb[ocee]r of Little Popo' accompanied him to Grand Popo and acted as his guide.[78] The French factor at Ouidah, who visited Little Popo in 1733, noted that 'Capne Fiterre who rules in the absence of the King, who has gone to war, promised me to favour all those who I would send there, being my friend'.[79] In early 1738, a French captain stated that his trade at Little Popo was authorised by the 'great pheter, the chief for the customs or duties of the country'.[80] Fiterre, or more commonly Fetera, was a title commonly used on the Gold Coast, probably from the Portuguese term for 'agent' (*feitor*). Barbot described it in the 1680s with reference to the Gold Coast, specifically Komenda and Accra. It was the title of the 'captain of the bodyguard of the king', who on the death of the king succeeds the latter as it was 'the rank closest to the throne.'[81] Obviously, Barbot's information derives from fifty years earlier and refers to the conditions in the old Ga kingdom on the Gold Coast rather than at Little Popo in the 1730s. Nevertheless, his information that the Fetera was second in rank to the king tallies with the statement from 1733 that the Captain Fetera whom he met at Little Popo represented the king when the latter was absent.

Second, in his letter from Little Popo dated April 1732, Hoeth mentions a 'Caboceer Quam' who was of great assistance to him: 'I think that I can make a good lodge here, with the help of Caboceer Quam, a Minase who

[75] Van Dantzig, *Dutch and the Guinea Coast*, no.326, NBKG 98: Elmina Journal, 8 January 1732, citing Hoeth, Little Popo, 14 Dec. 1731. For the date of Hoeth's arrival at Little Popo, 30 Nov. 1731, see *ibid.*, citing Capt. Moilives, Little Popo, 16 Dec. 1731. The 'Goude Put' left the coast on 24 Dec. 1731 with 475 slaves, but it is not clear how many were embarked at Jakin and how many at Little Popo. Cf. 'Voyages: The Trans-Atlantic Slave Trade Database' (2009): http://www.slavevoyages.org/tast/database/search.faces (accessed 25 Nov. 2011), voyage 10160: 'Goude Put' (1732).
[76] *Ibid.*, nos.322, 324, NBKG 98: Minutes Elmina Council, 10 Jan. 1732, 21 May 1732; nos.327, 331, 11 Jan. 1732, 28 April 1732.
[77] *Ibid.*, no.326, NBKG 98: Elmina Journal, 8 January 1732, citing Hoeth, Little Popo, 14 Dec. 1731.
[78] TNA: T70/1466, Diary of RAC Whydah Fort, 29 and 30 Dec. 1729.
[79] ANF: C.6/25, Levet, Juda, 26 Aug. 1733 ('lettre de nouvelles').
[80] ADCM: B.5729: Process-verbeaux du Phœnix, 30 Mar 1738, cited in Jean-Michel Deveau, *La traite Rochelaise* (Paris: Karthala, 1990), 210.
[81] Barbot, *Barbot*, ii, 594–5.

helps me very much in everything'.⁸² Possibly, Quam was the successor of caboceer Crakou whom Eytzen had met in 1717 – and perhaps he is the Quam Desu who is remembered in the local traditions as the leader of the Mina immigrants (as discussed in Chapter 2). These reports show that there were two notables in the coastal village who took care of the trade with the Europeans, a representative of the king at Glidji and the local caboceer.

In December 1734 the Dutch re-established their lodge at Keta, mainly for the ivory trade. It was subsequently fortified and called Singelenburg.⁸³ In his correspondence the local agent refers to another notable of Little Popo, 'Caboceer Adwoma', who he hoped would be useful for the promotion of the Dutch trade at Keta.⁸⁴

Political developments during Ashampo's reign, 1737 to 1772

King Ashampo (d. 1767) is one of the legendary figures in Glidji traditions, where he is celebrated as the archetypal warrior and his reign as the apogee of Ge military power.⁸⁵ The contemporary documents give relatively abundant detail about his activities both as a warrior and a trader, allowing a closer examination of his reign as follows.

Ashampo is first documented in 1737, in the context of a conflict with Dahomian forces which marked the beginning of a war between Little Popo and Dahomey that was to last until 1795. According to a report of the Dutch soldier Johan Joost Steirmark, who had been stationed at Fort Singelenburg at Keta, in early July 1737 a Dahomian army arrived at Keta in pursuit of 'a certain Popo Caboceer Asjenbo [= Ashampo] who had offended them and who was said to have gone to a certain island in the Rio Volta.'⁸⁶ A quarrel ensued between the Dutch at the fort and the Dahomians, which ended

---

⁸² Van Dantzig, *Dutch and the Guinea Coast*, no.330, NBKG 98: Elmina Journal, 18 April 1732, citing Hoeth, Little Popo, 5 April 1732. The editor notes that the name, 'Quam', is not fully legible.
⁸³ Van Dantzig, *Dutch and the Guinea Coast*, nos. 376, 377, 382, WIC 110: From, Quita, 10 Dec. 1734, 4 Feb. 1735, 18 Mar 1735; 384, Des Bordes, 31 May 1736; 388, Minutes Elmina Council, citing From, Quita, n.d.
⁸⁴ *Ibid.*, no. 382, WIC 110: From, Quita, 18 Mar 1735.
⁸⁵ Gayibor, *Le Genyi*, 104; Gayibor, 'Les rois', 205–6. See also Westermann, *Die Glidyi-Ewe*, 121–2; Agbanon II, *Histoire*, chpt.2. Ashampo's name appears in a variety of spellings in contemporary accounts, e.g. 'Asjambo', 'Assiambo', 'Aziampong', 'Sjampon', 'Schampa', 'Shampo', as well as in historical studies, e.g. 'Ashangmo' (Reindorf, *History*; Law, *Slave Coast*), 'Assingbon Dandje' (Agbanon II, *Histoire*), 'Asiōgbō-Dãdye' (Westermann, *Die Glidyi-Ewe*) and 'Assingbon Dandjin' (Gayibor, *Le Genyi*). According to Westerman, 'Asiōgbō' is the Ge version of the Ga name 'Ashangmo' (*Die Glidyi-Ewe*, 189). For simplicity's sake, I refer to him as 'Ashampo', which was often used in English documents.
⁸⁶ Van Dantzig, *Dutch and the Guinea Coast*, no. 393, WIC 111: Declaration of the Soldier Johan Joost Steirmark, Elmina, 4 Dec. 1737. For a retrospective version of this event from the Danish point of view, see Bjørn, 'Beretning 1788', 226. 'Asjenbo' is identified with Ashampo in local

in the destruction of the fort and the killing of the Dutch commander. The employees of the fort were taken prisoners by the Dahomians and the Europeans carried to Aflao and, two days later, Little Popo. At Little Popo, Steirmark managed to escape and flee to 'the Crom [= village] Ocoy of a certain Accra Negro Affory', that is Ofori, who is described as Ashampo's cousin. At another point in this report, Ofori is referred to as 'King Affory', suggesting that he was the ruler of the Ge at Glidji.[87] 'Ocoy' is possibly identifiable with Agoué (modern Agouégan), which (as noted before) may have been the camp of the Ge bandits documented in 1733. If it was, this would indicate that banditry was indeed a state-sponsored enterprise among the Ge at Little Popo. Ofori then informed Ashampo of the events at Keta and the latter marched 'with his own and the Crepeese [= Krepi] Negroes' against the Dahomian force and inflicted a devastating defeat on them, 'they completely routed the Dahommese, of whose 13,000 [sic!] men not a single one escaped.'[88]

The identities of the 'island' in the Volta where Ashampo sought refuge and of his Krepi allies are open to speculation. The former might be any place on the river, especially one settled by people who subsequently allied with Ashampo in his conflict with Anlo and Dahomey, such as the Ada or the Agave. As regards the Krepi, this name could refer to any group of Ewe people in the immediate interior. Some of them were controlled by Akwamu, now relocated in Peki territory, and were not friendly with Little Popo but allied with Anlo and Akwamu. Others however were controlled by or allied with Little Popo and fought on their side, as shown also by their participation in the raid against Ouidah in the 1720s.

Information about the reason of the Dahomians' pursuit of Ashampo is given by the English trader Robert Norris, who was active on the coast from the late 1760s, that is some thirty years after the event. According to him, Ashampo was a deserter from the Dahomian army where he had held 'a considerable post.' He had excited the jealousy of the king, Agaja, because 'he was the darling of the soldiers, and every tongue was busy in his praise.' Therefore, the king decided 'to cut him off'. Ashampo however was warned by one of his sisters, who belonged to the royal household, and fled, taking 'a considerable part of the army along with him into the Popoe country'. He was well received there and subsequently promoted

(cont.) tradition (Agbanon, *Histoire*, 19–33; Westermann, *Die Glidyi-Ewe*, 243).
[87] See above, pp. 106–7. N.B. A contemporary Danish document refers to Ofori as caboceer at Keta (Justesen, *Danish Sources*, X.14, V.-g.K. 881: Sekret Council Minutes, E.N. Boris, Christiansborg, 17 Aug. 1737.).
[88] Cf. Van Dantzig, *Dutch Dutch and the Guinea Coast*, no. 390, NBKG 190: Diary of Des Bordes, 1 Aug. 1737: 'It is estimated that at least 1,300 Daghomeese were captured.' For a version of the events from the Danish perspective, see Justesen, *Danish Sources*, X.15, V.-g.K. 123, Boris et al., Christiansborg, 30 Sept. 1737.

to the command of the Little Popo forces, which he held until his death in 1767.[89]

Despite some striking gaps in this account, such as the failure to mention that Ashampo was of Ge origin (as indicated by his name and in Steirmark's report) and that he subsequently became the ruler of Little Popo, the information given by Norris is nevertheless plausible. According to Snelgrave, after 1729 Agaja had reconstituted the strength of his army, which had been weakened by an invasion by Oyo in that year, by enlisting 'many Banditti of other nations.'[90] It is therefore possible that Ashampo had entered Agaja's service then or some time later, especially as the Ge at Little Popo had a history of hiring themselves out as mercenaries. The information that Ashampo brought part of the Dahomian force with him is supported by the existence of communities of 'Dahome' people in the Little Popo area, documented in the early twentieth century, who regard themselves as descendants of Ashampo's Dahomian army.[91] Some of these immigrants appear to have settled at Glidji, as indicated by the existence of a quarter called 'Agbome', like the Dahomian capital, there.[92] Others are said to have settled at Aklaku, some 6 miles/10km inland on the Gbaga river.[93]

By March 1738, Ashampo had become the ruler of Little Popo. This is indicated by a contemporary French report which describes him as 'the king of Little Popo' and also for the first time documents the name of the Ge capital, Glidji ('Grigry').[94] The internal politics are unclear, including Ashampo's relationship with his 'cousin' Ofori who seems to have lived until at least 1739.[95] In any case, Ashampo's military might, and particularly the army which he had brought from Dahomey, must have played a part in his ascent. Under Ashampo's leadership Little Popo soon began to engage in a struggle for territorial expansion, carried out on two fronts, to the west and to the east (and perhaps also on a third, to the interior, but this is not documented). In the east, Ashampo followed up his 1737 defeat of the Dahomian troops by a number of invasions of Dahomey, mainly directed

---

[89] Norris, *Memoirs*, 50–1. Norris' book deals mainly with his voyage to the Slave Coast in 1772, but he had previously visited the region in 1767.
[90] Snelgrave, *New Account*, 128. Cf. Law, *Slave Coast*, 292.
[91] Westermann, *Die Glidyi-Ewe*, 127; Agbanon, *Histoire*, 25–6.
[92] Ibid., 28 map.
[93] Westermann, 'Kindheitserinnerungen', 9 n. 19.
[94] ADCM: B.5729, Process-verbeaux du Phœnix, 30 Mar 1738, cited in H. Robert, *Les trafics coloniaux du port de la Rochelle au XVIIIe siècle* (Poitiers, 1960), 76–7. Cf. Gayibor 'Les rois', 205.
[95] The diary of Christianus Jacob Protten, who visited Little Popo between April and October 1739, includes a cryptic note, which is crossed out, saying '[I] heard Foli etc.', probably referring to king Ofori who was Protten's maternal uncle (UAH: R.15.N.2 no.11, Prottens Diarium, 1737–41, 10 April 1739). In Protten's diaries from 1757–61 no reference is made to 'Foli' but only to 'Aziampong' (ibid., R.15.N.8, 'Guinea Prottens Reise-Diarium' [1756–1761]). For Protten's kinship relations with Ofori and Ashampo, see Rømer, *Reliable Account*, 186; van Dantzig, *Dutch and the Guinea Coast*, no. 393, WIC 111: Declaration of the Soldier Johan Joost Steirmark, Elmina, 4 Dec. 1737.

against Ouidah. In these campaigns, he allied with Dahomey's enemies, such as the exiled Hueda (who from 1743 revived their war against Dahomey). In the west, his object was the extension of control over the Anlo region, where Little Popo's hold over Keta, the region's main outlet for the trade, remained precarious. This interest in Anlo can be explained by Anlo's position on the Volta, a major route for slaves and ivory from the interior.

The 1740s were auspicious for Little Popo. Dahomey suffered many problems in this period, internal as well as external, and Ashampo used this situation to his advantage. In 1740, he used the opportunity afforded by Agaja's death and the civil war which followed in Dahomey to threaten an attack: '[Ashampo] is already marching up with an army of 20,000 in order to fight with the Dahommese.'[96] It is however not clear whether anything came of this. The new king of Dahomey was Tegbesu. Between 1742 and 1748 Oyo renewed its war on Dahomey, which involved a number of invasions and seriously weakened the latter's defences.[97] One of these invasions occurred in early 1742. Ashampo seized this opportunity for an attack of his own, presumably against Ouidah.[98] In between these two campaigns against Dahomey, in 1741, he turned to the west and launched a campaign against Anlo.[99] According to Greene, the result of this campaign was the extension of Little Popo's authority over Keta and the Anlo region.[100] However, as discussed above, Keta appears to have fallen under Little Popo's control already by the mid-1730s. Therefore, the object of this campaign was probably the subjugation of Anlo, which continued to contest Little Popo's hold over Keta. Another major attack against Dahomey followed in August 1747, when Little Popo forces raided Ouidah beach, killing most of the Dahomian force stationed there, including its commander, before being driven off by the main garrison at Ouidah.[101] Soon afterwards Ashampo was reported to be encamped nearby intending to attack Ouidah, but this does not appear to have happened. The Danish trader Ludewig Ferdinand Rømer, who visited Little Popo in 1744, noted Ashampo's military advantage over Dahomey in the period. According to him, Ashampo could have completely destroyed Dahomey had it not been

[96] Van Dantzig, *Dutch and the Guinea Coast*, no. 420, NBKG 105: Elmina Journal, 1 Feb. 1741, citing letter by Jan Bronssema, Badagry, 11 Aug. 1740. Cf. Law, *Slave Coast*, 318. The number 20,000 is conventional, representing the number of cowries in a bag. See Marion Johnson, 'The Cowrie Currencies of West Africa, Part 1', *JAH*, 11/1 (1979), 17–49, p. 44.
[97] See Law, *Slave Coast*, 319–23.
[98] Van Dantzig, *Dutch and the Guinea Coast*, no. 434, NBKG 106: Elmina Journal, 23 May 1742, citing Raams and Verschueren, Accra, 21 May [1742]. Norris mistakenly dates this attack to 1743 (*Memoirs*, 36–9). See Law, *Slave Coast*, 318, 321.
[99] Van Dantzig, *Dutch and the Guinea Coast*, no. 422a, NBKG 105: Elmina Journal, 4 Dec. 1741, citing van Kuyl, Accra [n.d.].
[100] Greene, *Gender*, 56, 82. Cf. Gayibor, *Le Genyi*, 119–20; Kea, 'Akwamu-Anlo Relations', 37–8.
[101] Law, *Slave Coast*, 322, citing TNA: T70/423, Sundry Accounts, William's Fort, Whydah, 1 May-31 Aug. 1747 and 1 Sept.-31 Dec. 1747. Cf. Akinjogbin, *Dahomey*, 112. Norris mistakenly dates this attack to 1753 (*Memoirs*, 55–6).

for the refusal of his own subjects who feared that 'if Assiamboe became more powerful he [...] would become a tyrant.'[102]

However, in 1749 or 1750 Little Popo suffered a setback when Anlo managed to regain its independence. Keta tried to ally with Anlo but was prevented by an expeditionary force from Little Popo which attacked in April 1750 and returned in (or remained until) November 1750.[103] With independence, Anlo's expansionary ambitions were rekindled. They were mainly directed against its neighbour to the west, Ada, with whom it competed for the control of the Volta trade and fishing rights at the mouth of the river.[104] In December 1750, Anlo attacked the Agave, to the north-west. After initial success, however, Anlo's luck turned when the Agave engaged the support of Ada and a number of other allies, including the Danes, who then proceeded to defeat Anlo. Little Popo does not appear to have taken part in this conflict, which is remembered as the 'Nonobe War', although the Danes briefly considered whether to enlist Ashampo's assistance.[105] However, this was only the first in a series of wars in which Little Popo became actively involved. They involved complex political alliances, with Anlo receiving support from Akwamu and some of its Ewe neighbours, and, on the opposite side, Ada and Little Popo seeking support from Akwamu's enemies on the Gold Coast, most importantly Akyem but also Akuapem and Krobo. Asante also played a role, as the overlord and potential supporter of Akwamu and the opponent of Akyem, which it had conquered in 1742 but struggled to pacify in the period.[106]

In 1750, one of the RAC chief agents at Cape Coast Castle compared the relative military strength of Little Popo and Dahomey. He believed that the Dahomians had an advantage because they were 'all of a tribe subject to the Control of one prince' while 'the men of Ashampo's Allies [were] of different Countries & Interests.'[107] The small size of the Ge forces may indeed have been a fundamental problem for Ashampo, forcing him to rely on manpower from allies and subject groups – such as the Hueda and Keta – which were harder to control and less dependable.[108] However, during the

---

[102] Rømer, *Reliable Account*, 202.

[103] Justesen, *Danish Sources*, no. XI.95, J.C. Eminga, Ada, 21 Apr. 1750; no. XI.108, Johan Suurman, Keta, Nov. 1750 (noting that 'Asambo is encamped half a mile from [Keta]'); no. XI.110, Platfues et al., Christiansborg, 17 Dec. 1750; Gayibor, *Le Genyi*, 120, citing V.-g.K. 888: Christiansborg, 10 Jan. 1749; Greene, *Gender*, 82.

[104] *Ibid.*, 59. See also Grove/ Johansen, 'Historical Geography', 1390–94; Hernaes, *Slaves, Danes*, 23–31.

[105] Justesen, *Danish Sources*, XII.4, M. Hachsen, Christiansborg, 23 Aug. 1751; Greene, *Gender*, 57; Isert, *Letters*, 41 editor's n. 30. For a contemporary account, see Rømer, *Reliable Account*, 206; for local traditions, Härtter, 'Einige Bausteine', II, 477; Westermann, *Die Glidyi-Ewe*, 248–51.

[106] Kea, 'Akwamu-Anlo Relations', 36; Ivor Wilks, *Asante in the Nineteenth Century: The Structure and Evolution of a Political Order* (Cambridge, 1975), 24–25, 27–8.

[107] TNA: T70/1476, John Roberts, [Dixcove,] 26 June 1750.

[108] For information about Ashampo's relationships with the coastal settlements of Little Popo and Keta, see Rømer's description of his visits to Keta, Little Popo and Glidji in 1744 (Justesen, *Danish Sources*, XI.23: L.F. Rømer, Keta, 13 Aug. 1744).

1750s this does not seem to have been a problem, partly perhaps because in this period Dahomey's attention was distracted by a protracted war with Mahi, its north-eastern neighbour.[109] In 1755, there was another attack by the Little Popo-Hueda alliance against Ouidah. The raiders succeeded in killing the local Dahomian military commander before being driven off.[110] In 1758, Ashampo sent an embassy to the Gold Coast, specifically to the Dutch, the Danes and the chiefs at Accra, and to Akyem, to organise assistance for his struggle against Dahomey. To the Dutch and the Danish he applied for firearms and to Accra and Akyem for 'troops, powder, gold, and trade goods.'[111]

In the early 1760s, Little Popo's fortunes began to change. In 1763, it suffered a defeat in one of its campaigns against Dahomey, which had managed to consolidate itself by the late 1750s. This campaign took place on 12 July 1763, when an allied army from Little Popo and Hueda under the command of one of Ashampo's sons, Ofori, attacked Ouidah.[112] According to Norris, Ofori was accompanied by 'the whole flower of the Popoe chiefs', comprising 32 generals, but Ashampo himself was 'too old and infirm' to take part.[113] The battle is said to have started well for the attackers, but this changed when the English at William's Fort intervened with their artillery in support of the Dahomians, who then defeated the alliance. Thirty of Little Popo's officers were killed. Ofori himself is said to have survived the battle, but 'overwhelmed with grief and shame, sat down beneath a tree and shot himself; [thus] only one [of the officers] survived to conduct the shattered remains of their army back.'[114] Norris credits the local English chief factor with the victory because of his intervention.[115] This defeat proved decisive. From then on, Little Popo and the Hueda restricted themselves to raiding the beach and disturbing the trade, avoiding encounters with the Dahomian army.

If Norris is correct, Ashampo died in 1767. According to Biørn, he was succeeded by Amma.[116] Contemporary observers continued to refer

---

[109] Law, *Slave Coast*, 324; Law, 'Slave-Raiders and Middlemen, Monopolists and Free-Traders: The Supply of Slaves for the Atlantic Trade in Dahomey, c. 1715–1850', *JAH*, 30/1 (1989), 45–68, 53–4.

[110] Law, *Slave Coast*, 323.

[111] UAH: R.15.N.8, 'Guinea Prottens Reise-Diarium' (1756–1761), 11 March 1758, 12 March 1758, 14 March 1758; Kea, 'Akwamu-Anlo Relations', 37, citing '[NAN:] Elmina Journal. Letter from Accra, 11 Nov. 1858.'

[112] TNA: T70/1159, Day Book, William's Fort, Whydah (William Goodson, 12 July 1763). Agbanon identifies Ashampo's son who commanded the army as 'Foli Yawo' (*Histoire*, 40).

[113] Norris, *Memoirs*, 56–9. Cf. Burton, *Mission*, i, 112–4; Law, *Slave Coast*, 323–4.

[114] According to Burton, the tree under which Ofori shot himself still existed in the 1860s and was remembered as 'Foli Hun, or Foli's Bombax' (Burton, *Mission*, i, 112, 114). Cf. Forbes, *Dahomey*, i, 114.

[115] Norris, *Memoirs*, 59. The records of William's Fort show that the English had expended '4 Half Barrels Gunpowder 60l' in 'firing on the Popos' (TNA: T70/1159, Day Book, William's Fort, Whydah: William Goodson, 12 July 1763).

[116] Biørn, 'Beretning 1788', 226.

to Ashampo after 1767, perhaps because they did not know better. Another explanation might be that Ashampo's successor had more than one name.[117]

After Ashampo's death, Little Popo's military strength vis-a-vis its rivals to the east and the west continued to decline. On the western frontier, the turning point for Little Popo came in 1769, when another major conflict erupted in the Anlo area.[118] In February, Anlo attacked Ada and shortly afterwards threatened Keta, Little Popo's tributary. This prompted Little Popo's king to send an army, commanded by 'Caboseer Amoni', to Aflao in order to protect Keta and engage Anlo.[119] However, when the action began and Little Popo's allies, Ada, Akyem, Akuapem and Krobo, crossed the Volta into Anlo, the Little Popo forces failed to act. According to contemporary Danish sources, this was because they waited for the arrival of their important caboceers, without whom they 'cannot and must not move'. Due to this, the Ada and their allies were ambushed and defeated by the forces of Anlo and Tsiame.[120] The Anlo army then received reinforcements from Akwamu, enabling them to prevent Akyem from re-crossing the Volta. According to Kea, 'It was no doubt Akwamu participation in this war which obviated the danger of Popo intervention.'[121]

For Little Popo, its failure to act had consequences beyond the defeat of its allies. Greene argues that it was due to this failure that Keta left Little Popo's control a few years later and allied with Anlo to become a partner in the Anlo confederacy.[122] In September 1772, a Danish official at Keta reported that 'the Quitta and Augnas [= Anlo] negroes… have eaten fetish [= take a ritual oath]… to be united', which he thought inaugurated 'a new period in the Creepeiske system.'[123] This was a serious reverse for Little Popo which not only lost the revenue from Keta's trade but also manpower, with Keta's soldiers joining their opponent's side. And the opponent now was a powerful one because the Anlo confederacy included, besides Anlo, a number of its Ewe neighbours, in alliance with Akwamu. According to Kea, the beginnings of this alliance date back to the 1730s, after Akwamu relocation to the Peki area.[124] However, the 1769 conflict was the first

[117] See Gayibor, 'Les rois', 207.
[118] See Greene, *Gender*, 57–8, 82. Cf. Nørregård, *Danish Settlements*, 124; Gayibor, *Le Genyi*, 120–1.
[119] 'Caboseer Amoni' is probably identifiable with the Amoni listed in 1774 among the caboceers who received a fee for the Danish lodge at Little Popo (Gayibor, *Le Genyi*, 136 n.3, citing DNA: GK 156, I. Kiøge, N.H. Weile, Little Popo, 25 Aug. 1774). The name already appeared in 1728 ('Aumane'), in the records of the RAC lodge at Little Popo (cited above). Biørn's 'Amma' may be another spelling of it.
[120] Greene, *Gender*, 57–8, citing DNA: GK 165, E. Quist, Quitta, 13 May 1769; GK 165, Dahl, Ada, 25 April 1769; E. Quist, Quitta, 4 May 1769. See also DNA: GK 166, N. Scheven, Fredensborg [Ningo], 28 July 1769.
[121] Kea, 'Akwamu-Anlo Relations', 38.
[122] Greene, *Gender*, 59, 82.
[123] *Ibid.*, 83, citing DNA: GK 149, J. Kiøge, Quitta, 6 Sept. 1772.
[124] Kea, 'Akwamu-Anlo Relations', 33.

recorded instance that Anlo and Akwamu had successfully joined their forces. This signified an important shift in the power balance in the region, which Keta evidently realised. It chose to leave Little Popo's control because (unlike in 1750) Little Popo, faced by such a formidable opposition, was unable to prevent it.

On the eastern frontier, hostilities between Little Popo and the Hueda on the one hand and, on the other, Dahomey continued on a reduced scale, with raids by the former on the beach at Ouidah, aiming to disturb Dahomey's trade.[125] One of these occurred in between June and October 1767 and was reported by Archibald Dalzel, the new English chief factor who had arrived at Ouidah on the same day as Little Popo's army. The latter robbed French and Portuguese traders who had just landed their goods on the beach.[126] In May 1768, another attack by Little Popo was anticipated. According to Dalzel, '[t]he Popoes have paid us two Visits since I came here, and threaten us with a third'.[127] In mid-1769, Tegbesu, eager to improve Ouidah's trade, offered a peace treaty to Little Popo, mediated by Dalzel. A peace was eventually concluded and announced by Tegbesu in November (and again in December), but it proved to be short-lived.[128] In October 1770, Lionel Abson, who had succeeded Dalzel at Ouidah, reported that recently there had been four attacks by Little Popo. In the first 'they carried away Goods belonging to a French Captain', in the second they stole 'some Slaves belonging to a Portuguese Captain with burning & carrying away every canoe on the Beach', in the third 'they stayed five Days on the Beach successively & no Battle given on either side except a small skirmish wherein this Country People lost two Men', and in the fourth 'they carried away three White Men who were Tentkeepers to the Captains on the Waterside'.[129] According to a report by the French factor at Ouidah, there was another disturbance in 1772, when a Little Popo force blocked the path between Ouidah and the beach for a month.[130] However, in July of the same year another peace treaty was concluded between Dahomey and Little Popo. The Hueda apparently did not form a party to this treaty as they are not specifically mentioned.[131] As in 1769, this treaty was the initiative of Tegbesu. Nevertheless, the timing must have suited Little Popo, considering its difficulties on the western frontier, discussed above. Moreover, on the Gold Coast Asante (reinforced by Akwamu troops) invaded Little Popo's allies Akyem and

[125] Norris, *Memoirs*, 59–60; Law, *Slave Coast*, 324; Akinjogbin, *Dahomey*, 148–50.
[126] TNA: T70/31, incl. in Gilbert Petrie, Cape Coast Castle, 25 Oct. 1767: Archibald Dalzel, [Whydah, n.d.].
[127] *Ibid.*, 15 May 1768: Archibald Dalzel, William's Fort Whydah, 17 March 1768.
[128] Law, *Ouidah*, 64; Akinjobin, *Dahomey*, 152.
[129] TNA: T70/31, Lionel Abson, Williams Fort Whydah, 24 Oct. 1770.
[130] ANF: C.6/26, Bauduchiron, 'Mémoire d'Observations'.
[131] Law, *Ouidah*, 64; Akinjogbin, *Dahomey*, 152.

Akuapem, leaving Little Popo in a position of weakness in the face of the Akwamu-Anlo alliance.[132]

It is not clear what happened to Grand Popo in the period from 1733, after the Hueda had burnt part of the town. The Ge version of the events as told by Agbanon II states that Grand Popo fell under Ashampo's influence.[133] Hula traditions, however, categorically deny that Little Popo ever exercised control over Grand Popo.[134] Little Popo's forces had to pass through Grand Popo's territory when they attacked Dahomey, which suggests that Grand Popo had become either an ally or fallen under Little Popo's control. The latter would explain why in 1795 Grand Popo formed an alliance with Dahomey against Little Popo. It would also make sense in the context of Ashampo's expansionary policies: since he competed for the Volta trade, it seems likely that the trade of the Mono also interested him, especially given this river's proximity to Glidji. Whatever the exact nature of the relationship between Little Popo and Grand Popo, the latter's position between Little Popo, the Hueda and Dahomey cannot have been comfortable.

Little Popo's trade during Ashampo's reign, 1737 to 1767

In late 1737 or early 1738, the Dutch WIC established a lodge at Little Popo. This was a substitute for their fort, Singelenburg, at Keta, which had been destroyed by the Dahomians. The WIC wanted to re-occupy Keta, both for the ivory trade and to continue their successful experiments with the cultivation of indigo, but was prevented by the locals due to a conflict in which they were involved with the Ga at Accra.[135] The Danes, who in this conflict supported the Ga, used the opportunity to score off their Dutch rivals and establish themselves at Keta. Ashampo then requested the Dutch to establish a Dutch lodge at Little Popo, promising to compensate for their loss of Keta.[136] However, the lodge was short-lived and soon abandoned by the WIC because Ashampo and other Little Popo traders defaulted on their debts.[137] In 1740, the WIC agent at Badagry commented that 'no

---

[132] Wilks, *Asante*, 28, 131. Cf. Gayibor, *Le Genyi*, 122–3; Nørregård, *Danish Settlements*, 126.
[133] Agbanon, *Histoire*, 23–5.
[134] Gayibor, *Le Genyi*, 125.
[135] For this conflict, see Reindorf, *History*, 103–111; Wilks, 'Akwamu and Otublohum', 399. For indigo cultivation, see van Dantzig, *Dutch and the Guinea Coast*, no.396, NBKG 8: Minutes of Elmina Council, 6 Mar. 1738; also Robin Law, '"There's nothing grows in the West Indies but will grow here": European projects of plantation agriculture in West Africa, 1650s-1780s', *Commercial Agriculture*, ed. Law/ Schwarz/ Strickrodt, 116–37.
[136] Van Dantzig, *Dutch and the Guinea Coast*, nos. 394, 396, NBKG 8, Minutes of Elmina Council, 19 Dec. 1737, 6 Mar. 1738. The Dutch agent was documented at Little Popo in March 1738: ADCM: B.5729: Process-verbeaux du Phœnix, 30 Mar 1738, cited in Robert, *Les trafics coloniaux*, 76–7.
[137] NAN: NBKG 9, Minuut notulen DG & Raden 1742–1758: Elmina, 10 Feb. 1743.

whiteman will trade with [Ashampo ('Shampa')], because he is a real robber.'[138] Nevertheless, trade at Little Popo continued. The same agent reported the existence of another lodge at Little Popo, belonging to the Dutch captain Pieter de Moore: 'the King of Dahomme, if he could get hold of [de Moore], would massacre him in the most horrible manner, because he has several times sold gunpowder and muskets to Schampa.'[139] In 1743, the WIC decided to establish another lodge there, hoping to recover the debts.[140] Its success however was limited, if the testimony of Rømer, the Danish agent, is to be believed. Rømer visited Ashampo in August 1744 to negotiate another Danish lodge at Keta, the one established there in 1737 having proved short-lived.[141] He was disdainful about the Dutch establishment at Little Popo. According to him, the Dutch agent had arrived in early 1744 with two canoes and fifteen canoemen as well as trade goods worth ten to fifteen slaves, 'to build a lodge and as gifts for the King and the greatest negroes'. He had spent the goods as gifts but had not established a lodge, living in an African house instead, and his trade was a failure. He worked in what Rømer considered a 'remarkable fashion', borrowing slaves from people at Little Popo and, using his canoes and canoemen, sending them to Ouidah for sale to French or Portuguese vessels. After the return of his canoemen he paid his Little Popo suppliers, making a profit from the difference in the prices he paid at Little Popo and demanded at Ouidah. However, only one Frenchman had so far 'fallen into his clutches'.[142]

The French traded regularly at Little Popo between 1737 and 1744.[143] They were forced to do so by difficulties in their trade at Ouidah, due partly to the disturbances caused by the invasions by Oyo and Little Popo. According to a French document, by 1744 Little Popo had more trade than Ouidah.[144] However, this does not necessarily mean that the trade at Little Popo was going well, since Ouidah's trade virtually disappeared in the early

---

[138] Van Dantzig, *Dutch and the Guinea Coast*, no. 420, NBKG 105: Elmina Journal, 1 Feb. 1741, citing Assistant Bronssema, Pattackery, 11 Aug. 1740. For the identification of this statement with 'Schampa', see Law, *Slave Coast*, 318.
[139] *Ibid*.
[140] NAN: NBKG 9, Minuut notulen Directeur Generaal & Raden 1742–1758: Elmina, 10 Feb. 1743.
[141] Justesen, *Danish Sources*, XI.23: L.F. Römer, Keta, 13 Aug. 1744; Van Dantzig, *Dutch and the Guinea Coast*, no. 396, NBKG 8, Minutes of Elmina Council, 6 Mar. 1738.
[142] Justesen, *Danish Sources*, XI.23: L.F. Römer, Keta, 13 Aug. 1744. Römer identifies this vessel as the 'Duc de Bretagne', but this does not make sense as it had traded directly at Little Popo, leaving the place shortly before Rømer arrived. Mettas, *Répertoire*, ii, no. 1477; 'Voyages: The Trans-Atlantic Slave Trade Database' (2009): http://www.slavevoyages.org/tast/database/search.faces (accessed 7 Dec. 2011), voyage 31477.
[143] Mettas, *Répertoire*; 'Voyages: The Trans-Atlantic Slave Trade Database' (2009): http://www.slavevoyages.org/tast/database/search.faces (accessed 7 Dec. 2011).
[144] Akinjogbin, *Dahomey*, 115, citing ANF: C.6/25, Levet, Ouidah, 31 Jan. 1744. Cf. Law, *Slave Coast*, 318.

period of Tegbesu's reign.[145] The Danes focused on Keta, where a lodge (resulting from Rømer's negotiations with Ashampo) was established in late 1744. It was discontinued in 1746 because 'it brought nothing but expenses', but was re-established soon afterwards and functioned (with some interruptions) until 1784, when it was replaced by a fort.[146] From 1745 to 1749, there was an English lodge at Little Popo, run by Andrew Lewis Dettmar and John Dettmar. They were former employees of the RAC who had left the company because of disagreements with their governor. However, if they had hoped for more congenial conditions at Little Popo, they were disappointed. They were robbed, presumably by or on behalf of Ashampo, and prevented from leaving the place. According to a Danish report, 'they noted that the negroes at [Little Popo] had the mastery over the Whites, so that they could not know when the Negroes would take from them what they had brought to that place.'[147] This prompted the Dettmars to make an arrangement with the Danes to send the slaves and ivory purchased at Little Popo for safekeeping to the Danish headquarters at Christiansborg. Unable to escape from Ashampo's control, they died at Little Popo in April and November 1749 respectively. By then, they had sent 18 slaves and 3,600 lbs of ivory to Christiansborg.[148]

The Dettmars' experience seems to have discouraged European traders, causing a lull of Little Popo's trade. Hardly any ships are documented there during the period when they were there.[149] However, the deterrent effect was short-lived. By 1750 the Dutch and French were again active at Little Popo and there was also English interest.[150] George Stockwell, formerly the RAC's governor on the Gold Coast, planned to build a 'Castle', i.e. a fort, there in 1750. This project failed because his former RAC colleagues at Cape Coast Castle regarded it as an 'infringement' and successfully bribed Ashampo with 10 gallons of rum to prevent it.[151] But his successor at Cape Coast Castle, John Roberts, also became interested in Little Popo after he was ousted from his position in mid-1751. He planned to trade privately,

---

[145] Akinjogbin, *Dahomey*, 113; Law, 'Slave-Raiders and Middlemen', 51–4.
[146] Justesen, *Danish Sources*, no. 98, V.-g.K. 887: Letter Copy Book 13 Aug. 1744 – 4 Jan. 1745: 25 Sept. 1744; no. XI.95, J.C. Eminga, Ada, 21 Apr. 1750; no. XI.108, J. Suurman, Keta, Nov. 1750; nos. XII.1 and XII.8, M. Hachsen et al., Christiansborg, 7 May 1751 and 5 Jan. 1852; Nørregård, *Danish Settlements*, 106, 108–9, 124.
[147] Justesen, *Danish Sources*, XI.82: Platfues et al., Christiansborg, 12 April 1749.
[148] *Ibid.*, XI.93, V.-g.K. 124: J. Platfues et al., Christiansborg, 26 Nov. 1749; no. XII.8, V.-g.K. 125: Hachsen et al., Christiansborg, 5 Jan. 1752.
[149] The only exception is 'La Galère d'Afrique', which visited Little Popo between February and July 1749 (Mettas, *Répertoire*, vol. 2, no. 3172; 'Voyages: The Trans-Atlantic Slave Trade Database' (2009): http://www.slavevoyages.org/tast/database/search.faces, voyage 33172 [accessed 12 Jan. 2012]).
[150] TNA: T70/1476, J. Roberts to Capt. Bruce, 14 June 1750.
[151] TNA: T70/425, Cape Coast Castle Journal, 3 Feb. 1750 [= 1751], 24 Mar. 1751; T70/1476, J. Roberts to [R. Stockwell], Cape Coast Castle, 9 Aug. 1750; T70/1477, J. Roberts to S. Ashley, Cape Coast Castle, 5 Apr. 1751; Roberts to Capt. Cole, Cape Coast Castle, 5 April 1751.

together with some of his former RAC colleagues and partners in the West Indies, and to monopolise the rum trade on the Gold and Slave Coasts.[152] Little Popo and Ashampo became a focus of this project. In April 1751, Roberts described Little Popo as 'a place of great Trade', indicating the potential he saw for investment there.[153] He established a lodge, which however cannot have lasted very long as by 1756 he was bankrupt.[154] There was another ephemeral English lodge in May 1758.[155] English trade at Little Popo was carried on mainly under sail.[156] In 1758, the governor at Cape Coast Castle described Little Popo as 'a principal Place of Trade both for Slaves & Ivory'.[157] There was also a WIC lodge, although it cannot have been very profitable because in June 1758 it was reported that the agent wanted to relocate to Keta.[158] He appears to have done this, as three months later Ashampo forced a WIC agent to move his lodge from Keta to Little Popo. This lodge was active until at least the end of 1760 but was probably abandoned soon after this. During the period from September 1758 to June 1760, it purchased 120 slaves.[159] In 1762, there were plans for another WIC lodge but it is not clear whether anything became of this.[160] By 1763, there was an English lodge belonging to Richard Brew, then governor of the English fort at Anomabu.[161] It is not clear how long it lasted. It was still documented in 1766,[162] but had been abandoned by the time of Brew's death in 1776, as is suggested by the lack of reference to it by the executors of his will.

In 1764, an English report noted that French and Portuguese vessels regularly visited the place. This report also gave information about the origins of some of the slaves who were sold at Little Popo. They were 'sometimes' supplied by Akwamu, specifically when the trade route to Accra (the main outlet of Akwamu's trade) was disrupted by bandits.[163] The report's information about the French trade is contradicted by a French

---

[152] TNA: T70/1477, J. Roberts to G. Thomas, W. Sturgeon & B. Massiah, Cape Coast Town, 17 Sept. 1751.
[153] TNA: T70/1476, J. Roberts to S. Ashley, Cape Coast Castle, 5 Apr. 1751.
[154] TNA: T70/1526, J. Roberts, Garlick Hill, 24 Aug. 1756; T70/29, Committee to Ch. Bell, London, 4 Nov 1756
[155] TNA: T70/1528, W. Webster, Little Popo, 21 May 1758.
[156] TNA: T70/1517, T. Melvil, Cape Coast Castle, 26 Dec. 1751; T70/1522, T. Melvil, Cape Coast Castle, 21 June 1754; T70/1525, J. Knight, Liverpool, 3 Nov. 1756; T70/1528, Charles Bell, Cape Coast Castle, 20 Sept. 1757; UAH: R.15.N.8, 'Guinea Prottens Reise-Diarium' (1956–1761), 22 June 1757.
[157] TNA: T70/30, Nassau Senior, Cape Coast Castle, 15 June 1758.
[158] *Ibid.*; UAH: R.15.N.8, 'Guinea Prottens Reise-Diarium' (1956–1761), 16 July 1758.
[159] NAN: WIC 505, Resolutiën 1758–1764 aan kamer Amsterdam: J. van Gilst, Elmina, Nov. 1760.
[160] *Ibid.*: S. Elin, Elmina, [20] March 1762.
[161] TNA: T70/31, Charles Bell, Cape Coast Castle, 14 April 1763. Cf. Priestley, *West African Trade*, 72.
[162] TNA: T70/31, Gilbert Petrie, Cape Coast Castle, 13 Sept. 1766.
[163] *Ibid.*, William Mutter, Cape Coast Castle, 10 Jan. 1764. For banditry, see Kea, 'I am here', 124.

document from 1765, giving estimates of the volume of the European slave trade of the individual ports on the Slave Coast. The number for Little Popo is very low (100 slaves per year) compared to those for Keta (800), Grand Popo (2,000) and Ouidah (5,000).[164] An explanation may be that, rather than representing Little Popo's value to the Europeans generally, this reflects the decline of the French trade there in the period.[165] However, the high volume of slave exports for Grand Popo is a puzzle, and probably a mistake, given the lack of documentation for trade there in the period.

In 1771, a Dutch naval officer noted that Little Popo offered 'a good trade in slaves, the reason why the Portuguese also always call at this place.'[166] He also gave a rare description of the coastal settlement, 'which is very long and large and lying close to the beach'. In its centre were 'two large houses or Negro cases [Port. *casas*, i.e. houses], on one of which was flying a [Dutch] Prince's flag and on the other an English one.' The latter house may have been Brew's lodge. Or it could have belonged to a local person or notable, as must have been the case with the house with the Dutch flag, since the officer explicitly stated that the Dutch lodge 'has been abandoned for some time.'[167]

Afro-European relations during Ashampo's reign, 1737 to 1767

As the history of ephemeral lodges at Little Popo shows, Ashampo's success as a trader was limited, illustrating the complex relationship between warfare and the slave trade. On the one hand, Ashampo's military campaigns generated slaves who could be sold to the Europeans. However, this was local warfare and resulted in unreliable and fitful supplies of slaves. The old problem of the lack of strong connections with interior sources of slaves persisted. This put Ashampo under pressure as he was dependent on the external trade, both for supplies of firearms and of trade goods with which to attract followers and build the alliances necessary for his campaigns against Anlo and Dahomey, his rivals for control of the region and its trading ports.

On the other hand, it could be argued that the very attributes that made Ashampo an outstanding warrior also impeded his success as a

---

[164] ANF: C.6/29, 'Côte d'Afrique: État des esclaves que peuvent retirer de la Côte occidentale d'Afrique les nations de l'Europe, vers 1765', cited in K. D. Patterson, 'A Note on Slave Exports from the Costa Da Mina, 1760–1770', *BIFAN*, series B, 33, 2 (1971), 249–56. Cf. Akinjogbin, *Dahomey*, 139–40.

[165] According to Mettas, only two French vessels traded at Little Popo in the 1760s (*Répertoire*, i, no. 742; vol. 2, no. 3245).

[166] NAN: Archiv Admiraliteitscolleges, Collectie J. A. van der Velden 1.01.47.17, no.17: Particuliere aantekeningen van Gezagvoerder J. A. van der Velden, 4 July 1771.

[167] *Ibid*, no.16: Journaal van's lands fregat Boreas, 1770–1772, 7 July 1771.

trader. Throughout the period, Europeans merchants complained about his strong will, unpredictability and uncompromising nature, his lack of skill (or interest) in negotiation and cooperation.[168] In short, he tended to be a 'tyrant' with the Europeans as well as with his subjects. This made trade relations at Little Popo difficult, particularly as he controlled the trade even though he did not monopolise it. Europeans who wanted to trade at Little Popo had to get his permission and settle conditions with him, even to trade with others. As a result, Little Popo gained a bad reputation among the Europeans in the period, as illustrated by a Dutch trader's complaint from 1762 that it was 'known to the whole world' that conditions there were particularly difficult due to the 'excessive mandatory presents' requested by the king, the risk of being robbed and 'the wilfulness of the native people' to which traders had to submit 'only to be safe, to keep [their] life'.[169]

The continuing European interest in Little Popo despite these unfavourable conditions can be explained by two factors, the general state of the slave trade in this period, which was expanding, with the demand for slaves outstripping the supply,[170] and the problems at the neighbouring, more established ports on the Gold Coast and in Dahomey.[171] The result was an increasing competition between the European traders and a search for alternative sources of slaves. This worked to Ashampo's advantage, as he exploited the competition between the Europeans by robbing them if there was no other way for him to gain access to trade goods.[172]

The Europeans tried to control the risk of trading at Little Popo in various ways. One was the higher pricing of their goods, or lower pricing of slaves, to offset potential loss. This is suggested by a letter from Roberts, the RAC's governor at Cape Coast Castle, who in 1750 compared the prices of slaves at various ports on the Slave Coast. According to him, at Little Popo slaves cost 10 ounces besides the 'Dashé', i.e. custom payment to open trade (presumably paid to Ashampo), while at Epe (the port of the kingdom of Djeken, on the eastern Slave Coast) they cost 11 ounces and at Badagry (to the east of Epe) 12 ounces.[173]

[168] For a detailed discussion, see Strickrodt, 'In Search of a Moral Community', 113–15.
[169] NAN: WIC 505, Resolutiën 1758–1764 aan kamer Amsterdam: S. Elin, Elmina, [20] March 1762. For similar complaints, see e.g. Justesen, *Danish Sources*, XI.23: L.F. Römer, Keta, 13 Aug. 1744; XI.29: Opinions and votes of the members of the Secret Council in the matter of L. F. Römer's journey to Popo (Billsen, Christiansborg, 24 Sept. 1744). Cf. Rømer, *Reliable Account*, 176–7.
[170] Lovejoy/ Richardson, 'African Agency', 45–6; 'Voyages: The Trans-Atlantic Slave Trade Database' (2009): http://www.slavevoyages.org/tast/assessment/estimates.faces (accessed on 3 Mar. 2013).
[171] For Dahomey, see Law, 'Slave-Raiders and Middlemen', 52–3. For the Gold Coast, see Johannes Menne Postma, *The Dutch in the Atlantic Trade, 1600–1815* (Cambridge, 1990), 206–7.
[172] ADCM: B.5729: Process-verbeaux du Phœnix, 30 Mar 1738, cited in Robert, *Les trafics coloniaux*, 76–7 (cf. Deveau, *La traite rochelaise*, 210–12); NAH: WIC 505 Resolutiën 1758–1764 aan kamer Amsterdam: J. van Gilst, Nov. 1760; Rømer, *Reliable Account*, 176–7.
[173] TNA: T70/1476, J. Roberts, 14 June 1750. For Epe and Badagry, see Law, *Slave Coast*, 310–11.

Another way of managing risk was to deny Ashampo credit. There is no clear indication that credit was extended to Ashampo by the European traders. The only instance where credit is explicitly mentioned in the sources dates from 1758 when Ashampo sent an embassy to the Dutch and Danish at Accra (mentioned above) and this was not (strictly) in the context of trade but for a non-commercial purpose. The Dutch reaction is not recorded but can easily be surmised given their experience of Ashampo defaulting on his debts.[174] The Danes (also) refused, explaining that 'he who wants the guns should also take the other goods' and that they were unwilling to extend credit for such a large amount.[175] Credit, however, may not have been necessary for trade at Little Popo because the slaves were procured locally in warfare, rather than purchased from the interior.

European traders also attempted to use pawns to ensure their safety at Little Popo and on the western Slave Coast more generally. In 1744, the Danish company demanded Ashampo's son as collateral for their lodge at Keta. This was refused, but Ashampo proposed to give his son if they established a lodge at Little Popo. However, the Danes ignored this offer, evidently preferring to put some distance between themselves and Ashampo.[176]

Finally, Roberts sought to build a personal long-term relationship with Ashampo to minimise the risks of trading at Little Popo. In 1752, when he returned to London, he took with him one of Ashampo's sons, called 'Aqua', for education.[177] The practice of taking children of influential Africans to Europe for education has been described as 'a form of coastal insurance for the safeguarding of trade'.[178] For Roberts, this insurance potentially – if all turned out well – worked on several levels. First, while Ashampo's son was in England, he was in effect a pawn for the security of Roberts' agents and trade goods at Little Popo. Roberts himself noted that Aqua had been given to him as 'a hostage' for the establishment of a 'Fort'.[179] Second, after the boy's return to the coast, he would potentially provide a handle on his father, i.e. Roberts might be able to influence the father via the son. Roberts could also hope that after Ashampo's death, Aqua would succeed him and thus ensure Roberts a privileged position in Little Popo's

---

(cont.) The 'ounce' is the trade ounce, a unit of account used on the West African Coast which originally denoted the quantity of goods necessary to buy an ounce of gold. See Marion Johnson, 'The Ounce Trade in Eighteenth-Century West African Trade', *JAH*, 7/2 (1966), 197–214; Law, *Slave Coast*, 170.

[174] NAN: NBKG 9, Minuut notulen DG & Raden 1742–1758: Elmina, 10 Feb. 1743.

[175] UAH: R.15.N.8, 'Guinea Prottens Reise-Diarium' (1756–1761), 11 Mar. 1758, 12 Mar. 1758, 14 Mar. 1758; Kea, 'Akwamu-Anlo Relations', 37, citing '[NAN:] Elmina Journal. Letter from Accra, 11 Nov. 1758.' For non-commercial credit, see Law, 'Finance and Credit', 20–21.

[176] Justesen, *Danish Sources*, XI.18: Secret Council Minutes, Christiansborg: J. Billsen et al., 14 May 1744; XI.23: L.F. Römer, Keta, 13 Aug. 1744.

[177] TNA: T70/1478, J. Roberts, London, 31 Jan. 1753.

[178] Priestley, *West African Trade*, 19.

[179] TNA: T70/1526, J. Roberts, Garlick Hill, 24 Aug. 1756.

trade. Roberts' successor at Cape Coast Castle was clear about the potential benefits. According to him, Aqua was 'by all Acc[oun]ts a Black Man of much greater Family than any other that has hitherto been in England, besides as the Dutch Company have a factory [at Little Popo] it might be of some Service in strengthening our Interest.'[180]

The initiative for taking Aqua to England probably came from Roberts rather than Ashampo.[181] However, even if this was the case, Ashampo must have seen an advantage in this arrangement or else he would not have agreed to let his son (who in fact may have been a more remote relative) to be taken away to Europe. For him, this arrangement meant privileged access to European traders as it provided him with the broker that he had been trying to obtain by other means, such as detaining Europeans.[182] Further, the institution of child fosterage, which was widespread in Africa, implied binding moral obligations between legal parents and foster parents.[183] As indicated by the cases of children of notables on Gold Coast who were sent to Britain by the African Company, these obligations included continuing financial support from the company after their return to the African coast, from which their parents or seniors also profitted.[184]

The agreement had been for Aqua to remain in England for two or three years, but Roberts went bankrupt and refused to return the boy unless he was reimbursed for his costs. In May 1756 Ashampo became impatient and threatened to punish English traders if the boy was not returned.[185] The African Company's governor at Cape Coast Castle was concerned about possible consequences for British trade at Little Popo, but neither he nor the committee in London found themselves able to force Roberts to return the boy.[186] No action seems to have been taken until 1758, when Ashampo

[180] TNA: T70/30, Nassau Senior, Cape Coast Castle, 15 June 1758.
[181] Although there is no direct evidence relating to Ashampo's son, this is suggested by the case of another boy, from Dixcove on the Gold Coast, who was taken to England by Roberts at the same time. In this case, Roberts' initiative is documented (TNA: T70/1476, J. Roberts to E. Gregory, Dixcove, 8 July 1750; Priestley, *West African Trade*, 36–7). In the 1750s, the practice of educating the children of African notables in Britain was embraced with enthusiasm by the new Company of Merchants Trading to Africa (short: 'African Company'). However, the beginning of this trend dates back to the times of the old company, specifically to the adventure of William Ansah, a son of an important Anomabo caboceer who visited London in 1749 and with whom Roberts was personally acquainted. See Priestley, *West African Trade*, 20–1; Shumway, *Fante*, 79; Strickrodt, 'In Search of a Moral Community', 121–23.
[182] Justesen, *Danish Sources*, XI.23: L.F. Römer, Keta, 13 Aug. 1744; XI.82, XI.93: Platfues et al., Christiansborg, 12 April 1749, 26 Nov. 1749.
[183] For a discussion of how child fosterage was used to strengthen business relationships in the twentieth century, see A. Cohen, *Custom and Politics in Urban Africa: A Study of Hausa Migration in Yoruba Towns* (London, 1969), 86–92.
[184] TNA: T70/30, Ch. Bell, Cape Coast Castle, 20 March 1756. See also Strickrodt, 'In Search of a Moral Community', 122–23.
[185] TNA: T70/1525, J. Knight, London, Liverpool, 3 Nov. 1756.
[186] TNA: T70/30, Ch. Bell, Cape Coast Castle, 8 May 1756; T70/29, Committee of Merchants, London, 15 Aug. 1756; 4 Nov 1756; 17 Nov. 1756.

seized an English trader at Little Popo to force his son's return.[187] In doing so, he resorted to a practice that is well documented on the Gold and Slave Coasts, known as 'panyarring', by which a creditor held a community collectively responsible for a debt contracted by one of its members and seized another member for repayment.[188] This strategy worked. The matter was referred by the African Company's committee to the Board of Trade, which resolved it by ordering the company to pay Roberts £40 for his expenses and to arrange a passage for Ashampo's son to Little Popo.[189]

'Prince Ackwaw' returned to Africa in May 1759, having spent nearly seven years in England during which he had converted to Christianity. He was reportedly reluctant to leave.[190] He was richly fitted out with clothes and other 'necessaries', including fine suits, ruffled shirts, 'neat' shoes, beaver hats, black wigs, a silver watch and chain, a comb and snuff. He was also given a letter and presents for Ashampo, the latter comprising a robe of brocade, beer, brandy and gunpowder, the former expressing the company's hopes that Ashampo would use his influence to promote the British trade at Little Popo.[191] In total, Ashampo's presents and Aqua's necessaries cost the company about £100.[192] This impressive sum clearly indicates the company's recognition of the importance of good personal relations with Ashampo for the trade at Little Popo as well as the value they set on this trade. The importance of such relations for any activities at Little Popo was also emphasised by Rømer in his advice to the Moravian missionaries, who in the 1760s wanted to become active in the region: 'Asiambo's friendship is necessary.'[193]

The history of Afro-European trade relations at Little Popo during Ashampo's rule illustrates the difficulty of establishing relations of trust between Africans and Europeans. Although in theory trade between African and Europeans depended on the ability of Africans and Europeans to establish trust, in practice this was often difficult to establish, or broke down. Trade continued nevertheless at Little Popo in the period, but the inability to establish trust may have been a contributory reason why Little Popo did not become, in a sustained way, a major supplier of slaves in this period. However, developments in the latter part of Ashampo's reign, specifically the prolonged visit of his son to Britain, point to the emergence of a cosmopolitan culture which from the 1780s began to facilitate trade relations at Little Popo, as will be discussed in the following chapter.

[187] TNA: T70/1528, W. Webster, Little Popo, 21 May 1758.
[188] Law, 'On Pawning', 62.
[189] TNA: T70/30, Nassau Senior, Cape Coast Castle, 15 June 1758; T70/144, Minutes of Committee, 21 Feb. 1758, 2 May 1758.
[190] TNA: T70/1530, J. Roberts, Stanwell Place, 25 Feb., 29 Apr. 1759.
[191] TNA: T70/1529 and 1530: Bundle of bills and receipts, 3 May-12 July 1759; T70/29, Committee to Ashampo, King of Little Popo, London, 9 May 1759; Committee to Nassau Senior, London, 9 May 1759.
[192] TNA: T70/144, Minutes of Committee, 9 May 1759.
[193] UAH: R.15.N.5 no.19, L.F. Rømer, [n.d.], cited in J. Meder 10 Oct. 1767.

4

The era of the traders
1772 to c. 1807

For the period from 1772 to the abolition of the slave trade there is an exceptional abundance of documentation on the events on the western Slave Coast, which reflects its increasing importance in Afro-European trade. The region's rise in the trade had important repercussions for the communities there, shifting the power balance between the Ge king at Glidji and (African) traders in the coastal settlements in favour of the latter. This was the era of the traders, most importantly Lattie (d.1795), whose commercial success, new wealth and power was symbolised by the new, multi-storey houses that began to appear in the coastal settlement.

Little Popo, Anlo and the Danes, 1772 to 1792

In early 1772 the Danes established a lodge at Little Popo.[1] This must have been very desirable for Little Popo, given the difficulties it faced in its struggle against Anlo at that time. As noted in the previous chapter, in 1772 these difficulties resulted in loss of control over Keta, which then allied with Anlo in its attack on Aflao. This was against the background of the Asante invasion of Akyem, Little Popo's ally on the Gold Coast against Akwamu, and Anlo's alliance with Akwamu. In the same year, Little Popo concluded a peace treaty with Dahomey, presumably in consequence of these difficulties on the western border.[2] A European lodge meant supplies of firearms and gunpowder, access to credit and profits from trade which could be used towards war expenses. According to Biørn, reporting later in the century, the Danes also assisted Little Popo with money loans for

---

[1] Nørregård, *Danish Settlements*, 126, citing KODGKA, Indk. br. 1770–1773, no. 838, J.A. Kiøge, 26 March 1772.
[2] Law, *Ouidah*, 64; Akinjogbin, *Dahomey*, 152.

their wars.³ Although he does not give particular dates and has a tendency to exaggerate, Danish support of Little Popo in this period seems likely enough. For the Danes, this was an opportunity to expand their influence in the region, especially as Little Popo was not in the position to be as assertive in negotiations with the Europeans as it had been at the time of Rømer's meeting with Ashampo in the 1740s.

Anlo's power was on the rise in the period. According to Kea, between 1774 and 1781 it carried out successful campaigns against Little Popo, Ada and other lower Volta riverine communities.⁴ It is not clear when exactly the campaign against Little Popo occurred, possibly in 1774 but certainly before 1777. This was the year when the king of Little Popo sent notice of termination of the peace to Dahomey, indicating that by then Little Popo had recovered its strength. In September 1777, the French director at Ouidah reported, 'the blacks of Popo are almost always in war with those of Dahomey'.⁵ However, despite threats of raids on Ouidah beach in 1778, 1780 and 1784, no actual attack appears to have materialised. In 1789, there were reports that an attack against Ouidah itself was imminent, but these too proved to be false.⁶ A possible explanation for Little Popo's lack of action on the eastern frontier may be its preoccupation with developments to the west. There, Anlo had launched another attack against Ada on 26 October 1780, defeating it.⁷ Little Popo retaliated. In early 1781 the Danish Governor at Christiansborg reported that its king had led 'a large army' into the field and predicted Anlo's defeat.⁸ In May 1781 he wrote that the king had seized hegemony over all the Anlo towns to the mouth of the Volta.⁹ This is probably an exaggeration as Anloga was not under Little Popo's control; otherwise the 1784 war, in which the Danes allied with Little Popo to fight Anlo (see below), would have been unnecessary. He also implies that Keta had again fallen under Little Popo's authority, noting the importance of good relations with Little Popo's king, including regular rent payment,

---

³ TNA: T70/1565, A. R. Biørn, Christiansborg Castle, 12 May 1792.
⁴ Kea, 'Akwamu-Anlo Relations', 38, citing '[DNA:] Palaberbog 1773–76, entries for 2, 3, and 10 December 1774; V[estindiske] J[ournaler] No. 623, 1784.
⁵ ANF: C.6/26, Bauduchiron, 'Mémoire pour servir à faire de noveaux établissemens', 23 July 1777; *ibid.*, 'Mémoire d'Observations', Fontainebleu, 28 Sept. 1777.
⁶ Law, *Ouidah*, 47; Akinjogbin, *Dahomey*, 153.
⁷ Kea, 'Akwamu-Anlo Relations', 38–9; Nørregård, *Danish Settlements*, 146; Gayibor, *Le Genyi*, 127. Kea mistakenly dates this attack to 1781.
⁸ G[uineiske] J[ournaler] No. 113, 1781, cited in Kea, 'Akwamu-Anlo Relations', 39, n. 64.
⁹ Guineiske Sager og Aktstykker [ujournaliserede] 1765–1802, no.9, Kipnasse, Kiøbenhavn, 26 May 1781, cited in Kea, 'Akwamu-Anlo Relations', 39. Kipnasse wrongly identifies Little Popo's king with Ofoly Bossum ('Obly Bossum'), who was a 'prince' at Glidji, the king being another 'Obly'. However, the campaign was probably carried out by Ofoly Bossum rather than the king himself, whom Isert a few years later described as 'much over 80 and absolutely childish' (Isert, *Letters*, 99; Biørn, 'Beretning 1788', 226.) Reindorf identifies Ofoly Bossum as 'Ofoli Thosu' (Reindorf, *History*, 128; cf. Agbanon II, *Histoire*, 54, 55; Gayibor, *Le Genyi*, 90, 115 n.1, 164–5).

for the maintenance of the Danish lodge at Keta.[10] In the 1784 war, Keta initially supported Anlo, indicating that Little Popo's control of Keta was at best precarious. The Anlo then turned against the Danes, annoyed by their support of Ada, plundering their lodges in the Volta region. This prompted Kiøge to build a defensive fort at Ada, on the western bank of the Volta (rather than on the island where the lodge had been), which was begun in October 1783 and named Kongensten. He then proceeded to organise a great alliance to carry out a punitive expedition against Anlo, which became known as the 'Sagbadre War'.[11]

'Sagbadre' means 'swallow' and is said to derive from the nickname of a Danish official who had been mistreated by the Anlo, prompting the conflict.[12] The Ada-Danish alliance included, among others, Little Popo, Accra and Akuapem. Three employees of the Danish company participated in the campaign, among them Paul Erdmann Isert, who gave a first-hand account of it.[13] The commander of the allied army was Oto Brafo, the chief of Osu (Danish Accra).[14] The Anlo side comprised the Anlo confederacy. According to Isert, the Keta people had initially been allied with the Anlo, but during the campaign, when it became clear that this was the losing side, changed alliances and were either neutral or sided with the Ada-Danish alliance.[15] The war began on 30 March 1784 and ended six weeks later with the complete defeat of the Anlo forces. Several Anlo towns were destroyed, including Anloga, Woe, Tegbi and Pottebra, a fishing town of Keta.[16] A peace treaty, negotiated by Ofoly Bossum, a 'prince' at Glidji (see n.9), was concluded on 18 June 1784. It contained a number of conditions which in essence meant the imposition of a Danish trade monopoly in Anlo, including the construction of a Danish fort at Keta.[17]

Little Popo played an important role in this war and profited from it. It provided more than a quarter of the soldiers of the Ada-Danish alliance (1,100 out of 4,000), from various places including Aflao, Bé and Little Popo.[18] Further, Little Popo forces guarded the construction of Prindsen-

[10] Guineiske Sager og Aktstykker [ujournaliserede] 1765–1802, no.9, Kipnasse, Kiøbenhavn, 26 May 1781, cited in Kea, 'Akwamu-Anlo Relations', 39.
[11] Nørregård, *Danish Settlements*, 146. For contemporary accounts, see Isert, *Letters*, 60–1; ANF: C.6/27, Champagny, 'Mémoire' [1786].
[12] Westermann, *Die Glidyi-Ewe*, 250; Isert, *Letters*, 47 editor's n.1.
[13] Isert, *Letters*, 63–95. Cf. Nørregård, *Danish Settlements*, 146–8; Greene, *Gender*, 83.
[14] Isert, *Letters*, 65. For identification, see editor's note n.3.
[15] *Ibid.*, 81, 98 n.a.
[16] 'Pottebra' is called 'Kpotibra' by Agbanon II and 'Kpoduwa' by Gayibor, Greene and Akyeampong (*Histoire*, 54; Gayibor, *Le Genyi*, 130, 132; Greene, *Gender*, 83, 85, 88; Akyeampong, *Between the Sea*, 6, 39, 47–8, 72). According to Isert, it lay half-way between Keta and Aflao, a distance of 6 Danish miles (roughly 27.6 English miles/ 47km) (Isert, *Letters*, 82, 83). For its description as a fishing town of Keta, see TNA: T70/1565, A. R. Biørn, Christiansburg Castle, 6 May 1792.
[17] Isert, *Letters*, 97–8.
[18] *Ibid.*, 81, 65.

sten.[19] The rewards were handsome and manifold. First, its long-standing rival, Anlo, had been defeated and constrained. According to Biørn, the latter's territory was again limited to Anlo proper, 'from Greve, a place between the mouth [of the Volta] and Atocco, to Tebee [= Tegbi] town, but not further', and from the sea to 'the Krepee side', that is the northern bank of the Keta lagoon.[20] This means that Anlo was restricted to its limits in 1730, before it had extended its influence to the north and east. Little Popo's control reached westwards as far as Tegbi, 3 or 4 miles/ some 5 or 6km west of Keta.[21] The latter fell again under Little Popo's control, as is also indicated by the fact that Ofoly Bossum received a monthly stipend for Fort Prindsensten from the Danes.[22] Second, the Danish trade monopoly at Keta meant that Little Popo's commercial rival in the west was eliminated. Previously, the English, French and Portuguese had been trading there for slaves, ivory and provisions.[23] Isert states that the treaty banned only the trade in slaves and ivory with other European nations, but a subsequent complaint from the English suggests that the provisions trade was also affected because the Danes prohibited the Keta people from launching their canoes to meet English (and probably other European) vessels.[24] Third, Little Popo profitted financially. According to Nørregård, Prindsensten's construction cost six times as much as Kongensten's and the largest part of the money went to Little Popo for the military protection of the building work.[25] In addition, the King of Little Popo received presents from the Danish government in recognition of services.[26]

Shortly afterwards, however, Little Popo's relations with the Danes turned sour. The reason appears to have been Danish efforts to monopolise trade in the region, including Little Popo where they were keen to build a fort. Little Popo evidently wanted to preserve its (profitable) freedom of trade and requested the establishment of lodges from other European nations. In 1785 a deputation was sent to the English at Cape Coast Castle.[27] In the following year, a French visitor, Champagny, found the people eager for a French lodge but at the same time noted their aversion to any establishment that would tend to monopolise the trade, that is a fort.[28] Meanwhile, Biørn was hatching schemes to bring Little Popo into submission, including

---

[19] *Ibid.*, 105.
[20] Biørn, 'Beretning 1788', 222–3. Cf. Grove/Johansen, 'Historical Geography', 1402; Kea, 'Akwamu-Anlo Relations', 41.
[21] Greene, *Gender*, 60 map 4, 84 map 5.
[22] Biørn, 'Beretning 1788', 226. Cf. Kea, 'Akwamu-Anlo Relations', 40.
[23] TNA: T70/33, Governor and Council, Cape Coast Castle, 9 July 1785; Isert, *Letters*, 102.
[24] Isert, *Letters*, 102; TNA: T70/33, Governor and Council, Cape Coast Castle, 9 July 1785.
[25] Nørregård, *Danish Settlements*, 154; Isert, *Letters*, 105.
[26] Nørregård, *Danish Settlements*, 149.
[27] TNA: T70/33, Governor and Council, Cape Coast Castle, 9 July 1785.
[28] ANF: C.6/27, Champagny, 'Mémoire' [1786].

a plan to bribe Akwamu and Dahomey to invade it.[29] This plan was evidently discussed during the Danish mission to Akwamu in 1791, since the Akwamu's ruler's response included an offer of support for the establishment of a Danish fort at Little Popo.[30]

It is not clear when exactly the discord between the Danes and Little Popo began, but the conflict escalated in the late 1780s, when the Danes meddled in the royal succession at Glidji. According to Biørn, king Obly died in 1786. There were two candidates for succession, Ofoli Adjalu ('Offoli-adjalu') and Ohaittee, of whom the former prevailed.[31] Ohaittee fled to Keta, where he enlisted the support of the Danes and also applied to Akwamu for assistance.[32] According to Kea, in 1788 both Anlo and Akwamu were prepared to attack Little Popo to support Ohaittee, but the Danes prevented 'the outbreak of a full-scale war against Little Popo'.[33] Meanwhile, the Ge, annoyed with the Danish interference, started robbing the Danish lodge at Little Popo. Then they encouraged the inhabitants of Augoja and Pottebra, both fishing towns of Keta, to attack Fort Prindsensten, and sent a force to assist them.[34] The Augoja and Pottebra people, already hostile to the Danes because of their murder of a local notable a few years earlier, attacked Prindsensten several times.[35] Keta people apparently also participated in these attacks, which for them must have been a welcome opportunity to get back at the Danes. The Danish lodge at Aflao was also destroyed and, on 22 June 1790, a Danish agent was killed. The Danes, unable to retaliate with their own small military force, tried to organise mercenary forces to punish the people of the three towns. They first approached Akyem, but without success. Then they turned to Anlo, which agreed to become involved. In May 1791, an Anlo force set fire to Keta, Augoja and Pottebra, initiating a train of events that in February 1792

[29] Biørn, 'Beretning 1788', 227.
[30] Kea, 'Akwamu-Anlo Relations', 43.
[31] Biørn, 'Beretning 1788', 226.
[32] TNA: T70/1565, A. R. Biørn, Christiansborg Castle, 6 May 1792. Cf. Nørregård, *Danish Settlements*, 155. The spelling of the name varies in the literature: 'Okaitkie' (Nørregård), 'Okaytie' (Kea), 'Odaitke' and 'Okaitkia' (Gayibor, *Le Genyi*, 131).
[33] Kea, 'Akwamu-Anlo Relations', 42, citing DNA: Guineiske Sager og Aktstykker (ujournaliserede) 1765–1802; Kipnasse, Christiansborg, 4 Feb. 1789; Elmina Journal, A. Biørn, Christiansborg Castle, 6 May 1792, in A. Dalzel, Cape Coast Castle, 23 May 1792 [for original, see note below]; and another 'letter from A. Biørn' for which the reference is not clear.
[34] TNA: T70/1565, A.R. Biørn, Christiansborg Castle, 6 May 1792. 'Augoja' is presumably identifiable with one of the three towns which according to Isert lay between Keta and Pottebra: 'Little Ajuga', 'Great Ajuga' and 'New Ajuga' (*Letters*, 82). It has been identified with both modern Vodza and Kedzi (Grove/ Johansen, 'The Historical Geography', 1403 n.2). Kedzi seems plausible, since the English in the 1790s called it 'Acqueja' and in the mid-nineteenth century 'Kedger or Acquijah' (TNA: T70/1563, Governor and Council, Cape Coast Castle, 20 June 1791; FO84/893, incl. in Hamilton, Admiralty, 10 April 1852: T. G. Forbes, 'Philomel', at Whydah, 5 February 1852).
[35] TNA: T70/1565, A. R. Biørn, Christiansborg Castle, 6 May 1792; Greene, *Gender*, 85; Kea, 'Akwamu-Anlo Relations', 42; Nørregård, *Danish Settlements*, 154–5.

escalated into the battle which is remembered as the 'Keta War' or 'Some War'.[36] The latter name derives from the place where some of the inhabitants of these towns relocated (modern Agbosome, situated some miles in the interior between Blekesu and Aflao). In the battle, the troops from Keta, Augoja and Pottebra were reinforced by manpower from Kliko, Weta and Little Popo.[37] The Danes took an active part on the Anlo side, contributing thirty-five men from Prindsensten's garrison. Moreover, in July 1791 Biørn had sent an embassy to Akwamu to organise additional troops, which were promised him.[38] However, in the event they did not appear because Akwamu was engaged in another campaign against their own enemies, the Nyive.[39] The battle ended with a rout of the Anlo army, despite its superiority in numbers, with fifteen chiefs and many of the soldiers being killed.[40] Shortly afterwards an allied force of Little Popo, Keta, Augoja and Pottebra besieged Fort Prindsensten, intending to capture the fort's cannons. There was little the Danes could do, apart from complaining to their superiors in Denmark of their enemies' boundless arrogance.[41]

The outcome of the Keta War was a complete defeat for Anlo and the Danes. Anlo not only suffered great losses in the campaign, but subsequently the Anlo confederacy broke up, most of its former members making common cause with Keta, Augoja and Pottebra. Little Popo again controlled the coast up to Keta. The Danes had lost their lodges at Aflao and Little Popo and their influence east of the Volta, apart from Prindsensten which was cut off from all inland communication.[42] However, Biørn (who had meanwhile become governor of the Danish company on the coast) was unwilling to accept this. According to reports from the English at Cape Coast Castle, in early 1792 he began to prepare an army, apparently with a view to attacking Little Popo.[43] In March, the Danes and Anlo sent a joint embassy to Asante, requesting military support for a

[36] This is a simplified version of more complex developments. For a detailed discussion, see Greene, *Gender*, 85–6; Grove and Johansen, 'Historical Geography', 1405; Kea, 'Akwamu-Anlo Relations', 42; Nørregård, *Danish Settlements*, 155. For a contemporary account from the English point of view and the date, see TNA: T70/33, Governor & Council, Cape Coast Castle, 20 June 1791. (For another copy, see T70/1563.) For the Danish point of view, see TNA: T70/1565, A.R. Biørn, Christiansborg Castle, 6 May 1792. For a version of the events as recalled in local traditions, see Westermann, *Glidyi-Ewe*, 251 (although he erroneously dates this war to the first half of the nineteenth century).
[37] For a detailed account, see TNA: T70/1565, Biørn, Christiansborg Castle, 6 May 1792; Greene, *Gender*, 85; Nørregård, *Danish Settlements*, 156. Cf. Gayibor, *Le Genyi*, 134–5.
[38] Kea, 'Akwamu-Anlo Relations', 43, citing DNA: Biørn, Christiansborg, 16 July 1791; Guineiske Sager og Aktstykker (ujournaliserede) 1765–1802, no. 36, N. Jiellerup, Christiansborg, 1791; and 'A. Bioern, *op. cit.*', for which I was unable to find the reference.
[39] Kea, 'Akwamu-Anlo Relations', 44, 45.
[40] TNA: T70/1565, Biørn, Christiansborg Castle, 6 May 1792. Cf. Greene, *Gender*, 85.
[41] Kea, 'Akwamu-Anlo Relations', 45, citing DNA: Guineiske Sager og Aktstykker (ujournaliserede) 1765–1802, Biørn, et al., Christiansborg, 24 Jan. 1793.
[42] Kea, 'Akwamu-Anlo Relations', 45; Nørregård, *Danish Settlements*, 157.
[43] TNA: T70/33, Gordon, Cape Coast Castle, 9 Jan. 1792.

punitive expedition against Keta, Augoja and Pottebra.[44] Further, the Anlo sent an embassy to Akwamu, requesting them to join forces with Asante. The Danish appeal to Asante alarmed not just Little Popo and its allies but also the English and the Dutch on the Gold Coast, who feared the consequences of an Asante-Danish alliance for their trade. They had been informed of Biørn's plans by a deputation from the caboceers of English and Dutch Accra.[45] There followed an animated correspondence between the English, Dutch and Danish on the Gold Coast, which however failed to convince Biørn to abandon his plans.[46] On 3 May 1792, the English and the Dutch held an emergency conference, resulting in a resolution to actively support Little Popo and defend their commercial interests there. They agreed on a joint message to the Asantehene to try and convince him to abstain from interfering, as well as on a joint embassy to Little Popo to assure the people of their support.[47]

These efforts appear to have been successful, although it is not clear what exactly happened. The campaign against Little Popo did not materialise. In July 1792, Biørn was forced to resign his post by orders from Denmark. According to Nørregård, this was on account of debts which he and his colleagues had accumulated on the coast, rather than the Asante affair.[48] However, diplomatic pressure by the British government in Europe certainly contributed to the change of Danish policy on the coast.[49] At any rate, whatever the reasons, Little Popo emerged unscathed, although it desisted from further attacks against Anlo. According to Kea, this was due to reports of the arrival of an Asante army on the coast.[50]

In December 1792 the Anlo-Danish embassy returned from Asante with the message that the Asantehene had agreed to assist the Danes with 10,000 soldiers, in return for a substantial payment. Akwamu had likewise agreed to give their assistance.[51] Biørn's successor sent a large present to the Asantehene to persuade him to break off the campaign.[52]

---

[44] Kea, 'Akwamu-Anlo Relations', 45, citing DNA: Guineiske Sager og Aktstykker (ujournaliserede) 1765–1802, von Hager, Christiansborg, 14 Mar. 1793.
[45] TNA: T70/1565, William Roberts, James Fort Accra, 29 Mar. 1792.
[46] *Ibid.*, William Roberts, James Fort, Accra, 10 Apr. 1792; *ibid.*, Biorn, Christiansburg Castle, 10 Apr., 6 May, 12 May 1792.
[47] J.J. Crooks, *Records relating to the Gold Coast Settlements from 1750 to 1874* (London, 1973), 86–7: 'Danish Encroachments. May 3, 1792. At a conference held at Cape Coast Castle'.
[48] Nørregård, *Danish Settlements*, 157.
[49] TNA: T70/33, President, Cape Coast Castle, 12 Oct. 1792. Cf. Gayibor, *Le Genyi*, 137–8.
[50] Kea, 'Akwamu-Anlo Relations', 46.
[51] *Ibid.*, 45.
[52] Nørregård, *Danish Settlements*, 157.

Asante influence on the western Slave Coast, 1792 to 1810s

According to Kea, during the Anlo-Danish mission to Asante in 1792 Anlo became 'an ally (or protectorate?) of Asante.' He argues that Anlo's association with Asante prevented any expansionist interest of Little Popo in the districts west of Aflao after this date, 'but perhaps more important was the extension of Asante influence over Popo itself.'[53] For evidence, he refers to the accounts by M'Leod and Robertson from the early nineteenth century. The former, who visited Little Popo in 1803, observed that 'being a frontier town of Creppee, [it] is protected by the king of Ashantee.'[54] The latter, a trader whose experience of the coast dated to the late eighteenth and early nineteenth century, stated that Little Popo was 'tributary' to Asante.[55] For Kea, this clearly shows that between 1793 and 1800 Little Popo had become part of the Asante sphere of influence.[56] His argument is supported by information from a letter from a British trader at Little Popo in January 1794, noting a great demand for gunpowder on account of 'an Expedition going to be undertaken by the King of Ashantah [sic] in Conjunction with the [Little] Popo's [sic], against some Neighbouring Power.'[57]

If Little Popo had indeed fallen under Asante's influence in the period, it would probably have become what Christaller called a tributary country and Wilks refers to as an outer province.[58] Asante rule over such provinces was 'indirect', which means that Asante exacted regular tributary payments but did not interfere in their domestic affairs. The tribute was generally paid in slaves and sometimes also in other commodities such as salt and lime. According to Wilks, the local rulers of tributary provinces at the outer limits of Greater Asante, which Little Popo would have been, maintained their own military forces and were mainly responsible for defending their own, and Greater Asante's, outer frontier, but would not normally be drafted for service in other parts of Asante's territories.[59] This does not tally with the projected Asante-Little Popo expedition from 1794, although a possible explanation may be that this was to pre-empt an anticipated attack thought to be too powerful for the Little Popo forces (from Dahomey?).

The association of Little Popo with Asante had probably ended by the mid-1810s. This is indicated by Bowdich who noted that Asante's sphere

---

[53] Kea, 'Akwamu-Anlo Relations', 45–6.
[54] M'Leod, *Voyage*, 140.
[55] Robertson, *Notes*, 237.
[56] Kea, 'Akwamu-Anlo Relations', 46.
[57] TNA: T70/1569, John Searle, Popo Factory, 4 January 1794.
[58] Wilks, *Asante*, 46–7, 56–7, citing J. G. Christaller, *A Grammar of the Asante and Fante Language* (Basel, 1875), xii-xiv. Cf. Law, 'Dahomey', 158.
[59] Wilks, *Asante*, 63–73.

of influence included Akwamu east of the Volta but excluded Krepi and Anlo, and implicitly also Little Popo which lay further east.[60] Wilks argues that Bowdich was wrong in excluding Krepi, which also throws doubt on Little Popo's status.[61] However, by the early 1820s Little Popo had definitely freed itself from Asante influence, as indicated by reports from 1823 that the people were arming themselves against a threatened attack from Asante.[62]

Little Popo's conflict with Dahomey (continued), 1790s

Another explanation for Little Popo's disinterest in the Anlo region after 1792 may have been the conflict with Dahomey to the east. Akinjogbin suggests that raids by Dahomean forces on port towns such as Little Popo and Badagry were part of king Agonglo's attempt to increase trade at Ouidah, by preventing trade at other ports.[63] However, there is no record of Little Popo's having actually been attacked by Dahomey. In 1793 there was the threat of an invasion. A Dahomean force was reported to be encamped to the east of Grand Popo, but according to Thomas Miles, who ran a lodge at Little Popo, the locals showed no signs of apprehension, 'on the Contrary a party was sent with a view of harassing [the Dahomean] Rear, had they proceeded'. In the event, the anticipated attack did not materialise, the King of Dahomey turning against Agouna (north-west of Abomey) instead.[64]

An actual encounter between Little Popo and Dahomey, which this time was allied with Grand Popo, took place in May 1795. Miles reported that after '5 days hard engagement' Little Popo was 'totally defeated', three of its generals having been killed and the king and Lattie taken prisoners, 'their fate of course you may easily surmise.'[65] This event is recalled in Ge and Hula traditions. According to the version recorded by Agbanon II, giving the point of view of the Ge rulers at Glidji, Little Popo had not been attacked but had been in the offensive.[66] Their objective was twofold, with one force, led by Ofoly Bossum ('Foli Gbosu'), planning to attack Wogba (to the north of Glidji), while the other, led by Lattie, marched against Adamé, a Hula town on the western bank of the Mono (some miles north of Agbanaken). There are a couple of old cannons at Adamé which

[60] Bowdich, *Mission*, 221: map of Great Asante in first edition (1818). For a reprint, see Wilks, *Asante*, 44.
[61] Wilks, *Asante*, 57.
[62] *RGCG*, 1, 13 (28 Jan. 1823); also *ibid.*, 1, 15 (11 Feb. 1823).
[63] Akinjogbin, *Dahomey*, 181. Cf. Gayibor, *Le Genyi*, 95–116, who views the struggle of the Ge against Dahomey as 'resistance against the Fon occupation'.
[64] TNA:T70/1494, Thomas Miles, Popo, 10 Oct. 1793.
[65] TNA:T70/33, [Thomas] Miles, Accra 29 May [1795], quoted in Archibald Dalzel, Cape Coast Castle, 3 June 1795.
[66] Agbanon II, *Histoire*, 57.

according to local Hula traditions are relics of this conflict, having been taken there by 'a Chief of Little Popo', presumably referring to Lattie.[67] Hula traditions also give information about Lattie's fate. According to one version, he was transformed into a 'Tolègba', i.e. a divinity which still today is known by the name of Lattie and is one of the most powerful divinities of Adamé.[68] It is not clear how reliable the reference in the contemporary account to the death of the 'king' in this campaign is. According to Agbanon II, the king did not take part in this campaign, only Ofoly Bossum who however is said to have survived.[69] It is possible that the Europeans confused him with the king.

It is not clear what happened to Little Popo after this campaign, but the coastal settlement at least does not seem to have been invaded or suffered much. Miles was concerned that his lodge might be plundered, implying that there was disorder, although this may have been due simply to Lattie's death, who had been his landlord.[70] Another English lodge was also temporarily abandoned. However, by early 1796 the merchants were back and followed their business as usual, suggesting that in terms of trade at least the defeat did not have dramatic consequences for Little Popo.

Whether as a result of Asante influence (which may also explain why the Dahomeans did not follow up their victory by finally subjecting Little Popo) or the 1795 defeat, Little Popo desisted from any further expansionist moves westwards. With reference to the mid-1810s, Bowdich reported that Keta was 'included in' Anlo. According to him, the following Ewe ('Kerrapay', i.e. Krepi) towns lay between Keta and Little Popo, 'Egbiffeemee [= Agbosome?], to which several of the Quittas have retired, Edjenowah, Oöogloobooë, and Afflou or Afflahoo [= Aflao], a little way from the beach'. They were independent of each other as well as of Anlo.[71] Clapperton, who visited in the coast in 1825, noted that 'the authority of the Popoes formerly extended westward as far as Quitta – and is yet partially acknowledged, and custom paid, by most of the intervening towns'[72]

In the 1795 conflict with Little Popo, Grand Popo was reported to have

[67] GNA: ADM 1/2/361, incl. in no. 26: W.T.G. Lawson, 'Report' (1879), 70; Iroko, *Les hula*, 143–4. Cf. Agbanon, *Histoire*, 57.
[68] Iroko, *Les hula*, 114, 167–8.
[69] Agbanon, *Histoire*, 57–9. Cf. Gayibor, 'Les Rois', 207.
[70] TNA: T70/33, [Thomas] Miles, Accra, 29 May [1795], cited in Archibald Dalzel, Cape Coast Castle, 3 June 1795.
[71] Bowdich, *Mission*, 221. Cf. Kea, 'Akwamu-Anlo Relations', 53 n.162. In 1852, the British naval officer who concluded the anti-slave trade treaties listed the following places between Keta and Aflao (from west to east): 'Kedger or Acquijah [= Kedzi]', 'Block-ouse [= Blekesu]', 'Adiner [= 'Edina', the indigenous name of Elmina] Cooma, or Elmina Chica' and 'Adaffie [= Adafia]'. At the latter, he also met the chiefs of 'Daynoo [= Denu]' and 'Agin-no-hay [= Bowdich's 'Edjenowah'], independent Towns', which evidently lay nearby (TNA: FO84/893, incl. in Hamilton, [London] 10 April 1852: T. G. Forbes, 'Philomel', at Whydah, 5 Feb. 1852). All these towns are shown on W. T. G. Lawson's map: TNA: CO700/ GoldCoast13: Lawson, 'Sketch Map' (1879).(See Map 5).
[72] Clapperton, *Hugh Clapperton*, 88.

been allied with Dahomey. This must have been a relatively recent development, since Isert's account indicates that in the mid-1780s the relations between Little Popo and Grand Popo were harmonious. The religious authority of the king of Grand Popo was acknowledged by the inhabitants of Little Popo's coastal settlement.[73] In 1793, as noted before, a Dahomian army was encamped to the east of Grand Popo before proceeding to attack Agouna. It was possibly on this occasion that Grand Popo became associated with Dahomey, perhaps due to some grievance which the former felt against Little Popo. If this was the case, then Little Popo's 1795 campaign against Adamé may have been a punitive expedition in reaction to Grand Popo's alliance with Dahomey. As mentioned before, Robertson subsequently described Grand Popo as tributary to Dahomey. Although it is not clear how reliable this is, since he appears to confuse the Hula with the Hueda (who in the early eighteenth century had founded their successor kingdom to the north-east of Grand Popo), it nevertheless seems plausible that Grand Popo fell temporarily under Dahomey's influence.[74]

The development of Afro-European trade, 1772 to c.1807

As noted above, in 1772 a Danish lodge for the slave trade was established at Little Popo. According to Nørregård, a couple of years later there were some doubts as to whether it should be continued, implying that it was not profitable.[75] However, for the Danes the real value of this lodge was not commercial but strategic. Despite its temporary eclipse, Little Popo was a major military force in the region between the Volta and Mono rivers and therefore an important partner for the Danes who aspired to control the trade there. In the end, the lodge was maintained until the early 1790s, when the conflict associated with the Ohaittee affair forced the Danes to abandon it. The lodge at Aflao was also lost at this time.

Other Europeans, besides the Danes, also traded on the western Slave Coast in this period. In 1774, Kiøge reported that the English, the Dutch and the Portuguese 'now trade' at Little Popo.[76] In 1777, the French director at Ouidah reported that he had been approached by the king of Little Popo, requesting the establishment of a lodge in his country.[77] The French were interested, mainly because their trade suffered from the lack

---

[73] Isert, *Letters*, 95; Biørn, 'Beretning 1788', 226.
[74] Robertson, *Notes*, 237.
[75] *Ibid.*, 126.
[76] DNA: Sager til V.J. no. 126, 1776: Kiøbmand Kiøge, 22 March 1774, cited in Kea, 'Akwamu-Anlo Relations', 56. For English ships trading for slaves and provisions at Little Popo in the 1770s, see TNA: T70/1534, D. Mill, Sip Hawk off Popoe, 3 Feb. 1777; *ibid.*, Robert Norris to Richard Miles, S. Society, Whydah Road, 10 Sept. 1777.
[77] ANF: C.6/26, Bauduchiron, 'Mémoire d'Observations', Fontainebleau, 28 Sept. 1777.

of establishments on the Gold Coast, and for several years played with the idea of an establishment at Little Popo. In 1785, a mission was sent to the West African coast, which, among others things, was to investigate the possibilities for a lodge between the Volta and Ouidah, especially at Keta and Little Popo.[78] The agent who carried out the investigation, Champagny, found little competition there except for the Danes. These however he regarded as formidable rivals who would prevent any French establishment at Keta. Therefore, he proposed an establishment at Aflao, which he regarded as the only considerable place between Keta and Little Popo left after the Sagbadre War of 1784. In his view, Aflao's advantage, as compared to Little Popo, derived from its closeness to Keta, making it a suitable base for attempts to halt the expansion of Danish influence.[79] The French had recently begun to trade there, probably as a substitute for Keta from where they had been excluded by the Danes in 1784. There was not a permanent (onshore) lodge, but a vessel moored in the road, belonging to a French captain. It was profitable despite competition from a Danish lodge at Aflao. However, Champagny also noted disadvantages. Besides the Danish competition, these included an uncertainty about Aflao's resources and the lodge's profitability, and the absence of building materials, specifically shells for lime production and stones (the latter, however, being a general problem on the Slave Coast). Further, Aflao's distance from the shore was inconvenient, about three quarters of a mile/1.2km, although he thought this manageable, proposing to build the lodge halfway between the settlement and the sea to make it 'healthier and more independent.'[80] Ultimately, nothing became of these projects, either at Aflao or elsewhere on the western Slave Coast.

The Portuguese also traded on the western Slave Coast, specifically at Little Popo and Aflao, during the 1780s and 1790s, but documentation for their activities is scarce, coming from letters of English traders rather than the Portuguese themselves.[81] Among others, Robertson observed that they called at Little Popo 'for the purpose of buying slaves, and cowries to pay their expenses at Lagos, &c., where they commonly complete their cargoes.'[82]

An English lodge is documented at Little Popo by 1789, trading rum and gunpowder for ivory and slaves.[83] It belonged to the firm of Messrs Miles and Weuves of London, which had been established by two former employees of the African Company. The lodge was established and super-

[78] ANF: C.6/27, Champagny, 'Mémoire' [1786].
[79] For Isert's description of Aflao, see *Letters*, 98, 99.
[80] ANF: C.6/27, Champagny, 'Mémoire' [1786].
[81] See, for example, TNA: T70/1545, Lionel Abson, Whydah, 10 and 28 Nov. 1782.
[82] Robertson, *Notes*, 253. For references to Portuguese traders in the 1780s, see also TNA: T70/1545, letters by Lionel Abson to Richard Miles, 1782 and 1783.
[83] For a history of this lodge, see Strickrodt, 'Neglected Source', 294–301.

vised by Thomas Miles, a brother of one of the owners (Richard Miles), who at this time was a servant of the African Company and held the post of Governor of the English fort at Anomabo. He had established a wide business network with agents at Accra, Little Popo, Whydah, and Porto Novo, and also traded with the Danes at Keta. The 'Popo Factory', as it was called, probably owed its origins to business relations between Richard Miles and Lattie, a prominent trader at Little Popo. It had been established during the time when the former was Governor-in-Chief at Cape Coast Castle (1777–1785).[84] The records show that Lattie was closely involved in the operation of this lodge, functioning as a business landlord.[85] Apart from selling slaves to the lodge, he provided a wide range of services. He supplied servants as well as the house in which the lodge was accommodated (receiving rent for it). He gave advice to the local agent, solved problems with the local people and received royalties on all the slaves sold in the lodge, except those sold by Quam.[86] Besides trading slaves, the lodge purchased ivory and provisions, the latter being sold to European captains for the transatlantic passage. Maize ('corne') was the main article, but vegetables, fruits and livestock also played a role, including yams, plantains, bananas, pepper, palm nuts, (palm) oil, limes, okra, ducks, fowls, sheep, goats, hogs.[87] Further, wood and water were supplied to European vessels, although there were periods when water was judged to be 'both dear and bad here', in which case supplies were taken on the Gold Coast or at Keta.[88] In December 1790, another English agent, working for the private interest of the English Governor at Cape Coast, is documented at Little Popo, although this appears to have been only a temporary arrangement.[89] Besides these lodges, English vessels traded at Little Popo and Aflao under sail, for slaves, ivory and provisions.

As mentioned before, by 1792 the Danes had lost all their establishments to the east of the Volta apart from Fort Prindsensten at Keta. This or the following year marks the establishment of two more lodges at Little Popo, another English one and a Dutch one. The English lodge belonged

[84] For Richard Miles' career, see G. Metcalf, 'Gold, Assortments and the Trade Ounce,' *JAH*, 28 (1987), 27–41, pp.27–9; E. C. Martin, *The British West African Settlements, 1750–1821* (London, 1927), 43; TNA: T70/32, Richard Miles, 26 Jan. 1777; *ibid.*, Richard Miles, Cape Coast Castle, 2 April 1780; T70/1576, Minutes of committee meeting (London, n.d.). For the relations between Richard Miles and Lattie, see TNA: T70/1545, Lionel Abson, Whydah, 14 Dec. 1782; [Lionel Abson, Whydah] 5 Sept. [1783]; Lionel Abson, Whydah, 26 Sept. 1783.

[85] For the role of landlords in Afro-European trade, see V. R. Dorjahn and C. Fyfe, 'Landlord and Stranger: Change in Tenancy Relations in Sierra Leone', *JAH*, 3 (1962), 391–97.

[86] TNA: T70/584, 'Journal of Popo Factory,' p.4; T70/1484, Thomas Miles, Popo Factory, 26 Aug. 1793; T70/1498, Thomas Miles Notebooks: notebook 3 (softbound paper), inside cover; T70/1566, Lattie's Account with Popo Factory 1792–93 [30 Aug. 1793]; T70/1569, John Searle, 4 Jan. 1794.

[87] See TNA: T70/584, 'Journal of Popo Factory.'

[88] TNA: T70/1573, George Lawson, Popo, 17 Jan. 1796.

[89] TNA: T70/1560; James Hogg, Williams Fort Whydah, 4 Dec. 1790.

to a ship's captain.[90] The Dutch lodge was apparently a direct result of the Anglo-Dutch mission sent to Little Popo in May 1792, the local agent being the Dutch emissary. The lodge appears to have been his private enterprise, although he reportedly remained in the service of the WIC. Perhaps this was similar to the arrangement favoured by the WIC during Ashampo's reign, when WIC agents traded at Little Popo on commission (see Chapter 4). This lodge was active until early 1794.[91] The two remaining English lodges were temporarily abandoned in the wake of the 1795 conflict with Dahomey and Grand Popo, but re-established by early 1796. In February 1796 another lodge was established by a British captain and there were five vessels trading at the place, indicating that the 1795 defeat (and Lattie's death) had no long-term consequences for Little Popo's trade.[92] Richard Miles planned to continue his lodge, which he regarded as 'the best Adventure I have been engaged in, since leaving Africa'. However, these plans were abandoned due to the death of his brother, who had been intended to act as his local agent again.[93] Information from the records of the African Company suggests that Miles then continued his trade with Little Popo 'under sail'.[94] He remained active until at least 1810, trading ivory and, until 1807, probably also slaves. Although the places where he traded are not identified, it seems likely that he continued to be involved with Little Popo.[95] It is not recorded how long the other English lodge lasted.

By 1802, there was a lodge belonging to Jan Nieser, an Afro-Dutch trader from Elmina who between 1793–1806 resided at Accra, at Little Popo.[96] It was managed by one of his sons. Nieser had extended his commercial activities to the western Slave Coast already in the 1790s, when he was apparently involved in the Dutch lodge at Little Popo, although it is not clear to what degree, whether as a partner or just occasionally.[97] His own

---

[90] TNA: T70/1484, Thomas Miles, Accra, 20 Aug. 1793. See Strickrodt, 'Neglected Source', 299 n. 20.

[91] TNA: T70/1567, John Searle, Popo Factory, 18 Nov. 1793; T70/1569, John Searle, Popo Factory, 1 Feb. 1794. Cf. Strickrodt, 'Neglected Source', 299 n. 20.

[92] TNA: T70/1573, George Lawson, Popoe, 3 Feb. 1796. Cf. Akinjogbin, *Dahomey*, 181.

[93] TNA: T70/1571, Richard Miles, Wanstead, 1 Feb. 1795; T70/1572, Governor, Cape Coast Castle, 21 April 1796.

[94] One of his ships, commanded by captain George Lawson, arrived at Cape Coast Castle from Little Popo in 1797 and shortly afterwards returned there (TNA: T70/1574, [Cape Coast Castle:] Arrivals and departures 1 July – 30 Sept. 1797).

[95] PP Colonies Africa 1801–17, p.10, Report from Select Committee on Papers relative to the African Forts: An Account of Elephants Teeth imported into the Port of Portsmouth from Africa, in Ships of War.

[96] NAN: NBKG 1133, Jan Nieser, Harmony Hall, Accra, 25 Jan. 1802; J. T. Lever, 'Mulatto Influence on the Gold Coast in the Early Nineteenth Century: Jan Nieser of Elmina,' *African Historical Studies*, 3/2 (1970), 253–62, pp.254–5; L. W. Yarak, *Asante and the Dutch, 1744–1873* (Oxford, 1990), 143.

[97] TNA: T70/1484, J. Neicer, Accra, 26 Aug. 1793; Thomas Miles, Popo Factory, 31 Aug. 1793; Jan Neicer, Accra, 30 Sept. 1793; C. Alexander, Williams Factory, Whydah, 17 Nov. 1793; John Searle, Popo Factory, 18 Nov. 1793.

lodge was maintained until at least 1805, when he ordered a schooner boat from England for his trade with Little Popo.[98] It was probably abandonned in 1806 when he left Accra to re-settle at Elmina.

Grand Popo appears to have dropped out of the trade in the late eighteenth century, as is suggested by the use of 'Popo' to refer to Little Popo in this period. However, it is possible that slaves continued to be exported from the region by means of the lagoons, for embarkation onto ships either at Little Popo or Ouidah.

As can be seen from the above, in the 1780s and 1790s European commercial interest in the ports on the western Slave Coast increased, particularly in Little Popo.[99] As regards the volume of the slave trade, the records of the Danish company show that the numbers of slaves exported from Little Popo increased steadily from 1772 to 1787, with a peak in the years 1784–88, when the annual average was 170. The peak was in 1787, when 206 slaves were purchased.[100] These were the years immediately after the Sagbadre War and before the beginning of the conflict between the Ge and the Danes. Compared to the number of slaves exported annually from Little Popo in the 1760s, which according to the French report was 100, this was a significant rise. Moreover, from 1784 the Danes maintained a lodge at Aflao, where they purchased about 100 slaves annually between 1785 and 1788. However, despite this increase in slave exports, the ports on the western Slave Coast did not match the numbers of slaves supplied at the more established ports on the Gold Coast and the central ports of the Slave Coast. This is shown by a comparison with the Danish trade at Accra, where the annual average of slaves purchased was above 300, despite competition from the Dutch and English forts there.[101] Comments by the English and the French who were able to make comparisons with Ouidah also support this. In 1785, the English Governor at Cape Coast Castle noted that the (slave) trade at Little Popo was 'sometimes worthy of Attention.'[102] In 1786, Champagny reported a decline in Little Popo's

---

[98] NAN: NBKG 1134, Jan Nieser, Harmony Hall, Accra, 25 Sept. 1805. His son, Hendrik, is identifiable with the 'Dutch *Sambo*, of the name of Neiser,' whom M'Leod met at Little Popo in 1803 (*A Voyage*, 139). The meaning of 'Sambo' is explained as 'A person of colour, having three parts black, and one of white in his composition.' For further references to the lodge, see NAN: NBKG 1133, Jan Nieser, Harmony Hall, Accra, 31 March 1802; NBKG 1134, Jan Nieser, Elmina, 13 Sept. 1807; Jan Nieser, Elmina, 12 Sept. 1807.

[99] The 'Voyages' database shows a different trend but this is based on imputed figures and therefore unreliable: 'Voyages: The Trans-Atlantic Slave Trade Database' (2009): http://www.slavevoyages.org/tast/database/search.faces.

[100] Hernaes, *Slaves, Danes*, 396 Appendix III: 'Slave purchased by the danish forts and factories on the gold and slave coasts 1777–1789', citing 'Specification over de ved de Kongl. Danske Establissementer paa Kysten Guinea indhandlede slaver fra den Kongelige Guineske Handels gegyndelse pr. July 1777 til ult. Octobr. 1789', Dokumenter vedr. Kommissionen for Negerhandelens bedre Indretning & Ophævelse m.m, Vol.I (1783–1806); Gtk 1771–1816/RA.

[101] *Ibid.*

[102] TNA: T70/33, Governor and Council, Cape Coast Castle, 9 July 1785.

slave trade: 'The last French captains who maintained establishments there did only mediocre business, and the operations of a permanent factory established there by the Danes are not more successful; the English hardly stop here but to take provisions.' However, he thought this downturn might just be temporary because there was 'no place on the coast where the trade is not subject to similar variations'.[103]

Compared to Accra and Ouidah, Little Popo's handicap in the slave trade continued to be the same as in the late seventeenth century, that is the lack of strong links with the hinterland which could provide an abundant and steady flow of slaves. Information about the source of slaves sold on the western Slave Coast during this period was given by Kiøge in 1774. According to him, many came from the Ewe region ('Krepi'), 'some [are sold] to the black Negro merchants who convey them to Accra, some to Quitta, Way [= Woe] and Augona [= Anloga], who bring them to the ships, part to Popo [...] and finally a large number are brought down to Juda [= Ouidah].'[104] Robertson noted that 'a considerable number' of slaves, 'chiefly Crepees and Mahees', were sold at Little Popo.[105]

The increase in Little Popo's importance in the Atlantic trade in the last two decades of the eighteenth century can be explained by the problems which the Europeans were experiencing at Ouidah in this period. According to the governor of the English fort at Ouidah, Lionel Abson, these problems were due to the control which Kpengla, who had become king in 1774, began to exercise over the trade there by fixing the price of slaves. This prompted the slave traders from the interior to look for alternative outlets for their trade, including at Kpessie ('Peshi'), Little Popo and Keta. Moreover, he noted that at these places the traders were free to buy guns, powder and iron, which in Dahomey were prohibited for strangers, apart from iron worked into agricultural implements.[106]

In contrast to Ouidah, where the trade was strictly controlled by the Dahomean king, on the western Slave Coast the traders enjoyed relative freedom. As will be discussed in greater detail below, by the 1780s the authority of the king at Glidji over the coastal settlements was in decline, freeing the trade from the restrictions which the European traders had documented during Ashampo's reign. In 1803, M'Leod noted the positive consequences which the coastal settlement's quasi-independence from Glidji had for its trade, 'municipal laws are mild and equally favourable

---

[103] ANF: C.6/27, Champagny, 'Mémoire' [1786]. There is no record of French lodges at Little Popo. Possibly he is referring to ships moored in the road, like the one he documented at Aflao.
[104] DNA: Sager til V.J. no. 126, 1776: Kiøbmand Kiøge, 22 Mar. 1774, cited in Kea, 'Akwamu-Anlo Relations', 56.
[105] Robertson, *Notes*, 235.
[106] Dalzel, *History of Dahomy*, 214, citing Lionel Abson (see p. 155). Cf. Kea, 'Akwamu-Anlo Relations', 59; Law, 'Slave-Raiders, 56–7.

to the subjects of all countries; hence it enjoys a considerable share of the trade'.[107]

Further, the region also offered other exports and services which were valuable and even necessary for the slave traders.[108] Ivory was a major article of export from Little Popo in this period.[109] Most importantly for the slave traders, Little Popo was a main source for provisions in the period, supplying ship's crews and slaves for the trans-Atlantic passage as well as European agents on the coast, including the Gold Coast and Ouidah. This is documented by the records of the Miles lodge, discussed above. It was also noted by Abson at Ouidah, who in the early 1780s reported that due to the scarcity of livestock at Ouidah he supplied himself from Little Popo.[110] Little Popo's role in the trade in provisions was presumably boosted after Keta had been excluded from it after 1784. Further, the ports between the Volta and Mono (Keta, Pottebra, Aflao and Little Popo) provided cowries for the purchase of slaves at Ouidah and Lagos.[111] The cowries, which were used as local money, were imported into the coast by Dutch, English and French traders, who evidently also re-sold them to the Portuguese there.[112]

Finally, Little Popo continued to play an important strategic role for traders on the coast, for communication along the coast and as a supplier of canoemen. The latter were probably especially important for the traders of nations that did not have settlements on the Gold Coast, and consequently lacked access to canoemen necessary for the trade on the Slave Coast. A case from the early 1780s was documented by Abson, noting that a French vessel bound for Badagry had taken a canoe and canoemen at Little Popo.[113] The region's importance for communication along the coast in the period becomes clear from the records of the English fort at Ouidah, which shows that letters from there to the headquarters on the Gold Coast were sent by canoe to Little Popo, from where they were forwarded either by canoes going by sea along the coast or by overland messengers. It is noteworthy that while this was basically the same system as in the 1680s, it had evolved. Rather than just functioning as a place of trans-shipment for canoes and a resting place for canoemen, Little Popo now worked more independently, with local people providing and coordinating these services, similar to the duties of a postmaster. Abson's letters show that his letters for the Gold Coast were sent to Little

---

[107] M'Leod, *Voyage*, 140.
[108] See Eltis, 'Slave Trade', 28–35, for how other exports could in effect subsidise slave purchases.
[109] TNA: T70/1484, Thomas Miles, Popo Factory, 2 Sept. 1793; Adams, *Remarks*, 240; M'Leod, *Voyage*, 139 (noting the abundance of elephants in the area between Little Popo and Grand Popo).
[110] TNA: T70/1454, Lionel Abson, Whydah, 21 Oct. 1783, 18 Oct. 1783.
[111] TNA: T70/1560, Thomas Miles, Anomabu Fort, 6 Nov. 1789; T70/1484, Thomas Miles, Popo Factory, 2 Sept. 1793; T70/1569, George Lawson, London, 10 Oct. 1794.
[112] See Johnson, 'Cowrie Currencies', part 1, 17–49.
[113] TNA: T70/1545, Lionel Abson, William's Fort Whydah, 15 Mar. 1782.

Popo to an individual called Tom Young, probably an African, who forwarded them to the Gold Coast.[114] Lattie also provided messengers to the English for communication between Ouidah and Cape Coast.[115]

Society and internal politics at Little Popo, 1780s and 1790s

European visitors to Little Popo in the 1780s and 1790s noted the prosperity of the inhabitants, which derived from their successful engagement in the trade. According to Biørn, 'their exceedingly great trade makes them Capitalists [= rich people], and they live in a Superfluity of Superfluity.'[116] The visible signs of this new wealth were the European-style houses, built by local traders, which began to appear in the coastal settlement in this period.[117] Another consequence was perhaps less visible but nevertheless noted by the traders: the shift in the power balance between the Ge king at Glidji and the traders at the coastal settlement in favour of the latter, and also within the coastal settlement, where successful traders eclipsed the formal authority of the Mina chief(s).

In his 1788 report Biørn identifies many notables at Little Popo, besides the king, indicating that political authority in the kingdom was highly fragmented:

> Princes here are the King's brother, Offoli Bussu, Okannia Assiambo, Little Assiambo, Offoli, and yet another smaller Assiambo, who is a pawn at the main fort [= Christiansborg]. The main Kabusseerer here are Lathe [= Lattie], Tette-Obrim, Akoi, Odom and Quam, and also Kabusseer Odo and Great Ogie Koram over Labodee, each of whom, except the pawn Assiambo [,] has his town and some more than one or two, besides they are masters of a large number Krepee towns, as they can mobilize about 6,000 men besides their allies the Adampe, who likewise can make up so many people if not more.[118]

---

[114] *Ibid.*, Lionel Abson, William's Fort Whydah, 22 Dec. 1783. See also *ibid.*, Lionel Abson, Whydah, 10 Nov. 1782, 15 Aug. 1783, 21 Oct. 1783, 20 Nov. 1783.

[115] *Ibid.*, Lionel Abson, Whydah, 14 Dec. 1782, 5 Sept. [1783], 26 Sept. 1783.

[116] Biørn, 'Beretning 1788', 227 (transl. by Winsnes: Isert, *Letters*, 122, n. 3). Cf. Kea, 'Akwamu-Anlo Relations', 40; Isert, *Letters*, 122. For a definition of the contemporary meaning of 'Capitalist', see Raymond Williams, *Keywords: A Vocabulary of Culture and Society* (London, 1988), 50.

[117] The first multi-storey house at Little Popo is documented in 1784, belonging to 'Kabossie Akoi' (Isert, *Letters*, 124). In the early 1790s, Lattie was reported to have built himself 'a most excellent' new house, for which he ordered furniture from Europe (TNA: T70/1484, Thomas Miles, Popo Factory, 26 Aug. 1793).

[118] Biørn, 'Beretning 1788', 226 (my translation). Cf. Gayibor, *Le Genyi*, 178–9 (mistranslating *pant*, i.e. 'security, pawn', as 'secretary'). Kea gives the five principal towns of the kingdom of Little Popo as 'Little Popo (Anecho), Greghe (Gredgi or Gragi [= Glidji]), Popo Labodi, Popo Adannepugie and Popo Adannepragu', with Aflao and Bé ('Bay') as important dependencies ('Akwamu-Anlo-Relations', 39 n. 67, citing Biørn, 'Beretning 1788', 223, 226; P. Isert, *Voyages en Guinea*

Besides these local notables, the king of Grand Popo also held a share of authority at the coastal settlement until at least the late 1780s, although this was religious rather than political. He profited from the Afro-European trade there by exacting gifts from both the locals and the European traders.[119]

According to Isert, who visited Little Popo in October 1784, the king at Glidji was 'Obly', whom he described as old and doting.[120] The real power at Glidji appears to have rested with Ofoli Bossum, one of the 'princes' listed by Biørn and identified as 'a son of the late king Assiambo of Popo' by Isert. The latter described him as 'the chief' of Glidji, where 'he has his residence, to which he has now, to a certain degree, given the form of a fort.'[121] His importance in the kingdom is indicated by the role which he played during the Sagbadre War, discussed above. King Obly died in 1786 and was replaced by Ofoli Adjalu, whom Biørn identifies as a brother of Ofoli Bossum.[122] Therefore – following Isert's information that the latter was a son of Obly's predecessor Ashampo – Ofoli Adjalu too was a son of this Ashampo (although this information should perhaps not be taken too literally).

Isert describes the coastal settlement as 'a considerable Black settlement formed of five separate towns, each of which has its own kabossie [= caboceer]'.[123] Unfortunately, he fails to identify either the caboceers or the towns, but Biørn, quoted above, gives the names of five main caboceers (besides the Adangme caboceers), who may in fact have been the very ones Isert was referring to: Lattie, Tette-Obrim, Akoi, Odom and Quam. The contemporary documents give further details concerning all of them, apart only from Odom.

According to Isert, 'Kabossie Akoi' was 'an upright gentlemen [who] has recently built himself a proper palace, three storeys high.'[124] He is probably identifiable with 'Old Arqua', who is mentioned in a letter from the local agent at the Miles lodge in January 1794. This letter refers to Old Arqua's upcoming 'Custom', indicating that he had recently died.[125] The facts that he owned a European-style house and that his custom was to be a lavish one, demanding a large quantity of gunpowder, suggest that he was wealthy and probably a trader. This is corroborated by local traditions, according to which 'Akue' was an ivory trader and a nephew of Foli Bebe.[126] After

---

(cont.) [Paris, 1793], 119; Sager til G.J. no.37, 1799: 'General Mandtals og Gage Roulle', Christiansborg, 20 Sept. 1798; Sager til G.J. no.62, 1800: 'Mandtals Roulle', Christiansborg, 15 Jan. 1800. Cf. Gayibor, *Le Genyi*, 123, 125). This sounds plausible enough, Popo Labodi, Popo Adannepugie and Popo Adannepragu evidently being Adangme settlements, as indicated by their names.

[119] DNA: Guineisk Kompagnie 156, I. [sic] Kiøge, N.H. Weile, Little Popo, 25 Aug. 1774, cited in Gayibor, *Le Genyi*, 136 n.3; Isert, *Letters*, 127; Biørn, 'Beretning 1788', 226.
[120] Isert, *Letters*, 99.
[121] *Ibid.*, 97, 122.
[122] Biørn, 'Beretning 1788', 226.
[123] Isert, *Letters*, 121–2.
[124] *Ibid.*, 124. Cf. Strickrodt, 'Neglected Source', 308.
[125] TNA: T70/1569, John Searle to Thomas Miles, Popo Factory, 4 Jan. 1794.
[126] Agbanon II, *Histoire*, 45–47.

his marriage to the daughter of Amegadje, the founder of Degbenu, he settled at the latter place, which may have been one of the 'towns' referred to by Isert. His descendants became chiefs of Degbenu (where they live to this day). Although the direct link with Foli Bebe seems unlikely, his royal ancestry does not: he may in fact have been the 'son', Aqua, whom Ashampo sent to Britain in 1752 and who returned in 1759 (as discussed in the previous chapter). Like Lattie, who is discussed below, Akoi was the founder of a 'dynasty'. It is probably no coincidence that they were contemporaries and this illustrates how in this period individuals were able to transform their success in trade into political power.

There is little, but nevertheless revealing information about Tette-Obrim. According to Biørn, he received a monthly stipend for the Danish lodge at Little Popo, suggesting that (in the 1780s) he was the 'Danish chief' at the place.[127]

Quam is first documented in 1774, when he appears in the list of chiefs who received payments for the Danish lodge at Little Popo.[128] In 1786, Champagny noted that 'among the chiefs [at Little Popo]' is one who is named Coam [= Quam] who calls himself fidalgo or Caboceer of the place.'[129] He is also documented in the records of the Miles lodge from the early 1790s, where he is often referred to simply as 'the Caboceer.'[130] This suggests that he was either the most senior among the chiefs at the coastal settlement or the senior chief of the town or quarter where the Miles lodge was situated. This was probably Fantekome, which, as suggested by its name, was possibly the original settlement of Akan-speaking canoemen and which was probably another one of the five towns referred to by Isert. According to Agbanon II, the name 'Kwam' is one of the prerogatives of the Adjigo clan, whose members are said to have filled the office of the 'chief of the beach', collecting the customs from the European traders on behalf of the king at Glidji.[131] This is corroborated by the fact that a Mina named Quam who assisted European traders was documented there already in 1732.[132]

Of all the people documented at Little Popo in the period, Lattie is the one who is best-documented, reflecting his importance to the European traders at Little Popo.[133] He can be identified as Late Awoku, the ancestor of

[127] Biørn, 'Beretning 1788', 226.
[128] DNA: GK 156, I. [sic] Kiøge, N.H. Weile, Little Popo, 25 Aug. 1774, cited in Gayibor, *Le Genyi*, 136 n.3.
[129] ANF: C.6/27, Champagny, 'Mémoire' [1786].
[130] For references to Quam in the Thomas Miles papers, see TNA: T70/1484, p.1v; T70/1569, George Lawson, London, 10 Oct. 1794; T70/1569, John Searle, Popo Factory, 4 Jan. 1794; T70/1569, John Searle, Popo Factory, 23 Oct. 1794. Cf. Strickrodt, 'Neglected Source', 315.
[131] Agbanon II, *Histoire*, 137. Cf. Gayibor, *Le Genyi*, 181.
[132] Van Dantzig, *Dutch and the Guinea Coast*, no.330, Elmina Journal, 18 April 1732, citing Hoeth, Little Popo, 5 Apr. 1732. See chapter 3.
[133] Cf. Strickrodt, 'Neglected Source', 309–312.

the Lawson family in modern Aného. According to Isert, he was 'the most prominent Black' at Little Popo 'next after the king':

> [His] riches elevate him over all the other distinguished Blacks, and contrary to what is customary for rich Blacks, he is an energetic merchant and carries on his own considerable business. He understands three European languages, namely English, Portuguese and Danish, and, in order to be able to carry on his extensive business with more accuracy, he has at present one son in England and another in Portugal, where they are learning to write and calculate, skills he himself has not yet attained. He always has a warehouse full of supplies, and when an English ship is lying in the roadstead they lodge with him. When visiting him one is served in fully European style, and he always has European bread in his home, which is a rare experience among the Europeans in this land.[134]

Isert also gives details concerning his background. According to him, Lattie 'had risen from a lowly birth all the way to the position of kabossie [= caboceer] at [Little] Popo. He had served as a servant for the English in his youth, and having a keen mind he learned very quickly how to set about becoming rich and powerful.'[135] Information from local traditions and contemporary documents support this and give further detail. According to the Lawson family tradition, 'chief Latte Aoku' was married to 'Adaku, daughter of Ashongbo Dandjen, King of Glidji' and after his death was succeeded as chief by his son Akuete Zankli aka George A. Lawson.[136] According to Agbanon II, Adaku was not his wife but his mother, which however does not tally with the information given by Isert that he was of humble background. His father is identified as Bewu, the son of a hunter who had immigrated from Accra.[137] The link with Accra is corroborated by a contemporary report, noting Lattie's intention of visiting Accra 'to make Custom'.[138] According to Agbanon II, Lattie's service with the English took place on board a slaver. After his return to Little Popo, he is said to have moved from Agokpame (a few miles east of Glidji), where his grandfather and father had settled, to the coastal settlement to engage in the trade more successfully. He established himself at 'Adanliakpo', the place of the late Ata Ayi, a Ga man from Accra who had been 'the intermediary between [the king at Glidji] and the Whites': 'A few Fanti had settled there, engaging in the

[134] Isert, *Letters*, 122–3.
[135] *Ibid.*, 62.
[136] Jones/ Sebald, *African Family Archive*, 7.12., History of Akuete Zankli (alias G. A. Lawson I) [March 1906?].
[137] Agbanon II, *Histoire*, 39.
[138] TNA: T70/1572, John Searle, Popo Factory, 1 Feb. 179[4].

slave trade, who fled when they were chased away. They gave the name Fantekome to Adanliakpo.'[139] This can probably be interpreted to mean that the 'Fante' people fell under Lattie's control. According to a Danish document, Lattie was one of the caboceers who received payments for the Danish lodge at Little Popo in 1774, suggesting that by then he had returned from his service with the English (which may have been on a slave ship as recalled in the traditions or, given his friendship with Richard Miles, on the Gold Coast).[140]

Isert noted that Lattie's relations with English traders were particularly strong. They are well-documented and can be traced back to at least 1777, when it was noted that 'Lathe has been of great Service' to an English vessel trading at Little Popo.[141] By 1782 he was hiring out a 'boy' to the English for use as messenger between their fort at Ouidah and the headquarters at Cape Coast Castle.[142] In 1785, the English at Cape Coast Castle reported that he had established himself as the English caboceer at Little Popo, which they accepted.[143] His close involvement with the Miles lodge has been discussed above. Furthermore, he provided all kinds of services to English captains on the coast, supplying slaves and provisions, hiring out sailors for coasting voyages and facilitating relationships between English traders and women from Little Popo.[144]

Isert noted that Lattie had managed to transform his extraordinary success in the trade into political power. According to him 'A majority of the Krepees are now in Lattie's power because he supports them with money.' Due to this, he had gained 'as great a reputation as the King of [Little] Popo, and possibly even greater.'[145] In 1786, Champagny noted a tri-partite division of authority at Little Popo.

> Among the chiefs is one who is named Coam [= Quam] who calls himself fidalgo or Caboceer of the place. Laté, another chief of the place, has less authority but he would be more useful [for a French lodge] due to his superior intelligence and his perfect knowledge of European ways. I am not talking of the King, who does not reside in the village

---

[139] Agbanon II, *Histoire*, 39, 43. The plot said to have been given to Ata Ayi extended 'from Sosimé to Adanliakpo (Fantekome), on the beach' (39). According to Henrici, Sosime lay just east of Fantekome (*Das Deutsche Togogebiet*, 'Erläuterungen zur Karte', IV-V).
[140] DNA: GK 156, I. [*sic*] Kiøge, N.H. Weile, Little Popo, 25 Aug. 1774, cited in Gayibor, *Le Genyi*, 136 n.3.
[141] TNA: T70/1534, D. Mill, Ship Hawk off Popoe, 3 Feb. 1777.
[142] TNA: T70/1545, Lionel Abson, Whydah, 14 December 1782; [Lionel Abson, Whydah] 5 September [1783]; Lionel Abson, Whydah, 26 September 1783.
[143] TNA: T70/33, Governor and Council, Cape Coast Castle, 9 July 1785; T70/1565, Thomas Biddall, Cape Coast Castle, 7 April 1792.
[144] TNA: T70/1484, James Hogg, Ship Fly, 20 Oct. 1793; *ibid.*, Thomas Miles to James Hogg [n.d.]. Cf. Strickrodt, 'Neglected Source', 310–12.
[145] Isert, *Letters*, 87.

itself. Without authority, because he is without character, he is the least respected of the chiefs in his kingdom.[146]

The king referred to here was Obly, but information from the Miles papers indicate that his successor, Ofoli Adjalu, was politically equally remote from the coastal settlement.[147] Glidji traditions recall tensions between Lattie and the king at Glidji, the origins of which probably lay in the threat which the powerful trader posed to the king's authority.[148]

As noted above, Lattie was killed in the 1795 war against Grand Popo. For the following period between 1795 and 1807 there is hardly any documentation. An exception is the account by the British trader Robertson, which indicates that despite – or because of? – the local autonomy which the people of Little Popo enjoyed, the nominal authority of the king at Glidji continued to be acknowledged. 'The traders of Popo speak of their chief magistrate, Ama Adakoo, with great respect; and say, that Greghe, the capital, which is one day's journey from the shore, is a large and populous city; other reports say, that it does not contain more than seven or eight thousand inhabitants.'[149] The name of this personage, Ama Adakoo, is Ge and therefore he can probably be identified with the king at Glidji, rather than a notable at the coastal settlement.[150]

---

[146] ANF: C.6/27, Champagny, 'Mémoire' [1786].

[147] In the records of the Miles lodge, the king is conspicuous by his absence. Apparently he did not even receive the tax from the trade which theoretically was due to him (TNA: T70/584, 'Journal of Popo Factory'. See Strickrodt, 'Neglected Source', 308–9).

[148] Agbanon II, *Histoire*, 56–9.

[149] Robertson, *Notes*, 236.

[150] The first part of the name, 'Ama', is documented to have been the name of the king who succeeded Ashampo (Biørn, 'Beretning 1788', 226: 'Amma'). See also Westermann, 'Kindheitserinnerungen', 8. According to Agbanon II, it is one of the names used by the people belonging to a sub-clan of the Tugban who are responsible for the principal Ga divinities, Sakumo and Korle (Agbanon II, *Histoire*, 44–5, 135). 'Adakoo' is actually a female Ge name, which (as noted above) is also said to have been the name of Lattie's wife or mother. According to Agbanon II, it was Foli Dekpo who ruled from 1788 to 1813 (*Histoire*, 61). Cf. Gayibor, 'Les rois', 206.

5

Disintegration & reconstitution
Political developments, 1820s to 1870s

The next two chapters both deal with the nineteenth century. This one discusses political developments and lays the groundwork for the discussion of commercial developments, which follows in Chapter 6.

The civil war of 1823 and the foundation of Agoué

The political disunity at Little Popo observed by European visitors in the late eighteenth century became more pronounced in the early nineteenth century. In the 1820s a civil war flared up at Little Popo, as a result of which Agoué was founded.

The main obstacle to the reconstruction of the history of this war is the scarcity of contemporary documentation. Earlier historians have relied mainly on retrospective accounts from local oral traditions, which exist in abundance.[1] These accounts, which were recorded in writing in the early twentieth century, vary in detail and the point of view from which they are told.[2] In essence, however, they tell the story that was first published by Pierre Bouche:

---

[1] See Akibode, 'Contribution', 16–21; Cornevin, *Histoire*, 135; Gayibor, *Le Genyi*, 189–201; Gayibor, 'Les conflits politiques à Aného de 1821 à 1960', *Cahiers du CRA*, 8 (1994), 198–203; Jones, 'Little Popo and Agoué', 124; Pélofy, *Histoire*, 6; Archives Mgr Robert Codjo Sastre, Lokossa/ Benin: Pierrucci, ['Histoire d'Agoué'], 3–5.

[2] Accounts by the Adjigos include n.a., *Adjigovi*; Gaba, 'History'; Quam-Dessou, *Histoire*. Accounts by the Lawsons include 'History of Akuete Zankli (alias G. A. Lawson I)' in Jones/ Sebald, *African Family Archive*, no.7.12 (1906); n.a., 'La Courte Histoire'; n.a., 'Petite Histoire'. For an account from the perspective of the kings of Glidji, see Agbanon II, *Histoire*, 65–7. For accounts by members of the de Souza family, see N. F. de Souza, 'Contribution à l'Histoire de la famille de Souza', *ED*, 8 (1955), 18–9; S. de Souza, *La famille*, 35–6.

The foundation of Agoué dates only to the year 1821. A certain Feliz de Souza had a complaint about Comlagan, the chief of Petit Popo, and incited a revolt against him. Georges [Lawson], put at the head of this movement, succeeded in chasing away Comlagan. The latter established himself, with his followers, at Agoué and founded a small state where they have several times stood their ground, arms in hand, and asserted their independence.[3]

Bouche's account appeared in 1885 but goes back to information gathered at Agoué in 1874/5. He does not give his sources, but probably received his information from people at Agoué, that is the descendants of the defeated party, some fifty years after the event.

On the basis of contemporary newspaper accounts, in the *RGCG*, however, Bouche's story is wrong in several points, most importantly regarding the date of the civil war and the identity of George Lawson's adversary. According to contemporary reporting, the war occurred in 1823 rather than 1821. Further, George Lawson's adversary is named as 'Ansan', the 'caboceer of Dutch town' at Little Popo, rather than Komlagan who according to Bouche was the 'chief of Little Popo'. The first of the reports, from 11 February 1823, says that violence had broken out at Little Popo between the English and the Dutch parts of the town, 'many lives were lost and after destroying some of the houses the contending parties had encamped at some distance from each other.' George Lawson, 'the person who is agent to De Souza, the slave dealer', is identified as the leader of one of the parties.[4] The next report appeared on 18 March 1823. Based on information from a passenger on a ship from Little Popo, it states that the disturbances continued, 'the contending parties are so violent that they have hired an auxiliary force'. The Dutch town was reported to have been almost destroyed by fire. George Lawson, with support from '[s]ome of the districts of Creppee [= Ewe people]', appeared likely to win the conflict.[5] According to a report of 15 April 1823, the violence at Little Popo had 'to some degree subsided.' The caboceer of the Dutch town had evidently been defeated, and had left Little Popo with some of his followers. They had begun to build a town 'about halfway between Grand Popo and Little Popo.' A passing vessel found them 'actively employed, and traders had already some elephants' teeth and palm oil &c for sale.' George Lawson is reported to have threatened to drive the people away from their new settlement, 'but in consequence of the want of provisions his hired adherents had left him' and he apparently let the matter rest.[6] Five months later, a report of 20 September 1823 finally

[3] Bouche, *Sept ans*, 302. Cf. Bouche, 'Notes', 96.
[4] *RGCG*, 1/13 (28 Jan. 1823).
[5] Ibid., 1/15 (11 Feb. 1823).
[6] Ibid., 1/20 (18 Mar. 1823).

identifies the adversary of George Lawson as 'the caboceer Ansan.' His new settlement, 'on the right bank of the River Mansoo (or Great Popo river) [= the lagoon]' is described as a promising place for trade and a potential rival for Little Popo, 'as already they have given good tracts of their industry, and have diverted vessels from the old anchorage to call there'.[7] The name of the newly-founded town is not given in these articles, but in 1825 Clapperton, who passed through the region in November of that year, gave a brief account of the war and identified it as Agoué:

> the Caboceer of the Dutch part of the town, having become rich & powerful by an extensive trade with the Portuguese and Spaniards, at length refused to pay the usual customs on the arrival of the vessels, and set the Kings authority at defiance – a fight took place in consequence in April 1822 [sic] in which the Dutch town was burnt to the ground, and the inhabitants with their Caboceer driven away – they retreated along the beach about nine miles towards Whydah to a small village called Agwey – where they settled and built a considerable town – preserving their independence – making trade and twice or three times have returned to the attack on Popoe – but have every time been defeated and driven back with loss – They accuse the Popoez[e] of violating the graves of their fathers, and plundering the gold buried there – on the town being burnt and will hear of no accommodation until the matter is settled. The Popoes were commanded by George Lawson.[8]

As regards the date of the civil war and the foundation of Agoué, in the light of the information from the *RGCG*, this can be taken as 1823. It is of course possible that the quarrel had been drawn out and that there had been disturbances already before February 1823. This is perhaps suggested by Clapperton's reference to 1822 as the date of the civil war, though this might be merely a slip: 'Dutch town' at least was burnt only in 1823. A letter by George Lawson from late 1843 also indicates that the fighting had started at an earlier date, saying that the people of Agoué had been making war with him 'for 22 years.'[9] However, there is no contemporary or reliable documentation for a civil war having taken place in 1821, the date given by Bouche and often repeated by historians, and the contemporary reports clearly show that George Lawson's victory and the subsequent the foundation of Agoué by the defeated party occurred in 1823.[10]

[7] Ibid., 1/40 (20 Sept. 1823).
[8] Clapperton, *Hugh Clapperton*, 88–9.
[9] TNA: CO96/4, incl. 4 in no.8: Gov. Hill, Cape Coast Castle, 21 Mar. 1844: George Lawson Senr [Nov. 1843].
[10] Gayibor also gives 1821 as the date for the war, citing as his source a document 'in the archives of the de Souza family' (*Le Genyi*, 193, 194n., 199n.). This probably refers to a document quoted in his doctoral thesis which is not contemporary ('L'aire culturelle ajatado', 1210–11, appendix

Contemporary sources also give information about the identity of the rival parties. George Lawson, aka Akuete Zankli, is particularly well-documented.[11] He was a son of Lattie and according to information from several European observers had been trained or educated in his youth either on board an English vessel or in England. The earliest information comes from Clapperton, who describes him as 'a clever little fellow who was brought up on board an English vessel as cabin boy...'[12] An English trader reported to the Parliamentary Select Committee in 1842 that George Lawson 'was formerly a man-servant in England some years ago'.[13] The Wesleyan missionary Thomas Birch Freeman, who visited Little Popo in 1843 and met 'Lawson', reported that the latter had 'visited Europe many years back & has by some means obtained a little English Education.'[14] The information given by F. E. Forbes, a British naval officer who visited Little Popo in 1850, is consistent with this. Forbes makes it clear that his information, which is the most detailed available, comes directly from Lawson whom he credits with having 'a most astonishing memory.' 'He was a native of Popo, but educated in England, and became steward of a slaver in the time of its legal trade. Besides his pay, he had a shilling a head for each slave, as interpreter to the doctor. Seven months made the voyage to and from the port of Liverpool, landing the slaves at Jamaica.' According to Forbes, Lawson had returned to Little Popo in 1812.[15]

Forbes's account of Lawson's career is plausible. The practice of educating children of African notables in Europe or on a European vessel had a long tradition in West Africa generally and Little Popo specifically, as has been shown in the previous two chapters. The story of George Lawson's early

---

(cont.) 11: 'Francisco Félix de Souza à Petit-Popo'). Cf. Jones/ Sebald, *African Family Archive*, 7.10: 'The History of Francisco F. de Souza'.

[11] In retrospective family traditions, he is referred to as George Lawson or George A. Lawson (I.) aka Akuete Zankli. In the earliest extant letter by him, from 1806, he signed as 'George L. Lawson' (Jones/ Sebald, *African Family Archive*, 1.1, George L. Lawson, Ship L'Africain, Accra Road, 22 Dec. 1806). Letters written by him in the 1840s indicate that in this period he usually signed as 'George Lawson Senior', with the 'Senior' used to distinguish himself from his eldest son, George Latty Lawson (who sometimes but not always had a 'Junior' appended to his name). E.g., *ibid.*, 1.203, George Lawson Senior, Popo, 3 Jan. 1849; TNA: CO96/4, incl. 4 in no.8: Gov. Hill, Cape Coast Castle, 21 Mar. 1844: George Lawson Senior, Little Popo [Nov. 1843]. However, there is also evidence that he used the name 'George Latty Lawson' (Jones/ Sebald, *African Family Archive*, 1.168, George Latty Lawson Sr., New London, Popo, 20 Apr. 1848; UKHO: F. Struvé, OD9A, 'Report', 5: 'Mr George L. Lawson the father'). There is no contemporary documentation of him having used the name 'George A. Lawson', which however is used in two letters by a European trader at Agoué with reference to Lawson's eldest son (Jones/ Sebald, *African Family Archive*, 1.5, J.H. Ahkurst, Ahguay, 9 Feb. 1843; 1.9, J.H. Ahkurst, Ahguay, 17 June 1843).

[12] Clapperton, *Hugh Clapperton*, 89.

[13] PP Colonies Africa 1842, i, Report of the Select Committee on the West Coast of Africa, 91 (6 May 1842, Mr. John Arden Clegg).

[14] WMMS Thomas Birch Freeman, 'Journal', 164–6. Cf. Freeman, *Journal*, 279.

[15] Forbes, *Dahomey*, i, 100.

career is further supported by information from Isert, who reported in 1784 that two of Lattie's sons were being educated in Europe, one in Portugal and one in England.[16] If one of them – presumably the latter – was indeed George Lawson, this would mean that he was away from Little Popo for almost thirty years, although not necessarily continuously. This appears a long time but is nevertheless possible: assuming that he had been sent to England about 1784 at the age of about ten, this would mean that he was born in about 1774. Following this, he would have been just above eighty years old when he died in 1856. This would be consistent with the information given by Duncan, who in 1845 described him as being about seventy years old.[17]

The information concerning George Lawson's employment on an English vessel is supported by a letter, written by 'George L. Lawson' on board such a vessel off Accra in December 1806 to one of his brothers at Popo.[18] Although this letter announces his intention to return to the coast in the following year, it seems that this was not a permanent return or it was delayed. The date given by Forbes for George Lawson's final return to Little Popo, 1812, tallies with information given by his eldest son George Latty Lawson in early 1852, stating stated that he was 41 years old and 'a native' of Dutch town, Accra. This implies that he was born at Accra in 1810 or 1811 and his father was still away from Popo at this time (or at least not permanently settled there).[19]

As regards the name by which he was known to Europeans, 'George Lawson', this was evidently assumed from an English ship's captain of the same name who had been a business partner and friend of his father. Presumably, he had been under this particular captain's care during his stay in Britain or – more likely perhaps – during his employment on a vessel. It is not clear when exactly he had assumed this name. With reference to him, it was first documented in his letter from 1806.[20]

After his return to Little Popo, George Lawson presumably settled at Badji where he built his new residence. In his 1806 letter he had announced his

---

[16] Isert, *Letters*, 90.
[17] Duncan, *Travels*, i, 99. However, in 1852 he was described as about 68 years old: TNA: FO84/893, incl. in Hamilton, [London], 10 Apr. 1852: T. G. Forbes, 'Philomel', at Whydah, 5 Feb. 1852.
[18] Jones/ Sebald, *African Family Archive*, 1.1, George L. Lawson, Ship L. African, Accra Road, 22 Dec. 1806. The vessel can be identified as the 'L'Africaine', Capt. Vaughan, which is documented on the Gold Coast at this time. She arrived at Accra on 22 September, went to Cape Coast on 2 October and returned to Accra on 16 November. On 3 December she went again to Cape Coast, but documentation then ceases (TNA: T70/983: James Fort Accra & Vernons Fort Prampram: Day Book: Accounts from 1 July to 31 Dec. 1806).
[19] TNA: CO267/228, incls. in Governor Macdonald, Sierra Leone, 21 Apr. 1852: Copy of depositions taken before the Police Magistrate, Freetown, Sierra Leone, 10 Mar. 1852; 'Chief Justice's notes taken at the trial of Marman indicted for Slave dealing'.
[20] See Strickrodt, 'Neglected Source,' 312–3. For earlier speculations regarding George Lawson's name, see Agbanon II, *Histoire*, 43; Gayibor, *Le Genyi*, 183, Skinner, *Thomas George Lawson*, 10.

intention to build 'a castle' after his next return to the coast.[21] The residence was called 'New London', which may be an indication of where in Britain he had lived but beyond this it was evidently a political statement.[22] Like his father before him, George Lawson became well-known for the assistance and hospitality he offered, especially to British traders and naval officers.[23] Duncan reported that 'the old man professes great attachment for the English', acknowledging the British flag when British vessels arrived off Little Popo, but he added that 'the moment the flag of another nation is displayed, he, like the Vicar of Bray, acknowledges that also.'[24] Badji, which lay on a peninsula to the north-west of the Mina settlement on the beach (Aneho),[25] can therefore presumably be identified with the 'English Town' referred to in the *RGCG*.[26]

Like Bouche, the contemporary reports link George Lawson with Francisco Felix de Souza.[27] De Souza, a Brazilian who was the leading slave dealer on the Slave Coast, had been based at Little Popo on two occasions in the late eighteenth/ early nineteenth century; first, after his arrival on the coast around the turn of the century (before 1803), and then again by 1810 after a dispute with the Dahomean king Adandozan.[28] He had returned to Ouidah probably by 1820, but according to local and family traditions still owned a property at Little Popo. This was a peninsula situated opposite the settlement on the beach (Aneho) on the northern bank of the lagoon, which according to local tradition had been granted

[21] Jones/ Sebald, *African Family Archive*, 1.1, George L. Lawson, Ship L. African, Accra Road, 22 Dec. 1806.

[22] See Lawson, 'Report', 36. The name 'New London' is documented from the early 1840s: Jones/ Sebald, *African Family Archive*, 1.6. George Latty Lawson, New London, Popo, 5 Apr. 1843. Locally the place of the Lawsons' establishment is also known as 'Lolamé', meaning 'the crocodile attacks the man', because it abounded with crocodiles (Agbanon, *Histoire*, 43).

[23] Clapperton, *Hugh Clapperton*, 89; UKHO: OD8, Denham, 'Remarks and Sailing Directions' (1846), 83–4.

[24] Duncan, *Travels*, i, 100. The use of the Union Jack at Little Popo is also documented in a British naval officer's watercolour drawing from 1820, giving a view of the town from the sea (TNA: ADM344/960, no.1, Capt. B. Marwood Kelly, 'Town of Little Popoe N by E 25 Miles', H.M.S. Pheasant, 7 Sept. 1820). According to Denham, Lawson did not use the Union Jack as a trading signal but 'a large white flag with his initials G L in red' (UKHO: OD8, Denham, 'Remarks and Sailing Directions' [1846], 83–4.)

[25] Today Badji does not lie on a peninsula but merely on the southern bank of the lagoon. However, in the earlier period there was another arm of the lagoon which separated it from the Mina town/Aneho, now apparently dried up. See TNA: FO84/893, incl. in Hamilton, [London], 10 Apr. 1852: T. G. Forbes, 'Philomel', at Whydah, 5 Feb. 1852; Lawson, 'Report', 36; W. Stubenrauch, 'Map and sketch of Little Popo', 2 Feb. 1884; Gayibor, *Le Genyi*, 271.

[26] In modern Aného, there is also a quarter called 'Nlessi', i.e. 'English [Town]', lying on the beach towards the western limits of the town. However, this is not documented before 1879.

[27] Local traditions also recall the connection: Agbanon II, *Histoire*, 65; Jones/ Sebald, *African Family Archive*, 7.10: 'The History of Francisco F. de Souza'; n.a. *Adjigovi*, 6; de Souza, *La famille*, 35–6.

[28] See Robin Law, 'Francisco Felix de Souza in West Africa, 1820–1849', *Enslaving Connections*, ed. Curto/Lovejoy, 187–211, p. 192; Law, *Ouidah*, 165–66; L. N. Parés, 'Cartas do Daomé: Uma introdução', *Afro-Ásia*, 47 (2013), 295–395, pp. 384–85: no.13, Rei Adandozan to d. João, Abomey, 09.10.1810; for an English translation: A. L. Araujo, 'Dahomey, Portugal and Bahia: King Adandozan and the Atlantic Slave Trade', *Slavery and Abolition*, 33/1 (2012), 1–19, p. 10.

to him by Komlagan's predecessor, Sekpon.²⁹ De Souza named it Adjido, like his establishments at Ouidah and Badagry. His eldest son, Isidoro, is said to have been born there, his mother being the daughter of Akue, a local notable.³⁰ Through this marriage de Souza was related to George Lawson, who reportedly married Akué's younger daughter.³¹ Another of de Souza's sons, Antonio, was also closely related to the Lawsons.³² According to information given by Antonio himself, some of his wives were 'own sisters [i.e. full sisters, having the same father and mother], and half sisters of George Lawson of Popoe, and his own cousins.'³³ Although there is no contemporary documentation for de Souza's support of George Lawson in the conflict of 1823, it seems plausible, given their family and business relations as well as the situation at Little Popo in the 1840s and 1850s, when each of them (or their families) governed a part of the place independently of each other (see below).

The 'caboceer Ansan', who according to the *RGCG* was Lawson's adversary in the civil war, can probably be identified with John Ansa, a trader at Little Popo who first appears in the documents in 1777.³⁴ This is a letter from an English trader to the English Governor on the Gold Coast, which reports that both Lattie ('Lathe'), that is George Lawson's father, and 'Jno Ansah' had been of 'great service' to him. George Lawson's letter from 1806 throws some light on the relationship between John Ansa ('John Assa') and Lattie: 'John and our father [were] always great friend[s] [...] where [= when] our father used to have two English gentlemen [= traders] he used to send one of them to John…'³⁵ However, this letter also shows that after Lattie's death, the relationship between John Ansa and Lattie's children became problematic, since George Lawson reproaches his brother William Helu:

---

²⁹ N.a. *Adjigovi*, 5–6; Jones/ Sebald, *African Family Archive*, 7.10: 'Story of Francisco da Souza and George Lawson I.' Cf. Gayibor, *Le Genyi*, 168. There is no contemporary record of Sekpon.

³⁰ Agbanon II, *Histoire*, 47, 65–6. As discussed before, a notable or notables called 'Akue' ('Aqua', 'Ackwaw', 'Akoi', 'Arqua') was/were documented at Little Popo in the 1750s and the 1780s/1790s. This Akue may have been a descendant, if not the same person (see Chapters 3 and 4). According to Norberto de Souza, F.F. de Souza's wife was the daughter of Komlagan ('Contribution', 18). He gives Isidoro's birthday as 2 January 1802.

³¹ UKHO: Struvé, 'Report', 5; Agbanon, *Histoire*, 47.

³² Recently recorded family tradition recalls that Antonio's mother was Ahossi, 'a princess of Glidji' (de Souza, *La famille*, 59). But Burton noted that she was a 'a large woman from Agwe, dashed to the old Chacha. Her name was Akho-'si, i.e. King's Wife, but she had no connection with royalty' (Burton, *Mission*, i, 105–6 incl. notes). According to Simone de Souza, Antonio was born of the same mother as Ignacio. Norberto de Souza states that 'Ahosi Zanglanmio' was the mother of Maria and Ignacio but does not mention Antonio in the context ('Contribution', 18). See also Chapter 6, note 24.

³³ Fraser, 'the daily journal', 22 July 1851, in: Fraser, *Dahomey*, 32. It is probably George Latty Lawson, George Lawson's eldest son, who is referred to here.

³⁴ TNA: T70/1534, D. Mill, Ship Hawke, off Popoe, 3 Feb. 1777. See also Strickrodt, 'Neglected Source,' 306–7.

³⁵ Jones/Sebald, *African Family Archive*, 1.1, George L. Lawson, Ship L. African, Accra Road, 22 Dec. 1806.

> I am very much surprised to hear of your treatment to John Assa [...] I think it is a shame for you, not to use John Assa as our father did before us [...] I hear you like to keep all [English traders] to yourself and give him none which think it is a shame so to do, it is a putting an affront on John and our father's families. To hear the people talking about you so much of your misbehaviour to John.

The *RGCG* identifies Ansa as the caboceer of Dutch town. It is not clear when he had gained this status nor is there much information concerning Dutch town. However, its origins must have derived from the Dutch trade that had existed at Little Popo, with interruptions, since the 1730s. A glimpse of it, or its nucleus, was perhaps given by the Dutch naval officer from 1771, who noted a Dutch flag in the settlement on the beach despite the absence of Dutch traders in the period.[36] Indeed, this report is interesting because it mentions both a Dutch and an English flag, reflecting the division that in the 1820s became so problematic. Given the strong link between the Dutch, with their headquarters at Elmina, and the Mina canoemen, Dutch town may have been the quarter of the Mina at Little Popo. Further information comes from a letter by an American trader, Samuel Banks, who maintained a factory at Little Popo from September to December 1818, before the war. He mentions 'the Black Dutch caboceer' at Little Popo, describing him as 'an old Dotard.'[37] This description would fit John Ansa, who must have been quite old at this time. The letter also suggests that political relations at Little Popo were tense, due evidently to rivalry in the trade. The Dutch caboceer is reported to be extremely jealous, prohibiting another American trader who visited Popo at the time from any intercourse with other traders.

All this information seems to point to competition in trade as a likely explanation of the civil war at Little Popo. After the influential Lattie had died, his trade, mainly with the English, was continued by his son William Helu, while John Ansa, a trader and friend of the late Lattie, appears to have taken control of the trade with the Dutch. This arrangement was probably not very lucrative for the latter, and furthermore must have left much room for rivalry and quarrels as there were a number of other nations trading there as well, causing ill-feeling between these two traders (as shown by the letter of 1806). After the return of Lattie's son George Lawson in 1812, the situation evidently worsened. Like his father before him, George Lawson was very successful in the trade, in which he worked in association with F.F. de Souza. The resulting situation must have been one of great competition. As noted above, according to Clapperton the conflict was caused by the Dutch caboceer's refusal to pay the usual customs on the arrival of the

---

[36] See Chapter 3, p. 129. NAH: Archiv Admiraliteitscolleges, Collectie J. A. van der Velden 1.01.47.17, no.16: Journaal van 's lands fregat Boreas, 1770–1772, 7 July 1771.
[37] RIHS: Carrington Papers: Samuel Banks, Little Popo, Africa, 20 Dec. 1818.

vessels to the king and his defiance of the king's authority. This information, which is also recalled in the traditions of the kings at Glidji, points perhaps to the immediate cause of the war.[38]

An interesting problem is posed by the different information concerning the identity of Lawson's adversary as given in the contemporary accounts and the retrospective accounts from local traditions. While the former identify him as John Ansa, the caboceer of Dutch town, the latter name him Komlagan. According to Bouche, who, as noted above, gives the point of view of the Adjigo people at Agoué, Komlagan was the chief of Little Popo. Agbanon II, who represents the point of view of the king of Glidji, describes him as 'the chief of the beach at Aného', i.e. Little Popo.[39] According to the earliest version of the Lawson traditions that mentions him, dating probably from 1906, he was one in a sucession of 'Fantee Chiefs at Anecho beach... this title having been granted them by the King of Glidji.'[40] There is no mention of Komlagan in contemporary sources, although Bowdich, relying on second-hand information collected between 1816–18, notes the existence, behind Little Popo, of 'another smaller interior state, governed by a caboceer called Quaminagah.'[41] This name re-appears later in the century. According to Lawson's report from 1879, Agoué had been founded by 'Quamina Gang' who had to leave Little Popo after a civil war at Little Popo.[42] 'Quamina' (Kwamina) is the Akan name given to boys born on a Tuesday, of which 'Komlan' is the local version, i.e. 'Komlagan' is the local counterpart of 'Quaminagan'.[43]

There are several possible explanations for these different names given to Lawson's adversary.[44] First, Komlagan may have been a successor of John Ansa at Agoué and replaced him in the traditions as founder of the place, due perhaps to Ansa's death soon afterwards, or death without children. This telescoping of genealogies is a common phenomenon in traditions, as shown, among others, by the example of the founder of Glidji, Foli Bebe (as discussed in Chapter 2).[45] However, against this it could be argued that according to the traditions, Komlagan too died soon after the foundation of Agoué. Second, John Ansa and Komlagan might be two names for the same person. This is conceivable because, as shown in the cases of George Lawson and Pedro Kodjo/Pedro Pinto da Silveira (discussed below), African traders sometimes used different names in different spheres. However, as

[38] See Agbanon II, *Histoire*, 64.
[39] *Ibid.*
[40] Jones/ Sebald, *African Family Archive*, 7.12: 'History of Akuete Zankli (alias G.A. Lawson I).'
[41] Bowdich, *Mission*, 221–2.
[42] Lawson, 'Report', 39–40.
[43] Agbanon II, *Histoire*, 137. The suffix –gan means 'big' or 'great' and indicates seniority (Westermann, *Die Glidyi-Ewe*, 19).
[44] Cf. Gayibor, *Le Genyi*, 199.
[45] See Henige, *Chronology*, 27–38.

John Ansa and Komlagan are both African (Akan) names, this explanation does not seem convincing. Third, and more plausibly perhaps, Komlagan may be a name given retrospectively to John Ansa in the traditions. This is suggested by a version of the traditions recorded in the 1930s, according to which 'John Ansah Ahoussiadou' was the father of 'Comlanvi Toutouyê Dêgnon', although here it is the latter who is said to have founded Agoué while the former died at Little Popo, which the contemporary evidence shows to be wrong.[46] According to Bouche, Komlanvi was Komlagan's son and successor in the office of chief of Agoué.[47] It is possible that the name Komlagan, meaning 'big' or 'great' Komlan, was given to John Ansa retrospectively in relation to the name of his successor, Komlan, who then became Komlanvi or 'Little Komlan'.

Regarding the settlement of the refugees at Agoué, both contemporary sources and local traditions indicate that a settlement already existed there, on the northern bank of the lagoon. This is Agouégan, which according to W.T.G. Lawson was the 'original Agweh.'[48] Clapperton's account also suggests the existence of a settlement preceding the civil war at Little Popo, saying that the refugees retreated to 'a small village called Agwey – where they settled and built a considerable town…'[49] According to Glidji traditions, Agouégan had been founded by 'Kuadjo Kanli, the nephew of Foli Bebe, who came from Accra' and after a brief sojourn at Glidji had proceeded to found a settlement there.[50] This is plausible in the light of contemporary information, which shows that in the early eighteenth century Ga people engaging in banditry had encamped half-way between Little Popo and Grand Popo, which is the location of Agouégan and Agoué.[51] At the time of the civil war, there was said to have been a 'fishing post, called *cha*' where fish were caught and dried.[52] Observers from the second half of the nineteenth century noted that the indigenous name of the new settlement, situated on the beach opposite the old one, was 'Adjigo' rather than Agoué, Adjigo being the cult of the Mina immigrants.[53]

---

[46] ANT: 2APA Anécho, Affaires Politiques, Agouégan et environment; n.a., 'On nous a sommés de répondre, et nous répondons' (no date).
[47] Bouche, 'Notes', 96; Sept ans, 302. Cf. Pelofy, *Histoire*, 1, 3; Pierucci, ['Histoire'], 7.
[48] GNA: ADM 1/2/361, incl. in no. 26: Lawson, 'Report', 45.
[49] Clapperton, *Hugh Clapperton*, 89.
[50] Agbanon II, *Histoire*, 66.
[51] See Chapter 3. It is likely, however, that it existed even before this, as a Hula settlement: see Chapter 1.
[52] See Agbanon II, *Histoire*, 66.
[53] Bouche, *Sept ans*, 301. Cf. Bouche, 'Notes', 99; Zöller, *Das Togoland*, 182; Westermann, *Die Glidyi-Ewe*, 230 n.1; Agbanon II, *Histoire*, 63.

Agoué in the early 1830s

The earliest first-hand account of Agoué comes from C. H. van Züpthen, a trader based in Bahia who visited the place in June 1831. According to him, Agoué lay 'some hundred steps' behind the beach, with only the roofs of the houses visible from the sea. The caboceer's house stuck out and had a white flag on its roof. Van Zütphen indicated that the community prospered, noting that the inhabitants led 'a comfortable life', 'each has his property fenced in and a wealthy man has already several slaves'. He stated that their main occupation was the manufacture of cloth, but also mentions barracoons ('Baraken') on the beach, thus perhaps betraying another, more lucrative source of income: the engagement in the (illegal) slave trade.[54]

There is also information concerning the political situation in the town, including the identification of several individuals who played a role. First, there was 'the king', 'a very old man [and] unfit for service'. Second, there was the caboceer ('Cabiceiro'), called Joao Coparan, who was the king's son. He seems to have acted in the king's place, although 'the succession to the throne is inherited by the [king's] brother.' The caboceer received van Zütphen and his companion on their arrival at Agoué, walking 'under an umbrella which was carried above him; he wore a white felt hat and a fine cloth and was accompanied by many other blacks who were his servants.' During the visitors' fortnight's stay at Agoué, the caboceer acted as their landlord, discussing business with them, providing them with a house and visiting daily, 'partly to buy something, and partly from curiosity'. According to van Zütphen, he was 'no bad man of mind and manners, only is he, like all Africans, too keen on gold; he loves everything that is pretty, but he does not like to spend' – evidently, he was a proper trader. He lived in a two-storey house with a balcony (probably in the Brazilian style), spoke English well and also played chess.[55]

Finally, there was the caboceer's head servant ('moço grande'), Aité, who 'has a lot of weight with the caboceer, he speaks Portuguese well [and] was in Bahia for a long time'.[56] Like the caboceer, he lived in a two-storey house which was well furnished, including with English goods. He had eight wives, one of whom was 'the mulatto, daughter of Cha Cha [of Ouidah, i.e. Francisco Felix de Souza]'.[57]

---

[54] Van Zütphen, *Tagebuch*, 53–4, 56. The meaning of the word 'Barake' is ambiguous in van Zütphen's account, as he also uses it to signify 'hut' (e.g. p. 8). However, in his description of Lagos it is made clear that the 'Baraken' on the beach were used for the accommodation of slaves shortly before their embarkation on vessels (34).
[55] *Ibid.*
[56] *Ibid.*, 54.
[57] *Ibid.*, 58.

The description of the king, specifically his old age, agrees with the information given in 1818 by Samuel Banks about the Dutch caboceer (John Ansa) at Little Popo. It is likely that this was him – still alive but incapacitated. Traces of the Dutch connection were noted by van Zütphen, specifically the 'good Dutch Genever' with which the caboceer welcomed the European traders after their arrival at Agoué. However, more important was evidently the Brazilian influence, particularly that of Francisco Felix de Souza at Ouidah who was linked to the caboceer's influential servant, Aité, through family and presumably also business relations.[58] This connection with de Souza and the Brazilian slave trade network on the coast also helps to explain how John Ansa's followers managed so quickly to establish themselves in their new place and prosper.

Joao Coparan, the king's son and caboceer of Agoué, does not appear in any other sources, neither in contemporary records nor retrospective local traditions. This is baffling and raises the question whether he may (subsequently) have been known by another name. João is the Portuguese version of John, which was also the name of his father, John Ansa. In the 1840s and 1850s, there was another caboceer called 'John' at Agoué, John Quarvee, the caboceer of English town. (See below, pp. 178ff). However, although it would be neat to be able identify the one with the other, there is no evidence that positively links them. Another, perhaps more plausible, possibility would be the identification with Komlanvi, who (as noted above) according to traditions was a son and the successor of Komlagan/John Ansa. He was also known as Catraya (from Portuguese *catraia*, 'boat, small vessel'), and was succeeded by a brother or cousin, called Agunon, who ruled until 1835.[59] This interpretation appeals because, like Komlanvi, Joao Coparan was the caboceer's son and had a Portuguese name, but in the absence of further evidence, it is speculative.

The most intriguing character in van Zütphen's account is Aité. He is the first 'Afro-Brazilian' documented at Agoué, preceding Joaquim d'Almeida aka Zoki Azata and the other returnees by nearly a decade. (See below, pp. 179ff, and Chapter 6). As regards identification, it seems likely that this was Ayi Yovonou aka Pedro Felix d'Almeida, whose father was called Ayité Kissé and whose mother was connected to the royal family in Glidji.[60] The family was mainly resident in Little Popo.[61] According to local traditions, Ayi

---

[58] For another strategic marriage of one of de Souza's many children, to a slave trader settled at Ouidah in 1830, see Law, 'Francisco Felix de Souza', 197; Law, *Ouidah*, 172–3.

[59] Bouche, 'Notes', 96; *Sept ans*, 302 (cousin); Pelofy, *Histoire*, 1, 3; Pierucci, ['Histoire'], 7.

[60] Agbanon, *Histoire de Petit-Popo*, 46, 193; Emmanuel Azan Ajavon/ Paul Jaenavho Ajavon/ Pierre Jaenavho Ajavon, 'La Collectivité Ajavon' (Lomé, n.d. [2000]), 16; de Souza, *La famille*, 72. The names Ayi and Ayité seem to be used by males of the families tracing their origins to Ayi Manko (who was Ayité Kissé's father), with Ayi and Ayité being used in alternate generations.

[61] According to a history written in 1906 and preserved in the Lawson papers, Ayité Kissé was one of George Lawson's 'captains' at Flamani (Jones/ Sebald, *African Family Archive*, 7.12: Story of George Lawson I and his successors).

Yovonou/ Pedro Felix d'Almeida associated with de Souza and also knew Portuguese, although the story is inconsistently reported. De Souza family traditions say that he was an adoptive son of Francisco Felix de Souza, rather than a son-in-law, and grew up in the latter's household in Ouidah, learning Portuguese there. There is no mention of a visit to Brazil or a marriage to one of de Souza's daughters.[62]

At any rate, van Zütphen's account is interesting because it already indicates the political influences and potential divisions that characterized Agoué's community in the 1840s.

The foundation of Porto Seguro

In the 1840s another settlement on the western Slave Coast appeared in the documents. This is Porto Seguro (Agbodrafo), situated on the beach opposite the town of Togo some twenty kilometres west of Little Popo. It is first documented in 1841, in the form 'Sugru'.[63] Duncan, who visited the place in 1845, referred to it as 'a town of considerable size, though not of much trade.' He met the caboceer, 'a tall, stout, and good-natured looking man, about thirty-eight years of age.'[64] The caboceer was on bad terms with both the people of Agoué and with George Lawson at Little Popo. The latter he described as 'an inveterate enemy' and 'one of the principal slave-dealers on the coast', while the former were accused of having 'unjustly given his people a very bad name, which not only prevented white men from visiting and trading in his town, but all of the men-of-war from purchasing stock from him.'[65] In 1846 Denham noted that the settlement was surrounded by a barricade, indicating that the political climate was tense. He identified the chief as 'one John Jack', who gave the number of inhabitants as 1,000.[66]

There is no contemporary information concerning the date or circumstances of the foundation of this settlement, and (consequently) these points are subject to much speculation and controversy in retrospective accounts. According to Bouche, its origin was due to the same causes as in

---

[62] De Souza, *La famille*, 72. In the 1860s, Pedro Felix d'Almeida was living at Ouidah, but he returned to Little Popo after a dispute with King Glele (J. M. Turner, 'Les Brésiliens: The Impact of Former Brazilian Slaves upon Dahomey', Ph.D. thesis, Boston University, 1975, 109–10; cf. Law, *Ouidah*, 247).

[63] *PP* Colonies Africa 1842, 200: Capt. Laurence to Mr Dove, Sierra Leone, 4 June 1841, quoted by Rev. J. Beecham, 31 March 1842. Porto Seguro means 'safe haven' in Portuguese. However, as is discussed below, the town was founded by a man called Sedjro/ Seggiroe/ Sagrow, suggesting that the name may in fact derive from that of its founder and the European name was attached to it only later. (A similar case is that of Blekesu, which in English documents from the nineteenth century appears as 'Blockhouse'.)

[64] Duncan, *Travels*, i, 148.

[65] Ibid., 172–3.

[66] UKHO: OD8, Denham, 'Remarks and Sailing Directions' (1846), 81.

the case of Agoué, although it was founded later: 'Some of the partisans of Comla-gan established themselves little by little at this place, some fifteen kilometres to the west of Little Popo. The current caboceer is called Messau [= Mensa], he always recognizes a certain primacy of the [caboceer] of Agoué over himself.'[67] W.T.G. Lawson's version of events is slightly different and provides a date for Porto Seguro's foundation: 'The Town originated from a Civil war which occurred at Little Popo about the year 1825 when the original Chief had to leave the latter place.'[68] These two accounts are interesting because they illustrate the different views of this event held by the Adjigo people and the Lawsons respectively, which are expounded (in greater detail) in the accounts from the twentieth century. The point here is that the Lawsons argue that there had been a civil war, which is important for the legitimisation of their claim to political supremacy at Little Popo. According to them, this time the king at Glidji sided with Lawson's adversaries and followed them into exile. It was after this war that Akuete Zankli, aka George Lawson, 'became King of Anecho or *Ahwa-woto* (war-maker) and assumed the name George Akuete Lawson I.'[69] According to Lawson traditions recorded in the twentieth century, this war and the foundation of Porto Seguro took place in 1834.[70]

The traditions of the Adjigo people are divided about this event. Quam-Dessou denies that there was any war and thus the Lawsons' claim that Little Popo had become independent from Glidji and that George Lawson had been crowned king. According to him, some of Komlagan's followers who had remained at Little Popo after Komlagan's flight to Agoué subsequently disagreed with George Lawson and left for Porto Seguro 'little by little' and of their own free will.[71] According to Gaba, however, there was a war, which he describes in great (and implausible) detail. He gives 1836 as the date of Porto Seguro's foundation.[72]

Agbanon II, giving the point of view of the kings at Glidji, also avoids saying that there was a war, describing the disturbances at Little Popo as a quarrel ('querelle').[73] According to him, Porto Seguro was founded in 1835 after Kodjo Agbosu, one of Komlagan's successors, had been expelled from the town by George Lawson. Kodjo Agbosu is said to have requested a piece

---

[67] Bouche, 'Notes', 98–9.
[68] GNA: ADM 1/2/361, incl. in no. 26: Lawson, 'Report' (1879), 35.
[69] Jones/ Sebald, *African Family Archive*, 7.12: 'History of Akuete Zankli (alias G.A. Lawson I)'. Cf. n.a., 'La Courte Histoire', 42. However, according to 'Petit Histoire d'Aneho', George Lawson was proclaimed king already after the war of 1821 (60).
[70] See Jones/ Sebald, *African Family Archive*, 7.1: '[Chronological Tables] 1821–1884'; n.a., 'La Courte Histoire', 42.
[71] Cf. Quam-Dessou, *Histoire*, 34–5. He dates the foundation of Porto Seguro to 1835 and even gives the text of an alleged contract between the founder of the settlement and the ruler of Togo. (For another copy, see Agbanon II, *Histoire*, 180: 'Annexe II; Contrat de Fondation d'Agbodrafo').
[72] Gaba, 'History', 73–5.
[73] Agbanon II, *Histoire*, 67–9.

of land from the chief of Togoville, i.e. the town of Togo, who authorized him to establish himself on the beach opposite his place. Two sons of the king of Glidji are said to have followed, but not the king, Sowu, himself. Gaba refers to Lawson's opponent sometimes as Kodjo Agbosu and sometimes as Sedjro Agbosu, implying that these are two names for the same person. According to him, Kodjo/Sedjro Agbosu subsequently returned to Little Popo where he and Akuete Zankli made up and became 'the best of friends hereafter.'[74] This story is echoed by Quam-Dessou, who adds that Kodjo Agbosu was 'born of a Lawson [female].'[75] Intriguingly, Sedjro Agbosu is documented in the contemporary sources, which however only support the latter part of this story, that is the good understanding between him and George Lawson as well as his membership of the Lawson clan. His name first appears in the 1864 peace agreement between Little Popo and Agoué, which he signed as one of the headmen of Little Popo.[76] He also appears in several documents in the 'GLL' from the 1870s, where he is identified as one of the 'war generals' at Badji, which, as noted above, was the quarter of the Lawsons.[77]

Agbanon's information that the settlers requested land from the chief of Togo is supported by evidence from the late nineteenth century, when the chiefs of Togo requested the German officers who had established the protectorate there to restore their supremacy over the rebellious ruler of Porto Seguro, King Mensa.[78] The anti-slave trade treaty with Britain from 1852 was signed by three headmen of Porto Seguro, 'Ar-con-tee', 'A-kien' and 'James Bruce'.[79]

Little Popo in the 1840s and 1850s

From the 1840s, there is a relative abundance of information about the political situation at Little Popo. Most of it focuses on George Lawson, who

[74] Gaba, 'History', 73–5.
[75] Cf. Quam-Dessou, *Histoire*, 34.
[76] I have been unable to find the original of this treaty but there are several copies. They give different spellings of the names of the signees, due evidently to miscopying. See TNA: ADM123/66, incl. 3 in no 2, A.P. Eardley Wilmot, 'Rattlesnake', off Whydah, 11 July 1864: Agreement with Headmen of Little Popo, Little Popo, 13 Apr. 1864 ('Seggiroe'); CO96/66, incl. in Hammond, [London], 20 Sept. 1864: ('Leggiro'); *PP* Slave Trade 1864, Class A, incl.3 in no.128: ('Leggiro').
[77] See Jones/Sebald, *African Family Archive*, 2.10, Little Popo, 4 Oct. 1874. This document gives a list of the war generals appointed by G.B. Lawson and R.C. Lawson, including 'Old Sagrow [who] is the director & advisor.' For a reference to Badji, see 3.3, 'List of each company's Head Chief', New London Palace, Little Popo, 28 Aug. 1883. However, it is possible that this refers to a descendant rather than the person documented in 1864 and 1874, as must be the case in 7.5, '[List of Generals and Notables…] 20th September 1931', which includes 'Sedjro Agboku'.
[78] Sebald, *Togo*, 66. Cf. Henrici, *Das Deutsche Togogebiet*, 140–1.
[79] TNA: FO84/893, incl. in Hamilton, [London], 10 April 1852: T. G. Forbes: 'Schedule of Treaties' (1852).

172 • *Disintegration & reconstitution*

evidently played a central role in the political life of Little Popo in the period. The earliest information comes from the examination of traders, British naval officers and other officials by the Parliamentary Select Committee in 1842 but sometimes goes back to the 1830s or even earlier. A British trader who was asked whose sovereignty Popo was under, responded, 'I do not think it is under any sovereignty at all; there is a head man [= 'caboceer'] there, called Lawson, a black, a native...'[80] Another trader, who had been residing on the Gold Coast since about 1830, stated with regard to George Lawson, 'I know that he is a native of Popo, a man of influence there...'[81] A naval officer who had been serving on the West African coast between early 1838 and 1841, referred to George Lawson as 'the cabboceer, that is the king.'[82]

More interesting information however comes from accounts of actual visits to the place. In March 1843 Freeman visited Little Popo, which he described as a 'second class town' of 'very pretty appearance'.[83] He met George Lawson, 'one of the most influential and respectable Natives.'[84] In the original text of his journal, he refers to him as 'Lawson the Chief of Popo (Little),' which in the published version of the journal was changed to 'Lawson, one of the head-men of Popo.'[85] As noted in the introduction, it is not clear whether this and other (small but significant) changes were made by Freeman himself or by the editor, but the latter seems more likely. Freeman further noted that George Lawson was trying to establish a school at Little Popo in order to teach 'several young children the first rudiments of an English Education'. Asked whether he would welcome a teacher or missionary from the Methodist mission to support his venture, he responded in the affirmative.[86]

John Duncan, who visited the place in early 1845, also gives details concerning George Lawson's position in Little Popo society.

> Mr. Lawson, owing to his great trade and wealth acquired by the slave trade, is acknowledged as the leading man in Popoe, although they have a caboceer, or *dootay*, who is acknowledged as hereditary chief magistrate or ruler; for when Mr. Lawson interferes, the opinion or order of the caboceer is disregarded.[87]

---

[80] *PP* Colonies Africa 1842, Report of the Select Committee on the West Coast of Africa, 91 (6 May 1842: Mr. John Arden Clegg). Clegg had been engaged in the African trade since about 1825 but admittedly knew 'very little about Popo', having been there 'but twice altogether.' Cf. Jones, 'Little Popo and Agoué', especially 125–7.
[81] *Ibid.*, 660 (22 July 1842: Mr Gedge [questioned together with W. M. Hutton]).
[82] *Ibid.*, Commander Henry Broadhead, R. N., 13 May 1842. In the interview, Broadhead does not name George Lawson but from the context it is clear that it is he who is meant.
[83] WMMS: Freeman, 'Journal', 164–5.
[84] *Ibid.*, 165.
[85] *Ibid.* 63–4; Freeman, *Journal*, 243.
[86] WMMS: Freeman, 'Journal', 165–6. Cf. Freeman, *Journal*, 279.
[87] Duncan, *Travels*, i, 101.

It is noteworthy that Duncan uses the term 'magistrate', which earlier in the century had also been used by Robertson. 'Dootay' appears to be a version of the Ewe term *dutɔ́*, denoting 'chief magistrate, an elder, often a descendant of the founder of the town and as such the custodian of the country.'[88] If so, this refers to a person of authority in the coastal settlement itself rather than the king at Glidji. This is corroborated by information from 1883, indicating that there continued to be a Mina chief at Little Popo whose nominal authority was acknowledged. According to a document in the GLL, the Lawsons conceded that Jehowey aka Kodjovi ('Cudjovee') was 'the caboceer in the place'. He had held this position 'for the past 28 years', i.e. since about 1855; 'he is the one that stood in the country who knows everybody man or woman and knows that he is the caboceer of the town he has to call on him if he likes or not, he got to do it…'[89] A letter by W.T.G. Lawson from the same period states that Jehowey had been made 'yovogah', that is the 'chief of the whites' (a title also used at Ouidah), by his grandfather, i.e. George Lawson.[90] Jehowey himself explained to the Governor of the Gold Coast later this year:

> In the year 1854, or thereabout, I was proclaimed King of this town, paying tribute to the King of Gripi [Glidji], who has the sole right of this place, claiming this as his sea-beach; Chief G.A. Lawson 1st [= George Lawson] was created Field-Marshal […] for the protection of the English merchants and traders then residing on the beach. As such King I was appointed to collect and receive all duties upon produce exported by sea by the French, German, Portuguese, and other foreign merchants and traders from this place, and which are to be divided between myself and the King of Gripi, that George Arquartay Lawson Ist is to receive and collect all dues from the [English] houses alone.[91]

Ferdinand Struvé, sent by the British navy to the Slave Coast to survey the coastal lagoons, was based at Little Popo for several months between December 1849 and November 1850. In his report, he noted that the settlement was divided into two parts which were independent of each other, 'one calling itself "New London" and "English Town" the other "Ahjudo" and "Portuguese Slave Town" governed by a son of the present Viceroy [sic] of "Whydah", Mr José [sic] de Souza'. New London was ruled by George Lawson, who is variously referred to as 'King' and 'President', although due to ill health he 'deputed his Eldest Son to act for him'.[92]

[88] Westermann, *Wörterbuch der Ewe-Sprache*, 84, s. v. *dutɔ́*.
[89] Jones/Sebald, *African Family Archive*, 3.39, Minutes of a meeting, Little Popo, 30 Oct. [1883]. Cf. ibid., editors' 'Introduction', 175–181.
[90] Ibid., 3.53, W.T. G. Lawson, New London Palace, Little Popo, 24 Nov. 1883.
[91] TNA: PRO30/29.269 Conf. 4994, incl. 16 in no.72: Geyawhay, Little Popo, 2 Dec. 1883.
[92] UKHO: OD 9A, Struvé, 'Report', 5, 30, 31.

'Ahjudo' can be identified with the settlement of the de Souza family on the peninsula in the lagoon, which (as noted above) is said to have been founded by Francisco Felix de Souza in the early nineteenth century. It had been abandoned by him by 1820 when he returned to Ouidah, but in 1840 had been re-settled by his eldest son Isidoro, who established a factory for the slave trade there. Isidoro in turn had left Adjido for Ouidah following the death of his father in 1849 (which Struvé, who was based in New London, failed to note), but it continued to be settled by his family and other Portuguese slave traders and their slaves. By May 1850, Isidoro had succeeded his father as Chacha at Ouidah.[93]

Struvé reported that George Latty Lawson advised him to inform the 'Head Men' of 'Kingtown', Glidji ('Grivee'), of his plan to survey the lagoon to the west of Little Popo and have them in turn inform the people of the lagoon-side settlements where Struvé intended to pass.[94] This implies that Glidji's authority was recognised by these communities and also, nominally at least, by the Lawsons.

F. E. Forbes, who visited Little Popo in March 1850, described Little Popo as 'a republic, or rather the province of a republic.' According to him, 'The chief or president lives at a large town at a little distance; while the town of Little Popo is divided by the lagoon into Ajado, the slave town, under Portuguese directors, and New London, under a president (Mr. Lawson), whence palm oil is shipped.'[95] The terms 'republic' and 'president' imply that this ruler did not have the status of 'king', and perhaps also that his office was elected, rather than hereditary. This may mean that there was no paramount chief at Little Popo, or that although (perhaps) chieftaincy was a hereditary office, being open only to members of certain families or clans, the successor to these offices was elected from among the eligible candidates. On the other hand, Forbes had first-hand experience of the neighbouring kingdom of Dahomey with its strongly centralised state and a king who had absolute power over the lives and property of his subjects (and who used it). Therefore, it is also possible that he uses 'republic' in order to distinguish between Dahomey, which for his European readership would have been the stereotypical African kingdom, and Little Popo, where the king and the chiefs did not have absolute power but reached decisions in council. The description of Little Popo as a 'province' can be interpreted as a reference to its forming part of Genyi with its capital at Glidji, where the king, who like Lawson is referred to as 'president', resided.

Another naval officer, T. G. Forbes, who visited the region in January 1852 in order to conclude anti-slave trade treaties with the chiefs of the various towns on the western Slave Coast, refers to George Lawson as 'the

---

[93] Ibid., 17; Law, *Ouidah*, 215.
[94] UKHO: 9OD 9A [cf. n.92], Struvé, 'Report', 6.
[95] Forbes, *Dahomey*, i, 98.

Head Chief'.[96] He gives a detailed description of the ceremony of the conclusion of the treaty, which took place on 25 January in the courtyard of Lawson's 'most excellent house' at New London and involved 'the chiefs and headmen to the number of 500'. After having heard the treaty read, the chiefs consulted among themselves and then told the British officers, 'That they agreed to all Conditions and would sign the Treaty. That all they had heard read was very proper and for their good. That if we were going to leave the Country and had a Child would you refuse to take care of it'. According to Forbes, 'this sentence is spoken in parable – means "that if you had a King and he died, would you refuse to make another. That their King was dead and another not yet being made, would I say who was to be the King now that Slave Trade was for ever abolished."'[97] The treaty was signed by three people, George Lawson, Al-sham-bo-gar-gai and Al-sham-bo-Douavee.[98] The latter two were 'Chiefs, sons of the late King', which evidently refers to the king at Glidji.[99] Agbanon II identifies this king as Ekué Agbanon I, who ruled from 1849 to 1852 and was succeeded by Ganli Seddo (1854 to 1856).[100] Forbes's description shows that although George Lawson was the 'Head Chief' of Little Popo, his power was not absolute and decisions were taken jointly by a group of chiefs. Furthermore, theoretically at least he continued to acknowledge the political seniority of the king at Glidji, as is indicated by the reference to the forthcoming election of the king.

George Lawson died in 1856.[101] He was succeeded by his eldest son George Latty Lawson, who is well-documented as regards his activities in trade between 1843 and 1853, when he worked as an agent for the English trader John Marman (see Chapter 6). According to family traditions, he had been appointed 'prince regent' during his father's lifetime – the term is questionable, but it suggests that Lawson Senior was not well enough to conduct business during the last years of his life. This is supported by Struvé's report about his visit in 1849–1850, discussed above. It is also implied by information from the missionaries of the Wesleyan Methodist Missionary Society who became active at Little Popo, Glidji and Agoué in the mid-1850s, which does not mention George Lawson but only George Latty Lawson. The missionaries established a school at Little Popo about July 1854, which by the end of the year was boasting about fifty students. The

[96] TNA: FO84/893, incl. in Hamilton, [London], 10 Apr. 1852: T. G. Forbes, 'Philomel', at Whydah, 5 February 1852.
[97] Ibid.
[98] Ibid., T. G. Forbes: 'Schedule of Treaties' (1852).
[99] Ibid., T. G. Forbes, 'Philomel', at Whydah, 5 Feb. 1852. The first parts of the names, 'Al-sham-bo-gar-gai' and 'Al-sham-bo-Douavee', are obviously variant spellings of the name Ashampo, which is a prerogative of the royal family at Glidji. See Westermann, Die Glidyi-Ewe, 189.
[100] Agbanon II, Histoire, 71–8.
[101] TNA: CO267/270, T.G. Lawson, Freetown, 18 Apr. 1861.

good attendance was attributed to George Latty Lawson, 'in fact we cannot do without him.' Another son of George Lawson, Frederick L. Lawson, acted as interpreter for the missionaries.[102]

In March 1859, two Wesleyan Methodist missionaries, William West and Peter William Bernasko, visited Little Popo.[103] They were received by George Latty Lawson, 'the Chief'. They spent the afternoon discussing 'the responsibilities entailed on those in authority by the influence arising from their position' with him, followed by a prayer session in his house, 'which is a very nice one, and fitted up in European style.' On the following day, West held a public prayer meeting in Lawson's courtyard. However, he was disappointed by the small number of people who attended, and even more so when he found out that the school, rather than propagating the Christian faith, was mainly used to instruct members of the Lawson family to read and write.[104]

George Latty Lawson died on 3 June 1859, at the age of 48.[105] He was succeeded by one of his brothers, Thomas George Lawson, who however resided in the British colony of Sierra Leone and was unwilling to move to Little Popo. He had been at Sierra Leone since about 1825, under the care of an influential timber merchant, John McCormack. He had attended the Colonial Government School and become a Christian, and from 1846 served in the colonial government in various offices. In 1860 he applied to be naturalized as a British subject, which was granted.[106] His absence left the Lawson party at Little Popo in a position of weakness, which was to be exploited by Pedro Kodjo, a trader from Agoué (with family connections to Little Popo), as will be discussed below.

Agoué in the 1840s and 1850s

In March 1843, Freeman visited Agoué and described it – like Little Popo – as a 'second Class Town', with a population of between 1,500 and 1,600 inhabitants. Unlike Little Popo, however, Freeman was not too impressed by it: 'It is like most Native Towns on this Coast irregularly built and full of dirt and filth.' This negative impression may have been influenced by what he perceived to be the town's key business: 'Its main support is the Slave Trade

[102] WMMS: West Africa Correspondence, Box 262: Joseph Dawson, Little Popo, 23 Feb. 1855.
[103] *Ibid.*, Box 263: William West, Cape Coast, 6 June 1859.
[104] *Ibid.* West and Bernasko also visited the king at Glidji, who requested them to establish a school in the town. See also GNA: SC4/143, P.N. Bernasko [to T.B. Freeman], Little Popo, 18 May 1858.
[105] See GNA: SC4/146, P.W. Bernasko, Little Popo, 8 June 1859. In 1861 T. G. Lawson wrote that his brother had died 'in June last', which evidently is a mistake (TNA: CO267/270, T. G. Lawson, Freetown, 18 April 1861).
[106] TNA: CO267/270, T.G. Lawson, Freetown, 18 Apr. 1861; Jones/ Sebald, *African Family Archive*, 1.194, John McCormack [to George Lawson], Sierra Leone, 12 Nov. 1848, n. 54; Skinner, *Thomas George Lawson*, 13–16, ch. 2.

in the carrying on of which it is connected with Whydah.'[107]

In October 1843 there was a fire at Thomas Hutton's palm oil factory in Agoué. This incident generated an abundance of documentary material, which also gives some insight into the political situation at Agoué.[108] These documents show, firstly, that Agoué was divided into two parts, Portuguese town and English town, and, secondly, that the caboceer or head chief of Agoué had died by 25 September 1843.[109] One of the notables at Agoué explained: 'We have at present no Cabboceer here – all the minor Chiefs being on terms of equality.'[110] Five of these 'minor Chiefs' signed the letters to the British Governor at Cape Coast Castle and to the officers of the British navy: 'John Quarvil, Cabboceer of the English Town; Philip Decorsa, Acting Cabboceer of Portuguese Town; Quashie Sooquoo, Chief; Quashie Corley, State [late] Cabboceers Brother; Quashie Gah, Late Cabboceer's Son.'[111] This shows that not only was there no 'head chief' at Agoué at this time but also no caboceer of Portuguese town, suggesting that these two posts may in fact have been one and the same. Hutton's agent at Agoué, John Ahkurst, anticipated that the election of the new caboceer would be turbulent, but was not worried as he believed it would not concern English town.

> There is great talk here that a grand Palaver is about shortly to take place & which it is expected will cause some bloodshed, at least, so the people say – for my part I think it will amount to nothing beyond a Tongue fight – but true it is, they are making slugs [= shots], and other preparations. The cause of all this is – they are about to put a new Cabboceer on the stool, and there being so many who claim right thereto that it is supposed they will fight for it and the strongest party will get it. This however will have nothing to do with this English Town, at least I fancy not [.][112]

---

[107] WMMS: Freeman, 'Journal', 164–6.
[108] TNA: CO96/2, W. B. Hutton & Sons, [London], 20 Dec. 1843 (incls.); CO96/4, no.8, Hill, Cape Coast Castle, 21 March 1844 (incls.), CO96/4, no.31, Hill, Cape Coast Castle, 1 June 1844 (incls.); CO96/5, Canning, [London] 13 Jan. 1844 (incls.).
[109] TNA: CO96/2, incl. in T. Hutton, Cape Coast, 24 Oct. 1843: J.H. Ahkurst, Ahguay, 25 Sept. 1843.
[110] TNA: CO96/4, incl. 7 in no.8: Hill, Cape Coast Castle, 21 Mar. 1844: J. Quarvee, Ahguay, 28 Dec. 1843.
[111] TNA: CO96/2, incl. in T. Hutton, Cape Coast, 24 Oct. 1843: Chiefs of Ahguay, Ahguay, 8 Oct. 1843. For variations of the spelling of the names, see TNA: CO96/2, incl. in T. Hutton, Cape Coast, 24 Oct. 1843: Chiefs of Ahguay, Ahguay, 11 Oct. 1843: 'Jones Cuavi; Fellippe Decosta; Cuaci Sucu; Colle; Cuacigan.' Quashie/Cuaci is a variant of 'Kuassi' (= Akan 'Kwesi'), the name usually given to boys from the Adjigo clan born on a Sunday (Agbanon II, *Histoire*, 137).
[112] TNA: CO96/2, incl. in T. Hutton, Cape Coast, 24 October 1843: J.H. Ahkurst, Ahguay, 25 Sept. 1843.

However, the election was evidently not held for some time, as by December 1843 there was still no new caboceer.[113] In mid-May 1844 one of Hutton's agents at Agoué reported the death of 'Chief "Jakao"', due to which the negotiations about compensation for Hutton's damages were postponed 'until a fortnight has passed, on account of Custom making.'[114] It is not clear whether this refers to the head chief who had died by late September 1843 or to the newly elected chief or one of the minor chiefs, although the reference to a fortnight's custom-making suggests that this was somebody recently deceased. According to Bouche, from 1835 to 1844 Agoué was ruled by caboceer 'Toyi', who was succeeded by Kodjo-Dahoménou (1844–1846).[115]

The correspondence between the chiefs of Agoué on one hand, and, on the other, Hutton's agent at Agoué and the British officials was conducted by John Quarvee ('Quarvil', 'Cuavi', 'Quarver'), who called himself chief of 'English town': 'I have assumed and bear the title of English Cabboceer, and it is and will be my Chief aim to shew by my conduct that I am in heart a friend of the Sons of that Noble Nation.'[116] The second part of this statement was evidently aimed to placate the British, who put considerable pressure on the chiefs of Agoué, and Quarvee in particular, to find the party who had caused the fire and pay Hutton's damages. English town probably had its origin in the establishment of Hutton's factory at Agoué and the immigration of Sierra Leoneans. The Sierra Leoneans were former slaves, many of them Yoruba by origin, who had been captured by the British navy's anti-slave trade squadron from 'illegal' slave vessels, liberated and settled in the British colony of Sierra Leone. From the late 1830s, a considerable number of them immigrated into the Bight of Benin, to return to their homelands or seek a livelihood in the coastal settlements. The majority settled at Lagos and Abeokuta but others established themselves at other places, including Agoué.[117] At Agoué, at least some of them settled in the Saro or Salo quarter, the name of which derives from the local term for these immigrants. It lay to the south-east of the

---

[113] TNA: CO96/4, incl. 7 in no.8: Hill, Cape Coast Castle, 21 Mar. 1844: J. Quarvee, Ahguay, 28 Dec. 1843.
[114] TNA: CO96/4, incl.1 in no.31: Hill, Cape Coast Castle, 1 July 1844: J.W. Hanson, Ahguay, 13 May 1844.
[115] Bouche, *Sept ans*, 302. According to Pierucci, Toyi's original name was 'Yaovi Siko', and 'Jakao' may be a corruption of this (['History'], 8).
[116] TNA: CO96/4 incl. 2 in no.8: Hill, Cape Coast Castle, 21 March 1844: J. Quarvee, Ahguay, 14 Nov. 1843. 'Quarvee' is possibly a corruption of 'Kuaku-vi', as indicated by the spelling of his name in one of Hanson's letters: 'John Quacovie' (TNA: CO96/4, incl.1 in no.31: Hill, CCC, 1 July 1844: J.W. Hanson, Ahguay, 13 May 1844). 'Kuaku', a variant of the Akan name for boys born on a Wednesday, is one of the names used by Adjigo people (Agbanon, *Histoire*, 137). In 1859, it was noted that 'he is perfectly acquainted with Fante [= the language]' (WMMS: West Africa Correspondence, Box 263: William West, Cape Coast, 6 June 1859).
[117] Christopher Fyfe, *A History of Sierra Leone* (London, 1962), 212–3, 227–8, 317–8; J. Herskovits Kopytoff, *A Preface to Modern Nigeria: The 'Sierra Leoneans' in Yoruba, 1830–1890* (Madison and London, 1965), chap. 3.

settlement and is presumably identifiable with 'English Town', which would agree with the information given in Duncan's account that Hutton's factory lay 'on the south-side of the town, facing the sea, distant half a mile, over a bed of loose dry sand'.[118] In 1849 the Sierra Leoneans sent a representative, John Cole, with a petition to the recently appointed British Vice-Consul at Ouidah: 'Your Petitioners beg to say that they are Liberated Slaves from Sierra Leone under Queen's protection whom [sic] comes here into this Country with leave and we are now amongst the Portuguese.'[119] In 1859, a visiting missionary noted that the Sierra Leone people had 'located themselves in different parts of Ahguay.'[120]

'Portuguese town' owed its existence to the immigration and settlement of the Afro-Brazilians, comprising Portuguese, Brazilian and Spanish slave traders from Ouidah, who settled there after 1839, and liberated slaves from Brazil, who began to arrive in sizeable numbers after the slave revolts in Bahia in 1835.[121] However, as indicated by van Zütphen's account (and discussed above), at least one Afro-Brazilian, Aité, had settled there by 1831. Due to this Afro-Brazilian immigration, Agoué's population increased dramatically from the 1840s. By 1863, when the Catholic missionary Francesco Borghero visited the place, there were 'about a hundred Christians, all returned from Brazil after their liberation' at Agoué. Many of the immigrants were Yoruba, but there were also Fon, Mahi, Hausa and Krepi.[122] They founded new quarters, which probably formed part of 'Portuguese Town', where they settled largely according to their ethnic origin. Fonkome was settled by Fon, Mahi and Yoruba; Diata (or Idi-Ata) by Yoruba, and Hausakome by Hausa, Mahi and Yoruba, although it is not clear when exactly this happened.[123] Referring to the 1870s, Bouche noted that the (Brazilian) Muslims had their own quarter (probably Hausakome).[124] Further, there was Zokikome, the quarter of Joaquim d'Almeida, the most successful and prominent of the returnees ('Zoki' or 'Joqui' being a short form for Joaquim) (see Chapter 6). The settlement in several quarters according to ethnic origin is remarkable, especially in comparison with Ouidah, where the returnees established themselves mainly in one quarter, called Maro.[125] One part of the explanation is perhaps that Agoué was a recent foundation and rather small when the liberated slaves arrived, and that the number of the immigrants

---

[118] Duncan, *Travels*, i, 91.
[119] TNA: FO84/775, incl. in J. Duncan, British Fort Whydah, 22 Sept. 1849: Petition by George Cole, Ahguay, 14 Sept. 1849. For another copy, see CO96/20, incl. in Eddisbury, [London], 6 Feb. 1850.
[120] WMMS: West Africa Correspondence, Box 263: William West, Cape Coast, 6 June 1859.
[121] See Strickrodt, '"Afro-Brazilians"', 213–224.
[122] Borghero, *Journal*, 123, 124; Bouche, 'Notes', 98.
[123] Archives Mgr. Robert Codjo Sastre, Lokossa/ Benin: Pierucci, ['Histoire'], 13. For more detail about Agoué's quarters, see Akibode, 'Contribution', 20–9.
[124] Bouche, *Sept ans*, 302.
[125] Law, *Ouidah*, 180–1.

in proportion to that of the indigenous inhabitants was comparatively large. Another is probably the lack of a strong centralising political authority, such as existed in Ouidah.

It is clear that the big slave traders at Agoué, such as the de Souzas, Joaquim d'Almeida and (in the 1860s) Francisco José de Medeiros, must have had significant influence on the political life at Agoué, although there is little documentation for this. In the case of the de Souzas at least, this is suggested by the fact that after the fire at the Hutton factory in 1843, Francisco Felix de Souza requested the chiefs of Agoué to come to him at Ouidah in order to discuss the matter, which they promptly did.[126]

Duncan, who visited Agoué in 1845, does not throw any further light on its political organisation. However, he gives a (rather unsympathetic) description of the chief who welcomed him when he first arrived there in February 1845: 'a tall fat man, with bloodshot eyes… He wore a country cloth round his loins, and a light blue hat, too small for him. On his wrists he had heavy iron bracelets, rudely manufactured.'[127] Duncan does not identify this individual and therefore it is not clear whether this was the 'Portuguese caboceer', i.e. the head chief of Agoué, or the caboceer of English town, John Quarvee. In 1850, F. E. Forbes visited Agoué and described it as 'a small, not over clean town, although an extensive trading port.'[128] According to him, it was – like Little Popo – 'a republic, and as far as I could ascertain, ruled by a senate, with no direct head.'[129] In early 1852, T. G. Forbes visited the town in order to conclude the anti-slave trade treaty.[130] After his arrival on the morning of 23 January 1852, he sent a message to 'the Chiefs' and in response was told that 'next morning they would be prepared to hear the Treaty read.' Forbes and his companions stayed overnight at Thomas Hutton's factory. At midday on the following day, the chiefs and roughly two hundred followers assembled in Hutton's yard to have the treaty read to them. They reportedly agreed to its conditions, but nevertheless postponed its conclusion because they wanted 'to consult with a King who was over them, some three day journeys inland, but [I] could not find out either name of King or Town'.[131] This is presumably a reference to the king at Glidji, whose seniority Agoué acknowledged although in a practical sense he did not have any influence there. This is indicated by Borghero, who in

[126] TNA: incls. 3 and 5 in CO96/4 no.8: Hill, Cape Coast Castle, 21 Mar. 1844: Sergeant Cato and Private Derrick Holdbrook, Ahguay, 14 Nov. 1843; Francisco Felis de Souza, Whydah, 11 Nov. 1843.
[127] Duncan, *Travels*, i, 91–2.
[128] Forbes, *Dahomey*, i, 104. Forbes' visit to Agoué took place on 7 March 1850 and lasted only a few hours.
[129] *Ibid.*, 102.
[130] TNA: FO84/893, incl. in Hamilton, [London], 10 Apr. 1852: T. G. Forbes, 'Philomel', at Whydah, 5 February 1852 (23/24 Jan. 1852).
[131] *Ibid.*

1863 observed that the caboceer of Agoué 'recognizes himself dependent on the king of Glidji, but in fact he is independent and governs Agoué and his territory with entire independence.'[132] However, if the chiefs of Agoué really were referring to the king at Glidji on this occasion, they considerably exaggerated the distance to the king's residence. It is also conceivable that they were merely playing for time, possibly in order to consult the slave traders at Ouidah, with whom – as Freeman had noted – they were closely linked in the slave trade.

To avoid delay, Forbes decided to proceed along the coast to conclude the treaties with the other settlements and then return to Agoué. During his absence, on 26 January 1852, there was a fire at Agoué which destroyed the town, 'Mr. Hutton's Wooden house being the only one left standing, but very much shaken from the explosion of Powder Magazine'.[133] According to Bouche, all the houses but three were destroyed by this fire, which was remembered as the 'fire of Marcellina', after the name of the woman at whose house it first broke out.[134] Forbes returned to Agoué on 1 February and 'after a little palavering' the treaty was concluded.[135] It was signed by five people, 'John Quaver English Caboceer', 'Atta-catri-ger Portuguese [Caboceer]', 'John Ephraim', 'Ar-dotai' and 'Atoo'.[136] The name of the Portuguese caboceer, 'Atta-catri-ger', appears to be a corruption of Ata Cataraya-gan, with Ata being a title used for the Adjigo chief, signifying 'father' or 'lord'.[137] As noted above, according to local traditions Cataraya was the name of the second chief of Agoué, that is Komlagan's successor, suggesting that Atta-catri-ger was a descendant of the former. At this time Hanto-Tona ruled (1846–1858).[138]

In March 1859, West and Bernasko, the missionaries, visited Agoué. According to them, 'Ahguay, although in appearance but one town, is divided into two and called by the respective names of English, and Portuguese towns.'[139] The chief of English town is identified as 'Old King John', that is John Quarvee, the title 'king' clearly indicating his political aspirations. He is reported to have supported the foundation of a school at English Town a few months earlier, which was attended by 65 children. At the time of the missionaries' visit, a new 'Caboceer' of Portuguese town was due to be inaugurated. Trouble was anticipated as John Quarvee

---

[132] Borghero, *Journal*, 123.

[133] TNA: FO84/893, incl. in Hamilton, [London], 10 April 1852: T. G. Forbes, 'Philomel', at Whydah, 5 Feb. 1852 (27 Jan. 1852).

[134] Bouche, *Sept ans*, 302–3.

[135] TNA: FO84/893, incl. in Hamilton, [London], 10 April 1852: T. G. Forbes, 'Philomel', at Whydah, 5 Feb. 1852 (1 Feb. 1852).

[136] *Ibid.*, T. G. Forbes: 'Schedule of Treaties' (1852). Cf. Cornevin, *Histoire du Dahomey*, 278–9.

[137] H. M. Kponton, 'Histoire des guin d'Aného et de Glidji', *Traditions Historiques du Bas-Togo*, ed. N. L. Gayibor (Niamey, 1992), 237–61, p. 257.

[138] Bouche, *Sept ans*, 302; Pelofy, *Histoire*, 6, Pierucci, ['Histoire'], 7.

[139] WMMS: West Africa Correspondence, Box 263: William West, Cape Coast, 6 June 1859.

was expected to interfere in the succession, but in the end this did not happen and inauguration went without disturbances. The new caboceer of Portuguese town is not named but can be identified as Kumi Aguidi, who is first documented in May 1860.[140] The missionaries also mention another person of influence at English Town, 'Miss Havie', 'a lady of considerable influence [...] who at the commencement of the school sent seven of her young slaves to be instructed. The golden trinkets about her person, were more numerous and costly than any I had seen, except at Cape Coast or Elmina.'[141] Miss Havie's importance in Agoué's political life is also suggested by the fact that she was one of the notables who in 1861 and 1864 signed the peace agreements with Little Popo, which were negotiated by the British navy.[142]

In October 1859, a British naval officer, William Bowden, visited Agoué to warn the local chiefs about slaves being shipped from their town. His report throws more light on the relationship between the English and the Portuguese towns as well as the political situation at Agoué more generally.[143] He first met the English caboceer, i.e. John Quarvee, who rather meekly assured him that he 'had nothing to do with Slaves, and had always acted up to the Treaty, that none of his people were concerned in it, that his part of the town was smallest; and poorest, and that he had no influence in the Portuguese town.' Bowden then saw the 'Portuguese Caboceer', probably Kumi Aguidi, whose initial response less compliant: '[H]e said he had heard of a treaty, but never saw it, that the old Caboceer was dead, and that he belonged to another family...' However, Bowden reminded him of the British naval power and threatened reprisals, citing Lagos as an example, which made the caboceer more 'humble'. He agreed to have the treaty read to his followers, which was done on following day: 'both Caboceers with their Chiefs and followers, came to the Mission house, where the Treaty was read, and explained; and they promised to keep it strictly.' The Portuguese caboceer's statement that he was of a different family seems to contradict information from van Zütphen and retrospective local traditions that the office of the caboceer was the prerogative of one particular family, but possibly 'family' here just refers to different branches of the ruling family.

[140] TNA: FO84/1115, incl. in Slave Trade no.30: G. Brand, Lagos, 2 May 1860: The 'inhabitants and merchants of Agoué', Agoué, 5 Mar. 1860. According to Bouche, 'Coumin-Aguidi' became caboceer of Agoué after the death of Hanto-Tona in 1858 (*Sept ans*, 302; Bouche, 'Notes', 96).
[141] WMMS: West Africa Correspondence, Box 263: William West, Cape Coast, 6 June 1859.
[142] In some of the copies of the treaties, including that published in the Parliamentary Papers, she appears as a male, evidently due to miscopying. See TNA: ADM123/66, incl. 2 in no 2, A.P. Eardley Wilmot, 'Rattlesnake', off Whydah, 11 July 1864: Agreement with Chiefs of Aghwey, 20 April 1864 ('Iley Vi, her mark'); CO96/66, incl. in Hammond, [London], 20 Sept. 1864: ('Iley Vi, his mark'); *PP* Slave Trade 1864, Class A, incl.3 in no.128: ('Iley Vi, his mark').
[143] TNA: FO84/1123, incl. 2 in Admiralty, [London] 29 Feb. 1860: W. Bowden, 'Medusa', Lagos, 21 Nov. 1859.

After the meeting, the English caboceer privately approached Bowden and requested 'that an English Agent, or Commandant might be sent to govern them, and instruct them in what was right, as at Lagos, & Quitta.' Lagos had been bombarded by the British in 1851, on the pretext that the local ruler, Kosoko, continued to engage in the slave trade. He was deposed and another king installed, Akitoye, whom the British regarded as a compliant ally. The British had also established a consulate.[144] Keta had fallen under British jurisdiction in 1850, when the British took over the Danish settlements on the West African Coast, including Fort Prindsensten. John Quarvee was playing with fire when requesting the British intervention, evidently hoping that their support would propel him to power at Agoué. In a letter to the Wesleyan missionaries from November 1859, he signed as 'English Caboceer of British Ahguay'.[145]

Grand Popo in the 1840s and 1850s

Grand Popo remained an independent state in this period. Contemporary documents show that neither George Lawson at Little Popo nor the de Souzas at Ouidah nor the king of Dahomey had any influence there. This is suggested by an episode in 1846, when the English trader John Marman had (unspecified) problems at Grand Popo and requested the assistance of Antonio de Souza at Ouidah. The latter however was unable to help, replying that 'I have not interposition [at] all over the Grand Popo people, which are not subject of this kingdom...'[146] Marman's agent at Little Popo was George Latty Lawson and it can be assumed that if the Lawsons had had any influence with the people of Grand Popo, they would have interfered on Marman's behalf. Similarly, in 1851 goods belonging to Thomas Hutton were confiscated at Grand Popo when the canoemen refused to pay the toll for passing along the lagoon. According to one of the canoemen involved, 'I tell the people [= collectors of the toll at Grand Popo], that Mr Hutton pay the King of Dahomey; they said it was no matter, whether Mr Hutton pay the King of Dahomey or not.'[147] In 1852, the king of Dahomey told officers of the British navy that his dominions extended no further than to the Bouche du Roi, to the east of Grand Popo.[148]

In this year, the anti-slave trade treaty with the British navy was signed

---

[144] See Kristin Mann, *Slavery and the Birth of an African City: Lagos, 1760–1900* (Bloomington and Indianapolis, 2007), chapt. 3, particularly 91–102; Robert S. Smith, *The Lagos Consulate, 1851–1861* (London and Basingstoke 1978), chap. 2.
[145] WMMS: West Africa Correspondence, Box 263: John QuanVee, Ahguay, 11 Nov. 1859, quoted in William West, Cape Coast, 10 Feb. 1860.
[146] Jones/ Sebald, *African Family Archive*, 1.57, Antonio de Souza, Whydah, 15 Feb. 1846.
[147] Fraser, *Dahomey*, 124–5 (7 Nov. 1851).
[148] TNA: FO84/886, Geezo, King of Dahomey, Dahomey, Cannah, 12 Jan. 1852.

by two chiefs, 'Al-lee-far' and 'John Bassora'.[149] In 1860 a British naval officer, who visited the place to remind the chiefs of the terms of treaty, noted that 'Al-Lee Far […] it appears is now King'.[150] The latter resided at Agbanaken, which is described as 'a large town about two miles from one of the branches of the lagoon & some 4 miles from the beach. There are several other Villages & towns on both sides of the Vista [.] Al Lee Far is the head or king of all the Country near.' By then, John Bassora had associated himself with 'French town' (which presumably had its origin in the establishment of Régis's factory there in late 1857 or early 1858) and called himself 'John Bassard'. The two notables had quarrelled and Bassard refused to attend the meeting at Al-lee-far's place because 'they were not friends.'[151]

The war between Agoué and Little Popo, 1860 to 1866

The relationship between Agoué on the one hand and, on the other, Little Popo and Glidji seems to have been one of (mainly) suppressed enmity until 1860. In 1825 Clapperton noted that after their defeat in the civil war at Little Popo, the people of Agoué had 'twice or three times' returned to attack Little Popo.[152] According to Bouche, Komlagan himself undertook two expeditions, his successor Catraya also fought Little Popo and Hanto-Tona undertook one expedition against Little Popo.[153] The suspicion and bad feeling which existed between the two places is also indicated by the fact that after the fires at Agoué in 1843, the local chiefs immediately suspected that they had been caused by the Little Popo people.[154] For the Lawsons, Agoué remained off limits until at least the late 1840s, as indicated by George Latty Lawson's statement in 1848 that 'I am sorry to say that Ahguay is not a place for one to venture'.[155]

In 1860 open conflict erupted between the two places following a civil war at Agoué. The defeated party, led by Pedro Kodjo aka Pedro Pinto da Silveira, took refuge in Little Popo, where he called upon the people of Little Popo, Glidji and other places to join the fight against Agoué and further hired mercenaries from Anlo.[156] This war lasted until 1866, after

---

[149] TNA: FO84/893, incl. in Hamilton, [London], 10 Apr. 1852: T. G. Forbes: 'Schedule of Treaties' (1852).
[150] TNA: FO84/1124, incl. in Admiralty, [London] 13 July 1860: W. Bowden, 'Medusa', Whydah, 31 Jan. 1860.
[151] *Ibid*.
[152] Clapperton, *Hugh Clapperton*, 89.
[153] Bouche, 'Notes', 96.
[154] TNA: CO96/2, incl. in T. Hutton, Cape Coast, 24 Oct. 1843: J. H. Ahkurst, Ahguay, 3 Oct. 1843.
[155] Jones/ Sebald, *African Family Archive*, 1.178, G. L. Lawson, New London, Popo, 3 Sept. 1848.
[156] Pedro Kodjo (Cudjoe/Kodgo/Cogio/Quadjo/Kuadjo) was known by a number of names

which it seems to have petered out, or at least the documentation has.

Retrospective accounts agree that the war at Agoué was caused by Pedro Kodjo but give different explanations. According to Agoué traditions, Pedro Kodjo harboured a grudge against Kumi Aguidi, the caboceer, because the latter had been elected chief in preference to himself. According to Bouche, writing about fifteen years after the event, Pedro Kodjo decided to topple the new caboceer, 'he armed his slaves and opened the fire against the town, but a lively riposte forced him to flee and seek refuge at Little Popo.'[157] According to Agbanon II, who gives the viewpoint from Glidji and Little Popo, where Pedro Kodjo sought refuge, the war had developed from a quarrel between the latter and Joaquim d'Almeida, a wealthy slave trader at Agoué, over a debt. However, while it is plausible that competition for the lucrative trade was the underlying cause of the conflict, this account is evidently wrong as regards its direct cause, since d'Almeida had died in 1857.[158] A possible explanation is that this story is based on the support which the d'Almeida family along with most of the Afro-Brazilians in the town gave Kumi Aguidi during the war.

There is abundant contemporary documentation of this war, due to the involvement of officers of the British navy and missionaries of the Société des Missions Africaines at Ouidah, who at various points attempted to negotiate a peace. The beginning of the war is documented because the houses and property of two British subjects, Joseph Dawson, the former Wesleyan Methodist missionary who had meanwhile turned trader, and Bernasko, who still was a missionary, were among its first casualties. Dawson and Bernasko requested assistance from a British man of war, which caused fears among the people of Agoué that they would be punished. These fears were by no means unreasonable, given the tenor of the 1859 interview between the naval officer and Kumi Aguidi. Therefore, they wrote a number of explanatory letters to the British Consul at Lagos and offered to pay for the damages suffered by the missionary and ex-missionary.[159] One of these letters, signed by 33 'inhabitants and merchants' of Agoué as well as Kumi Aguidi, gives a detailed account of the events.[160]

(cont.) which were used in different spheres. 'Pedro Kodjo' appears to have been his local name, that is the name by which he was known among the indigenous population at Agoué and Little Popo (Borghero, *Journal*, 124–5; Bouche, *Sept ans*, 303; Zöller, *Das Togoland*, 166, 168, 171). 'Pedro Pinto da Silveira' appears to have been his Afro-Brazilian and business name (TNA: FO84/1115, incl. in Slave Trade no.30: Consul G. Brand, Lagos, 2 May 1860: The 'inhabitants and merchants of Agoué', Agoué, 5 Mar. 1860; Burton, *Mission*, i, 75n.) 'Kodjo Landjékpo' is used in retrospective accounts from local traditions but is not documented in the contemporary sources (Agbanon II, *Histoire*, 46, 81; Pierucci, ['Histoire'], 19).

[157] Bouche, 'Notes', 96. Cf. Bouche, *Sept ans*, 303; Pelofy, 'Histoire', 7–8; Pierucci, ['Histoire'], 19–20.

[158] Agbanon II, *Histoire*, 81–5. Joaquim d'Almeida had died by 9 July 1857, when his will was read at Bahia. See Verger, *Os Libertos*, 121.

[159] TNA: FO84/1115, Slave Trade no.30, G. Brand, Lagos, 2 May 1860 (incls.).

[160] *Ibid.*, incl. in Slave Trade no.30: G. Brand, Lagos, 2 May 1860: 'Inhabitants and merchants

Another, slightly different, version of the events was given by the chiefs of Agoué in 1866.[161] These accounts suggest that the immediate occasion of the conflict was Pedro Kodjo's imprisonment on 1 March 1860 of a diviner from Mahi who had been in Kumi Aguidi's service at Agoué. The reason for Pedro Kodjo's action was a debt owed to him by the diviner. Pedro Kodjo defied Kumi Aguidi's request to release the man, prompting Kumi Aguidi to seize one of Pedro Kodjo's dependants in order to force him to comply. However, this failed to have the desired effect; instead of giving up his prisoner, Pedro Kodjo and his followers attacked Agoué on 3 March 1860. On the following day they were forced to admit defeat, at least temporarily, and fled to Little Popo.

There is little information regarding Pedro Kodjo's life and career before the civil war, and almost all of it is retrospective. According to Bouche, he was a rich and influential slave trader who had spent some time in Brazil, where he had learnt the trade of a cooper.[162] This implies that he was a returned ex-slave, which however is contested in local and family traditions. Ouidah sources state that he had been in the service of F. F. de Souza at Ouidah and trained as a cooper there.[163] Recent family traditions also note that he had been trained at Ouidah rather than in Brazil, but some of his children had been sent to the latter place for education.[164] According to Agbanon II, Pedro Kodjo's mother was Sasi Aheba, the daughter of Sekpon who, as noted before, is said to have been one of the chiefs of the beach at Little Popo.[165] The letter by the chiefs of Agoué from 1866 gives further detail, stating that Pedro Kodjo 'is a native of Little Popo, and because his mother was a daughter of one of the late Caboceers of Ahgway, he obtained a piece of house [sic?] to the windward of our town.'[166] Zöller met Pedro Kodjo in the 1880s and noted that he was 'close to ninety', which would mean he was born in the late eighteenth or early nineteenth century.[167] Burton, writing in 1863, noted that he was 'a well-known slaver' and that one of his sons, Domingo Francisco da Silveira, managed the affairs of José Francisco dos Santos aka José Alfaiate

---

(cont.) of Agoué', Agoué, 5 Mar. 1860. Apart from Kumi Aguidi, all the signatories of this letter were Afro-Brazilians, as shown by their Portuguese names. Among them is Francisco José de Medeiros, who also signed the peace agreement of the chiefs of Agoué from 1864 as a witness. This disproves the statement by Agbanon II that de Medeiros was one of Pedro Kodjo's followers (*Histoire*, 81). For de Medeiros, see Chapter 6, pp. 207–8.

[161] TNA: ADM123/73, incl. in no. 8: Caboceer Kumi, Ahguay, 17 Mar. 1866: The chiefs of Agoué, Ahgway, 16 Jan. 1866.

[162] Bouche, *Sept ans*, 303. Cf. Bouche, 'Notes', 96; Zöller, *Das Togoland*, 171.

[163] Reynier, 'Eléments sur la reorganisation du commandement indigène à Ouidah (1917)', *Mémoire du Bénin*, 2 (Cotonou, 1993), 29–73, p.43.

[164] Léon da Silveira, p.c., 29 Aug. 2000, Aného, Togo.

[165] Agbanon II, *Histoire*, 46.

[166] TNA: ADM123/73 incl. in no.8: Caboceer Kumei, Ahguay, 17 Mar. 1866: Chiefs of Ahgway, Ahgway, 16 Jan. 1866.

[167] Zöller, *Das Togoland*, 171.

at Ouidah.[168] According to Dolben, a British naval officer who visited Little Popo in 1861, there was a close connection between Pedro Kodjo and the King of Dahomey (or more likely perhaps the traders at Ouidah): 'several bags of cowries were sent down [from the King of Dahomey] to Kodgo some little time ago. Kodgo stated that they were in return for goods, that the Dahomey people stole from him, when they had war with Little Popo.'[169] Dolben refers to him as 'a Portuguese mulatto', an error probably based on his name and his ability to speak Portuguese, which was also noted by Borghero.[170] The relations between Pedro Kodjo and the Ouidah traders suffered during the war, in which the latter sided with Agoué, as is suggested by Dolben. This is confirmed by Borghero, who in 1863 noted that Pedro Kodjo was the bogeyman with whom the people in Dahomey frightened their children when they misbehaved.[171]

Dawson and Bernasko claimed that the destruction of their house and property had been carried out on Kumi Aguidi's orders. The chiefs of Agoué denied this, explaining that it had happened by mistake: 'Our boys and people who came from bush to see the war, unfortunately supposed that Messrs Dawson & Bernasko had something to do with Pedro Kudjo, broke into their stores and plundered'.[172] However, there may have been more to it because the war would have been a good opportunity for Kumi Aguidi to rid Agoué of the English influence and teach John Quarvee and the inhabitants of English town a lesson. At the very least, this incident shows that there was suspicion and ill-feeling against the people of English Town, as they were supposed to have played a part in the rebellion and supported the adversaries of the local authority. On 11 March 1860 a vessel of the British navy proceeded to Agoué, together with Bernasko and Dawson, to negotiate an agreement between the latter and the chiefs of Agoué. It was agreed that Kumi Aguidi should pay $2,500 in compensation, which was half the amount Bernasko and Dawson had originally demanded.[173] However, Kumi Aguidi found it impossible to fulfil his part of the agreement, due to the disruption of the trade by the war. In April 1860 he wrote to the British Consul at Lagos, complaining that 'since we had civil war here no vessels ever anchored in this Place' and requesting the consul 'to give notice to all captains who come there to call here for

[168] Burton, *Mission*, i, 75n.
[169] TNA: FO84/1184, incl. 2 in Admiralty, 15 Apr. 1862: W.D.M. Dolben, 'Bloodhound', Cape Coast Castle, 18 Oct. 1861. Cf. *PP* Slave Trade 1862, incl. 2 in no.91: Edmonstone, 'Arrogant', Fernando Po, 3 March 1862: Dolben, 'Bloodhound', Cape Coast Castle, 18 Oct. 1861.
[170] Borghero, *Journal*, 125.
[171] *Ibid.*
[172] TNA: ADM123/73, incl. in no. 8: Caboceer Kumi, Ahguay, 17 Mar. 1866: The chiefs of Agoué, Ahgway, 16 Jan. 1866. See also FO84/1115, incl. in Slave Trade no.30: G. Brand, Lagos, 2 May 1860 (incls.).
[173] TNA: FO84/1115, incl. in Slave Trade no.30: G. Brand, Lagos, 2 May 1860: C.O. Allingham, 'Spitfire', off Quittah, 14 Apr. 1860.

trade, as the people get plenty of palm oil for trade and no vessel'.[174]

Meanwhile, Pedro Kodjo and his followers were rallying forces at Little Popo. In May 1860, Bernasko reported that they were 'very busy gathering troops to attack Ahguay. So the roads leading from this to all those places are very dangerous. The people of Little Popo, and Griji are preparing daily too to join this party to fight Ahguay.' He feared that the war would continue for a long time because these people had 'no powerful King over them', who, as is implied, would be able to impose a peace. Further, he noted that these developments had particularly serious consequences for the Sierra Leonean settlers, many of whom left for Ouidah or Lagos.[175]

According to information given by Thomas George Lawson in 1861, the war between Little Popo and Agoué began in October 1860.[176] This is confirmed by information from a Wesleyan missionary, who on 13 November 1860 noted that 'the civil war has recently broken out between the Popoes and the people of Ahguey.'[177] In the traditions of the Anlo, who were engaged as mercenaries by Pedro Kodjo, this is remembered as the first 'Agoué war'.[178] In January 1861, Bernasko reported 'that all the places from *Little Popo* to *Awoonah* [= Anlo] have concerted to join the fight against *Ahquay*.'[179] In October 1861, the naval officer Dolben visited the region to attempt to negotiate a peace agreement. It is not clear what had caused this initiative, but presumably it was connected with a letter by Thomas George Lawson from April 1861 which offered the sovereignty of Little Popo to the British and requested British protection in the war with Agoué. Lawson portrayed this war as a conflict between the slave traders at Agoué and their allies on the one hand and, on the other, the inhabitants of Little Popo who were engaged in 'legitimate' commerce, i.e. trade in commodities other than slaves.[180] However, Dolben first visited Agoué and was soon convinced that it was Pedro Kodjo and the people of Little Popo who were the aggressors and that the people of Agoué had merely defended themselves.[181] Dolben then went to Little Popo

---

[174] *Ibid.*, 'Caboceer Ecoome', Ahgway, 27 Apr. 1860.
[175] WMMS: West Africa Correspondence Box 263: Peter Bernasko, Whydah, 30 May 1860. For an example of a Sierra Leonean forced to leave Agoué at this time, see TNA: FO84/1115, incl. in Slave Trade no.41, Brand, Lagos, 5 June 1860: T. D. Reynolds, Great Popo, 29 May 1860; Jones/Sebald, *African Family Archive*, 1.128, J.H. Ahkurst, Ahguay, 2 Mar. 1848, n.40.
[176] TNA: CO267/270, T.G. Lawson, Freetown, 18 Apr. 1861.
[177] WMMS: West Africa Correspondence, Box 263: Henry Wharton, Cape Coast, 13 Nov. 1860.
[178] Greene, *Gender*, 133 n.62. Cf. Härtter, 'Einige Bausteine', II, p.480.
[179] *The Report of the Wesleyan-Methodist Missionary Society for the Year ending April, 1861* (London [1861]), 85 (author's emphasis).
[180] TNA: CO267/270, T.G. Lawson, Freetown, 18 Apr. 1861.
[181] TNA: FO84/1184, incl. 2 in Admiralty, [London], 15 April 1862: W. D. M. Dolben, 'Bloodhound', Cape Coast Castle, 18 Oct. 1861. This was published in the Parliamentary Papers in an abridged version: *PP* Slave Trade 1862, Class A, incl. 2 in no.91, Edmonstone, 'Arrogant', Fernando Po, 3 March 1862: W. D. M. Dolben, 'Bloodhound', Cape Coast Castle, 18 Oct. 1861.

to have the chiefs there sign the peace agreement, which however was refused. Dolben's report of his negotiations give an interesting insight in the political situation at Little Popo at the time.

> I proceeded to [Little Popo,] landed, & sent for the Chiefs: afterwards also for Kodgo, as I found that the Chiefs would do nothing without his opinion. The first question I asked was if they acknowledged Lawson [= Thomas George Lawson, who was in Sierra Leone] as rightful King, which they answered in the affirmative. I then told them, that he had asked for English protection for his Village & that if they would sign a paper which I read to them (similar to that signed by the people of Aghwey) that they would be under our protection so long as they kept peace. I had not told them that the Aghwey Chiefs had signed – so they said that I must get them to sign a treaty first. I then told them that I had one signed on board by them. At last after some palaver amongst themselves they said, that Lawson did not do right in writing to England without consulting them first – that they could look after themselves & did not want peace. They had a regular camp outside with about 500 men in it commanded by Pedro Kodgo & they were about to make another attack on Aghwey. I should think it very probable that if Lawson returns, he will meet with a similar reception, as King Pepple did in the Bonny. I belief that the Chiefs would acknowledge him, but that Kodgo has so much authority (which of course he would partially if not entirely lose by Lawson's return) that he will never allow him to land if he can help it.[182]

Pedro Kodjo was reported to have attacked Agoué again afterwards, which, according to the chiefs of Agoué, was the fourth time he had done so. Dolben had not been given orders to protect Agoué and therefore did not interfere in these events but only watched them, which annoyed and disappointed the chiefs, who felt that having signed the peace agreement they were entitled to British protection.[183] It is likely that it was during this attack that Agoué was burnt to the ground. Irénée Laffitte, one of the missionaries of the Société des Missions Africaines at Ouidah who visited Agoué in 1862, reported that the town had been burnt in the previous year. At the time of his visit, 'the Portuguese town had hardly begun to emerge from its ruins.'[184] Although there is no record of further attacks for the following three years, the situation remained tense and trade interrupted. Both parties patrolled the lagoon with war canoes, blocking the

---

[182] *Ibid*. King Pepple was exiled, returned, but exercised little authority.
[183] TNA: ADM123/73, incl. in no.8: Caboceer Kumei, Ahguay, 17 Mar. 1866: Chiefs of Ahgway, 16 Jan. 1866.
[184] Laffitte, *Le Pays*, 42; also Borghero, *Journal*, 125.

passage.¹⁸⁵ In early 1863 Borghero, another missionary of the Société de Missions Africaines at Ouidah, visited the region in an attempt to establish peace between the two towns. He had been requested to do so by 'several of the principal merchants of Ouidah' because the war 'very much hampered their trade and communication on the coast of Agoué'.¹⁸⁶ At Agoué, the caboceer, evidently Kumi Aguidi, and chiefs also requested his assistance in negotiating a peace. They gave Borghero 'full power to negotiate', leaving the terms of agreement at his discretion. Borghero then went to Little Popo. He travelled by canoe along the lagoon to Adjido, where the canoemen from Agoué remained because 'they would be killed if they went to Little Popo.' This implies that Adjido was neutral in the war and generally independent from Little Popo. He used another set of canoemen to cross the lagoon from Adjido to Little Popo, where he met Pedro Kodjo, the 'Caboceer of Little Popo' and discussed 'the Agoué affair' with him. However, Pedro Kodjo refused a definitive statement and requested time for reflection. Borghero allowed him two days, using this time to explore the country around Porto Seguro. When he returned to Little Popo on 11 February 1863, Pedro Kodjo was still reluctant. Running out of patience, Borghero threatened him with the anger of God, which appeared to 'terrify' Pedro Kodjo and induced him to come to an agreement. Originally, he had insisted that he should be reimbursed all the damages and expenses which he had suffered in the war, but now he compromised: 'He said that, if Agoué wants peace, he would consent not to attack any more if he himself was not attacked. But he declared all reconciliation on his part impossible.' He then shook hands with Borghero, took the cross that the latter was carrying and swore to keep his promise. Borghero returned to Agoué where he reported the outcome of his negotiations to the chiefs. In his account he also noted that it was not the Little Popo people themselves who were engaged in the war but that Pedro Kodjo had hired mercenaries from the neighbouring areas.¹⁸⁷

In 1864 a vessel of the British navy went to Agoué to demand payment of the debt which the chiefs still owed to Bernasko and Dawson.¹⁸⁸ The naval officer used the occasion to make another attempt to negotiate a peace deal between the two towns. According to the chiefs of Agoué, four attacks had been made by Little Popo on Agoué, three before the peace agreement with the British navy in 1861 and one afterwards. This time, the peace treaty was signed by both Agoué and Little Popo. Both towns

---

¹⁸⁵ Laffitte, *Le Pays*, 53–59.
¹⁸⁶ Borghero, *Journal*, 122–7. In the conflict, Borghero (and the Catholic missionaries generally) sided with Agoué, which impressed him as 'one of the most favourable points for the establishment of a mission' (124).
¹⁸⁷ *Ibid*.
¹⁸⁸ TNA: ADM123/66, no.2, A. P. E. Wilmot, 'Rattlesnake', off Whydah, 11 July 1864 (incls.). Cf. *PP* Slave Trade 1864, Class A, no.128: Wilmot to the Secretary to the Admiralty, 'Rattlesnake', off Whydah, 11 July 1864 (incls.).

promised to abstain from attacks. Agoué reserved the right, in the event of 'the person calling himself Pedro Cudjoe, or any other person from Little Popo, attacking or molesting our town without the concurrence of the Head Men of Little Popo', to defend itself and 'deal with the person or persons according to our native laws, without making war on Little Popo.' Nine notables, including Kumi Aguidi, signed the treaty. Francisco José de Medeiros and Joseph Dawson signed as witnesses. The chiefs of Little Popo for their part initially agreed that if anybody from Little Popo who they found difficult to punish, attacked Agoué, they would 'give the person or persons up to the first British man-of war arriving here, to be conveyed without restraint during the passage to Whydah, where they will be landed and allowed to follow their own desires.' However, subsequently the chiefs revoked their promise, explaining that it would be impossible for them to surrender Pedro Kodjo because 'he is a native of this place, Little Popo, and there would be great disturbance between us and his family, and it would raise a civil war.' Instead, they promised 'not to make any more war, and if he declares war we will stop him, and if he is determined on it, we will give information to any of Her Majesty's ships of war in order that they may interfere.' Three 'Headmen of Little Popo' signed this agreement: Tobi Lawson, a member of the Lawson family; Segiro Agboku, who (as noted above) was one of the war generals at Badji; and Kwavi/Ouavi Hauta, who according to information from the GLL was one of the (late) George Lawson's 'captains' at Flamani.[189] James W. Lawson, another member of the Lawson family, and Joseph Dawson signed as witnesses.

A few months later, however, on 25 July 1864, the chiefs of Little Popo notified the British navy that the people of Agoué had abducted three people belonging to Little Popo and therefore broken the treaty, 'so the Treaty between us and Aghwey is no more.'[190] Due to this, the British navy regarded the treaty as annulled and did not feel themselves bound to protect Agoué any more, of which however they failed to notify the Agoué chiefs.[191] According to the latter, Pedro Kodjo again threatened to attack Agoué, but in the event nothing happened until 25 December 1865, when he approached with an army of mercenaries from Anlo. The Agoué people informed Dawson of the impending attack, who was able to call assistance from the British navy. One of the cruisers anchored off Agoué and fired on Pedro Kodjo's forces when they attacked, 'which frightened them away for that day and having burnt two villages on the other side of the Lagoon.'[192]

[189] Ibid.; Jones/ Sebald, *African Family Archive*, 7.12: Story of George Lawson I and his successors.
[190] TNA: ADM123/66, no. 4, The Chiefs of Little Popo, Little Popo, 25 July 1864.
[191] TNA: ADM123/73, no.11, G. S. P. Hornby, 16 Mar. 1866.
[192] Ibid., incl. in no.8, Caboceer Kumei, Ahguay, 17 Mar. 1866: Chiefs of Ahgway, 16 January 1866. This account is corroborated by a letter from a naval officer (TNA: FO84/1267, incl. in Admiralty, [London], 10 April 1866: Hornby, Accra, 11 Mar. 1866).

According to Greene, this conflict was called the 'Second Agoué War' by the Anlo.[193]

A few days later another naval officer arrived to arrange a truce between the two parties to 'enable the English property to be embarked before they proceed to hostilities'.[194] According to the chiefs of Agoué, he first went to Little Popo to talk to the chiefs there and then proceeded to Agoué.

> ... to our astonishment Captn. Peile and one Officer from the 'Torch' came to us with message from the hired Angwoona [= Anlo] and the Little Popo cheifs [sic], the message was as follows; – 'Both the hired cheifs & those of Little Popo wish us to send them Boy & Girl well dressed up with costly beads &c if we do not wish for any more war and that must be the term on which they would enter into friendly treaty with us.' Captn. Peile also desired us to sign a treaty to that effect and also to bind ourselves in the treaty that in case we go and attack Popo we were not to set fire into the Town nor to touch any thing belonging to the Europeans or any British subject and that all the former Treaties with us were cancelled.[195]

'Seeing the absurdity of this message', the chiefs of Agoué refused to sign this or any further treaties with the British navy and the people of Little Popo, explaining that they had always been the victims of attack, and that the British navy had not helped them but left them to fend for themselves. They then sent a letter to the Senior Officer of the West African Stations, giving their version of the history of the war and an explanation for their refusal to sign the treaty:

> We beg therefore to give you our reasons for refusing Captn Peile; – 1st because he dismashed [= dismissed] all the former interfereance [sic] &c &c made by the other Officers who have been before him, & also left us to fight our battles when he could easily have stopped by or driving the hired troops of the Angwoonah away as they were helping an evil doer and disturber of peace. 2nd Because he did not examin [sic] the case between us before he entered into the Treaty with the Angwoonas & the Little Popo cheifs [sic]. 3rd we refused to send the Boy & girl requested by the Cheifs of Angwoona & Little Popo, because the doing a thing of the kind one town binds himself to become tributary and why should we

---

[193] Greene, *Gender*, 133, Gustav Härtter, 'Einige Bausteine', III, *Beiträge zur Kolonialpolitik und Kolonialwirtschaft*, 3 (1901–02), 492–514, p. 494.

[194] TNA: FO84/1267, incl. in Admiralty, [London], 10 April 1866: Hornby, Accra, 11 Mar. 1866.

[195] TNA: ADM123/73, incl. in no.8: Caboceer Kumei, Ahguay, 17 Mar. 1866: Chiefs of Ahgway, 16 Jan. 1866.

submit to the parties whom we have beaten every time when they came to attack? 4th not last, we refused, because if a treaty made with one Town or country can be cancelled ~~without~~ [*sic*] by one of the party with whom the treaty is made without the knowledge of the Town or country it is not worth anymore of it; – further if the promise of Commodore or his orders can be cancelled by junior officer, we saw no reason of having any thing to do further with such Officer [.][196]

Another attack by Little Popo and Anlo mercenaries was launched on 8 January 1866 but was defeated.[197] The British navy was exasperated and refused to get involved any more. In March 1866 the Senior Officer informed the chiefs of Little Popo, Anlo ('Angola') and Agoué that 'Her Majesty's Officers have no wish to take part in either side in quarrels between Native tribes' and requested to be given eight weeks' notice if they were determined to continue to fight, in order to enable him to warn the European merchants in the area to remove their property out of the reach of harm. After the expiration of the eight weeks, the navy would not interfere in any way.[198] However, he did not abstain from giving a final piece of good advice to the chiefs of Agoué: 'as fighting is a bad thing, I think you had better make peace and keep up a brisk trade.'[199] This is the last time that reference is made to this conflict in the documents, perhaps because it ended soon afterwards. Another possibility, however, is that the war continued but documentation ceased after the British had lost interest in it.

Pedro Kodjo settled at Little Popo, where he came to play an important role in local – and briefly also in international – politics. He had lost his fortune in this war.[200] According to Agbanon II, he was reduced to trading pigs which he imported from Europe, fattened and then sold mainly to slave traders. This, however, is an apocryphal story, as the slave trade had ended by then.[201] At Agoué, Kumi Aguidi died in June 1873 and was succeeded in November 1873 by Atahounlé, often spelled 'Atanlé'.[202] According to Bouche, Kumi Aguidi's death and the choice of his successor

---

[196] *Ibid.*
[197] *Ibid.*
[198] *Ibid.*, no.9, G. S. P. Hornby, 15 Mar. 1866.
[199] *Ibid.* no.11, G. S. P. Hornby, 16 Mar. 1866.
[200] Zöller, *Das Togoland*, 181.
[201] Agbanon II, *Histoire*, 85.
[202] Bouche gives two different dates for Kumi Aguidi's death and the succession of Atahounlé. According to the article from 1875, Kumi Aguidi reigned until the end of December 1873 and was succeeded by Atanhounlé in the beginning of 1874 ('Notes', 97). In the 1885 account, however, he states that Kumi Aguidi died on 15 June 1873 and was succeeded by Atahounlé on 30 November 1873 (*Sept ans*, 302). The latter seems plausible, especially given that there had been a conflict about the succession, which presumably delayed the elections. It is possible that Kumi Aguidi died during the smallpox epidemic of 1873 (*ibid.*, 207, 301).

prompted new disorder. The civil war would have flared up again had not Atahounlé been eventually chosen due to the resolution of the Sierra Leoneans and the Mina chief of war.[203] The 'chief of war' can probably be identified with Todegereapu, whom Zöller met in 1884 and who signed the treaty for the French protectorate in 1885.[204] No further reference is made in the documents to John Quarvee. By the time of Bouche's sojourn at Agoué in 1874 there was a new English caboceer, Kouasi-Gazouza.[205]

The incidence of warfare both between and within states was not unique for this section of the West African coast in the period. Parallels can be drawn to elsewhere, such as the civil wars in Lagos in 1845, Badagry in 1851 and Bonny in the 1850s and 1860s.[206] It was a common contemporary British perception to see these wars as conflicts between slave traders and legitimate traders, but this interpretation has been subject to criticism from historians.[207] In the case of the western Slave Coast, the war of the 1820s was obviously too early to be connected with the transition from the slave trade to legitimate trade. In that of the 1860s it is interesting that Lawson presented it as a conflict between slave traders at Agoué and legitimate traders at Little Popo, although this was evidently a case of Lawson being aware of British prejudices and trying to appeal to them. However, in a looser way it is possible to make a connection between the 1860s wars and the problems of the commercial transition, in that the declining profitability of the trade may have led to increased conflicts over shares of trade, and maybe over taxes, and hence political office.[208]

---

[203] Bouche, 'Notes', 97.

[204] ANB: 1E12.4.1, 'Rapport de Monsieur Pornain, Lieutenant de Vaisseau, Adjudant du Commandant Superieur sur sa mission aux Popos pour y etablir le protectorat de la France' (1885); Pierucci, ['Histoire'], 34, 35; Zöller, *Das Togoland*, 181.

[205] Bouche, *Sept ans*, 189. For the name 'Kouasi'/Kuassi, see n. 111.

[206] See e.g., Smith, *Lagos Consulate*, 1–33; Caroline Sorensen-Gilmour, 'Badagry: 1784–1863: The Political and Commercial History of a Lagoonside Community in South-West Nigeria' (unpubl. PhD thesis, University of Stirling, 1995), chap. 9; K. Onukwa Dike, *Trade and Politics in the Niger Delta 1830–1885* (Oxford 1956), 128–202; Martin Lynn, 'Factionalism, Imperialism and the Making and Breaking of Bonny Kingship c. 1830–1885', *Revue Française d'Histoire d'Outre-mer*, 82 (1995), 1–24.

[207] See Robin Law, 'The Historiography of the Commercial Transition in Nineteenth-Century West Africa', *African Historiography: Essays in Honour of Jacob Ade Ajayi*, ed. Toyin Falola (Longman, 1993), 91–115.

[208] This has been suggested by Wariboko with regard to interstate wars in the Niger Delta and by Latham with regard to conflict within Old Calabar. See Waibinte E. Wariboko, 'New Calabar: The Transition from Slave- to Produce-Trading and the Political Problems in the Eastern Delta, 1848–1891', *Ports of the Slave Trade (Bights of Benin and Biafra)*, ed. Robin Law and Silke Strickrodt (Centre of Commonwealth Studies, University of Stirling, 1999), 153–68; A. J. H. Latham, *Old Calabar 1600–1891: The Impact of the International Economy upon a Traditional Society* (Oxford, 1973).

6

From slaves to palm oil
Afro-European trade, c. 1807 to 1870s

In 1807 Great Britain abolished its slave trade, making it illegal for British subjects to engage in the slave trade from 1 May 1807. From then on, there followed a number of acts and treaties with other countries which progressively restricted the slave trade. At the Congress of Vienna in 1815, the European nations stated their desire for the universal abolition of the trade while reserving their right to do so in their own time. In the same year, Portugal agreed to abolish the slave trade north of the equator. In order to enforce the abolition of the trade, British men of war patrolled the West African coast, among others, capturing suspicious vessels. From the 1840s they were joined, theoretically at least, by French, American and Portuguese cruisers. Captured vessels were sent for adjudication to the court of mixed commission at Sierra Leone and, after 1842, also to other places such as Luanda.

Initially, however, these developments did not have great consequences for trade on the western Slave Coast, which continued to export slaves as well as ivory and provisions. If anything, the region's trade was boosted because, in order to avoid the surveillance of the British cruisers, slaves were sent from the established ports on the Gold Coast to the western Slave Coast to be shipped from there. This was noted by a British trader in 1830: 'At Accra there is a great deal [of slaving]; the slaves are sent down, perhaps as far as [Little] Popoe, by small canoes…'[1] Another trader, who had been active on the coast between 1818 and the late 1830s, reported that 'There has been no slaving on the Gold Coast till you come down to [Little] Popo and Whydah', although in the late 1830s 'there was very little [slave trade]'. According to him, Little Popo's main trade was in ivory and dollars.[2] As

---

[1] PP Colonies Africa 1810–1830, p.82, Report from Select Committee on the Settlements of Sierra Leone and other Settlements on the West Coast of Africa (Capt. Isaac Spence, 5 July 1830).
[2] PP Colonies Africa 1842, i, p.108, Report from the Select Committee on the Coast of West Africa (Capt. H. Dring, 10 March 1842). Cf. *ibid.*, 120 (Capt. J. Courtland, 10 May 1842).

noted in the previous chapter, von Zütphen's account from 1831 hints at Agoué's involvement in the slave trade in the period. A British naval officer who had been engaged in the suppression of the trade on the coast until 1838 reported that a considerable slave trade was carried on between Cape St Paul and Benin, at Ouidah, Little Popo, Grand Popo and Lagos, 'all that is a bad country.'[3]

Besides the slave trade, the ivory trade also continued to flourish on the western Slave Coast in this period.[4] In 1818, three factories competed for ivory at Little Popo, two of these American and one Danish.[5] One of the American agents, Samuel Banks, arrived in early September 1818 and purchased roughly 2,300kg ivory within three months. However, he found this trade 'very inferior to what I had every reason to expect', due to the stiff competition. The Danish factory belonged to Philip Wilhelm Wrisberg, who had formerly been employed by the Danish trade company on the coast, including as commandant of Fort Prindsensten at Keta.[6] This factory had been established in late October or November 1818 but can have lasted only briefly, as Wrisberg returned to Europe in March 1819.[7] He had planned to establish a soap factory (using palm oil) at Little Popo, but fearing that this could be 'connected with troubles' – possibly a reference to the political unrest at Little Popo in the period – he decided to establish it at Keta instead.[8] With regard to Grand Popo, the British naval officer Edward Bold reported in the early 1820s that ivory abounded 'in endless quantities', being sent to the coast from 'the inland towns to the Northward'. There was little competition in the trade at Grand Popo, as only 'a few vessels' called there.[9] However, his reliability is questionable, particularly as he appears to confuse Grand Popo with Little Popo. In this period, the ivory exported from the western Slave Coast seems to have come from the near neighbourhood as well as from the interior. This at least is suggested by the

---

[3] PP Colonies Africa 1842, i, p.24, Report from the Select Committee on the Coast of West Africa (Capt. A.T. E.Vidal, R.N., 22 April 1842).

[4] For a discussion of the West African ivory trade in the period, see Marion Johnson, 'Ivory and the Nineteenth Century Transformation in West Africa', *Figuring African Trade: Proceedings on the Symposium on the Quantification and Structure of the Import and Export and Long Distance Trade of Africa in the Nineteenth Century (c. 1800–1913)*, ed. G. Liesegang et al. (Berlin, 1986), 89–139.

[5] RIHS: Carrington Papers: Samuel Banks, Little Popo, Africa, 20 Dec. 1818. Cf. Brooks, *Yankee Traders*, 240; Jones, 'Little Popo and Agoué', 122.

[6] For Wrisberg, see Daniel Hopkins, *Peter Thonning and Denmark's Guinea Commission: A Study in Ninteenth-Century African Colonial Geography* (Leiden and Boston, 2013), 143, 291–2, 296–8.

[7] *Ibid.*, 298; RIHS: Carrington Papers: Samuel Banks, Little Popo, Africa, 20 Dec. 1818.

[8] DNA: Sager til Guineisk Journal, 1817, no.1497, Gov. J. E. Richter, [Christiansborg] 2. 8. 1816; *ibid.* 1820, no.1815, Gov. Reiersen, [Christiansborg] 25.10.1818; *ibid.*, 1822, no.191, P. Wrisberg, Copenhagen, 11.11.1822; Nørregård, *Danish Settlements*, 191, 193. The factory at Keta probably became active in 1823 and was abandoned by July 1825 (Sager til Guineisk Journal, 1825, no.512, Gov. Richelieu, [Christiansborg], 25.1.1825, placed in *ibid.*, 1837, no.559; *ibid.*, 1826, no.756, P.W. Wrisberg, 28.7.1826 (incls.). See also TNA: CO96/24, Alderley, [London] 19 July 1851 (incls.).

[9] Bold, *Merchant's and Mariner's African Guide*, 61.

account of a British trader, who in 1803 noted that 'the wild elephants were very numerous' on the northern bank of the lagoon between Ouidah and Little Popo. From the 1820s this bank began to be cultivated by the settlers at Agoué, and the elephants would have been driven away.[10]

Further, Little Popo continued to export maize on a large scale as well as other provisions. According to Bold, 'like Accra, [it] possesses inexhaustible quantities of the Indian wheat [= maize] obtainable at a very low rate. It is a place that merits the attention of vessels, being a very superior port of trade.'[11] In 1819, Robertson noted that since the 'partial cessation' of the slave trade, Little Popo had increased exports in alternative products, including gold, which has 'latterly found its way here, in small quantities', ivory, palm-oil, gums, wax, and provisions. He found that despite the difficult landing for traders, 'these people continue respectable.'[12]

The export of dollars and other kinds of specie, such as doubloons, from the western Slave Coast, as noted by one of the British traders in 1842, indicates the activity of slave traders in the region and the comfortable coexistence – and cooperation – of the illegal trade and the 'legitimate' commerce.[13] The cash was imported by the slave traders in order to pay for slaves (and, according to a complaint from the British consul at Lagos in the 1850s, comprised the proceeds from the sales of slaves in the Americas).[14] Alternatively, since the African suppliers/ brokers preferred to be paid in trade goods, and particularly cowries, the local currency, the illegal traders purchased these articles from 'legitimate' traders on the coast, paying cash, and then bartered these goods for slaves. This practice was one of the major issues considered by the British parliamentary enquiry of 1842, but it nevertheless continued into the 1860s.

The illegal slave trade after the Equipment Act of 1839

Unlike the abolition of the slave trade in 1807, the Equipment Act of 1839 had considerable impact on the economic life of the western Slave Coast. This act gave cruisers of the British anti-slave trade patrols the right to detain Portuguese vessels that carried equipment for the trade. This meant that Portuguese vessels could no longer hang around on the coast prior to

---

[10] M'Leod, *A Voyage*, 139.
[11] Bold, *The Merchant's and Mariner's African Guide*, 62.
[12] Robertson, *Notes*, 235–6.
[13] See Martin Lynn, *Commerce and Economic Change in West Africa: The Palm Oil Trade in the Nineteenth Century* (Cambridge, 1997), 68–70; Lynn, 'The West African palm oil trade in the nineteenth century and the 'crisis of adaptation', *From Slave Trade to 'Legitimate' Commerce*, ed. Law, 57–77; Elisée Soumonni, 'The compatibility of the slave and palm oil trades in Dahomey, 1818–1856', *ibid.*, 78–92.
[14] *PP* Slave Trade 1854–5, Class B, Consul Campbell, Lagos, 27 March 1854.

taking in slaves, which was a special problem for Ouidah, the centre of the illegal trade on the Slave Coast.[15] Thus the slave traders there were forced to decentralise their trade and shift their activities along the lagoon to places to the east and west of this town. From Ouidah, slaves were now transported into neighbouring regions, including the western Slave Coast, in order to be embarked from any point that was not watched by the British navy. The coastal lagoons played a crucial role in this arrangement, which relied on the flexibility and swiftness of the slave traders to outmanoeuvre the cruisers. This was described by Freeman in 1845:

> The great ease with which slaves may be conveyed along the lagoon, to any given point on the line of coast in question, and the absence of rocks or high banks which would offer any hindrance to the launching off a canoe from any great point offer great facilities to the Slave Dealers, and enable them repeatedly to elude the most active vigilance of the two or three British cruisers stationed in the western part of the Bight. It is just as easy for a Slave Dealer to ship a cargo of slaves from any point many miles distant from any town or village, as to ship from Whydah, Porto Novo, Lagos or any other place on the shore of the Bight; and the rapidity with which the Slave Dealers <u>Do</u> ship a cargo of slaves is astonishing. [...] When the dealers learn, by their spies, that one of their vessels is at hand, and that a cruiser is also on any part of the coast, so that they may apprehend the danger of a capture, they watch for an opportunity while the Slave-ship hovers about in the offing, sometimes for several days, and when any point can be pronounced <u>clear</u>, slaves are hastened along the lagoon or down or up the plain betwixt the lagoon and the beach, and several large canoes well manned, glide down or up <u>in-shore</u>, just outside of the breakers to the point fixed upon for shipping: signals are made, the vessel stands in for a few hours, takes in her cargo and sails off in triumph.[16]

Duncan, who visited the western Slave Coast in the same year, gives an illustration of this practice in his account. Travelling along the lagoon from Agoué to Ouidah on 18 February 1845, at the toll station at Grand Popo he fell in with 'a very large canoe [...] from Whydah, in which were several Spanish slave merchants, accompanied by a number of young slaves, apparently between 12 and 15 years of age', proceeding westwards.[17]

---

[15] *PP*, Colonies Africa 1842, i, 226, Report of the Select Committee on the West Coast of Africa (Lieut. R. Levinge, R.N., 3 June 1842); Eltis, *Economic Growth*, 83, 89.

[16] WMMS: Special Series Biographical, West Africa: Papers of T. B. Freeman: T. B. Freeman, London, 5 May 1845, cited in T.B. Freeman, 'West Africa', unpubl. ms, 218–20 (author's emphasis). See also UKHO: OD 9A, Struvé, 'Report' (1849/1850), 30–1.

[17] Duncan, 'Note', 146. He confuses Grand Popo with Little Popo, but from the location (east of Agoué) it is clear that the former is meant. Cf. Duncan, *Travels*, i, 110–1, which gives the number of slaves in the canoe as 'about twenty'. For the account of a slave who was transported from

Slaves were shipped not only from Little Popo, which throughout the eighteenth century had been the main port in the region, but also from other places, some of which entered documentation for the first time (such as Porto Seguro, Baguida and Sekko). Grand Popo reappears in the sources in this period. Agoué became particularly important in this trade; Freeman noted that 'Its main support is the Slave Trade in the carrying on of which it is connected with Whydah', while Duncan rather nonchalantly remarked that 'Nothing of interest struck me in Ahguay, the slave-trading being the principal traffic.'[18] Agoué first came to the attention of the Royal Navy's anti-slave trade patrol after the Equipment Act, in 1840, when it was identified as one of the 'slave ports' in the Bight of Benin.[19] In 1841, an English trader listed the places on the West African coast where trade was carried on – or, more precisely, where the slaves were shipped:

> I believe you will find there is no more of the slave trade from [the Gallinas] until you come to Atocco, on Cape St. Paul's, where a factory stands; thence to Awey [= Woe, west of Keta], thence to – [*sic*], thence to Sugru [= Porto Seguro], thence to Little Popo, which is a place of note; thence to Augua [= Agoué], thence to Great Popo, and thence to Whydah. [...] Whydah is the central place, and the root of the slave trade in the Bight of Benin.'[20]

The first of the traders from Ouidah to extend their activities to the western Slave Coast was Francisco Felix de Souza, the Chacha of Ouidah (d. 1849). This is not surprising, given that he was the most influential of the traders on the coast in the period and able to draw on old connections with Little Popo and George Lawson and probably also with Agoué, where in the 1830s his son-in-law had been the caboceer's head servant (see Chapter 6). De Souza himself did not relocate, but sent his eldest son, Isidoro, to act as his agent at Little Popo. Isidoro, who after being educated in Brazil had served his father at Badagry and Ouidah, re-occupied the factory at Adjido apparently in 1840.[21] Duncan, who visited this place in 1845, decribed it as 'a

---

(cont.) Ouidah via the lagoon to be shipped elsewhere in this period, see Baquaqua, *Biography*. Although Baquaqua does not identify the place he was shipped from, his description of it as 'a very beautiful place' suggests that this was Little Popo, which was noted for its 'very pretty appearance' (148–9, incl. n.201; WMMS: Freeman, 'Journal', 164–5).

[18] WMMS: Freeman, 'Journal', 164–6; Duncan, *Travels*, i, 93.

[19] PP, Slave Trade 1841, A, no.109: case of the Brazilian schooner *Gratidão*. See also PP, Slave Trade 1840, A, no.125: case of the Brazilian schooner *Calliope*.

[20] PP, Colonies Africa 1842, i, p.200–1, Report from the Select Committee on the Coast of West Africa (Rev. J. Beecham, 31 May 1842, citing Capt. Laurence, Sierra Leone, 4 June 1841).

[21] Law, 'Francisco Felix de Souza', 201.

large slave establishment with several baracoons.'[22] In the early 1840s, other traders were reported to be active at Little Popo, probably in cooperation with Isidoro: Felis Cosme Madail, Joseph Moreyra Sampayo and José de Taparica.[23] Another son of Francisco Felix de Souza, Antonio, also became active on the western Slave Coast in the 1840s, presumably also as an agent for his father.[24] Contemporary information suggests that he oscillated between Ouidah, Little Popo and Agoué.[25] By 1844, the de Souzas had a house at Agoué, where Antonio appears to have resided at least from time to time.[26] This house was presumably situated in the Zomayi quarter, which belonged to the de Souzas. According to Pierucci, it had been founded by Francisco Felix de Souza, who stopped there sometimes during his trips from Ouidah to Little Popo and also used it to bulk his slaves before shipping them.[27]

However, the most important trader at Agoué in the period was probably Joaquim d'Almeida (d.1857), who had formerly been enslaved in Brazil. D'Almeida, or 'Zoki Azata' as he was called on the coast, was a Mahi from Hoko (a town roughly 62 miles/100km to the north of Abomey, in present-day Bénin) who as a child had been captured by the Dahomeans and sold into slavery. He had been shipped to Bahia, where he had been purchased by Manoel Joaquim d'Almeida, the captain of a slave ship who traded between Brazil and the West African Coast. Joaquim d'Almeida had been employed in this trade and became a trusted servant of his master, whose name he assumed. After being liberated, he continued to trade between Bahia and the Bight of Benin.[28] He first appears in the records of the British navy in the 1840, when he was said to engage in the slave trade at 'Agui' together with several other traders: Tobias Barretto Brandão, Elias Domingo de Carvalho, Antonio Caetano Coelho, Seçar Medair and Antonio Verra dos Santos.[29] He finally returned to the West African Coast in

[22] Duncan, *Travels*, i, 102.
[23] *PP*, Slave Trade 1840, Class A, no.85: case of the brig *Plant*; *PP*, Slave Trade 1844, Class A, no.73: case of the Spanish brigantine *San Pedro*.
[24] De Souza had several sons by the name of Antonio, but most likely it is Antonio Felix 'Kokou' who is referred to here. According F. E. Forbes, who visited the coast in 1849, three of the Chacha's sons were 'wealthy and slave-merchants': Isidoro, Antonio 'Kokou' ('Cockoo') and Ignatio (*PP*, Slave Trade 1849–50, Classs B, incl. 10 in no.9: Lieut. Forbes, 'Bonetta', at sea, 5 Nov. 1849). According to Simone de Souza, another son, called San Anthonio, was also engaged in trade at Little Popo, but there are no references to him in the contemporary records (*La famille*, 46).
[25] Jones/ Sebald, *African Family Archive*, 1.11: J.H. Ahkurst, Ahguay, 1 Oct. 1843; 1.15: James W. Hansen, Ahguay, 31 Oct. 1843; 1.16: Hansen, Ahguay, 12 Nov. 1843; 1.17: Hansen, Ahguay, 23 Oct. 1843; 1.20: Hansen, Ahguay, 4 Jan. 1844; 1.21: Hansen, Ahguay, 10 Jan. 1844; 1.218: George Latty Lawson, Little Popo, 30 March 1849.
[26] WMMS: Special Series Biographical, West Africa: Papers of T. B. Freeman: Revd. William Allen to T. B. Freeman, Ahguay, 18 Jan. 1844, cited in T. B. Freeman, 'West Africa,' 248.
[27] Pierucci, ['History'], 9–10.
[28] Verger, *Os libertos*, 43–4. Verger gives 'Gbego Sokpa' as Joaquim d'Ameida's original name. For a discussion of d'Almeida's career on the coast, see Turner, 'Les Brésiliens', 102–5; Guran, *Agudás*, 85–7.
[29] *PP*, Slave Trade 1841, Class A, no.109: case of the Brazilian schooner *Gratidão*.

1845 and settled at Agoué, where (as noted above, in Chapter 5) he founded his own quarter, Zokikome.[30] He was only one of many liberated slaves who settled at Agoué in the period and engaged in the illegal trade, but he was exceptional in that he was the only one who entered the overseas dimension and came to the notice of the British navy, shipping slaves himself rather than just buying and reselling them locally on a small scale.[31] In 1845, Duncan reported that a 'large ship of great tonnage and sailing qualities, in order to compete with H.M. cruisers, is now building [at Agoué].'[32] He does not state who built it, but it seems likely that it was at d'Almeida's initiative. The construction of slave vessels in Africa was one way of trying to avoid British surveillance, or at least to cut the risk by avoiding the voyage to the West African coast. Another way was the practice of buying vessels on the West African coast from legitimate traders, which became a standard practice in the period.

Other important traders who became active on the western Slave Coast in the 1840s include José Francisco dos Santos ('Alfaiate') and Domingo Mustiche. Dos Santos was a Brazilian who traded as an agent for merchants in Bahia and Rio de Janeiro, as well as on his own account. He was established at Ouidah but letters from his business correspondence show that in the mid-1840s he also shipped slaves from Little Popo and Agoué.[33] One of these shipments took place at Agoué in March 1845, when more than 300 slaves were embarked on board the Spanish vessel 'Pepito', which however was captured by the British navy. According to the naval officer in charge, 450 more slaves were waiting to be embarked when the vessel was captured.[34]

Domingo Mustiche, a Spaniard, was established at Little Popo by 1846/7. In 1855 the British Consul at Lagos, Benjamin Campbell, noted that he worked as an agent for a Barcelona firm by the name of Vidal as well as on his own account, but it is not clear how reliable this is since Vidal was also the name of Régis's agent at Ouidah in 1856 and possibly the Consul confused this.[35] In 1852, George Latty Lawson gave a graphic description of 'Don Domingo Musticke's slave factory' at Little Popo, where in about 1847 he had sold two Krepi (= Ewe) slaves:

---

[30] According to family tradition, Joaquim d'Almeida first arrived at Agoué in 1835, but there is no evidence of this in the contemporary records. The date is inscribed in a memorial plaque that has been erected by the family at Agoué (see Guran, *Agudás*, 87).
[31] See Strickrodt, 'Afro-Brazilians', 221, 226–7.
[32] Duncan, 'Note', 145.
[33] The number of slaves that dos Santos annually shipped from Ouidah, Agoué and Little Popo rose from 27 in 1844 to 296 in 1847. See Verger, *Les afro-américains*, 53–86. Cf. Jones, 'Little Popo', 130.
[34] Verger, *Les afro-américains*, 61 (no.5, J. Dos Santos to Sr Manoël Pereira [Bahia], Ouidah, 25 March 1845); TNA: FO84/610, incl. in Hamilton, [London] 5 June 1845: H. B. Young, 'Hydra', off Quitta, 7 March 1845; Duncan, 'Note', 149; Duncan, *Travels*, i, 142.
[35] *PP*, Slave Trade 1855–6, Class B, no.9: Consul Campbell, Lagos, 28 Aug. 1855.

This yard was called a Barracoon. The man was fastened by an iron collar on his neck. He was chained to others slaves [sic] in the Barracoon. This is the usual way of securing slaves. The Cre[e]pee woman had a string round her neck, she was fastened to some other women. In this way, slave women are generally fastened. I saw these Creepee people in Don Domingo's yard during a period of six months. They were amongst a lot, about one hundred and fifty people in the yard. Sometimes I have seen two or three hundred people, in his yard. They were blacks, natives of Africa. Don Domingo Musticke was a large slave dealer. After six months I missed the Creepee people and all the others from the yard, I believe they were shipped off a little further down the Coast about three miles from Popo. I have seen Don Domingo Musticke shipping slaves at Popo, about one mile and a half or two miles from the town. Sometimes he shipped slaves in a Brig at other times in a Felucca. The vessels are not ordinary traders. They come at certain times for slaves.[36]

According to Lawson, Mustiche subsequently based himself at Agoué. However, he appears to have kept his establishment at Little Popo, as is suggested by a report from 1855 stating that he had establishments at both places.[37]

By 1848, Joaquim d'Almeida had established himself at Ouidah, where in cooperation with a former associate of Francisco Felix de Souza, Quenum, he broke de Souza's trade monopoly and traded very successfully.[38] In 1849, after de Souza's death, Forbes described d'Almeida as 'a slave-merchant on an extensive scale' and 'the richest resident in Whydah'.[39] In the following year, he referred to Agoué as a 'slave-port, almost a monopoly of José [sic] d'Almeida', while Grand Popo was 'almost a monopoly' of Joaquim Antonio, a Spanish trader based at Ouidah, and Little Popo 'almost a monopoly of Isidoro de Souza.'[40] However, following his father's death on 8 May 1849, Isidoro had left his establishment at Little Popo for Ouidah, where a year later he succeeded his father as Chacha.[41] Soon afterwards the de Souzas seem to have lost interest in the

---

[36] TNA: CO267/228, incl. in Macdonald, Sierra Leone, 10 March 1852: 'Copy of depositions taken before the Police Magistrate, Freetown, Sierra Leone, 10 March 1852'.
[37] *PP*, Slave Trade 1855–6, Class B, no.9: Consul B. Campbell, Lagos, 28 Aug. 1855.
[38] This is indicated by the traditions of the Quenum family at Ouidah, which exist in several versions that vary in the details but agree in the essence. See E. Foa, *Le Dahomey* (Paris, 1895), 23; Reynier, 'Eléments', 29–73, p.63; M. Quenum, *Les ancêtres de la famille Quenum* (Langres, 1981), 60–1. For a detailed discussion, see Law, 'Francisco Felix de Souza', 201–4; Law, *Ouidah*, 196–202.
[39] *PP*, Slave Trade 1849–50, Class B, incl.10 in no.9: Lieut. Forbes, Bonetta', at sea, 5 Nov. 1849.
[40] Forbes, *Dahomey*, i, 102; *PP*, Slave Trade 1849–50, Class A, incl.2 in no.220: Journal of Lieut. Forbes (4 July 1850); *ibid.*, incl.10 in no.9: Lieut. Forbes, 'Bonetta', at sea, 5 Nov. 1849.
[41] Shortly before Isidoro left for Ouidah, his house was accidentally destroyed by a fire and its remains were plundered (Jones/ Sebald, *African Family Archive*, 1.225: George Latty Lawson, 10 May 1849). It is conceivable that it was this incident as well as his father's death which prompted

western Slave Coast, focusing instead on the ports to the east of Ouidah. By 1852, Isidoro was reported to have monopolised the trade of Godomé and Antonio that of Cotonou.[42]

In 1850, the British took over the Danish settlements on the coast, including Fort Prindsensten at Keta, extending their jurisdiction (as they assumed at the time) to Kedzi, two or three miles east of Keta.[43] The main reason for their purchase of these settlements was the fear that unless they did so themselves, a commercial rival, particularly the French, might do it to the detriment of British trade interests. However, part of the reason was also the advantage which the British hoped this extension of their influence would have for their anti-slave trade campaign.[44] At any rate, one of the consequences of the British take-over of Fort Prindsensten (from then on called 'Keta Fort') was that the traders who had been active in the Keta region moved further east, into the western Slave Coast, in order to avoid the punishment for trading slaves in British territory. Among them was João Gonçalves Baeta, a trader from Bahia. Between 1840 and 1850 he had been active at Atoko, west of Cape St. Paul, where Governor Winniett met him during his tour of the new British acquisitions in 1850. According to Winniett, Baeta was 'desirous to carry on legal trade in palm oil, &c., under the British flag.'[45] However, by January 1851 he had relocated to Blekesu, just outside British jurisdiction, where he continued to engage in the slave trade.[46]

In early 1852, between 23 January and 2 February, Britain concluded anti-slave trade treaties with the towns on the western Slave Coast. This had been preceded by a British naval blockade of the ports in the Bight of Benin (from Keta in the west to beyond Lagos in the east, excepting only Badagry), starting at the beginning of the year and preventing all

---

(cont.) Isidoro's relocation to Ouidah. Curiously, Struvé, who was at Little Popo at the time, dates the fire to 26 May 1850 (UKHO: OD 9A, Struvé, 'Report', 26 May 1850). For the date of F. F. de Souza's death, see Law, 'Francisco Felix de Souza', 205.

[42] Fraser, 'Commercial Report' [May 1852], in: Fraser, Dahomey, 198.

[43] TNA: FO84/893, incl. in Hamilton, [London] 10 April 1852: Lieut. T. G. Forbes, 'Philomel', at Whydah, 5 Feb. 1852. In this period the eastern limits of British jurisdiction were notoriously ill-defined and caused some headaches to British officials both on the Gold Coast and in London. In 1860, it was eventually agreed that British authority reached no further than 'the range of the guns of the Fort of Quittah' (TNA: CO96/47, no.65, E. B. Andrews, Cape Coast Castle, 28 June 1860).

[44] TNA: CO96/17, Eddisbury, [London] 12 July 1849.

[45] PP 1850 [1171] XXXVIII, Papers respecting the Cession to Great Britain of the Danish Possessions on the Coast of Africa, 5 (Journal of Governor Winniett, 10 March 1850). The ruins of Baeta's house at Atoko still existed in the early twentieth century, as did a well which according to local tradition he had built to provide water for his slaves (C. Spiess, 'Ein Erinnerungsblatt an die Tage des Sklavenhandels in Westafrika', *Globus: Illustrierte Zeitschrift für Länder- und Völkerkunde* 92, 13 [3 Oct. 1907], 205–8, p.205).

[46] TNA: CO96/22, J. Bannerman, Cape Coast Castle, 17 Jan. 1851. Cf. Jones, 'Little Popo', pp. 129, 134 n.75. According to Spiess, Baeta founded the 'slave place Gadome' there ('Ein Erinnerungsblatt,' 205).

trade.⁴⁷ The treaties were concluded by T. G. Forbes, the naval officer, and the British Vice-Consul at Ouidah, Louis Fraser, with the chiefs of the following places, from west to east: Blekesu ('Blockhouse'/'Block-ouse'), Elmina Chica ('Adinner Cooma, Elmina Chica or Little Elmina'), Adafia ('Adaffie'), 'Aguinerweh', Denu ('Daynoo'), Aflao ('Afflowhow or Flohow'), Porto Seguro ('Aboadrafo' or 'Porto Segoora'), Gomaluta (Gunkope), Little Popo, Agoué ('Ahgwey') and Grand Popo.⁴⁸ Forbes's report is interesting for the information it gives, among others, concerning slave-trading establishments in the region at this time. He noted that 'Bajado', said to lie six miles from the beach, was 'a noted Slave Depôt, the place where the Slaves were housed for the Slave Ship lately taken by HMS "Flying Fish"; the Natives of this Village are a set of Robbers, trapping parties who pass unarmed.'⁴⁹ The location of this place, between Porto Seguro and Bé, suggests that this refers to Baguida (which would be the first time it is documented), although the latter lay only about a mile from the beach. According to W. T. G. Lawson's report from 1879, Baguida was 'originally built by one Boy Salvador alias William Lawson', which combined with the information given by Forbes indicates that the Lawsons were active in the illegal slave trade.⁵⁰ The slave vessel referred to by Forbes was the 'Pepita', a brig from Havana, which was caught in the act of embarking slaves on 14 July 1851, with 70 slaves on board.⁵¹

At Blekesu, Forbes was treated to refreshments at the local 'Portuguese factory'. Finding good accommodation there, he and his companions spent the night there. This establishment probably belonged to Baeta, who soon afterwards relocated to Agoué.⁵² At the eastern limits of the western Slave Coast, at Grand Popo, he found that a 'Senôr Carvallio' was established at 'Guévé or Quw-vay', which can probably be identified with Hévé, to the northern bank of the lagoon opposite the coastal settlement. As to the identity of Senôr Carvallio, this is not quite clear because there were at least two people named Carvalho in the region in the period, who furthermore shared some of the same initials. One was José Pereira Monteiro do Carvalho, who in 1860 acted as agent for the 'Companhia União Africana' at Agoué and probably on the western Slave Coast more

---

⁴⁷ TNA: FO84/892, incl. in Admiralty, [London] 7 Jan. 1852: H. W. Bruce, HM Steam Ship Penelope, Sierra Leone, 6 Dec. 1851 ('Notification of Blockade').
⁴⁸ See TNA: FO84/893, incl. in Hamilton, [London] 10 April 1852: Lieut. T. G. Forbes, 'Schedule of Treaties'; *ibid.*, Lieut. T. G. Forbes, 'Philomel', at Whydah, 5 Feb. 1852; Fraser, 'Windward Treaties', 22 Jan. – 2 Feb. 1852, in: Fraser, *Dahomey*, 148–50. For copies of the treaties, see *State Papers* 1852–53, 673–91.
⁴⁹ TNA: FO84/893, incl. in Hamilton, [London] 10 April 1852: Lieut. T. G. Forbes, 'Philomel', at Whydah, 5 Feb. 1852. Cf. Borghero, *Journal*, 124–5, who reports the prevalence of robbers to the west of Porto Seguro.
⁵⁰ GNA: ADM1/2/361, no.26: Lawson, 'Report' (1879), 26.
⁵¹ TNA: FO84/866, Admiralty, [London] 17 Nov. 1851 (incls.).
⁵² *PP*, Slave Trade 1855–6, Class B, no.30, Consul Campbell, Lagos, 1 Feb. 1856.

generally.⁵³ The other was Manoel Joaquim de Carvalho, a Brazilian slave trader who subsequently became Régis's agent at Porto Novo. This connection with Régis suggests that it was probably this Carvalho whom Forbes met in 1852, as Régis subsequently established a factory at Grand Popo/ Hévé.⁵⁴ Hévé was still 'Mr Carvalho's place' three years later, in 1855, when the Wesleyan Methodists were requested to open a school there.⁵⁵

Following the conclusion of the treaties, these places were exempted from the blockade and declared free for legitimate trade from 11 February 1852.⁵⁶ Further, the chiefs were given presents from the British government, comprising a cane embossed with the royal arms, a broad-brimmed hat, 112 pounds of cowries and a bale of blue bafts (i.e. cotton cloth) each. All chiefs received the same amounts except George Lawson of Little Popo, whose bale of bafts was bigger.⁵⁷

Despite the 1852 treaties, however, the places on the western Slave Coast continued to export slaves. In 1854, this prompted the British Consul at Lagos to complain about 'the continued shipment of Cargoes of Slaves from the neighbourhood of the Ports of Whydah, Ahguay, and Great and Little Popo.'⁵⁸ However, with regard to Little Popo this appears to have been wrong. Although the naval officers as well as the British consul continue to name it as a potential place for illegal shipments of slaves into the 1860s, it seems to have stopped functioning as such after the 1852 treaty. There is no record of shipments having taken place from there, which may have been due to the close watch of the cruisers but more likely to the risks involved in breaking the 1852 treaty, particularly for the Lawsons. There is only one record of an attempt at shipping slaves, and this is based on rather thin evidence. This incident dates from August 1857 and involved the 'William Clarke', a brigantine under American colours, which came under the suspicion of intending to ship slaves when she was observed loading large amounts of water at Little Popo. This was subsequently confirmed by some deserters from her crew, who claimed that she was 'ready to take in her cargo of Slaves, which was to be 600 most of them down here [at Little

⁵³ TNA: FO84/1115, Consul G. Brand, Lagos, 2 May 1860. For a more detailed discussion, see Strickrodt, 'Afro-Brazilians', 9–10.
⁵⁴ Newbury, *Western Slave Coast*, 63–4, 68n., 69.
⁵⁵ WMMS: West Africa Correspondence: Box 262: Joseph Dawson, Little Popo, 23 Feb.1855.
⁵⁶ TNA: FO84/893, incl. in Admiralty, [London], 10 April 1852: H.W. Bruce, off Whydah, 11 Feb. 1852.
⁵⁷ TNA: FO84/925, incl. in Admiralty, [London], 31 March 1853: H. W. Bruce, Penelope, Ascension, 23 April (incl.). The canes were probably similar to those given to Anlo chiefs when Fort Prindsensteen became British: 'malacca canes 5 feet long polished […] complete with silver heads bearing Her Majesty's arms stamped and embossed' (CO96/26, G. Baillie, [London] 12 May 1852). See also FO84/1124, incl. in Admiralty, [London] 13 July 1860: W. Bowden, 'Medusa', Whydah, 31 Jan. 1860. Such canes evidently had a tradition in the region; in the 1780s, the king of Grand Popo was reported to carry 'a Spanish manila cane with a silver knob' (Isert, *Letters,* 94).
⁵⁸ TNA: FO84/950, Slave Trade no.21, Consul B. Campbell, Consulate Lagos, 12 Aug. 1854.

Popo] ready [for shipment].'⁵⁹ In consequence, the vessel was captured and sent to Sierra Leone, although the reliability of the deserters' report seems questionable.

One of the consequences of the 1852 treaty was that slaves were shipped from places outside the settlements, because the chiefs hoped that in this way they could circumvent the provisions of the treaty.⁶⁰ Among these new embarkation places was Sekko, to the east of Agoué and north of the lagoon. It is first documented in 1853, when a naval officer reported his suspicions that slaves 'are kept in small lots & assembled at or near Secco, 3 miles to Leeward of Aghwey'. According to him, there had been three embarkations from there in the first half of the year. He furthermore pointed to the comfortable coexistence of the illegal trade and the legitimate commerce when noting with regard to Agoué that while it was certainly 'the most suspicious place at present' it also 'appears to have most of the English trade [on the Slave Coast]'.⁶¹

During the 1850s there was a decline of the slave trade due to the closure of the markets in Brazil. Many of the slave traders on the coast went into the palm oil trade. In May 1857, the commander of the Bights Division of the British navy reported that the slave trade was practically finished on the Slave Coast, but singled out Agoué as one of the places most likely to ship a cargo of slaves if opportunity offered.⁶² In the same year, however, a new impetus was given to the illegal trade due to a brief revival of the Cuban market. This Cuban trade was organized in a new way. It was carried on by organisations in Cuba with connections in the United States, which used American vessels and the American flag to elude the search of the British cruisers. On the West African coast, the new trade apparently also involved a change of traders, with new people moving in and replacing the established traders, who one by one disappear from the records of the British navy in this period. This was due to various reasons: while some of the established traders presumably died, such as Joaquim d'Almeida in 1857, others, such as José Francisco dos Santos, gave up the slave trade and went into the palm oil trade. Others again left the coast, such as João Gonçalves Baeta, who by 1862 had apparently returned to Bahia where he became an agent for dos Santos.⁶³

The British navy's report on the state of the trade from February 1858

---

⁵⁹ TNA: FO84/1040, incl. in Admiralty, [London] 9 Oct. 1857: G. Day, 'Firefly', off Little Popo, 23 Aug. 1857 (incls.).
⁶⁰ TNA: FO84/950, Slave Trade no.21, Consul B. Campbell, Consulate Lagos, 12 August 1854.
⁶¹ TNA: FO84/926, incl. in Hamilton, [London] 25 October 1853: C.G. Phillips, Journal, 25 April to 30 June 1853.
⁶² PP, Slave Trade 1857–8, A, no.155, Commander Hope, 23 May 1857.
⁶³ The dos Santos correspondence includes nine letters addressed to 'J. Gbr. Baêta'. If this refers to João Gonçalves Baeta (as Verger assumed), this would mean that Baeta had returned to Bahia between July 1859 (when he was last recorded at Agoué by the British navy) and 1862 (the date of the first letter to him at Bahia). See Verger, *Les afro-américains*, 53–100.

noted the increasing numbers of vessels under the American flag arriving on the coast and the collection of slaves 'at the Depôts in the neighbourhood of Whydah, Little Popo, Ahgwey, and the adjacent villages.'[64] Already by September 1857, the British Consul at Lagos had felt it necessary to issue a warning to the chiefs of Adaffie and Agoué because slave shipments had taken place. With regard to Agoué, he noted that 'it is notoriously known [that the chiefs] allowed in the years 1853 and 1854 several cargoes of slaves to be shipped in Canoes on board Vessels' and 'the Chiefs of Ahguay have again within the last six months permitted Slaves to be embarked from their Shores.'[65] In December 1857, a schooner under American colours, the 'Hanover', reportedly intended to ship slaves at Adafia, where 80 slaves had been collected. However, this was foiled by the British navy, which discovered the slaves. They were then moved to Porto Seguro and Agoué for embarkment there, but the schooner as was unable to slip the navy's watch and therefore left the Bights in March 1858 with only a small cargo of palm oil.[66] In May 1858, another American schooner, the 'Lydia Gibbs', was captured by the British navy after she had landed $25,000 at Agoué for the purchase of slaves.[67] According to the officer who captured her, she was fully equipped for 600 slaves, who had been taken from the town to the beach on the day of the vessel's capture (29 May 1858).[68] In September of the same year, three slave vessels were reported to have shipped slaves from Agoué 'or its immediate neighbourhood', two of whom escaped from the coast. This prompted a visit from a British naval officer, William Bowden, in November 1859, to remind the chiefs of the consequences of breaking the treaty. Two slave traders, 'Mr Maderes' and 'Mr Swarey', were living in the town at this time. Bowden urged the chief to evict them. After initial reluctance the chief gave in, promising to do so if he found that they were engaged in the trade.[69] 'Mr Maderes' was Francisco José de Medeiros (d. 1875), a Portuguese from the island of Madeira who had been based for a long time in Cuba, where he had engaged in the slave trade. According to Pierucci, at Agoué he bought Baeta's house and continued his trade, which

---

[64] TNA: FO84/1070, incl. in Admiralty, [London] 8 Nov. 1858: F.W. Grey, 'Boscawen', Sierra Leone, 11 February 1858.
[65] TNA: FO84/1031, incl. in Slave Trade no.40, Consul B. Campbell, Consulate Lagos, 3 Oct. 1857: Consul B. Campbell to the Chiefs of Ahguay, Lagos, 15 Sept. 1857.
[66] *PP*, Slave Trade 1858–9, Class A, no.131, Commodore Wise, 6 Aug. 1858, Report of slave trade, July 1857 – June 1858.
[67] TNA: FO84/1069, incl. in Admiralty, [London], 13 July 1858: Commander J. A. Close, 'Trident', Whydah, 31 May 1858; *PP* Slave Trade 1858–9, Class A, no.131, Commodore Wise, 6 Aug. 1858, Report of slave trade, July 1857 – June 1858.
[68] TNA: FO84/1069, incl. in Admiralty, [London], 13 July 1858: Commander J. A. Close, 'Trident', Whydah, 31 May 1858.
[69] TNA: FO84/1070, incl. in Admiralty, [London] 28 Dec. 1859: Commodore Wise, 'Vesuvius', Ascension, 23 Nov. 1859; FO84/1123, incl.2 in: Secretary of the Admiralty, [London] 29 Feb. 1860: Commander W. Bowden, 'Medusa', Lagos, 21 Nov. 1859. For his account, see Chapter 5.

is plausible as Baeta is last documented there earlier in 1859.[70] The identification of 'Mr Swarey' is less certain because there are two possibilities, Samuel da Costa Soares (d.1894) and João Soares Pereira, both of whom are said to have cooperated with de Medeiros. The former, a Portuguese by origin and a naturalized citizen of the United States, was one of the 'old' slave traders and based at Ouidah.[71] According to family traditions, he had established himself at Agoué before settling at Ouidah, but there is no record of this in the contemporary sources.[72] João Soares Pereira was also Portuguese and is otherwise first documented in 1863, when he also had an establishment at Ouidah.[73]

In January 1860, Bowden visited Grand Popo to warn the chiefs there of the consequences if they continued to ship slaves. According to him, the king, Al-lee-far, remembered the treaty and produced the cane with the royal arms that had been presented to him on its ratification, but his copy of the treaty had been eaten by insects. Al-lee-far and the chiefs denied that shipments had taken place from Grand Popo's beach, but if they had, this was without their knowledge or participation.[74]

In 1860, the British abandoned Keta fort, causing concern among the British naval squadron's leadership that the slave trade in the Anlo region would be revived, with Dzelukofe ('Jella Coffee') 'certain to become once more a great Export for Slaves'.[75] In his report on the slave trade for the second half of 1860, the Senior Officer noted that although slaves were collected all along the Slave Coast, they were principally embarked from 'Elmina Chica about 10 Miles to the Eastward of Quittah to Porto Novo on the Eastern part of the Bights, still great and little Popo, Whydah, Jackin, and Delmina [= Elmina, which however was on the Gold Coast and not a slave port anymore]'. Often they were not collected in barracoons, as had been done previously, but 'scattered about among the houses, so as to appear as Domestic Slaves.' The slave traders were mostly based at Whydah, with the exception of 'a Senor Madeiras', i.e. José Francisco de Medeiros, active at Agoué, and 'a Senor Limas a Brazilian', i.e. Cesar Cequeira de Lima (d.1862), living 'about a mile' from Keta Fort.[76]

---

[70] Pierucci, ['Histoire'], 26. The date for his death comes from his tombstone at the Catholic cemetery at Agoué.
[71] TNA: FO84/1031, Consul B. Campbell, Lagos, 27 July 1857.
[72] Turner, 'Les Brésiliens', 125–6. Cf. Guran, *Agudás*, 21.
[73] Burton, *Mission*, i, 74 n.
[74] TNA: FO84/1124, incl. in Admiralty, [London] 13 July 1860: W. Bowden, 'Medusa', Whydah, 31 Jan. 1860.
[75] *Ibid.*, incl. in Admiralty, [London] 11 Sept. 1860: Commodore Edmonstone, 'Arrogant', Ascension, 25 July 1860.
[76] TNA: FO84/1148, incl. in Admiralty, [London] 16 May 1861: Commodore Edmonstone, 'Arrogant' at Sierra Leone, 24 March 1861, Report on the slave trade, 1 July – 31 Dec.1860. For the identification of 'Senor Limas', see D.E.K. Amenumey, 'Geraldo da Lima: A Reappraisal', *THSG*, 9 (1968), 65–78; Greene, *Gender*, 127–8.

In early 1863, his successor proposed a strict blockade of the coast from Little Popo to Porto Novo, which on second thoughts he extended 'as far as Cape St Paul's, or even to the River Volta, to make it effectual'. This was to stop the king of Dahomey from engaging in the slave trade. According to him, besides trading at Lagos the King 'deals largely with the Portuguese at Aghwey and Great Popoe.'[77] In December 1864, the officer was able to report that the blockade had been successful, not a single shipment having been made in the past year.[78]

The illegal slave trade in the Bight of Benin was effectively finished in 1863. The last successful shipment was made from Godomé, to the east of Ouidah, in October of this year. The last confirmed shipment of slaves from the western Slave Coast took place at Agoué on 20 October 1862, when about 1,100 slaves were embarked.[79] However, according to the British navy the slave traders kept hoping and trying for some time after this.[80] The Senior Officer reported that in May 1864 a suspect steamer, supposed to be the 'Ciceron', had attempted to communicate by signal with Porto Seguro but was prevented from doing so by one of the cruisers. In this period, Francisco Olympio da Silva (d. 1908), a Brazilian who had formerly worked for Baeta, was established at Porto Seguro. Borghero, who visited the place in 1863 and met Olympio (who according to family traditions dropped the 'da Silva' from his name in an attempt to fool the British navy), noted that due to its isolated situation it had often been chosen as a point of embarkation for slaves.[81] Another suspect vessel appeared off Little Popo in June of the same year but left after spotting the anti-slave trade patrol's cruisers.[82] A third incident occurred in March 1866, when the Portuguese barque 'Dahomey' was taken at Agoué by the British navy, on the suspicion of intending to ship 600 slaves. However, the evidence for this was very thin and the master was subsequently acquitted by the mixed commission at Sierra Leone.[83] Nevertheless, the fact that de Medeiros and Soares Pereira,

---

[77] TNA: FO84/1207, incl. in Admiralty, [London] 17 February 1863: Commodore Wilmot, 'Rattlesnake', at Sea, 10 February 1863.
[78] PP 1864–5, Class A, no.151, Commodore Wilmot, 'Rattlesnake', at Ascension, 1 December 1864, Annual report on the slave trade on the West Coast of Africa.
[79] TNA, FO84/1175, incl. in: Secretary of the Admiralty, [London] 25 Jan. 1864: Rear Admiral B. Walker, 'Narcissus', Simons Bay, 17 Nov. 1863. According to the British Consul at Lagos, a shipment of 650 slaves was made from Agoué in late 1863, but there is no confirmation of this in the records the British navy (TNA, FO84/1221, Consul G. Stanhope Freeman, Lagos, 8 Jan. 1864). According to Bouche, the slave trade stopped in 1865 (*Sept ans*, 197).
[80] PP Slave Trade 1864–5, Class A, no.151, Commodore Wilmot, 'Rattlesnake', at Ascension, 1 December 1864, Annual report on the slave trade on the West Coast of Africa.
[81] Boghero, *Journal*, 124–5; Burton, *Mission*, 74; Guran, *Agudás*, 56–68. For the date of his death, see Pelofy, *Histoire*, 23. His tombstone at Agoué, which is of recent date, gives it as 1907.
[82] PP Slave Trade 1864–5, Class A, no.151, Commodore Wilmot, 'Rattlesnake', at Ascension, 1 December 1864, Annual report on the slave trade on the West Coast of Africa.
[83] TNA: FO84/1267, incl. in Secretary of Admiralty, [London] 12 April 1866: Commander M. S. L. Peile, 'Espoir', Lagos, 7 March 1866; PP Slave Trade 1867, Class A, no.48, Commodore Hornby, Sierra Leone, 12 Feb. 1867.

'the last of the rich traders', maintained their establishment at Agoué until 1867 suggests that they did indeed keep trying, or at least hoping, until then. In 1867, they finally reduced their establishment at Agoué. De Medeiros reportedly explained to a naval officer, 'The Slave Trade is finished for the present, so I am going into the legal trade; your cruisers have not stopped it, but there is no demand from Cuba.'[84]

The development of 'legitimate' commerce on the western Slave Coast

Agricultural produce had been an important part of the exports from the western Slave Coast from the beginning of Afro-European commercial enterprise in the region. Little Popo had been a supplier of provisions to European factors on the coast as well as ships during the Middle Passage throughout the period of the slave trade, most importantly of corn, but also of vegetables, fruit and livestock. The abundance of corn at Little Popo was noted in a document that dates right back to the beginning of Afro-European enterprise there.[85] The documents from the late eighteenth century also show that provisions had been a major export from Little Popo (see Chapter 4). A Danish trader had even made an attempt to maintain plantations at Little Popo in the late eighteenth century, i.e. before 1792, but there is no information as to what was grown there.[86]

Palm oil had been exported from the West African coast before the nineteenth century, although only on a small-scale, for the provision of slaves during the Middle Passage. The export of palm oil on a large scale from the western Slave Coast, and the Slave Coast more generally, was initiated by the English firm of Messrs W. B. Hutton & Sons of London in the 1830s.[87] W. M. Hutton, the head of the house in London, stated in 1847 that his firm had first engaged in the palm oil trade '12 or 13 years ago', that is in 1834 or 1835.[88] Messrs. Hutton had two agents on the coast, Thomas Hutton, who was based at Cape Coast, and John Marman, a ship's captain who was based at Accra.[89] In about 1836 Marman estab-

---

[84] PP, Slave Trade 1867, A, no.65, Commodore Hornby, Elephant Bay, 7 June 1867.
[85] Law, *English in West Africa*, part 1, no. 495, Petly Wyborne, Guydah, 26 June 1683.
[86] Monrad, *Description*, 237. Cf. Ray A. Kea, 'Plantations and Labour in the South-East Gold Coast from the Late Eighteenth Century to the Mid-Nineteenth Century', *From Slave Trade*, ed. Law, 119–43, p.129; Jones, 'Little Popo and Agoué', 122.
[87] Cf. Lynn, *Commerce*, 22, 87.
[88] TNA: CO96/12, W. M. Hutton, London, 25 March 1847. Cf. Lynn, *Commerce*, 22.
[89] Thomas Hutton was the nephew of W. M. Hutton. His mother was African (*PP* Colonies Africa 1842, i, 667 [22 July 1842, W. M. Hutton]; Lynn, *Commerce*, 87; Manning, *Slavery*, 51). In 1843, W. M. Hutton stated that Thomas Hutton 'had resided for some years upon the Gold Coast', implying that formerly he had resided elsewhere, possibly in England (being educated and employed by Messrs Hutton) (TNA: CO96/2, W. B. Hutton & Sons, London, 20 Dec. 1843).

lished a factory for the firm at Little Popo, mainly for the palm oil trade but also for the purchase of corn and ivory. However, he had evidently been purchasing palm oil at Little Popo before, by means of 'floating trade.'[90] In 1842, W. M. Hutton stated that his firm had been connected with Little Popo 'in the way of trade' for 'about eight years', i.e. since about 1834.[91] The factory at Little Popo was situated in George Lawson's house, that is in Badji and on the lagoon rather than on the sea. It was managed by Lawson's eldest son, George Latty Lawson.[92] A description of this establishment was given by Duncan, who visited the place in February and March 1845. According to him, George Lawson's two sons (one of them presumably George Latty Lawson) lived next door to their father and traded extensively 'in all sorts of goods of British manufacture', in exchange for palm oil and ivory: 'Their houses are good, and in every way arranged to imitate our English style. They also enjoy every luxury which can be procured from European nations, as well as those of their own country.'[93] Apart from supervising Messrs Hutton's factory, Marman also had a private interest in Little Popo. He was married to George Lawson's daughter Sashey, who traded on his account in a separate establishment.[94] There is little information about this arrangement, but it probably existed by the early 1840s.[95]

Hutton's factory at Little Popo was soon followed by establishments at other places on the Slave Coast. In 1838, a factory was opened at Ouidah.[96] It appears to have been based on an arrangement between Marman and de Souza, reportedly made in 1837 during one of Marman's visits to Ouidah when de Souza offered to provide him with palm oil in exchange for goods, 'as the slave trade was so bad.'[97] This factory was destroyed in 1841 during an attack by a British cruiser on de Souza's flagstaff (which was suspected

---

[90] For Marman's activities on the coast, see Silke Strickrodt, 'British Abolitionist Policy on the Ground in West Africa in the Mid-Nineteenth Century', *Changing Worlds*, ed. Falola/ Childs, 183–200, pp. 184–5; Strickrodt, 'Aballow's Story'.
[91] *PP* Colonies Africa 1842, i, 212 (2 June 1842, W. M. Hutton).
[92] *Ibid.*, 660 (Mr. Gedge, 22 July 1842).
[93] Duncan, *Travels*, i, 99–100.
[94] TNA: CO267/228, incl. in Governor Macdonald, Sierra Leone, 21 April 1852: 'Chief Justice's notes taken at the trial of Marman indicted for Slave dealing.' Marman also had a wife in London, Elizabeth Marman, and one in Accra, Abena, with whom he managed his large establishment there.
[95] This date is inferred from evidence deriving from Marman's court case in 1851, when he was accused of slave dealing. It refers to events 'about 8 years ago' and mentions that he was married to Sashey at the time (TNA: CO96/23, no 87, incl. in Governor Hill, Cape Coast Castle, 24 Nov. 1851: B. Cruickshank, Cape Coast Castle, 24 Nov. 1851: Aballow's deposition, 12 Nov. 1851; see Strickrodt, 'Aballow's Story', 392, 398–99. However, in the GLL 'Mrs Marmon', referring to Sashey, is first documented in 1847 (1.68, J. H. Ahkurst, Ahguay, 22 [no month] 1847).
[96] TNA: CO96/24, W. M. Hutton, London, 25 July 1851; Lynn, *Commerce*, 22, 87.
[97] *PP* Colonies Africa 1842, i, Report from the Select Committee on Papers Relating to the African Forts, 116 (10 May 1842, Capt. Henry Seward).

to be used to signal to slave vessels) and abandoned.[98] However, it was re-established in April or May 1842, when Thomas Hutton took possession of the abandoned English fort there.[99]

A British naval officer, who had been engaged in the Bight of Benin between early 1838 and July 1841, gave an account of the development of the palm oil trade in this period and compared the exports of Little Popo and Ouidah. He noted that these two places and Lagos were 'the three principal slave ports' but regarded the slave trade as being 'comparatively at an end'. With regard to Little Popo, he explained this with the 'great' increase in the palm-oil trade: 'I think the cabboceer, that is, the king [George Lawson], is becoming aware of the superior advantage of the legal trade over the slave trade, the one being a steady commerce, the other only a chance thing.' According to him, Little Popo was the only place on the coast in this period where the palm oil trade was carried on to a considerable extent: 'At Whydah, which is a much larger slaving port, there is very little trade in palm oil; perhaps to one puncheon at Whydah, 10 go off from Popo; at least such is my idea, speaking from what I have heard'.[100]

The French naval officer Bouët-Willaumez, who made three voyages to the West African coast between 1837 and 1846, also noted that 'a lot' of palm oil was collected at Little Popo.[101] Further information concerning the amount of palm oil exported from Little Popo comes from W. M. Hutton. When questioned in 1842 about the development of Little Popo's exports, he replied,

> The growth of the trade is very gradual; that is to say, the increase of the trade in the products of Africa. In comparison with about eight years ago [when his firm began to trade at Popo], I dare say, the quantity of palm oil from that portion of the coast may have trebled; still at present the quantity is not large, comparatively, for instance, with Bonny. Bonny exports from 15,000 to 20,000 tons of palm oil, and we think it a great deal if we can get 300 or 400 from Popo.[102]

From 1842, Messrs Hutton's enterprise on the coast was growing fast. Marman started a factory at Badagry, perhaps as a substitute for the one that had been given up at Ouidah in 1841. He was reportedly forced to abandon

---

[98] Ibid., 667–8 (22 July 1842, W. M. Hutton); ibid., 125 (13 May 1842, Commander H. Broadhead, R.N.).
[99] Ibid., 668 (22 July 1842, Mr. Forster citing letters by Mr. Topp, 12 May 1842; Capt. Grove, 17 April 1842). Newbury mistakenly gives 1845 as the date for Hutton's occupation of the abandoned English fort: *Western Slave Coast*, 33.
[100] PP, Colonies Africa 1842, i, 125–6 (13 May 1842, Commander H. Broadhead, R.N.).
[101] E. Bouët-Willaumez, *Commerce et traite des noirs aux côtes occidentales d'Afrique* (Genève, 1978), 123.
[102] PP Colonies Africa 1842, i, 212 (2 June 1842, W. M. Hutton).

it by May 1842, but the trade with Badagry continued and by early 1845 the factory had been re-established by Thomas Hutton.[103] Another factory was established at Agoué, although it is not clear exactly when. It is documented reliably from early 1843, but there is an earlier reference to Thomas Hutton's local agent, John Henry Ahkurst, which suggests that it may have been established by April 1842.[104] The factory house which was made of wood and had been prefabricated in England, came to be known locally as the 'board house'. It was one of the few buildings which survived the fire of January 1852, in which Hutton was estimated to have lost about £10,000.[105]

Initially, the factories at Little Popo and Agoué appear to have been Messrs Hutton's main establishments on the Slave Coast. Between these two places, conditions were more favourable at Little Popo, due to the political stability there in the 1840s. The trade there was controlled by the Lawsons, who effectively ruled the place, while the situation of the factory at Agoué was more hazardous, owing to the political instability and frequent disturbances, which were probably fuelled (partly at least) by the anti-British feeling of the local slave traders. For example, in 1848 Ahkurst told a visitor that the country was 'generally in an unsettled state' and showed him a place 'where the natives had a short time previous attempted to burn down his factory but had only succeeded in destroying one shed.'[106] There were also suspicions that the fire at the factory in 1843 had been due to arson.[107] Another incident was reported in August 1851, when the factory was blockaded by the inhabitants for more than a week.[108] Generally, the situation at Agoué was so precarious that Ahkurst was afraid to leave the factory unguarded.[109]

By early 1843, Messrs Hutton's agents were also purchasing palm oil at Porto Seguro and in the Anlo area, at Keta and Woe ('Awey', near Cape St. Paul). By April of this year a factory had been established at Porto Seguro.

---

[103] *Ibid.*, 116 (10 May 1842, Capt. Henry Seward), Duncan, *Travels*, 143. For references to Messrs Hutton's trade at Badagry, see GLL.

[104] Jones/ Sebald, *African Family Archive*, 1.4, J. H. Ahkurst, Ahguay, 7 Feb. 1843; *PP* Colonies Africa 1842, i, 668 (22 July 1842, Mr. Forster, citing a letter by Capt. Grove, 17 April 1842). There is an earlier letter, dated 12 December 1841, but the dating is not reliable: Jones/ Sebald, *African Family Archive*, 1.2, J.H. Ahkurst, Ahguay, 12 Dec. 1841, incl. n.5.

[105] TNA: FO84/893, incl. in Hamilton, [London] Admiralty, 10 April 1852: T. G. Forbes, 'Philomel', Whydah, 5 Feb. 1852; WMMS: West Africa Correspondance, Box 263: William West, Cape Coast, 10 Feb. 1860 (citing John Quan Veé, Ahguay, 11 Nov. 1859); Bouche, *Sept ans*, 302–3. The factory house was destroyed by another fire in 1859. This was after Hutton's death and the purchase of the house by the Wesleyan Methodist Missionary Society, which had planned to move their headquarters on the coast from Ouidah to Agoué.

[106] TNA: CO96/14, incl. in H. S. Ward, [London], 4 July 1848: Abraham Middleton, Badagry, W[est] Coast Africa, 1 Mar. 1848.

[107] TNA: CO96/2, W. B. Hutton & Sons, [London], 20 Dec. 1843 (incls.); CO96/4, no.8, Gov. Hill, Cape Coast Castle, 21 March 1844 (incls.), CO96/4, no.31, Gov. Hill, Cape Coast Castle, 1 June 1844 (incls.); CO96/5, Canning, [London] 13 Jan. 1844 (incls.).

[108] FO84/886, incl. 13 in Slave Trade no. 3, Beecroft, 19 Feb. 1852: G. A. F. Prior, Whydah, 12 Aug. 1851.

[109] Jones/ Sebald, *African Family Archive*, 1.179, J.H. Ahkurst, Ahguay, 4 Sept. 1848.

Duncan's report of his visit to Porto Seguro in March 1845 suggests that no agent was settled there at this time, although there was a house belonging to a Mr Henrique, who had his main residence at Agoué.[110] According to Duncan, the inhabitants were eager to have a factory at their place and the chief offered to build him a house and store if he remained there and established one.[111] However, there must have been an agent there again soon afterwards, as is shown by references in the GLL to the collection of palm oil there in December 1845 and again in May 1849.[112] One of these references also indicates that the factory at Porto Seguro was subordinate to the one at Little Popo, as the oil collected there was sent to Little Popo by canoes via the lagoon or, when the lagoon was low, by sea. A resident agent for Thomas Hutton is documented there in 1852.[113]

Further, palm oil was collected at 'Fish Town' or Gunkope/Gomalouta, Aflao and Adafia. In May 1849, the factor at Agoué reported that 'Bruce at fish town' has 'some' palm oil to sell.[114] Bruce can probably be identified with James Bruce, one of the caboceers of Porto Seguro who signed the anti-slave trade treaty of 1852 (see Chapter 5). A factory had been established at Aflao by December 1845 and in Adafia by early 1852.[115] According to the British naval officer who visited Adafia in January 1852, the factory there belonged to Thomas Hutton, but two or three months later George Latty Lawson stated that it was Marman's (like the one at Kedzi, in the Anlo area).[116] This discrepancy may have been due to Marman being imprisoned at Accra at this time, charged with slave dealing. It is only of minor consequence anyway, because all these factories probably ran on the account of Messrs Hutton in London. The local agent, G. T. Ward, was documented at Adafia in July 1853, suggesting that the factory was still active at this time.[117]

---

[110] Duncan describes Henrique as a 'half-brother to Mr. Ingram, late Governor in the Gambia' but does not say what he was doing on the coast (Duncan, *Travels*, 148, 170). His Portuguese-sounding name and the fact that he maintained houses at both Agoué and Porto Seguro probably made him suspicious to the British anti-slave trade patrols. For further references, see Jones/ Sebald, *African Family Archive*, 1.47, George Latty Lawson, Popo, New London, 27 Dec. 1845; 1.33, James W. Hansen, Ahguay, 22 Nov. 1844 ('Senhor Erique').

[111] Duncan, *Travels*, i, 172.

[112] Jones/ Sebald, *African Family Archive*, 1.47, George Latty Lawson, Popo, New London, 27 Dec. 1845; 1.228, J. H. Ahkurst, Ahguay, 30 May 1849.

[113] TNA: FO84/893, incl. in Hamilton, [London], 10 April 1852: T. G. Forbes, 'Philomel', Whydah, 5 Feb. 1852.

[114] Jones/ Sebald, *African Family Archive*, 1.228, J. H. Ahkurst, Ahguay, 30 May 1849.

[115] *Ibid.*, 1.46, James M. [W.?] Hansen, Ahguay, 26 Dec. 1845. Hansen had made a trip to Aflao earlier in this year: *ibid.*, 1.39, James W. Hansen, Ahguay, 22 Oct. 1845; TNA: FO84/893, incl. in Hamilton, [London], 10 April 1852: T. G. Forbes, 'Philomel', Whydah, 5 Feb. 1852.

[116] TNA: CO267/228, incl. in Governor Macdonald, Sierra Leone, 21 April 1852: 'Chief Justice's notes taken at the trial of Marman indicted for Slave dealing'; TNA: FO84/893, incl. in Hamilton, [London] Admiralty, 10 April 1852: Lieut. T. G. Forbes, 'Philomel', Whydah, 5 Feb. 1852.

[117] Jones/ Sebald, *African Family Archive*, 1.259, G. T. Ward, Adaffie, 17 June 1853; 1.260, G. T. Ward, 10 July 1853.

At Grand Popo, the purchase of palm oil by Messrs Hutton is first documented in October 1845, when it was reported that one of their vessels was 'at Grand Popo taking palm oil from Antonio [de Souza].'[118] In October 1849, Ahkurst wrote to George Latty Lawson that he was 'glad to hear that you are doing a little at Grand Popo', suggesting that Messrs Hutton's trade at Grand Popo was managed by George Latty Lawson and that the oil was sent to Little Popo.[119] Grand Popo's main revenue however seems to have derived not from this trade but from the duties that were levied on traders, goods and, most of all, slaves that passed along the lagoon through the area. This is indicated by the T. G. Forbes' report of the conclusion of the anti-slave trade treaty in 1852.[120] According to this, the chief of Grand Popo (= Al-lee-far?) inquired how he was expected to act if he saw slaves passing his town, explaining that 'his Revenue was kept up by a Tax placed upon all Slaves passing either along the Coast or from the interior [...] That his Revenue would be stopped [by the treaty], wished it would be explained how he was to support himself.' In response, Forbes pointed to the benefits of increased cultivation and trade in agricultural produce, noting that the chief 'had hundreds and thousands of Acres of land, which by a little cultivation would produce a great quantity of Palm Oil and Cotton, and by placing a small Duty thereon, he would obtain a larger revenue than the one he at present receives through the Slave Trade.' According to Forbes, the chief appeared to be 'much pleased' with this, but (as noted above) by 1860 the British navy found it necessary to remind the chiefs of the treaty.[121]

There is little information concerning the sources of the palm oil exported from the western Slave Coast. Most of it came from the interior, partly by overland porterage and partly by canoes via the lagoon and rivers. In 1842, a British ship's captain stated that while on the Windward Coast (i.e. to the west of the Gold Coast) oil palms grew near the coast, on the Leeward Coast (i.e. to the east of the Gold Coast) they were 'some distance from the coast.'[122] This is corroborated by information from a naval officer, citing the slave traders and Marman, 'who possesses great information of the coast', as his sources. According to him, the palm oil was 'brought down to the coast on the heads of the natives, from a great distance, each native carrying a calibash [sic], which is a pumpkin hollowed out, which perhaps holds a couple of gallons'.[123] In 1845 Duncan reported that oil palms were

---

[118] *Ibid.*, 1.187, A. J. Beart, Ahguay, 15 Oct. 1848.
[119] *Ibid.*, 1.238, J. H. Ahkurst, Ahguay, 13 Oct. 1849.
[120] TNA: FO84/893, incl. in Hamilton, [London] Admiralty, 10 April 1852: Lieut. T. G. Forbes, 'Philomel', Whydah, 5 Feb. 1852.
[121] TNA: FO84/1124, Admiralty, [London] 13 July 1860: Commander W. Bowden, 'Medusa', Whydah, 31 January 1860.
[122] *PP* Colonies Africa 1842, i, 113 (10 May 1842, Capt. H. Dring).
[123] *Ibid.*, 125–6 (13 May 1842, Commander H. Broadhead, R.N.).

'cultivated' at Porto Seguro, 'on account of the nuts, used for oil.'[124] Bouët's map from 1851 shows oil palm forests to the north of the lagoon between Glidji and the Mono river.[125] In his report from 1879, W.T.G. Lawson noted that the market at Gbome ('Pomeh') on Lake Togo played an important role in the trade. Palm oil and kernels were brought there from the interior, totalling 'not less than upwards of twenty puncheons of oil [...] besides several tons of Kernels on each market day', and then presumably shipped to the coastal entrepôts by canoe along the lagoon.[126] (Palm kernels were exported from the Bight of Benin only from the 1850s.[127]) In the 1890s, Klose gave further information, which can probably be extrapolated to the earlier period. According to him, Little Popo's trade was mainly carried on by African middlemen who bought the produce in the great markets on the lagoon and the rivers, such as at Glidji, Vogan, Dekpo, and Hahoté. He explicitly noted the central role of the lagoon in this trade, as a means the transportation. However, oil was also sent to Little Popo from markets that were farther removed from the lagoon, 'such as the whole stretch of coast which comprises the area of the oil palms, the hinterland of Little Popo, Sagada, Tshegbo and other central points.'[128]

The importance of small suppliers in the palm oil trade is indicated by the great role which cowries played as an article imported into the region in exchange for palm oil.[129] Bouët-Willaumez observed that 'At Little Popo, as on the coast that follows [to the east] and even a little on the Gold Coast, one will note that the cowries play a great role among the articles of a cargo'.[130] This is supported by the documents in the GLL, which show that cowries played a crucial role for Messrs Hutton's factories on the coast.[131] The importance of cowrie currency in this trade was due to its great capability for subdivision, which made it suitable for small-scale transactions.

Why did the western Slave Coast play this pioneering role in the palm oil trade on the Slave Coast? There are several possible explanations and the answer probably lies in a combination of some or all of them. First, agricultural produce had been exported from the region before. This means that there was a fertile hinterland, the local people were used to cultivating it for

---

[124] Duncan, *Travels*, i, 148.

[125] A. Bouët, *Sketch of the Slave Coast* (1851), in B. Schnapper, *La politique et le commerce français dans le Golfe de Guinée de 1838 à 1871* (Paris, 1961), map 10, opp. p.192.

[126] GNA: ADM1/2/361, no. 26: Lawson, 'Report' (1879), 27.

[127] Law, *Dahomey*, 196 n.50.

[128] Klose, *Togo*, 70.

[129] See Robin Law, '"Legitimate" Trade and Gender Relations in Yorubaland and Dahomey', *From Slave Trade*, ed. Law, 195–214, p.199. He uses the case of Dahomey and Yorubaland to argue that there is a direct link between the importance of small-scale production of palm-oil and the role of cowries among the goods imported in exchange for palm oil.

[130] Bouët-Willaumez, *Commerce*, 123.

[131] See Jones/ Sebald, *African Family Archive*, 27–28.

a surplus and there already existed a transportation network for the export of bulky goods. Palm oil is bulky, which made transport difficult, especially once it had been collected in the factories and filled into puncheons. Information from the GLL shows that the puncheons used in the period contained just over 100 gallons imperial, which means that one puncheon weighed over 300kg.[132] The role of the lagoon for the transport was particularly important, as illustrated by a letter from George Latty Lawson to Marman in March 1849, noting that 'Our head trades man has been up from the bush who told me there is plenty of palm oil in the country only they are wanting once or twice raining that they might have sufficient water in the river to enable them to bring the oil in the canoes.'[133] In this respect, the ports on the western Slave Coast had a definite advantage over Ouidah because the lagoon ran close to the sea and its various branches connected the coastal entrepôts with the market towns in the interior.

Another reason may be external rather than internal: the western Slave Coast pioneered in the palm oil trade by default because the important ports to the east, Ouidah and Lagos, were still committed to the slave trade and there was resistance against the legitimate trade and traders there.[134] In contrast, on the western Slave Coast, and particularly at Little Popo, the trade in slaves and palm oil appears to have run smoothly in combination (and cooperation), due mainly to George Lawson, who on the one hand cultivated good relations with the British while, on the other hand, continuing to engage in the slave trade. The political situation at Agoué may not have been quite as favourable but it was still under control, quite literally, owing to the presence of the British cruisers on the coast. The threat of reprisals was a real one to Agoué, due to its exposed situation on the beach.

Lastly, part of the explanation may be found in the family connections between the pioneering trader, John Marman, and his agents in the region, the Lawsons, which may have preceded Marman's trade relations with the region. Marman first knew George Latty Lawson, and possibly his sister Sashie, from Accra, where they were all living at the time: George Latty Lawson at Dutch Accra, Sashie at Osu ('Danish Accra') and Marman at James Town ('British Accra'). According to George Latty Lawson, he had first met Marman in 1832 at Accra.[135] It is conceivable that Marman used this acquaintance to start his trade on the western Slave Coast – at least it must have facilitated his business there considerably, given the influence of

---

[132] See Jones/ Sebald, *African Family Archive*, 1.6, George Latty Lawson, New London, Popo, 5 April 1843; 1.47, George Latty Lawson, New London, Popo, 9 Dec. 1845. (1 ton = 320 imperial gallons.)
[133] *Ibid.*, 1.217, George Latty Lawson, New London, Popo, 30 March 1849.
[134] See Manning, *Slavery*, 53.
[135] TNA: CO267/228, incls. in Governor Macdonald, Sierra Leone, 21 April 1852: Copy of depositions taken before the Police Magistrate, Freetown, Sierra Leone, 10 March 1852; 'Chief Justice's notes taken at the trial of Marman indicted for Slave dealing'.

the Lawsons in the region.[136] Moreover, through his marriage with Sashey, Marman was also linked with de Souza, who (as noted before) had married a sister of a wife of George Lawson.

Besides palm oil, Messrs Hutton's agents on the coast also purchased other commodities for export, mainly corn and ivory but also cotton (and cash). Ebony is also documented, in September 1843, when Hutton's agent at Agoué mentioned that a vessel purchased 20 billets, 'the first shipd [sic] during my residence here'.[137]

Corn, that is maize, was an important article exported by Messrs Hutton's factories at Little Popo and Porto Seguro. There are two references to this in the GLL. In April 1843, George Latty Lawson notified Marman that he had shipped one hundred 100 puncheons of corn (containing '920 of small measures'), of which eighty had been supplied by the factory at Porto Seguro. However, Lawson was disappointed, as 'the corn does not come on so far as we expected'.[138] In March or May 1846, he informed Marman that the corn trade was ' very very dull indeed' and therefore had only been able to purchase just above 1,800kg.[139] The documents do not give information about the purpose for which the corn was exported, but it is likely that it was sold to slave traders to be used as provisions for slaves during the Atlantic crossing. This would have been just one of many ways by which Messrs Hutton's agents on the coast facilitated the slave trade by cooperating with the traders, which soon attracted the attention of the British navy and British authorities on the Gold Coast. At Ouidah, it was found that Hutton's agents not only lent canoes to the slave traders for the embarkation of slaves but also informed them about the movements of cruisers.[140] Marman himself was suspected of having sold slaves from his establishment at Accra to traders at Little Popo, for which he was charged in 1851 and subsequently stood trial at Sierra Leone.[141] The large cash-trade of Messrs Hutton's factories on the Slave Coast also raised suspicions, since

---

[136] An insight into the relationship between the Lawsons and Marman was given at Marman's trial in 1852, when George Latty Lawson stated that Marman was to him 'more like a father than anything else' (*ibid.*). This is interesting in the light of a similar statement made at a court case at Lagos in 1879, in which one client described his relationship to his patron as follows: 'He agreed promising to be as a father to us and help us in any difficulty. We were to be his sons and do what he wished us to do' (Kristin Mann, 'Owners, Slaves and the Struggle for Labour in the Commercial Transition at Lagos', *From Slave Trade*, ed. Law, 144–71, p.161).

[137] TNA: CO96/2, incl. in Thomas Hutton, Cape Coast, 24 Oct. 1843: J.H. Ahkurst, Ahguay, 25 Sept. 1843.

[138] Jones/ Sebald, *African Family Archive*, 1.6, G.L. Lawson, New London, Popo, 5 April 1843.

[139] *Ibid.*, 1.59, G. L. Lawson, New London, Popo, 18 March [May?] 1846. An imperial bushel is 36.369 litres, or, if it was used as a weight, so many kilograms.

[140] TNA: FO84/775, John Duncan, British Fort Whydah, 21 Aug. 1849; FO84/836, incl. in Admiralty, [London], 15 March 1851: Capt. John Adams, 'Gladiator', Badagry, 25 Dec. 1850; FO84/892, incl. in Admiralty, [London] 19 Jan. 1852: Capt. John Adams, 'Gladiator', at Ascension, 22 Nov. 1851.

[141] See Strickrodt, 'British Abolitionist Policy'.

it implied that they did business with the slave traders, who imported the cash into the region.[142]

Ivory was also purchased by Messrs Hutton's factories at Little Popo and Agoué but references to this trade in the GLL are rare and incidental. This can be interpreted in two ways; either this trade did not play a great role or it ran smoothly and was therefore not mentioned.[143] Referring to Little Popo, H. Seward, a British ship's captain, stated in 1842 that 'they generally have a good quantity of ivory there', while another, who had last traded there in 1837 or 1838, noted that 'a little ivory' was available.[144] Regarding the sources of the ivory, Bouche stated in the 1870s that Atakpame, lying a six to eight days' march in the interior, was a major source.[145]

The export of cotton was initiated by Thomas Hutton in the early 1850s at Agoué. In January 1851, he wrote that he had begun to purchase raw cotton for one string of cowries (i.e. forty shells) per pound. He found this price rather high but paid it to encourage the trade, hoping eventually to be able to bring it down.[146] However, manufactured cotton, that is cotton cloth (also referred to as 'Popo cloth'), had been an article of export from the region before. Seward reported that it was exported from Little Popo to the Gold Coast, apparently both by Africans and Europeans. According to him, it was bought at Little Popo for English goods and sold on the Gold Coast for palm oil and gold dust.[147]

The cultivation of cotton is documented in the region between Agoué and Porto Seguro. In the mid-1840s, Duncan explicitly mentioned it at Agoué, Little Popo ('to a considerable extent'), on the lagoon west of Glidji and Zalive, and at Ekpoui (on the eastern bank of Lake Togo).[148] In 1852 the English Vice-Consul at Ouidah noted that there was no cotton in Dahomey, 'Ahgwey, Little Popo and Porto Segoora, being the places for that commodity.'[149]

In 1842, W. M. Hutton observed that Hamburg firms had begun to trade palm oil in the Bight of Benin 'some four or five years ago', but he hoped that 'we need not call it a considerable one yet'. Bremen had also entered this trade.[150] However, on the western Slave Coast in the

---

[142] Lynn, *Commerce*, 216 n.44.
[143] Duncan, *Travels*, i, 93; Jones/ Sebald, *African Family Archive*, 1.294, James W. Hansen, Ahguay [probably 1845].
[144] PP Colonies Africa 1842, i, 117 (10 May 1842, Capt. H. Seward); *ibid.*, 112 (10 May 1842, Capt. Dring). See also *ibid.*, 120 (10 May 1842, Capt. Courtland). Cf. Bouët-Willaumez, *Commerce*, 123.
[145] Bouche, 'Notes', 94.
[146] Jones/ Sebald, *African Family Archive*, 1.251, Thomas Hutton, Ahguay, 23 [Jan.] 1851. For an overview of the monetary values in the region in the period, see Fraser, *Dahomey*, 271–2.
[147] PP, Colonies Africa 1842, i, 117 (10 May 1842, Capt. H. Seward).
[148] Duncan, *Travels*, i, 145.
[149] Fraser, 'Commercial Report' [May 1852], in: Fraser, *Dahomey*, 196.
[150] PP, Colonies Africa 1842, i, 217 (W. M. Hutton, 2 June 1842). Cf. Lynn, *Commerce*, 14–15.

1840s, Messrs Hutton seem to have managed to monopolise the palm oil trade, or at least to control it to a considerable degree. There is only one reference in the GLL to an 'interloping' trader at Agoué in this period, in June 1849. This was Walter Hanson, a Gold Coast trader whose brother James had been an agent at Hutton's Agoué factory between 1843 and 1846. He clearly was not welcome, as shown by Ahkurst's comment that 'he cant stay long, if he does we must outpay him, for these small traders do a deal of harm.'[151] The lack of further references to Hanson's activities in the region suggests that Messrs Hutton's agents successfully dealt him.[152] However, it is possible that traders at Ouidah purchased oil at Little Popo in the period.[153]

In the early 1850s Messrs Hutton's trade 'empire' fell apart. In London, W. M. Hutton died in 1851 and the firm W. B. Hutton & Sons was wound up.[154] The events on the West African coast were even more dramatic. As noted before, in November 1851 Marman was investigated on charges of slave dealing. Although he was acquitted in the subsequent trial at Sierra Leone, his trading career was apparently finished, and with it the factory at Little Popo.[155] George Latty Lawson, his agent at Little Popo, had been the prosecution's main witness during the trial, which probably finished their relations, if not to those between Marman and George Latty Lawson's sister. In 1852, Marman was judged bankrupt.[156] Thomas Hutton was experiencing his own troubles in the period. As already mentioned, he suffered great losses by the fire that destroyed Agoué in early 1852 and probably abandoned the factory soon afterwards.[157] Moreover, in the early 1850s there were personal problems between him and Marman's eldest son, Gerard Wilkins Marman, because the latter had seduced his wife and mother of his five children. This led to a court case because Hutton alleged that his wife, who had evidently left him for Marman junior, took with her property

---

[151] Jones/ Sebald, *African Family Archive*, 1.230, J.H. Ahkurst to G.L. Lawson, Ahguay, 16 June 1849.
[152] In the 1850s and early 1860s, Hanson was documented to be active in trade further east, at Ouidah, Badagry and Lagos. See TNA: FO84/976, Slave Trade no.17, Consul B. Campbell, Consulate, Lagos, 6 Sept. 1855 (incl.); FO84/1115, Slave Trade no.15, Consul G. Brand, Lagos, 7 April 1860 (incl.); FO84/1207, Admiralty, (London), 17 Feb. 1863 (incl.). In 1851, he was described as the clerk of Antonio de Souza at Ouidah (Fraser, 'Scraps from the daily memoranda', 26 Dec. 1851, in Fraser, *Dahomey*, 139). For James W. Hansen, see Duncan, *Travels*, i, 148; Jones/ Sebald, *African Family Archive*.
[153] Duncan, 'Note', 147; Duncan, *Travels*, i, 113.
[154] Lynn, *Commerce*, 87.
[155] See Strickrodt, 'British Abolitionist Policy'.
[156] TNA: CO96/43 no.17, incl in Sir B. Pine, Accra, 5 March 1858: John Marmon, James Town, Accra, 5 March 1858. Bankruptcies were frequent on the Gold Coast in the period. See S. B. Kaplow, 'The Mudfish and the Crocodile: Underdevelopment of a West African Bourgeoisie', *Science and Society*, 41 (1977), 317–33, pp. 323–28.
[157] TNA: FO84/893, incl. in Hamilton, [London] Admiralty, 10 April 1852: T. G. Forbes, 'Philomel', Whydah, 5 Feb. 1852.

of 'a very considerable value' that belonged to him.[158] He nevertheless planned to continue the trade with Little Popo and in June 1853 requested George Latty Lawson's assistance in supplying palm oil for a vessel which he intended to send out from London.[159] However, this project evidently failed since he too went bankrupt.[160] He died a short time later, on 6 November 1856, being drowned at Lagos when the canoe which was to take him to a vessel bound for Europe was upset in the surf.[161] Further, (as noted before) the important agents for the firm at Little Popo, George Lawson and his son George Latty Lawson, also died, the former in 1856 and the latter in 1859.

In the 1850s, the centre of the palm oil trade on the Slave Coast shifted to the east.[162] The western Slave Coast attracted a small number of palm oil traders from Europe and the Gold Coast in this and the following decade. Among the first new traders there appears to have been the French firm Victor Régis, of Marseille, which had occupied the French fort at Ouidah in 1842. Régis' first attempt to establish a factory in the region was apparently made in 1856, at Agoué.[163] In the same year it was reported that Thomas Hutton's son (presumably A. Calvert Hutton) had a factory there, which suggests perhaps that he was in fact Régis' agent and that Régis used the connections established by Thomas Hutton for their trade at Agoué.[164] It is not clear how long this factory lasted but probably not very long – it certainly did not survive the outbreak of the war at Agoué. In late 1857 or early 1858 Régis established a factory in Grand Popo, probably at Hévé.[165] In 1860, it was reported that 'the French have the trade almost entirely in their own hands at Popo.'[166] In the 1860s, Régis' factory at Agoué was reestablished and further factories at Little Popo and Porto Seguro founded, although the exact dates are not clear.[167]

Joseph Dawson, the Wesleyan Methodist missionary turned trader (who came from Cape Coast and was probably a descendant of the British governor whose name he bore) is documented to have started a factory at

---

[158] TNA: CO96/30, Gov. Hill, Cape Coast Castle, 1 Aug. 1854.
[159] Jones/ Sebald, *African Family Archive*, 1.258, Thomas Hutton, London, 1 June 1853.
[160] TNA: FO84/1115, incl. in Slave Trade no 41, Consul Brand, 5 June 1869: Petition of Thomas D. Reynolds, 29 May 1860.
[161] TNA: CO96/40, E. G. Banner, London, 15 Oct. 1856.
[162] Lynn, *Commerce*, 22.
[163] Schnapper, *La politique*, 180.
[164] TNA: FO84/1002, Consul B. Campbell, Consulate, Lagos, 29 July 1856.
[165] TNA: FO84/1061, incl. in Slave Trade No 19, Consul B. Campbell, Consulate, Lagos, 6 May 1858: Commander Aplin, 'Hecla', Lagos, 4 May 1858; Schnapper, *La politique*, 166.
[166] PP 1864–5, Class A, no.151, Commodore Wilmot, 'Rattlesnake', at Ascension, 1 Dec. 1864: Annual Report on the Slave Trade on the West Coast of Africa.
[167] Cornevin, *Histoire du Togo*, 131, 133; Schnapper, *La politique*, 166; Percy Ernst Schramm, *Deutschland und Übersee; der deutsche Handel mit den anderen Kontinenten, insbesondere Afrika, von Karl V. bis zu Bismarck* (Braunschweig, 1950), 252. Schramm gives the following dates for the foundation of the factories: 1864 Little Popo, 1868 Agoué and Porto Seguro. Cornevin gives 1865 for Porto Seguro and 1868 for Little Popo.

Agoué by 1859, which however finished with the 1860s war, when his house and property were destroyed. As noted above, this war crippled Agoué's trade in the early 1860s. In June 1860, the British consul at Lagos reported that Agoué's trade was 'completely paralyzed', forcing 'a very considerable number' of Agoué people to seek employment at Lagos.[168] In mid-1864, a British naval officer reported that 'All trade has been stopped for more than a year.'[169] Little Popo's trade also appears to have suffered from this war. There is just one factory documented in this period, belonging to the Dutch.[170] Despite the absence of competition it was reported to have but little trade, due mainly to the lack of suitable trade goods. It was taken over by a French firm in 1863 but abandoned as a failure shortly afterwards.[171]

By March 1859, a merchant named Byl was established at Agbanaken, but it is not clear who he was or where he came from.[172] He is possibly identifiable with the 'Mr Byll' listed among the people who gave presents to the new Lawson chief at Little Popo in 1869.[173] Whoever he was, he made his mark. By 1879 there was a place called 'Byll's town', lying on the beach to the south of Agbanaken, just east of the coastal settlement of Grand Popo.[174] His descendants still live in the region. According to their traditions, he was an English trader, but it is also possible that he was from Sierra Leone or the Gold Coast.[175] By 1872, Messrs F. and A. Swanzy, an English firm which had been active on the Gold Coast since 1847, had established factories at Porto Seguro, Agoué, Little Popo as well as Keta and Ouidah, although the exact dates are not clear.[176]

The transition from the slave trade to the palm oil trade initially posed no problems for the western Slave Coast. This is indicated by its pioneering role in the palm-oil trade. Further, the problems which this transition potentially posed for the economic life in the region were offset or at least delayed by

[168] TNA: FO84/1115, Slave Trade no.41: Consul Brand, Lagos, 5 June 1860.
[169] TNA: ADM123/66 no.2, Commodore A.P. Eardley Wilmot, 'Rattlesnake', off Whydah, 11 July 1864.
[170] *PP* Slave Trade 1862, Class A, incl. 5 in no. 91: Lieut. Dolben, 'Bloodhound,' at Sea, Aghwey, 16 Nov. 1861; TNA: FO84/1175, incl. in Slave Trade no.17: Consul Stanhope Freeman, Lagos, 10 Aug. 1862: Commander Parry, 'Griffon', Little Popo, 6 Aug. 1862; FO84/1186, incl. in Admiralty, [London], 14 October 1862: Commander J. L. Parry, 'Griffon', Little Popo, 6 Aug. 1862; Borghero, *Journal*, 124.
[171] Laffitte, *Le Pays*, 59–60.
[172] WMMS: West Africa Correspondence, Box 263: William West, Cape Coast, 6 June 1859.
[173] Jones/ Sebald, *African Family Archive*, 2.5: List of presents (to A.B. Lawson?). There are further references to a person or persons of this name in the GLL, probably relatives or descendants of Mr Byll.
[174] GNA: ADM1/2/361, no. 26: Lawson, 'Report' (1879), 64. Cf. Bouche, *Sept ans*, 301.
[175] Pelofy, *Histoire*, 6, editor's note 12.
[176] Pedler, *The Lion and the Unicorn in Africa: A History of the Origins of the United Africa Company 1787–1931* (London, 1974), 45. The Swanzy family's connection with the Gold Coast reaches back to the 1790s, when the father of F. and A. Swanzy was employed by the African Company. See H. Swanzy, 'A Trading Family in the Nineteenth Century Gold Coast', *TGCTHS*, 2 (1956), 87–120.

the fact that the slave trade continued while the large-scale palm-oil trade had begun; from the 1830s to the 1860s these two trades were carried on side by side or, indeed, in co-operation.[177] Only in the 1870s, after the ending of the illegal trade and the civil war between Little Popo and Agoué, did the consequences of this transition become clear, i.e. that some places were better able to adapt to the new conditions than others. Little Popo and Porto Seguro managed well. Agoué, however, was unable to establish itself in the palm oil trade due to the lack of water transport to the interior. In contrast, Grand Popo began to thrive, owing to its situation on the Mono river. This was observed in a report from 1875 by the British Governor of the Gold Coast. According to him, Porto Seguro, 'the first town of any importance to leeward of Ouittah', exported principally 'palm oil and palm-nut kernels, but there is also a trade in cotton, guinea grains, &c.' Little Popo's trade was stated to be of the same kind, but larger. Agoué's once considerable trade was deteriorating, 'in consequence of the produce being now carried from the interior to Grand Popo.' Grand Popo's trade flourished, 'there is a large trade in palm oil and palm nut kernels in exchange for spirits, which are imported in large quantities. [...] The King of Agbanakey – a small place up the Lagoon – claims a small export duty, which is paid by all resident merchants.'[178]

The decline of Agoué's trade and the revival of Grand Popo's trade can be explained by access to water transport into the interior, or, in the case of Agoué, the lack of it.[179] According to Bouche, by the mid-1870s Agoué's economy was based on the cultivation of the farms to the north of the lagoon and the sale of provisions to vessels and to Dahomey.[180] This is corroborated by other observers. In 1879, W.T.G. Lawson described Agoué as 'a trading Port', which however seems to refer exclusively to the provisions trade, as he fails to mention any European factories there. According to him, there were 'many fine buildings built by the Portuguese but they are now mostly in ruins'.[181] Six years later, Zöller explicitly noted the lack of European factories and European trade at Agoué.[182] This contrasts with developments in the Grand Popo territory, where there were three or even four important trading places by the late 1870s. Among them was Agbanaken, the royal capital, which had developed a flourishing trade in palm oil and kernels due to its advantageous position on the Mono.

---

[177] Cf. David Northrup, 'The Compatibility of the Slave and Palm Oil Trades in the Bight of Biafra', *JAH*, 17 (1976), 353–64; Elisée Soumonni, 'The Compatibility of the Slave and Palm Oil Trades in Dahomey, 1818–1856', *From Slave Trade*, ed. Law, 78–92.
[178] TNA: FO84/1465, G. Strahan, Government House, Cape Coast, 22 Nov. 1875.
[179] See Bouche, 'Notes', 98.
[180] Bouche, *Sept ans*, 305. Cyprien Fabre et Cie of Marseille left Agoué (where they had probably established themselves in the late 1860s or early 1870s) in 1874, when they sold their house and plot there to the Catholic Mission.
[181] GNA: ADM1/2/361, no.26: Lawson, 'Report' (1879), 39–40.
[182] Zöller, *Das Togoland*, 182.

According to Lawson, many traders from Ge/ Little Popo, Ouidah and other places had settled there, although there was but one 'good house [European built?]'.[183] At Grand Popo, the port town, Lawson counted four European and four 'native' factories, and the mail steamers called 'about three weeks out of four.' Hévé, lying opposite Grand Popo on the northern bank of the lagoon, 'possesses one fine brick built house a French Trading Establishment one of the oldest Establishments on the Coast', probably referring to Régis' factory. Further, there was 'Byll's Town', already mentioned, which boasted 'three good European built houses and three trading establishments.'[184]

Agoué's brief economic boom in the mid-nineteenth century was closely bound up with the illegal slave trade and the link by the lagoon with Ouidah (as Freeman had noted so perceptively already in 1843). However, although it was unable to succeed in the palm oil trade after the abolition of the slave trade, it found a niche in the regional, and also international trade by supplying provisions. This was observed by Zöller, who in 1885 noted the 'high degree of cultivation, which at Agoué can be found north of the lagoon and which makes the lack of trade less perceptible.' Due to this, Agoué continued to thrive in the period. This is further indicated by the fact that of all the places on the Slave Coast which he had visited (including Keta and Little Popo), Zöller rated it as the second-most populous settlement, after Ouidah.[185]

---

[183] GNA: ADM1/2/361, no.26: Lawson, 'Report' (1879), 68–9.
[184] *Ibid.*, 64–5, 67.
[185] Zöller, *Das Togoland*, 182–3. Zöller estimated Agoué's population at 9,000 inhabitants, which however is exaggerated. According to Bouche, Agoué had 6,000 inhabitants before the small-pox epidemic of 1873 killed nearly a quarter of them (*Sept ans*, 207, 301).

Epilogue

The colonial partition & its consequences 1870s to c. 1900

In the 1870s, two developments occurred which had profound consequences for the political and economic life on the western Slave Coast and would eventually lead to the partition of the region among three European colonial powers. These were, first, the incorporation of the Anlo region to the west into the British Gold Coast territory and, second, the establishment of increasing numbers of foreign traders on the western Slave Coast. These developments were interconnected, the latter being mainly a result of the former.

The incorporation of the Anlo region into the British Gold Coast territory in June 1874 was part of the extension and consolidation of British political power on the Gold and Slave Coasts, the beginnings of which can be traced back to the British anti-slave trade campaign.[1] Aspects of this process were the bombardment of Lagos in 1851, the blockade of the ports and places on the Slave Coast in early 1852, the 1852 treaties for the abolition of the slave trade, the annexation of Lagos in 1861. In 1872, the British took over the Dutch settlements on the Gold Coast. A month after the incorporation of Anlo, the Crown Colony of the Gold Coast and Lagos was created by Royal Proclamation.[2] Between July 1876 and May 1877, the British also blockaded the coast from Porto Seguro to Porto Novo, in order to force the king of Dahomey to pay a fine.[3]

---

[1] On the Gold Coast, this can be traced back even further, to George Maclean's term of office as President of the Council at Cape Coast Castle (1828 to 1843). Beginning with the 1831 peace treaty with Asante, he 'acquired or assumed large responsibility' for the other Gold Coast states that were party to it, which was then formalised by the 'Bond' of 1844. See G. E. Metcalfe, *Great Britain and Ghana: Documents of Ghana History 1807–1957* (Accra, 1964), 129.

[2] For the background of British policy in the region in the period, see Hargreaves, *Prelude*, 166–74. For Lagos, see Mann, *Slavery*, chap. 3; Newbury, *Western Slave Coast*, 49–76, esp. 65–7.

[3] See Catherine Coquery, 'Le blocus de Whydah (1876–1877) et la rivalité franco-anglaise au Dahomey', *CEA*, 2/7 (1962), 373–419; Hargreaves, *Prelude*, 201–7; Newbury, *Western Slave Coast*, 103–5.

The incorporation of Anlo into the British Gold Coast territory meant that a stiff duty was now imposed on spirits and other goods imported into the region.[4] This prompted many of the traders who were established at Keta to move further east out of the British territory, which extended to Adafia, or at least to establish branches there. Some of these traders, French, German and Sierra Leonean, moved to Little Popo. The first German, or, more correctly, Hanseatic, firm, Friedrich M. Vietor Söhne from Bremen, established itself there in this period.[5] S. B. Cole, a Sierra Leonean trader, also arrived at Little Popo then.[6] However, many of the traders from Keta moved only a short distance beyond the boundary, to Denu, which within a few years became a flourishing trading place.[7] This situation gave rise to large-scale smuggling of goods into the British territory, in which, incidentally, a person from Agoué, Geraldo de Lima aka Atitsogbi, a former slave who had turned slave trader, played a central role.[8] In order to end the smuggling business, in December 1879 the British pushed the limits of their territory further east, incorporating the territories of Agbosome and Aflao.[9] The rationale of this move was to widen the distance between the Keta lagoon and the border, in order to render the transport of smuggled goods more difficult and hazardous. The relocation of the British frontier prompted the traders at Denu to move yet further east. It was then, in the early 1880s, that a number of European firms established themselves at Little Popo and Porto Seguro. However, just as before many also settled just outside the border in

[4] See A. B. Ellis, *A History of the Gold Coast of West Africa* (London, 1893), 350, 359; Zöller, *Das Togoland*, 82–3. Cf. W. E. F. Ward, *A History of Ghana* (London, 1966), 313–14.

[5] The exact date of the firm's arrival is not clear. Sebald gives December 1873 (*Togo*, 32, citing August Vogt, *Westafrika in vorkolonialer Zeit; Freuden und Leiden eines Bielefelder Kaufmanns vor fünfzig Jahren in Togo, der früheren Sklavenküste in den Jahre 1873–77* [Bielefeld, n.d. (1926)], 26). According to information from Cole from 1884, the firm's agent Rottmann had arrived following the British Asante war (TNA: 30/29.269 Conf. 4994, no.72, incl.9: 'Notes by Sir S. Rowe of a Conversation with Mr. S. B. Cole at Little Popo', 15 Feb. 1884). In March 1875, the firm leased a newly built factory house from the chiefs of Little Popo (*ibid.*, no.72, incl.10: Notes taken by S[amuel] R[owe], Little Popo, 10 Feb. 1884: 'Agreement of M. Roltmann [= Rottmann] with T. A. Severin, dated March 3, 1875'). Cf. Jones, 'Between Three Stools', 2. Schramm gives 1856 as the date of Vietor's establishment at Little Popo, possibly in an attempt to show that the German firms predated the French at Little Popo (*Deutschland*, 253–5).

[6] TNA: 30/29.269 Conf. 4994, no.72, incl.9: 'Notes by Sir S. Rowe of a Conversation with Mr. S. B. Cole at Little Popo', 15 Feb. 1884.

[7] For a description of Denu in this period, see GNA: ADM1/2/361, no.26: Lawson, 'Report' (1879), 21. The name of the place, 'Denu', means in fact 'customs/toll station', but it predates these developments. It was documented in 1852 by T. G. Forbes ('Daynoo') (TNA: FO84/893, incl. in Hamilton, [London] Admiralty, 10 April 1852: T. G. Forbes, 'Philomel', Whydah, 5 Feb. 1852).

[8] Amenumey, 'Geraldo da Lima'; Ellis, *History*, 358–61; Gayibor, *Le Genyi*, 217–21; Greene, *Gender*, 127–34.

[9] For the treaties, see TNA: CO876/35, no.24: Memorandum of provisional agreement between H. T. Ussher and the chiefs and headmen of Afflowhoo, 1 Dec. 1879; *ibid.*, no.25: Articles of a final agreement between H. T. Ussher and the king and chiefs of Agbosomé, 2 Dec. 1879; *ibid.*, no.26: Articles of a final agreement between H. T. Ussher and the chiefs and headmen of Afflowhoo, 6 Dec. 1879.

order to capitalise on the customs differences, prompting trade to spring up at Baguida, Baguida Beach and Bé Beach (Lomé).[10]

The extension of British authority along the coast gave the starting signal for the European 'scramble' for the settlements on the Slave Coast, whether the British wanted it or not. It caused alarm among both the European traders and local people. Already in 1874, German traders had requested protection from their government against the British encroachments, but Bismarck was not yet interested.[11] The French government was more responsive to the complaints of their traders, especially after the blockade of the coast by British cruisers in 1876/7, when fears of a British invasion of Dahomey, and its consequences for the French trade, had prompted French traders to pay half of the fine which the British had demanded from the king of Dahomey. This episode caused the French to conclude a treaty for the cession of Cotonou, which in February 1879 was formally attached to French Gabon. A treaty for a French protectorate over Porto Novo was signed in April 1882 and ratified in early 1883.[12]

At Little Popo, British expansion caused anxiety not only among the French traders but also among the rivals of the Lawson party, which was possibly fanned by French traders. In order to understand subsequent developments, a brief discussion of the political situation there is necessary. By the 1870s, political authority in both the kingdom of Little Popo and its main coastal port was fragmented. The kingdom was divided into three 'semi-independent' districts, Porto Seguro, Little Popo and Agoué, where the king at Glidji was nominally acknowledged but had little real influence. According to W.T.G. Lawson, who was not, however, a disinterested observer, the actual power rested with '[t]he Chiefs of [the coastal settlement of] Little Popo', i.e. by implication the Lawsons, who 'from their pecuniary influence absorbed and still retain the ruling power of the Geng Country'.[13] Other reports from the period do, however, indicate that the political situation at the coastal settlement was not that simple. According to a report from Strahan, the Governor of the Gold Coast, from 1875, 'There is here a divided Government, under two chiefs, each of whom governs his part of the town. An appeal by Europeans to the Courts of this place is useless, as the chiefs appear to have no power to enforce their decrees.'[14] The nature of this division of authority becomes clear from contemporary documents. On the one side, there were the Lawsons, who after an 'interregnum' of ten years,

---

[10] See Newbury, *Western Slave Coast*, 101. NB: He gives the wrong date for the extension of British jurisdiction of Adafia; it was 1874 rather than 1867. (Cf. Ellis, *History*, 350, 359; Ward, *History*, 313.)
[11] Schramm, *Deutschland*, 256; Newbury, *Western Slave Coast*, 110.
[12] Coquery, 'Le blocus', 373–419; Hargreaves, *Prelude*, 201–7; Newbury, *Western Slave Coast*, 103–8.
[13] GNA: ADM1/2/361, no.26: Lawson, 'Report' (1879), 29, 38–9, 44.
[14] TNA: FO84/1465, Gov. G. Strahan, Government House, Cape Coast, 22 Nov. 1875.

after the death of George Latty Lawson, had elected a new chief in 1869, Alexander Boevi Lawson. He died in 1883, but during the last years of his life had been unable to carry out his duties due to illness and had in effect been replaced by Edward Lawson (d. 1882). T. G. Lawson, who had become the head of the family after George Latty Lawson's death, had preferred to remain at Sierra Leone, where he was employed in colonial government service. Nevertheless, he continued to be acknowledged by the Lawsons at Little Popo as 'a sort of counsellor "in absentia"'.[15] On the other side, there was Pedro Kodjo, who had settled at Little Popo after the war with Agoué and, as shown by the testimony of the naval officer who visited the place in 1864, had gained considerable political influence there.[16] He had associated with or gained influence over Jehowey aka Kodjovi, the Mina chief and collector of customs at the coastal settlement.[17] To make things worse, the king at Glidji died in the early 1880s, and there appears to have been a brief interregnum before he was replaced.[18]

This was the situation when the French traders, prompted by Bareste, the French Vice-Consul at Sierra Leone, decided to secure requests for protection from the chiefs of Little Popo, Porto Seguro and Grand Popo in order to forestall British moves. This was done in August 1881, with 'discreet support' from French officials and missionaries on the coast but without the knowledge of the government in France.[19] The request from Little Popo was signed by Pedro Kodjo and probably also by Jehowey. The former had urged the Lawsons to do the same, but without success.[20] The Lawsons not only refused to sign but also contacted the British authorities on the Gold Coast, once again requesting British protection.[21] At the same time, some of the Sierra Leonean traders on the western Slave Coast also began

---

[15] See Jones, 'Between Three Stools', 2, 5.
[16] TNA: FO84/1184, incl. 2 in Admiralty, 15 April 1862: W.D.M. Dolben, 'Bloodhound', Cape Coast Castle, 18 Oct. 1861. Cf. PP Slave Trade 1862, incl. 2 in no.91: Edmonstone, 'Arrogant', Fernando Po, 3 Mar. 1862: Lieut. Dolben, 'Bloodhound', Cape Coast Castle, 18 Oct. 1861.
[17] Jones/ Sebald, *African Family Archive*, 3.39, Minutes of a meeting, Little Popo, 30 Oct. [1883]. Cf. *ibid.*, editors' 'Introduction', 175–81; TNA: PRO30/29.269 Conf. 4994, incl. 16 in no.72: Geyawhay, Little Popo, 2 Dec. 1883.
[18] See Jones, 'Between Three Stools', 8. Cf. Gayibor, 'Les rois', 212; Newbury, *Western Slave Coast*, 113.
[19] Hargreaves, *Prelude*, 324–5; Newbury, *Western Slave Coast*, 110. Hargreaves gives the following dates for these requests: Agoué, 6 Aug. 1884; Little Popo, 18. Aug.; Porto Seguro, 20 Aug.; Great Popo, 24 Aug. (325 n.1).
[20] Edmund Lawson to T. G. Lawson, Little Popo, 5 Sept. 1881, quoted in TNA: PRO30/29.269, Conf. 4994, no.72, incl. 32: S. Rowe, [London] 25 May 1884. Cf. Jones, 'Between Three Stools', 5.
[21] According to Rowe, T. G. Lawson wrote a letter (to him?) on 3 October 1881 and Edmund Lawson visited Accra in December 1881. T.G. Lawson had 'offered' Little Popo to the British already in 1861 and (as Rowe seems to suggest) again in 1862 (TNA: CO267/270, T. G. Lawson, Freetown, 18 April 1861; T. G. Lawson, 10 March 1862, cited in TNA: PRO30/29.269, Conf. 4994, no.72, incl.32: S. Rowe, [London] 25 May 1884).

to request British protection.²² However, the British governor on the Gold Coast, Samuel Rowe, was unable to react because (unknown to the French) he was not authorised to acquire new protectorates. Meanwhile, the French government delayed action until 1883, and then accepted only the request for protection from Grand Popo. Nothing was done about the requests from the places further west because there were 'doubts', which evidently did not reach Governor Rowe on the Gold Coast.²³ In early August 1883, Rowe was alarmed by the information that a French man-of-war was about to establish protectorates at Little Popo as well as Grand Popo.²⁴ This prompted him to send W.T.G. Lawson, the son of T. G. Lawson who (like his father) had been a civil servant in the British settlements and who was then at Lagos, to Little Popo, with confidential instructions 'to do all in his power to encourage his relations and the people of the place to have confidence in the good intentions which Her Majesty's Government has always entertained towards them.' More explicit instructions were not deemed necessary, since Lawson himself was 'so much interested in the furtherance of British influence in Little Popo.'²⁵ Lawson arrived at Little Popo on Lagos on 24 August 1883. According to his own report to the lieutenant-governor at Lagos, he found the country 'in a most confused state, no particular Chief or King, and no unity, and the whole country at the mercy of usurpers, who are intriguing with the French Government.'²⁶ More detail about the situation comes from the report of a naval officer, Lieut. Comm. Blennerhasset, who had visited Little Popo in April of that year. According to him, the Lawsons, 'although numerous and supported by members of the British factories, apparently have not sufficient influence to maintain their just position', while their rival Pedro Kodjo had the support of the French and German traders, who were all 'Europeans or half-cast[e]s'. The representatives of the British factories were all 'gentlemen of colour', that is probably (mainly) Sierra Leoneans.²⁷ In May 1883, shortly after Blennerhasset's visit, Alexander Boévi Lawson, the Lawson chief, had died. However, W.T.G. Lawson acted promptly. On 31 August 1883, the Lawson people appointed him 'the rightful heir and Chief of this town', meaning that he was to be 'Regent of this town and Chief of this family till some one is permanently appointed in the room of G.L. Lawson [sic].'²⁸ In October 1883, they elected a new 'king', Daniel Cummings Lawson, who subsequently

---

²² See Jones, 'Between Three Stools', 5.
²³ Hargreaves, *Prelude*, 325; Newbury, *Western Slave Coast*, 107–8, 111.
²⁴ TNA: PRO30/29.269 Conf. 4994, no.10, incl.13: Gov. S. Rowe, Accra, 9 Aug. 1883.
²⁵ The published instruction for Lawson's visit was to gather further information on the distance between the Keta and Little Popo lagoons (TNA: PRO30/29.269, Conf. 4994, no.10, incl.13: S. Rowe, Accra, 9 Aug. 1883). Cf. Jones, 'Between Three Stools', 6.
²⁶ TNA: PRO30/29.269, Conf. 4994, no.10, incl.8: Mr. Lawson, Little Popo, 8 Sept. 1883.
²⁷ GNA: ADM 1/2/368, no.96, Blennerhasset, 20 April 1883. Cf. Jones, 'Between Three Stools', 6.
²⁸ TNA: PRO30/29.269, Conf. 4994, no.10, incl.11: Extract from the *Lagos Times* of September 12, 1883.

assumed the royal name George Akwete Lawson III, whilst W.T.G. Lawson took the title of 'Principle [sic] Minister'.[29] These developments gave a boost to the Lawson party and were a set-back for their rivals, forcing the French trader Cantaloup (Cyprien Fabre's agent) to admit that 'his candidate's [Pedro Kodjo's] claims were weaker than those of the Lawsons'. According to Hargreaves, by the end of 1883 Cantaloup was prepared to give up his hopes for a French protectorate at Little Popo.[30]

Meanwhile, in early 1883, the German traders, aggrieved by problems with the payment of customs duties (among other things), which were caused by the political disunity at Little Popo, had sent a request for the visit of an occasional warship to the German Foreign Office.[31] This set in motion the process that eventually was to produce the German colony of Togoland, although nobody at the time, not even the German traders on the coast, appears to have intended it. In response to the traders' complaints, the German government took two steps which were to have important consequences for the developments on the western Slave Coast. First, it appointed an Imperial Commissioner, Gustav Nachtigal, who was to investigate the traders' complaints.[32] Secondly, it sent the war-covette S.M.S. 'Sophie', Captain Stubenrauch, to Little Popo, to provide immediate relief. The outcome was the infamous episode of S.M.S. 'Sophie' at Little Popo, which can be briefly described as a German naval officer's attempt to impose order on a West African community – which however, as G. A. Lawson III tried to explain to him, was 'next to impossible' given 'the present state of affairs in the country'.[33] The result was unexpected and overwhelming, an illustration of the proverbial German efficiency. It included a request for German protection signed by Pedro Kodjo and his allies, the deportation of W.T.G. Lawson to Lagos, the imprisonment of two advisers of G.A. Lawson III who were subsequently taken to Germany as hostages, and the killing of one follower of the Lawson party and wounding of one or two others by German marines. G. A. Lawson III himself was badly shaken by the experience and the French traders' hopes for a French protectorate at Little Popo were boosted, since Stubenrauch's actions had diminished the British threat.[34] At this stage, Germany itself did not intend to establish a protectorate at Little Popo but accepted the precedence of French claims.

Five months later, in July 1884, the hostages returned by S.M.S. 'Möwe',

---

[29] Jones, 'Between Three Stools', 7.
[30] Hargreaves, *Prelude*, 326.
[31] Newbury, *Western Slave Coast*, 111–3.
[32] For the European background, see Hargreaves, *Prelude*, 316–21.
[33] TNA: PRO30/29.269 Conf. 4994, n.17, incl.2: King Lawson III to commander Stubenrauch, New London Palace, Little Popo, 1 Feb. 1884.
[34] For versions of this event, see TNA: PRO.30/29.269 Conf. 4994; *Gold Coast Times*, 8 Feb. 1884, 'Little Popo, Latest Intelligence', cited in Jones, 'Between Three Stools', 10 n.43; Yves Marguerat, *La naissance du Togo selon les documents de l'époque; premier periode: l'ombre de l'Angleterre* (Lomé, 1993), 236–290.

together with Nachtigal, the German Imperial Commissioner.[35] The latter had been instructed to visit Little Popo in order to arrange terms for the release of the hostages, but was precluded from accepting the protectorate since any collision with French interests was to be avoided. In Europe, the German government was keen to be friends with the French in the period and had assured the latter that the request for protection would not be accepted (which people on the coast however did not know). However, to the west of Little Popo, where there were no French traders, matters were different. According to Nachtigal's report, German traders there insisted that they were threatened by an imminent British move to end the smuggling into the Gold Coast from Bé Beach (Lomé), Baguida and Porto Seguro. In order to forestall this, Nachtigal proceeded to Baguida where the situation appeared critical, prompting him to arrange requests for German protection from the King of Togo (town), Mlapa, and the chiefs of Baguida. On 5 July the treaty was signed by which Mlapa accepted the German protectorate over his territory, extending from 'the eastern frontier of Porte [sic] Seguro to the western frontier of Lome or Beybeach.'[36] The German flag was hoisted and Heinrich Randad, the local agent for Wölber & Brohm, appointed provisional consul. By accepting the protectorate at Togo and Baguida, Nachtigal had exceeded his instructions but the German government nevertheless accepted it in October 1884. Nachtigal then returned to Little Popo, where he finally released the hostages.[37]

Randad, the new German provisional consul, swiftly proceeded to claim protectorates at Porto Seguro and Little Popo as well. So however did the French, who were becoming disturbed by the German traders' talk of taking over the whole of the Slave Coast. By the end of 1884, both the German and the French flags were raised over these two places. At Little Popo, the Kodjovi people claimed German protection, while the Lawsons, despairing of British support, now sided with the French. The British had now dropped out of the scramble for 'the Popos' and confined themselves to trying to negotiate assurances that the Lawsons would not suffer from having supported their cause.[38]

The subsequent events had little to do with the communities, inhabitants or traders in the region but were decided entirely by diplomats in Europe. After considering and rejecting a number of possible exchanges of territory, the French and German governments eventually agreed that the Germans were to have Little Popo and Porto Seguro while France added the possession of Agoué to that of Grand Popo.[39] This agreement came

---

[35] See Hargreaves, *Prelude*, 327; Newbury, *Western Slave Coast*, 114–5.
[36] For the text of the treaty, see *ibid.*, 209–10. Cf. Hargreaves, *Prelude*, 327–8.
[37] *Ibid.*, 328; Jones, 'Between Three Stools', 11.
[38] Hargreaves, *Prelude*, 328; Jones, 'Between Three Stools', 11–6.
[39] Newbury, *Western Slave Coast*, 115.

into effect on 24 December 1885. The boundary was finally delimited in early 1887. The way it was done shows the complete disregard which the colonial officials on the spot had for the concerns of their 'protected' people. The French–German protocol from 24 December 1885 had determined a point between Agoué and Little Popo where the border was to run, but also requested that indigenous boundaries should be considered. The boundary officials, however, decided for their own convenience (since they thought it very difficult and awkward to determine to which 'tribe' the various places belonged), to choose a suitable meridian instead. The resulting boundary ran from Hilakondji, situated on the beach just east of Little Popo, straight north as far as the ninth parallel, that is about 186 miles/300km inland. The German Foreign Office found this 'unbelievable', but nevertheless accepted it.[40]

This frontier was modified in 1897, when the French ceded the area north of the lagoon and west of the Mono river to the Germans, giving them to access to the Mono river.[41] Among other things, this meant that Agbanaken, the capital of the Hula kingdom, now fell under German rule, while the kingdom's coastal port of Grand Popo remained under the French. Furthermore, Agoué, which the French kept, was now cut off from its hinterland, where the farms which formed the basis of its economic life were situated. Agoué was now trapped on the mainly barren sandspit between the sea and the lagoon, the latter having become the part of the new boundary. There were agreements between the French and the Germans that the local people, who had their farms and their great market, Agouégan, north of the lagoon, were exempted from paying duties on the agricultural produce carried across the border to Agoué, but this lasted only as long, or as briefly, as the good understanding between the French and the Germans. Moreover, duties had to be paid on livestock, for which there was no exemption, and especially the tax on goats became a source of grievance. As a result of this situation, European, Afro-Brazilian and African traders as well as a large number of locals left Agoué, which was economically ruined.[42]

The question could be posed as to whether this colonial partition grew out of the earlier history of the region or whether it came from 'outside'? The most influential argument for the former view is by Hopkins, who

---

[40] Sebald, *Togo*, 69–70; Newbury, *Western Slave Coast*, 115.
[41] Newbury, *Western Slave Coast*, 169.
[42] ANB: 1E12.8, no.1, Poiret, Grand Popo, 11 Jan. 1900: 'Rapport sur Agoué'. Cf. Manning, *Slavery*, 166–7. For illustrations of incidents on this border, see ANB: 1E12.8, no.18, L'Administrateur Comandant le cercle de Grand-Popo (Rouhaud), Grand-Popo, 14 Sept. 1909; nos. 20, 21, L'Administrateur Comandant le cercle de Grand-Popo (Ch. Deroux), Grand-Popo, 17 Sept. 1909, 18 Sept. 1909; no.23, 'Situation politique pendant le mois de Novembre 1909', Cercle de Grand-Popo (n.d.); nos. 24, 28, L'Administrateur de Grand-Popo, Grand-Popo, 6 Dec. 1909; 28 Dec. 1909; 5E3, Gov. Mecklenburg, Lomé, 12 Oct. 1913.

claims that the partition was a logical consequence of the transformation of trade in the nineteenth century. Tensions between African suppliers and European traders arose basically as a result of the transition from the slave trade to 'legitimate' commerce (the 'crisis of adaptation'), when the position of the established ruling elites who had controlled the slave trade was undermined both by the lower profitability of the new trade and by the opening up of the trade to people who had formerly been excluded from it, creating new tensions between European traders and their African suppliers. These tensions were exacerbated by the collapse of West African produce prices from the 1860s, and particularly during the 'Great Depression' (1873–1896), which reduced profit margins and to which European traders reacted by trying to break the power of the African coastal middlemen. The breakdown of local authority and problems of disorder also prompted requests for intervention for the protection of trade.[43]

On the one hand, the events on the western Slave Coast, and more specifically at Little Popo, can be plausibly read in this way. The local problems multiplied with the increasing settlement there of European firms, itself a result of the 'new' trade in agricultural produce. With the declining profitability of this trade, the control of customs duties became more critical for local traders, which increased the rivalry between the two factions, led by the Lawsons and Pedro Kodjo. In order to bolster their positions, the rivals requested protection from the various European powers, the former first from the British and subsequently from the French, while the latter first turned to the French and later to the Germans. By protection they initially understood support rather than annexation, but this implication of the European powers in local politics began the process which led to the colonial take-over.

On the other hand, it can be argued that locally the situation had not really changed from earlier times. The political disorder that existed at Little Popo in the 1870s had already been there, as illustrated by the events in the 1820s, when the conflict between two rival factions there escalated into a civil war. The authority of the king at Glidji had already been eclipsed by 'upstart' traders in the coastal settlement in the 1780s.[44] Therefore, these problems could be seen as being inherent in the devel-

---

[43] Hopkins, *Economic History*, chapter 4. In an earlier article dealing with late nineteenth-century Yorubaland, Hopkins used the term 'crisis of adaptation' to describe the situation of the region's elite, while in his book he refers to 'acute problems of adaptation': 'Economic imperialism in West Africa: Lagos, 1880–1892', *Economic History Review*, 21 (1968), 580–608; *Economic History*, 142. For the argument that falling produce prices exacerbated conflict over political office, with reference to Calabar, see Latham, *Old Calabar*. For a discussion of local requests for protection, in the case of Douala, see Austen/ Derrick, *Middlemen*, 88–91.

[44] Hopkins himself noted that although the new trade in agricultural produce accelerated social change in coastal communities, it did not initiate it, for enterprising individuals had also been able to exploit the opportunities provided by the Atlantic slave trade for their own advantage (*Economic History*, 147).

opment of Afro-European trade more generally rather than being peculiar to this period. Moreover, requests for European protection from African notables keen to increase their local standing were nothing new either. British protection had been requested by the people of Gunkope already in 1852, by John Quarvee at Agoué in 1859 and by T. G. Lawson at Little Popo in 1861 and perhaps again in 1862.[45] German traders on the coast had also demanded intervention by their government to protect their trade interests against British 'encroachments' in the 1870s but this had been ignored by Bismarck. What had changed in this period was the attitude of the European governments, which became much more interventionist and aggressive. While in the earlier period the requests for protection had been disregarded, they were now accepted and even actively sought after, with European traders and officials actually handing out request forms to African chiefs. In this respect, colonial partition mainly reflected European rivalry rather than local problems and can be seen as coming from 'outside' the region.

Whatever its origins, the partition in its consequences was a watershed, resulting in the disruption of established trading patterns and the marginalisation of established trading settlements. It was especially disruptive on the western Slave Coast, and arguably more so than in other regions in West Africa, precisely because it was a partition rather than merely a European take-over. The region was divided among three colonial powers, which meant the establishment of two colonial frontiers and, more importantly, several different customs zones.[46] It is sometimes held that the artificial colonial frontiers did not matter much to the African people, who disregarded them and followed their business much as they had done before, across the borders. However, the case of the western Slave Coast shows that this was not always the case. On the one hand, the Africans exploited these new borders for their own profit, by smuggling, as illustrated especially clearly by the activities of Geraldo de Lima on the border of the British Gold Coast territory.[47] On the other hand, however, the borders, and particularly the customs duties that went with them, had a very real negative effect on some of the established trading places in the region, as shown by the almost instant ruin of Agoué's economy. Moreover, subsequent colonial devel-

[45] TNA: FO84/893, incl. in Hamilton, [London], 10 April 1852: T.G. Forbes, 'Philomel', at Whydah, 5 February 1852; FO84/1123, incl. 2 in Admiralty, [London] 29 Feb. 1860: William Bowden, 'Medusa', Lagos, 21 Nov. 1859; CO267/270, T. G. Lawson, Freetown, 18 April 1861; T. G. Lawson, 10 March 1862, cited in TNA: PRO30/29.269, Conf. 4994, no.72, incl. 32: S. Rowe, [London] 25 May 1884.
[46] The customs zones in the region in the early colonial period are a complex matter, constantly changing according to the various customs agreements concluded between the English, French and Germans. See Newbury, *Western Slave Coast*, 115–21, 158–9.
[47] See also Paul Nugent, 'Arbitrary Lines and the People's Minds: A Dissenting View on Colonial Boundaries in West Africa', *African Boundaries: Barriers, Conduits, and Opportunities*, ed. Nugent and A. I. Asiwaju (London, 1996), 35–67 (pp. 55–60).

opment policies, especially the construction of piers and railways, affected the very basis of the established economic and commercial structure in the region. This is shown by the cases of Little Popo and Grand Popo, which initially were able to cope quite well with the partition due to their favourable situation as regards water links with the interior (which is why they had become trading settlements in the first place). However, with the construction of piers at Cotonou and Lomé, which facilitated the embarkation and disembarkation of people and goods and therefore attracted trade, they too became marginalised. The wooden pier at Cotonou was built by the French in 1893 and affected Grand Popo (as well as Ouidah). There were plans for a similar pier at Grand Popo, for which the government gave concessions in 1893 and 1896, but nothing came of this.[48] Little Popo, on the other hand, lost out to Lomé, whose pier was opened in January 1904.[49] However, it had started to become marginalised even before this, as indicated by the relocation of the German colonial administration from Little Popo, where it had installed itself after the German-French agreement of December 1885, to Lomé in 1897. The building of railway lines further contributed to the economic decline of Little Popo and Grand Popo, because they made water transport by river and lagoons, which had been their principal asset, less important. The railway line from Cotonou to Dan, just north of Abomey, was opened in July 1905. As a result of this, the traffic from Grand Popo to Djalloukou, one of the large entrepôts for imported salt, declined, since the entrepôt for salt moved to the end of the railway line. Probably even worse was the effect of the railway branch lines along the coast, which facilitated the transport of produce for shipment from Cotonou and Lomé.[50]

Today the once thriving trading settlements of Aného/Little Popo, Agoué and Grand Popo strike the visitor as run-down but with a certain seedy charm, places where nothing much ever happens. The local communities are keen to change this. The desire for economic regeneration was a major stimulus for the organisation of the international colloquium at Aného in September 2000, which was co-organised by the local 'Association pour le Développement de la Commune d'Aného (ADECAN)'. The discussion of the possibilities for regeneration and ways to attract investors were high on the agenda. The exploitation of the town's history and its role in the slave trade by developing projects of cultural tourism is an obvious possibility, as is already practised successfully at Ouidah and a number of Ghanaian towns, especially Cape Coast and Elmina.

[48] Newbury, *Western Slave Coast*, 144.
[49] Djamoudja Nangbadi, 'Histoire d'une capitale africaine: Lomé des origines à nos jours' (thèse de doctorat, Université de Poitiers, 1994), 221.
[50] See Manning, *Slavery*, 145–7. The railway line between Cotonou and Ouidah was opened in 1903 and extended to Segbohoué (on Lake Ahéme) in 1906. The line connecting Lomé and Aného opened in 1905.

However, if the predictions of one of the participants in the colloquium, the geographer Adoté Blivi, are correct, such projects of regeneration may prove irrelevant. According to him, due to global warming, Aného, which is already visibly threatened by coastal erosion, will disappear into the rising sea in the near future.[51]

---

[51] Blivi, 'Vulnerabilité', 652–3.

Bibliography

Archival sources

BÉNIN

Archives Nationales du Bénin, Porto Novo
Série E: Affaires politiques, sous-série 1E-5E, 1ère partie
1E2   Abomey.
1E8   Colonie du Dahomey.
1E9   Grand Popo.
1E12   Mono.
5E   Delimitation des frontières et relations extérieures.

Archives Mgr Robert Codjo Sastre, Lokossa
Pélofy, Isidore, 'Familles d'Agoué venues du Brésil et de Cuba et du Sierra Leone' (ms, [1944?] 97pp).
——, 'Histoire d'Agoué' (ms, 14pp).
Pierucci, J., ['Histoire d'Agoué'] (ms, 1953, 48pp).

DENMARK

National Archives, Copenhagen
Sager til Guineisk Journal, 1817–26.

FRANCE

Archives Nationales de la France, Section d'Outre-Mer, Aix-en-Provence
Archives des Colonies
C.6, Letters received, Sénégal ancien.
C.6/25-7, Papers concerning Juda [Ouidah], Ardres [Porto-Novo] etc., 1712–1806.
C.6/26, Sr Bauduchiron, 'Mémoire pour servir à faire de noveaux établissemens à la Côte de Guinée', 23 July 1777.
Sr Bauduchiron, 'Mémoire d'Observations sur ceux faits par Sr Baud Duchiron, pour les noveaux Etablissmens à faire à la Côte de Guinée', Fontainebleu, 28 Sept. 1777.

C.6/27, M. de Champagny, 'Mémoire contenant des observations sur quelques points de la Côte de Guinée, visités en 1786 par la Corvette le Pandour, et sur la possibilité d'y faire des Etablissmens'.

Bibliothèque Nationale, Paris
Fonds français: 24223: 'Journal du voiage de Guinée et Cayenne, par le Chevalier Des Marchais Capitaine comandant la fregatte de la Compagnie des Indes, l'Expédition, pendant les Années 1724, 1725 et 1726'.

GERMANY

Unitätsarchiv Herrnhut
R.15.N.2 no.11   Prottens Diarium, 1737–41.
R.15.N.5 no.19   Erstes Schreiben Meders an das Direktorium aus Fort Christiansburg (sic), 11. Juli 1761.
                  Meder 10.10.1737 an das Unitäts-Direktorium.
R.15.N.8   'Guinea Prottens Reise-Diarium' (1756–1761).

GHANA

National Archives of Ghana, Accra
ADM 1/2   Despatches – Enclosures from Governor to Secretary of State.
SC 4   Freeman Papers.

NETHERLANDS

National Archives, The Hague
Archief Admiraliteitscolleges, Collectie J. A. van der Velden 1.01.47.17.
NBKG 9   Minuutnotulen DG & Raden 1742–1758.
NBKG 198   Register der Rapporten 1758–1770.
NBKG 1132–1135   Correspondentie Jan Nieser, 1787–1819.
WIC 505   Resolutiën 1758–1764 aan kamer Amsterdam.
WIC 961   Correspondentie met de buitenforten den Journaal Elmina 1760, Lamer Zeeland: Poposche correspondentie.

TOGO

Archives Nationales du Togo, Lomé
2APA   Affaires Politiques et Administratives.
FA1   Fonds allemand: Kaiserliches Gouvernement von Togo.

UNITED KINGDOM

The National Archives, London
ADM123   Admiralty Records: Africa Station, Correspondence.
ADM344   Hydrographic Department: Coastal and Riverine Views.
CO96   Colonial Office and predecessors: Gold Coast: Original Correspondence to 1951.
CO267   Colonial Office and predecessors: Sierra Leone: Original Correspondence, 1664–1946.
CO700   Colonial Office and predecessors: Maps and Plans, series 1.

CO879	War and Colonial Department and Colonial Office: Africa, confidential prints to 1934.
FO2	Foreign Office: Political and Other Departments: General Correspondence before 1906, Africa.
FO84	Foreign Office: Slave Trade Department and successors: General Correspondence before 1906.
PRO30/29	Domestic Records of the TNA, Gifts, Deposits, Notes and Transcripts: Leveson-Gower, First Earl of Granville and predecessors and successor: Papers.
T70	Records created and inherited by HM Treasury: Company of Royal Adventurers of England Trading with Africa and Successors.

United Kingdom Hydrographic Office, Taunton

L5971	H. M. Denham and A. Middleton, 'Avon's Survey of the Bight of Benin 1846. Sheet 1: Cape St. Paul's to Little Popoe'.
L5972	H.M. Denham and A. Middleton, 'Avon's Survey of the Bight of Benin 1846. Sheet 2: Porourah to Lagos'.
L7791	F. Struvé, 'West Coast of Africa: Plan of the Coastal Lagoon between Whydah and Cape St. Paul, Bight of Benin, surveyed in the years 1849 and 1850'.
OD 8	H. M. Denham, 'Remarks and Sailing Directions for the Bight of Benin, West Coast of Africa, resulting from the Survey HMS Avon, 1846'.
OD 9	F. Struvé, 'Report of the Expedition surveying and exploring the coastal lagoons in the Bight of Benin, mainly between Whydah and Cape St Paul, 1849–1850'.

Wesleyan Methodist Missionary Society Archive, School of Oriental and African Studies, London
Special Series Biographical, West Africa: Papers of Thomas Birch Freeman.
West Africa Correspondence, Gold Coast / Gold Coast and Lagos.
Reports of the Wesleyan Methodist Missionary Society.

USA

Rhode Island Historical Society, Providence, Rhode Island
Carrington Papers.

Government Publications

Parliamentary Papers 1850 [1171] XXXVIII, Papers respecting the Cession to Great Britain of the Danish Possessions on the Coast of Africa.

Parliamentary Papers **(Irish University Press, 1968)**
Colonies Africa series.
Slave Trade series.

Report of the Committee of Council appointed for consideration of all matters relating to Trade and Foreign Plantations ... [on] the State of the Trade to Africa (House of Commons, London, 1789).
State Papers 1852–53 ('Great Britain and West Coast of Africa').

Collections of contemporary documents

Brásio, António, ed., *Monumenta Missionaria Africana*, 1st series 14 vols, 2nd series 5 vols (Lisbon, 1952–85).
Crooks, J. J., *Records relating to the Gold Coast Settlements from 1750 to 1874* (London, 1973).
Curtin, Philip (ed.), *Africa Remembered: Narratives by West Africans from the Era of the Slave Trade* (Madison, Wisc., 1967).
Jones, Adam, transl. and ed., *German Sources for West African History 1599–1669* (Wiesbaden, 1983).
——, transl. and ed., *Brandenburg Sources for West African History 1680–1700* (Wiesbaden, 1985).
——, transcr., transl. and ed., *West Africa in the Mid-Seventeenth Century; An Anonymous Dutch Manuscript* (African Studies Association Press, 1995).
——, and Peter Sebald, eds, *An African Family Archive: The Lawsons of Little Popo / Aneho (Togo), 1841–1938* (Oxford, 2005).
Justesen, Ole, ed., *Danish Sources for the History of Ghana, 1657–1754*, 2 vols (Copenhagen, 2005).
Law, Robin, ed., *Correspondence from the Royal African Company's Factories at Offra and Whydah on the Slave Coast of West Africa, in the Public Record Office, London, 1678–93* (Edinburgh, 1990).
——, ed., *Correspondence of the Royal African Company's Chief Merchants at Cabo Corso Castle with William's Fort Whydah, and the Little Popo Factory, 1727–1728: An annotated transcription of Ms. Francklin 1055/1 in the Bedfordshire County Record Office* (African Studies Program, University of Wisconsin-Madison, 1991).
——, ed., *Further Correspondence of the Royal African Company of England relating to the 'Slave Coast', 1681–99: Selected Documents from Ms. Rawlinson c. 745–747 in the Bodleian Library, Oxford* (African Studies Program, University of Wisconsin-Madison, 1992).
——, ed., *The English in West Africa: The local correspondence of the Royal African Company of England, 1681–1699*, 3 vols (Oxford, 1997, 2001, 2006).
Marguerat, Yves, *La naissance du Togo selon les documents de l'époque: premier periode: l'ombre de l'Angleterre* (Lomé, 1993).
Metcalfe, G.E., *Great Britain and Ghana; Documents of Ghana History 1807–1957* (Accra, 1964).
Newbury, C.W., *British Policy towards West Africa: Select Documents 1786–1874* (Oxford, 1965).
Parés, Luis Nicolau, 'Cartas do Daomé: Uma introdução', *Afro-Ásia*, 47 (2013), 295–395.
Peres, Damião, ed., *Os mais antigos roteiros da Guiné* (Lisbon, 1952).
Reynier, 'Eléments sur la réorganisation du commandement indigène à Ouidah (1917)', *Mémoire du Bénin* 2 (Cotonou, 1993), 29–73.
Van Dantzig, Albert, comp. and transl., *The Dutch and the Guinea Coast 1674–1742: A Collection of Documents from the General State Archive at The Hague* (Accra, 1978).

Books and articles before 1900

Aarestrup, N. U., 'Report to the Company (1774)', *TA*, 3 (Copenhagen, 1797–98), 161–92.
Adams, John, *Remarks on the Country Extending from Cape Palmas to the River Congo; with an Appendix containing a New Account of the European Trade with the West Coast of Africa* (London, 1823).
African Pilot, or Sailing Directions for the Western Coast of Africa, Part 1: From Cape Spartel to the River Cameroons (London, 1856; 5th ed., 1890; 7th ed., 1907).
Baquaqua, Mahommah Gardo, *The Biography of Mahommah Gardo Baquaqua; His Passage from Slavery to Freedom in Africa and America*, ed. Robin Law and Paul Lovejoy (Princeton, 2001).
Barbot, Jean, *Barbot on Guinea: The Writings of Jean Barbot on West Africa, 1678–1712*, ed. Paul

Hair, Adam Jones and Robin Law, 2 vols (London, 1992).
Biørn, A. R., 'Biørn's beretning 1788 om de danske Forter og Negrier; Nogle Bidrag til Kundskab om de Danske Stracking paa Guinea Kysten', *TA*, 3 (Copenhagen, 1797–98), 193–230.
Bold, Edward, *The Merchants' and Mariners' African Guide: The Coast, Bays, Harbours, and Adjacent Islands of West Africa* (1822, repr. Cambridge, 2011).
Borghero, Francesco, *Journal de Francesco Borghero, premier missionaire du Dahomey, 1861–1865*, ed. Renzo Mandirola and Yves Morel (Paris, 1997).
——, 'Relation sur l'établissement des missions dans le Vicariat apostolique du Dahomé' (3 Dec. 1863), *Journal de Francesco Borghero, premier missionnaire au Dahomey, 1861–1865*, ed. by Renzo Mandirola & Yves Morel (Paris, 1997), 235–81.
——, 'Lettre au sujet d'une carte de la Côte des Esclaves addressée à M. d'Avezac par M. l'abbé Borghéro, missionaire', Lyon, 14 April 1866, in: (M. l'Abbé) Laffitte, *Le Dahomé, souvenirs de voyage et de mission* (Tours, 1873), xi–xxvii.
Bosman, William, *A New and Accurate Description of the Coast of Guinea: Divided into The Gold, The Slave, and The Ivory Coasts* (1705), introd. John Ralph Willis, ed. John D. Fage and R. E. Bradbury (London, 1967).
Bouche, Pierre, 'Notes sur les républiques minas de la Côte des Esclaves', ed. J. E. Bouche, *Bulletin de la Société de Géographie*, 6th series, 10 (July-Dec. 1875), 93–100.
——, *Sept ans en Afrique occidentale: la Côte des Esclaves et le Dahomey* (Paris, 1885).
Bouët-Willaumez, E., *Commerce et traite des noirs aux côtes occidentales d'Afrique* (Paris, 1848).
Bowdich, Thomas Edward, *Mission from Cape Coast Castle to Ashantee* (1819), ed. W. E. F. Ward (London, 1966).
Bowen, T. J., *Central Africa. Adventures and Missionary Labours in Several Countries in the Interior of Africa, from 1849 to 1856* (1857, repr. London, 1968).
Burton, Richard, *A Mission to Gelele, King of Dahomey*, 2 vols (London, 1864).
Clapperton, Hugh, *Hugh Clapperton into the Interior of Africa: Records of the Second Expedition, 1825–27*, ed. Jamie Bruce Lockhart and Paul E. Lovejoy (Leiden: Brill, 2005).
Christaller, J. G. et al., *A Dictionary, English, Tshi (Asante), Akra; Tshi (Chwee) comprising as Dialects: Akán (Asànté, Akán, Akuapém &c) and Fànté; Akra (Accra) connected with Adangme; Gold Coast, W. Africa* (Basel, 1874).
——, *Dictionary of the Asante and Fante Language* (Basel, 1881).
Dalzel, Archibald, *The History of Dahomy, an Inland Kingdom of Africa, compiled from authentic memoirs* (London, 1793).
Delbée, 'Journal du voyage du Sieur Delbée', in vol. 2 of Jean Clodoré, *Relation de ce qui s'est passé dans les isles & terre-ferme de l'Amerique, pendant la dernière guerre avec l'Angleterre* (Paris, 1671), 347–558.
Ducasse, Jean-Baptiste, 'Relation du voyage de Guynée fait en 1687 sur la frégate "La Tempeste" par le Sieur du Casse', *L'Établissement d'Issigny 1687–1702*, ed. P. Roussier (Paris, 1935), 1–47.
Duncan, John, 'Note of a Journey from Cape Coast to Whydah, on the West Coast of Africa', *Journal of the Royal Geographical Society of London* 16 (1846), 143–153.
——, *Travels in Western Africa in 1845 & 1846: Comprising a Journey from Whydah, through the Kingdom of Dahomey, to Adofoodia, in the Interior*, 2 vols (1847, repr. London, 1968).
Ellis, A. B., *The Ewe-Speaking Peoples of the Slave Coast of West Africa* (1890, repr. Chicago, 1965).
——, *A History of the Gold Coast of West Africa* (London 1893).
Foa, Edouard, *Le Dahomey* (Paris, 1895).
Forbes, Frederick E., *Dahomey and the Dahomans, being the Journal of two Missions to the Kingdom of the King of Dahomey and Residence at his Capital in the Years 1849 and 1850*, 2 vols (1851, repr. London, 1966).
Fraser, Louis, *Dahomey and the Ending of the Trans-Atlantic Slave Trade: The Journals and Correspondence of Vice-Consul Louis Fraser, 1851–1852*, ed. Robin Law (Oxford, 2012).
Freeman, Thomas Birch, *Journal of Various Visits to the Kingdoms of Ashanti, Aku, & Dahomi, in Western Africa* (1844, repr. London, 1968).

Gonzales, Père, 'Relation abregée du voyages des Pères de l'Ordre des Frères Prêcheurs, missionaires en Afrique et en Guinée', *L'Année dominicaine*, 14 (1702; new ed., Lyon, 1900), 462–75.
Henrici, Ernst, *Das deutsche Togogebiet und meine Afrikareise 1887* (1888, British Library, n.d.).
——, *Lehrbuch der Ephe-Sprache (Ewe). Anlo-, Anecho- und Dahome-Mundart mit Glossar und einer Karte der Sklavenküste* (1891, repr. Charleston, S. C., n.d.)
Isert, Paul Erdmann, *Letters on West Africa and the Slave Trade: Paul Isert's Journey to Guinea and the Caribbean Islands in Columbia (1788)*, transl. and ed. Selena Axelrod Winsnes (Legon-Accra, 2007).
Klose, Heinrich, *Togo unter deutscher Flagge* (Berlin, 1899).
Koelle, Sigismund Wilhelm, *Polyglotta Africana* (1854, 2nd ed. Graz, 1963).
Labarthe, P., *Voyage à la Côte de Guinée, ou description des côtes d'Afrique, depuis le Cap Tagrin jusqu'au Cap de Lopez-Gonzalves* (Paris, 1803).
Labat, Jean Baptiste, *Voyage du Chevalier de Marchais en Guinée, isles voisines, et à Cayenne, fait en 1725, 1726 et 1727*, 4 vols (1730, 2nd ed. Amsterdam, 1731).
Laffitte, l'Abbé, *Le Dahomé : souvenirs de voyage et de mission* (Tours, 1873).
——, *Le pays des nègres et la Côte des Esclaves* (Tours, 1885).
Lind, H.G., 'Undersøgelser foretagne op ad Flodan Volta i 1827 og 1828', *Archiv for Sovaesenet* VI (Copenhagen, 1834), 1–6.
De Marees, Pieter, *Description and Historical Account of the Gold Kingdom of Guinea* (1602), transl. and ed. Albert van Dantzig and Adam Jones (Oxford University Press for the British Academy), 1987.
M'Leod, John, *A Voyage to Africa, with Some Account of the Manners and Customs of the Dahomian People* (1820, repr., London, 1971).
Monrad, H. C., *A Description of the Guinea Coast and its Inhabitants*, transl. Selena Axelrod Winsnes (1822, Legon, 2008).
Müller, Wilhelm Johann, 'Description of the Fetu Country', *German Sources for West African History 1599–1669*, transl. and ed. Adam Jones (Wiesbaden, 1983), 134–328.
Norris, Robert, *Memoirs of the Reign of Bossa Ahadee, King of Dahomy* (London, 1789).
Pereira, Duarte Pacheco, *Esmeraldo de Situ Orbis*, trans. and ed. George H.T. Kimble (London, 1937).
Phillips, Thomas, 'A Journal of a Voyage made in the Hannibal of London, Ann. 1693, 1694, From England to Cape Monseradoe, in Africa; And then along the Coast of Guiney to Whidaw, the Island of St. Thomas, and so forward to Barbadoes', *A Collection of Voyages and Travels, some now first printed from original manuscripts, others now first published in English*, comp. Awnsham Churchill and John Churchill (1732, repr. London, 1746).
Pornain, 'Rapport de Monsieur Pornain Lieutenant de vaisseau, Adjudant du Commandant Superieur sur sa mission aux Popos pour y etablir le protectorat de la France' [April 1885], *Mémoires du Bénin*, 1 (1993), 45–67.
Rask, Johannes, *A Brief and Truthful Description of a Journey to and from Guinea*, vol. 1 of *Two Views from Christiansborg Castle: H.C. Monrad (1805–1809), Johannes Rask (1708–1713)*, transl. Selena Axelrod Winsnes (1754, Legon, 2008)
Reindorf, Carl Christian, *The History of the Gold Coast and Asante* (1895/1951, repr. Accra, 1966).
Robertson, G.A., *Notes on Africa, particularly those parts which are situated between Cape Verde and the River Congo* (1819, repr. n. p., 2007).
Rømer, Ludewig Ferdinand, *A Reliable Account of the Coast of Guinea (1760)*, transl. and ed. Selena Axelrod Winsnes (Oxford, 2000).
De Sandoval, Alonso, *Naturaleza, policia sagrada I profana, costumbres I ritos, disciplina I catechismo evangelico de todos Etiopes* (Seville, 1627).
Snelgrave, William, *A New Account of Some Parts of Guinea, and the Slave Trade* (London, 1734).
Stubenrauch, Korv.-Kapt., 'Aus den Reiseberichten S.M.S. "Sophie", Korv.-Kapt. Stubenrauch. Bemerkungen über die hydrographischen und kartographischen Verhältnisse an der Küste von Guinea', *Annalen der Hydrographie und Maritimen Metereologie* 12 (1884), 193–8.

Tilleman, Erick, *En kort og enfoldig beretnig om det landskab Giunea og dets beskaffenhed (1697);A Short and Simple Account of the Country Guinea and its Nature,* transl. and by Selena Axelrod Winsnes (African Studies Program, University of Wisconsin-Madison, 1994).
Van Zütphen, C. H., *Tagebuch einer Reise von Bahia nach Afrika* (Düsseldorf, 1835).
Zöller, Hugo, *Das Togoland und die Slavenküste* (Berlin and Stuttgart, 1885).
——, *Als Jurnalist [sic] und Forscher in Deutschlands großer Kolonialzeit* (Leipzig, 1930).

Newspapers and journals

The African Times: Journal of the African-Aid Society (London), 1862–5.
Annalen der Hydrographie und Maritimen Metereologie (Hamburg), vols 11–13, 1883–5.
Annual Reports of the Wesleyan Methodist Missionary Society (London), 1855–1863.
Globus: Illustrierte Zeitschrift für Länder- und Völkerkunde, vol. 13, 1907.
Royal Gold Coast Gazette and Commercial Intelligencer (Cape Coast), April 1822 – Jan. 1823.

Maps

Akolly, Adjavou Agbo, *Renovations urbaine & économique Aného: evolution spatiale, 1/10.000è* (Lomé, June 1982).
République du Bénin: Carte générale au 1: 600 000 (Cotonou: IGN, 1989).
Togo: Carte générale au 1: 500 000 (Lomé: IGN, 1989).

Internet sources

House of Commons Parliamentary Papers (2005–2014): http://parlipapers.chadwyck.co.uk/marketing/index.jsp
'Voyages: The Trans-Atlantic Slave Trade Database' (2009): http://slavevoyages.org/tast/index.faces

Local and family histories

Agbanon II, Fio, *Histoire de Petit-Popo et du royaume guin (1934)*, ed. N. L. Gayibor (Lomé, 1991).
Ajavon, Emmanuel Azon, Paul Jaenavho Ajavon and Pierre Jaenavho Ajavon, 'La Collectivité Ajavon', Lomé: n.d. [2000].
Gaba, Kue Agbota, 'The History of Anecho Ancien & Mordern [sic] [fro]m the earliest days in the 20 century [on] the Gold Coast to the later days of stool disputes and peace settlement between the Adjigos (Fanties) & the [L]awsons the Nugos (Akagbans)', ed. K. O'Rhodes (Anecho, September 1942).
Gayibor, Nicoué Lodjou, ed., *Les traditions historiques du Bas-Togo* (Niamey, 1992).
Kponton, Hubert Messanvi, 'Histoire des guin d'Aného et de Glidji', *Traditions Historiques du Bas-Togo,* ed. N. L. Gayibor, 237–61.
n.a., *Adjigovi* (n.p., 1933).
n.a., 'La Courte Histoire de Generation de la Famille Lawson' (1921), *Rivalités politiques et politique coloniale de la France au Togo,* comp. Gayibor, 40–53.
n.a., 'Petite Histoire d'Aneho' (1966), *Rivalités politiques et politique coloniale de la France au Togo,* comp. N. L. Gayibor, 54–61.

Quam-Dessou, *Histoire de la ville d'Anécho* (Lomé, 1981).
Quénum, Maximilien, *Les ancêtres de la famille Quénum* (Langres, 1981).
De Souza, Norberto Francisco, 'Contribution à l'Histoire de la Famille de Souza', *ED*, 8 (1995), 15–21.
De Souza, Simone, *La famille de Souza du Bénin – Togo* (Cotonou, 1992).

Books and articles after 1900

Akinjogbin, I. A., *Dahomey and its Neighbours 1708–1818* (Cambridge, 1967).
Akyeampong, Emmanuel Kwaku, *Between the Sea and the Lagoon: An Eco-Social History of the Anlo of Southeastern Ghana, c. 1850 to Recent Times* (Athens and Oxford, 2001).
Alagoa, E. J., 'Long-Distance Trade and States in the Niger Delta', *JAH*, 11/3 (1970), 319–29.
Alpern, Stanley B., 'The European Introduction of Crops into West Africa in Precolonial times', *HiA*, 19 (1992), 13–43.
——, 'Exotic Plants of Western Africa: Where They Came From and When', *HiA*, 35 (2008), 63–102.
Amenumey, D. E. K., 'Geraldo da Lima: A Reappraisal', *THSG*, 9 (1968), 65–78.
——, *The Ewe in Pre-Colonial Times* (Accra, 1986).
Araujo, Ana Lucia, 'Dahomey, Portugal and Bahia: King Adandozan and the Atlantic Slave Trade', *Slavery and Abolition*, 33/1 (2012), 1–19.
Austen, Ralph, *African Economic History: Internal Development and External Dependency* (Oxford and Portsmouth, NH, 1987).
—— and Jonathan Derrick, *Middlemen of the Cameroons Rivers: The Duala and their Hinterland c. 1600–1960* (Cambridge, 1999).
Austin, Gareth, 'Resources, Techniques, and Strategies South of the Sahara: Revising the Factor Endowments Perspective on African Economic Development, 1500–2000', *Economic History Review*, 61/3 (2008), 587–624.
Bailey, Anne C., *African Voices and the Atlantic Slave Trade: Beyond the Silence and the Shame* (Boston, 2005).
Bagodo, Obare, 'Archaeological Reconnaissance of the Lower Mono Valley: A Preliminary Report', *West African Journal of Archaeology*, 22 (1993), 24–36.
Barnes, Sandra 'The Economic Significance of Inland Coastal Fishing in Seventeenth-Century Lagos', *The Changing Worlds of Atlantic Africa: Essays in Honor of Robin Law*, ed. T. Falola and M. D. Childs (Durham, N. C., 2009), 51–66.
Baylin, Bernard; 'The Idea of Atlantic History', *Itinerario*, 20/1 (1996), 38–44.
Bayly, C. A., '"Archaic" and "Modern" Globalization in the Eurasian and African Arena, c.1750–1850', *Globalization in World History*, ed. Hopkins, 47–73.
Bellagamba, Alice, Sandra E. Greene, Martin A. Klein, eds, *African Voices on Slavery and the Slave Trade*, vol.1 (Cambridge, 2013).
Blivi, Adoté, 'Vulnerabilité de la côte togolais à l'elevation du niveau marin: une analyse de prévision et d'impact', *Le tricentenaire d'Aného*, ed. Gayibor, 643–60.
Boco, Pamphile, *Proverbes de la sagesse fon (Sud-Bénin)*, 4 vols (Cotonou, 2000)
Bourgoignie, G. I., *Les hommes de l'eau: Ethno-écologie au Dahomey lacustre* (Paris, 1973).
Brivio, Alessandra, 'Nos grand pères achetaient des esclaves…'. Le culte Mami Tchamba au Togo et Bénin', *Gradhiva: Revue d'anthropologie et de muséologie* (Musée de Quai Branly, Paris), nouvelle série 8 (2008), 65–79.
Brooks, George E., *Yankee Traders, Old Coasters and African Middlemen: A History of American Legitimate Trade with West Africa in the Nineteenth Century* (Boston, 1970).
——, *Eurafricans in Western Africa: Commerce, Social Status, Gender, and Religious Observance from the Sixteenth to the Eighteenth Century* (Athens and Oxford, 2003).
Candido, Mariana P., *An African Slaving Port and the Atlantic World: Benguela and its Hinterland* (Cambridge, 2013).
Canny, Nicholas and Philip Morgan (eds), *The Oxford Handbook of the Atlantic World,*

1450–1850 (Oxford, 2011).
Capo, Hounkpatin C., 'Le Gbe est une langue unique', *Africa*, 53/2 (1983), 47–57.
Chauveau, Jean-Pierre, 'Une histoire maritime africaine est-elle possible? Historiographie et histoire de la navigation et de la pêche africaine à la côte occidentale depuis le XVe siècle', *CEA*, 26 (1–2), 101/102 (1986), 173–235.
Chouin, Gérard L. and Christopher R. DeCorse, 'Prelude to the Atlantic Trade: New Perspectives on Southern Ghana's Pre-Atlantic History', *JAH*, 51/2 (2010), 123–4.
Cohen, Abner, *Custom and Politics in Urban Africa: A Study of Hausa Migration in Yoruba Towns* (London, 1969).
Conrad, Sebastian, *Globalgeschichte: Eine Einführung* (München, 2013), 18–19.
Cooper, Frederick, 'What is the Concept of Globalization Good for? An African Historian's Perspective', *African Affairs*, 100/399 (2001), 189–213.
Coquery, Catherine, 'Le blocus de Whydah (1876–1877) et la rivalité franco-anglaise au Dahomey', *CEA*, 2/7 (1962), 373–419.
Cornevin, Robert, *Histoire du Togo* (Paris, 1959).
——, *Histoire du Dahomey* (Paris, 1962).
Curtin, Philip, *The Atlantic Slave Trade: A Census* (Madison, Wis., 1969).
——, *Cross-Cultural Trade in World Perspective* (Cambridge, 1984).
Daaku, Kwame Yeboa, *Trade and Politics on the Gold Coast, 1600–1720: A Study of the African Reaction to European Trade* (Oxford, 1970).
Da Cunha, Manuela Carneiro, *Negros, estrangeiros: Os escravos libertos e sua volta à África* (São Paulo, 1985).
Dakubu, M. E. K., *Ga-English Dictionary* (Legon, 1973).
Debien, G. & J. Houdaille, 'Les origines des esclaves aux Antilles, no.32: Sur une sucrérie da la Guyane en 1690', *BIFAN*, series B, 26 (1964), 166–94.
Debrunner, H. W., *Presence and Prestige: Africans in Europe: A History of Africans in Europe before 1918* (Basel, 1979).
DeCorse, Christopher R., *An Archaeology of Elmina: Africans and Europeans on the Gold Coast, 1400–1900* (Washington and London, 2001).
Dike, K. Onukwa, *Trade and Politics in the Niger Delta 1830–1885* (Oxford 1956).
Dorjahn, V. R. and Christopher Fyfe, 'Landlord and Stranger: Change in Tenancy Relations in Sierra Leone', *JAH*, 3 (1962), 391–7.
Eltis, David, *Economic Growth and the Ending of the Transatlantic Slave Trade* (New York and Oxford, 1987).
——, *The Rise of African Slavery in the Americas* (Cambridge, 2000).
——, 'The Slave Trade and Commercial Agriculture in an African Context', *Commercial Agriculture*, ed. Law/ Schwarz/ Strickrodt, 28–53.
Everts, Natalie, 'Social Outcomes of Trade Relations: Encounters between Africans and Europeans in the Hubs of the Slave Trade on the Guinea Coast', *Migration, Trade, and Slavery in an Expanding World: Essays in Honour of Pieter Emmer*, ed. W. Klooster (Leiden, Boston, 2009), 141–62.
——, 'A Motley Company: Differing Identities among Euro-Africans in Eighteenth Century Elmina', *Brokers of Change*, ed. Green, 53–69.
——, 'Incorporating Euro-Africans in Akan Lineages and a Modest Development towards a Euro-African Identity in Eighteenth-Century Elmina', *THSG*, new series, 14 (2012), 79–104.
Fage, J. D., 'Some Remarks on Beads and Trade in Lower Guinea in the Sixteenth & Seventeenth Centuries', *JAH*, 3/2 (1962), 343–7.
Feinberg, Harvey, *Africans and Europeans in West Africa: Elminans and Dutchmen on the Gold Coast during the Eighteenth Century* (Philadelphia, 1989).
Field, M. J., *The Social Organization of the Gã People* (n. p., 1940).
Ford, John, *The Role of the Trypanosomiases in African Ecology: A Study of the Tsetse-Fly Problem* (Oxford, 1971).
Freitag, Ulrike and Achim von Oppen, '"Translocality": An Approach to Connection and Transfer in Area Studies', *Translocality: The Study of Globalising Processes from a Southern*

Perspective, ed. Freitag/von Oppen (Leiden, 2010), 1–21.
Fyfe, Christopher, *A History of Sierra Leone* (London, 1962).
Gayibor, Nicoué Lodjou,'Esquisse d'une histoire economique des ewe de l'ere precoloniale', *Annales de l'Université du Bénin, Togo*, 5 (1978), 129–44.
——, 'Agokoli et la dispersion de Notsé', *Peuples du Golfe du Bénin*, ed. de Medeiros, 47–70.
——, *Le Genyi: Un royaume oublié de la Côte de Guinée au temps de la traite des noirs* (Lomé, 1990).
——, 'Toponymie et toponymes anciens de la Côte des Esclaves', *Toponymie historique et glossonymes actuels de l'ancienne Côte des Esclaves (XVe-XIXe s.)*, ed. Gayibor (Lomé, 1990), 25–42+VIII.
——, 'Les conflits politiques à Aného de 1821 à 1960', *Cahiers du CRA*, 8 (1994), 198–203.
——, 'Les Rois de Glidji: Une chronologie revisée', *HiA*, 22 (1995), 197–222.
——, *Histoire des Togolais (Vol. 1) Des Origines à 1884* (Lomé, 1997).
——, 'Les villes négrières de l'ancienne Côte des Esclaves d'Ada à Grand-Popo', *Ports of the Slave Trade*, ed. Law/ Strickrodt, 35–47.
——, ed., *Rivalités politiques et politique coloniale de la France au Togo: Textes et Documents sur les conflits politiques à Aného de 1884 à 1960* (Lomé, 2000).
—— ed., *Le tricentenaire d'Aného et du pays guin; Actes du colloque internationale sur le tricentenaire du pays guin (Aného 10–20 septembre 2000)*, 2 vols (Lomé, 2001).
Green, Toby, *The Rise of the Trans-Atlantic Slave Trade in Western Africa, 1300–1589* (Cambridge, 2012).
——, (ed.), *Brokers of Change: Atlantic Commerce and Cultures in Pre-Colonial Western Africa* (NewYork, 2012).
Greene, Sandra E., 'Land, Lineage and Clan in Early Anlo', *Africa*, 51/1 (1981), 451–64.
——, 'Social Change in Eighteenth-Century Anlo: The Rule of Technology, Markets and Military Conflicts', *Africa*, 58/1 (1988), 70–86.
——, *Gender, Ethnicity and Social Change on the Upper Slave Coast: A History of the Anlo-Ewe* (Portsmouth, NH and London, 1996).
——, *Sacred Sites and the Colonial Encounter: A History of Meaning and Memory in Ghana* (Bloomington and Indianapolis, 2002).
Grivot, R., 'L'industrie du sel dans la subdivision de Grand-Popo', *Notes Africaines*, 21 (Jan. 1944), 23–4.
——, 'La pêche chez les Pedah du lac Ahémé', *BIFAN*, 11 (1949), 106–28.
Grove, J. M. and A. M. Johansen, 'The Historical Geography of theVolta Delta, Ghana, during the Period of Danish Influence', *BIFAN*, 30 (1968), 1376–1421.
Gutkind, Peter C.W., 'Trade and Labour in Early PrecolonialAfrican History:The Canoemen of Southern Ghana', *The Workers of African Trade*, ed. Catherine Coquery-Vidrovitch and Paul E. Lovejoy (Beverly Hills, 1985), 25–47.
Hancock, David, *Citizens of the World: London Merchants and the Integration of the British Atlantic Community, 1735–1785* (Cambridge, 1997).
Hargreaves, John D., *Prelude to the Partition of West Africa* (London, 1963).
Harrison Church, R. J., *West Africa: A Study of the Environment and of Man's Use of It* (London, 1974).
Härtter, Gustav, 'Einige Bausteine zur Geschichte der Evhestämme (Togo)', *Beiträge zur Kolonialpolitik und Kolonialwirtschaft*, 3 (1901–1902), I: 432–48, II: 464–80, III: 492–514.
——, 'Der Fischfang in Evheland', *Zeitschrift für Ethnologie*, 1 & 2 (1906), 51–63.
Henige, David P., *The Chronology of Oral Tradition: Quest for a Chimera* (Oxford, 1974).
Hernaes, Per O., *Slaves, Danes and African Coast Society* (Trondheim, 1998).
Hieke, Ernst, *Zur Geschichte des deutschen Handels mit Ostafrika: Das hamburgische Handelshaus Wm. O'Swald & Co, Teil 1: 1831–1870* (Hamburg, 1939).
Hill, Polly, 'Ewe Seine Fishermen', *Studies in Rural Capitalism in West Africa*, ed. Polly Hill (Cambridge, 1970), 30–52
Hill, M. B. and J. E.Webb, 'The Ecology of Lagos Lagoon, II. The Topography and Physical Features', *Philosophical Transactions of the Royal Society of London*, B, 241, 683 (4 Sept 1958), 319–33.

Hogendorn, Jan and Marion Johnson, *The Shell Money of the Slave Trade* (Cambridge, 1986).
Hopkins, A. G., *An Economic History of West Africa* (1973, new ed., London, 1996).
—— (ed.), *Globalization in World History* (London, 2002).
——, 'Introduction: Globalization', in *Globalization in World History*, ed. Hopkins, 1–10.
—— (ed.), *Global History: Interactions between the Universal and the Local* (Basingstoke, 2006).
——, 'The New Economic History of Africa', *JAH*, 50 (2009), 155–77.
Hopkins, Daniel, *Peter Thonning and Demark's Guinea Commission: A Study in Ninteenth-Century African Colonial Geography* (Leiden and Boston, 2013).
Iroko, A. Félix, 'La Côte des Esclaves: Un espace regional pour une histoire internationale', *Toponomie historique et glossonymes actuels de l'ancienne Côte des Esclaves (Xve-XIXe s.)*, ed. Nicoué Lodjou (Lomé, 1990), 43–54.
——, *Les Hula du XIVe au XIXe siècle* (Cotonou, 2001).
Johnson, Marion, 'Ashanti East of the Volta', *THSG*, 8 (1965), 33–59.
——, 'The Ounce Trade in Eighteenth-Century West African Trade', *JAH*, 7/2 (1966), 197–214.
——, 'The Cowrie Currencies of West Africa', part 1: *JAH*, 11/1 (1970), 17–49; part 2: *JAH*, 11/3 (1970), 331–53.
——, 'News from Nowhere: Duncan and "Adofoodia"', *HiA*, 1 (1974), 55–66.
——, 'Ivory and the Nineteenth Century Transformation in West Africa', *Figuring African Trade: Proceedings on the Symposium on the Quantification and Structure of the Import and Export and Long Distance Trade of Africa in the 19th Century (c.1800–1913)*, ed. G. Liesegang et al. (Berlin, 1986), 89–139.
Jones, Adam, *Zur Quellenproblematik der Geschichte Westafrikas, 1450–1900* (Stuttgart, 1990).
——, 'Little Popo and Agoué at the End of the Atlantic Slave Trade: Glimpses from the Lawson Correspondence and Other Sources', *Ports of the Slave Trade*, ed. Law/ Strickrodt, 122–34.
—— and Silke Strickrodt, 'Introduction: Recent Research on the Early Modern History of Atlantic Africa', *THSG*, new series, 4 (2012), 1–12.
Kahl, Wilhelm, 'Eingeborenenfischerei im westafrikanischen Küstenmeer und Lagunengebiet und ihre Ertragsfähigkeit', *Beiträge zur Kolonialforschung*, 1 (1942), 75–92.
Kaplow, Susan B., 'The Mudfish and the Crocodile: Underdevelopment of a West African Bourgeoisie', *Science and Society*, 41/3 (1977), 317–33.
Karl-Augustt, Emmanuel, 'Les populations du Mono béninois', *Peuples du Golfe du Bénin*, ed. de Medeiros, 243–68.
Kea, Ray A., 'Akwamu – Anlo Relations, *c.* 1750–1813', *THSG*, 10 (1969), 29–63.
——, 'Firearms and Warfare on the Gold and Slave Coasts from the Sixteenth to the Nineteenth Centuries', *JAH,* 12/2 (1971), 185–213.
——, *Settlements, Trade, and Polities in the Seventeenth-Century Gold Coast* (Baltimore, 1982).
——, 'I am Here to Plunder on the General Road: Bandits and Banditry in the Pre-Nineteenth Century Gold Coast', *Bandits, Rebellion and Social Protest in Africa*, ed. Donald Crummey (London, 1986), 109–32.
——, 'Plantations and Labour in the South-East Gold Coast from the Late Eighteenth Century to the Mid-Nineteenth Century', *From Slave Trade*, ed. Law, 119–43.
Kelly, Kenneth G., 'Change and Continuity in Coastal Bénin', *West Africa during the Atlantic Slave Trade: Archaeological Perspectives*, ed. Christopher deCorse (London and New York, 2001), 81–100.
Kimble, David, *A Political History of Ghana; The Rise of Gold Coast Nationalism 1850–1928* (Oxford, 1963).
Latham, A. J. H., *Old Calabar 1600–1891: The Impact of the International Economy upon a Traditional Society* (Oxford, 1873).
Law, Robin, 'Royal Monopoly and Private Enterprise in the Atlantic Slave Trade: The Case of Dahomey', *JAH*, 18/4 (1977), 555–77.
——, 'Trade and Politics behind the Slave Coast: The Lagoon Traffic and the Rise of Lagos, 1500–1800', *JAH*, 24/3 (1983), 321–48.
——, 'Problems of Plagiarism, Harmonization and Misunderstanding in Contemporary

European Sources: Early (pre-1680s) Sources for the "Slave Coast" of West Africa', *European Sources for Sub-Saharan Africa before 1900: Use and Abuse (Paideuma 33)*, ed. Beatrix Heintze and Adam Jones (1987), 337–58.

——, 'Between the Sea and the Lagoons: The Interaction of Maritime and Inland Navigation on the Precolonial Slave Coast', *CEA* 114, XXIX-2 (1989), 209–37.

——, 'The Slave-Trader as Historian: Robert Norris and the History of Dahomey', *HiA*, 16 (1989), 219–35.

——, 'The Gold Trade of Whydah in the Seventeenth and Eighteenth Centuries', *West African Economic and Social History: Studies in Memory of Marion Johnson*, ed. David Henige and T.C. McCaskie (African Studies Program, University of Wisconsin, Madison, 1990), 105–18.

——, *The Slave Coast of West Africa, 1550–1750: The Impact of the Atlantic Slave Trade on an African Society* (Oxford, 1991).

——, 'Religion, Trade and Politics on the "Slave Coast": Roman Catholic Missions in Allada and Whydah in the Seventeenth Century', *Journal of Religion in Africa*, 21/1 (1991), 42–77.

——, 'The Historiography of the Commercial Transition in Nineteenth-Century West Africa', *African Historiography: Essays in Honour of Jacob Ade Ajayi*, ed. Toyin Falola (Harlow, 1993), 91–115.

——, 'Dahomey and the North-West', *Cahiers du CRA*, 8 (1994), 149–67.

——, 'A Lagoonside Port on the Eighteenth-century Slave Coast: The Early History of Badagri', *Canadian Journal of African Studies*, 28 (1994), 35–59.

—— (ed.), *From Slave Trade to 'Legitimate' Commerce: The Commercial Transition in Nineteenth-Century West Africa* (Cambridge, 1995).

——, 'Introduction', *From Slave Trade to 'Legitimate' Commerce*, ed. Law, 1–31.

——, '"Legitimate" Trade and Gender Relations in Yorubaland and Dahomey', *From Slave Trade to 'Legitimate' Commerce*, ed. Law, 195–214.

——, 'Finance and Credit and Pre-Colonial Dahomey', *Credit, Currencies and Culture: African Financial Institutions in Historical Perspective*, ed. Endre Stiansen and Jane I. Guyer (Stockholm, 1999), 15–37.

——, 'Individualising the Atlantic Slave Trade: The Biography of Mahommah Gardo Baquaqua of Djougou (1854)', *Transactions of the Royal Historical Society*, 12 (2002), 113–40.

——, 'Francisco Felix de Souza in West Africa, 1800–1849', *Enslaving Connections: Western Africa and Brazil during the Era of Slavery*, ed. José C. Curto and Paul E. Lovejoy (Amherst, NY, 2003), 187–211.

——, 'Pawning and Enslavement for Debt in the Precolonial Slave Coast', *Pawnship, Slavery, and Colonialism in Africa*, ed. Paul E. Lovejoy and Toyin Falola (Trenton, N.J. and Asmara, 2003), 55–69.

——, *Ouidah: The Social History of a West African Slaving 'Port', 1727–1892* (Athens and Oxford, 2004).

——, 'Ethnicities of Enslaved Africans in the Diaspora: On the Meanings of "Mina" (Again)', *HiA*, 32 (2005), 247–67.

——, 'West Africa's Discovery of the Atlantic', *IJAHS*, 44/1 (2011), 1–25.

——, 'Ouidah as a Multiethnic Community', *The Black Urban Atlantic in the Age of the Slave Trade*, ed. Jorge Cañizarres-Esguerra, Matt D. Childs, James Sidbury (Philadelphia, 2013), 42–62.

—— and Kristin Mann, 'West Africa in the Atlantic Community: The Case of the Slave Coast', *William and Mary Quarterly*, 56 (1999), 307–34.

—— and Silke Strickrodt (eds), *Ports of the Slave Trade (Bights of Benin and Biafra)* (Stirling, 1999).

——, Suzanne Schwarz and Silke Strickrodt (eds), *Commercial Agriculture, the Slave Trade and Slavery in Atlantic Africa* (Woodbridge and Rochester, NY, 2013).

Lawrance, Benjamin N. (ed.), *The Ewe of Togo and Benin* (Accra, 2005).

Le Herissé, A., *L'Ancien royaume du Dahomey* (Paris, 1911).

Lever, J. T., 'Mulatto Influence on the Gold Coast in the Early Nineteenth Century: Jan Nieser of Elmina,' *African Historical Studies*, 3/2 (1970), 253–62.

L[ombard], J[aques], 'A propos de l'etymologie d'Agoué', *ED,* 16 (1956), 3–6.
Lovejoy, Paul E. and David Richardson, 'Trust, Pawnship, and Atlantic History: The Institutional Foundations of the Old Calabar Slave Trade', *American Historical Review*, 104 (1999), 333–55.
——, 'Letters of the Old Calabar Slave Trade 1760–1789', *Genius in Bondage: Literature of the Early Black Atlantic*, ed.Vincent Carretta and Philip Gould (Lexington, KY, 2001), 89–115.
——, 'The Business of Slaving: Pawnship in Western Africa, c.1600–1810', *JAH*, 42/1 (2001), 67–89.
——, '"This Horrid Hole": Royal Authority, Commerce and Credit at Bonny, 1690–1840', *JAH*, 45/3 (2004), 363–92.
——, 'From Slaves to Palm Oil: Afro-European Commercial Relations in the Bight of Biafra, 1741–1841', *Maritime Empires*, ed. David Killingray, Margarette Lincoln and Nigel Rigby (Manchester, 2004), 13–29.
——, 'African Agency and the Liverpool Slave Trade', *Liverpool and Transatlantic Slavery*, ed. David Richardson, Suzanne Schwarz and Anthony Tibbles (Liverpool: Liverpool UP, 2007), 43–65.
Lynn, Martin, 'Change and Continuity in the British Palm Oil Trade with West Africa, 1830–1855', *JAH*, 32/3 (1981), 331–48.
——, 'From Sail to Steam: The Impact of the Steamship Services on the British Palm Oil Trade with West Africa, 1850–1890', *JAH*, 30/2 (1989), 227–45.
——, 'The West African Palm Oil Trade in the Nineteenth Century and the 'Crisis of Adaptation', *From Slave Trade to 'Legitimate' Commerce*, ed. Law, 57–77.
——, 'Factionalism, Imperialism and the Making and Breaking of Bonny Kingship c.1830–1885', *Revue Française d'Histoire d'Outre-mer*, 82 (1995), 1–24.
——, *Commerce and Economic Change in West Africa: The Palm Oil Trade in the Nineteenth Century* (Cambridge, 1997).
Mann, Kristin, 'Owners, Slaves and the Struggle for Labour in the Commercial Transition at Lagos', *From Slave Trade to 'Legitimate' Commerce*, ed. Law, 144–71.
——, *Slavery and the Birth of an African City: Lagos, 1760–1900* (Bloomington and Indianapolis, 2007).
—— and Edna G. Bay (eds), *Rethinking the African Diaspora: The Making of a Black Atlantic World in the Bight of Benin and Brazil* (London and Portland, OR, 2001).
Manning, Patrick, *Slavery, Colonialism and Economic Growth in Dahomey, 1640–1960* (Cambridge, 1982).
——, 'Merchants, Porters, and Canoemen in the Bight of Benin: Links in the West African Trade Network', *The Workers of African Trade*, ed. Catherine Coquery-Vidrovitch and Paul E. Lovejoy (Beverly Hills, 1985), 51–74.
Manoukian, Madeline, *The Ewe-Speaking People of Togoland and the Gold Coast* (London, 1952).
Manshard, Walther, 'Die Küsten- und Flußfischerei Ghanas', *Die Erde: Zeitschrift der Gesellschaft für Erdkunde zu Berlin*, 89/1 (1958), 21–33.
Martin, Eveline C., *The British West African Settlements, 1750–1821* (London, 1927).
McCarthy, Mary, *Social Change and the Growth of British Power on the Gold Coast: The Fante States 1807–1874* (Lanham MD, 1972).
De Medeiros, François, ed., *Peuples du Golfe du Bénin (Aja-Ewé)* (Paris, 1984).
Metcalf, George, 'Gold, Assortments and the Trade Ounce: Fante Merchants and the Problem of Supply and Demand in the 1770s', *JAH*, 28 (1987), 27–41
Mettas, Jean, *Répertoire des expéditions négrières françaises au XVIIIe siècle*, vol. 1: *Nantes* (ed. Serge Daget), vol. 2: *Ports autres que Nantes* (ed. Serge and Michèle Daget) (Paris, 1978, 1984).
Middleton, John, 'Merchants: An Essay in Historical Ethnography', *The Journal of the Royal Anthropological Institute*, 9/3 (2003), 509–26.
Miller, Joseph C., 'A Historical Appreciation of the Biographical Turn', *Biography and the Black Atlantic*, ed. Lisa A. Lindsay and John Wood Sweet (Philadelphia, 2014), 19–47.
Monroe, J. Cameron, 'Continuity, Revolution or Evolution on the Slave Coast of West

Africa? Royal Architecture and Political Order in Precolonial Dahomey', *JAH*, 48/3 (2007), 349–73.

——, 'Building the State in Dahomey: Power and Landscape on the Bight of Benin', *Power and Landscape in Atlantic West Africa: Archaeological Perspectives*, ed. Monroe and Akinwumi Ogundiran (Cambridge, 2012), 192–221.

Morgan, W. B. and J. C. Pugh, *West Africa* (London, 1969).

Mouléro, T., 'Histoire et légendes des Djêkens', *ED,* 8 (October 1996), 39–56.

Newbury, C. W., *The Western Slave Coast and its Rulers: European Trade and Administration among the Yoruba and Adja-speaking Peoples of South-Western Nigeria, Southern Dahomey and Togo* (Oxford, 1961).

Norman, Neil L., 'Hueda (Whydah) Country and Town: Archaeological Perspectives on the Rise and Collapse of an African Atlantic Kingdom', *IJAHS*, 42/3 (2009), 387–410.

Nørregård, Georg, *Danish Settlements in West Africa* (Boston, Mass., 1966).

Northrup, David, 'The Compatibility of the Slave and Palm Oil Trades in the Bight of Biafra', *JAH*, 17 (1976), 353–64.

——, *Africa's Discovery of Europe 1450–1850* (2002, 2nd ed., New York, 2009).

Nouhouayi, Albert, 'Zagnanado (Agonlin) et la Route de Esclaves', *Le Bénin et la Route d' Esclave,* ed. Elisée Soumonni *et al.* (Cotonou, n.d.), 113–7.

Nugent, Paul, 'Arbitrary Lines and the People's Minds: A Dissenting View on Colonial Boundaries in West Africa', *African Boundaries: Barriers, Conduits, and Opportunities*, ed. Nugent and A. I. Asiwaju (London, 1996), 35–67.

Parés, Luis Nicolau, 'The Hula "Problem": Ethnicity on the Pre-Colonial Slave Coast', *The Changing Worlds of Atlantic Africa: Essays in Honour of Robin Law*, ed. Toyin Falola and Matt D. Childs (Durham, N. C., 2009), 323–46.

Parker, John, *Making the Town: Ga State and Society in Early Colonial Accra* (Portsmouth, NH, 2000).

Patterson, K. David, 'A Note on Slave Exports from the Costa Da Mina, 1760–1770', *BIFAN*, series B, 33/2 (1971), 249–56.

Pazzi, Roberto, 'Aperçu sur l'implantation actuelle et les migrations anciennes des peuples de l'aire culturelle Aja-Tado', *Peuples du Golfe du Bénin*, ed. de Medeiros, 10–19.

Pedler, F., *The Lion and the Unicorn in Africa: A History of the Origins of the United African Company, 1787–1931* (London, 1974).

Pélofy, Isidore, *Histoire d'Agoué (République du Bénin)*, ed. Régina Byll-Cataria (Leipzig, 2002).

Person, Yves, 'La toponymie ancienne de la côte entre le Volta et Lagos', *CEA*, 60, XV-4 (1975), 715–21.

Pognon, André, 'Le Problème "Popo"', *ED,* 8 (1955), 11–14.

Polanyi, Karl with Abraham Rotstein, *Dahomey and the Slave Trade: An Analysis of an Archaic Economy* (Seattle and London, 1966).

Postma, Johannes Menne, *The Dutch in the Atlantic Trade, 1600–1815* (Cambridge, 1990).

Pouwels, Randall Lee, 'A Reply to Spear on Early Swahili History', *IJAHS*, 34/3 (2001), 639–46.

Priestley, Margaret, *West African Trade and Coast Society: A Family Study* (London, 1969).

Richard-Molard, Jaques, *Afrique Occidentale Française* (Paris, 1949).

Rivallain, Josette, 'Le sel dans les villages côtiers et lagunaires du bas Dahomey: sa fabrication, sa place dans e circuit du sel africain', *Annales de l'Université d'Abidjan*, série 1 (Histoire), 8 (1980), 81–124.

Rosenthal, Judy, *Possession, Ecstasy and Law in Ewe Voodoo* (Charlottesville and London, 1998).

Ryder, A. F. C., *Benin and the Europeans 1485–1897* (London, 1969).

Sastre, Robert Codjo, *Le premier siège de la préfecture apostolique du Dahomey. Survol de l'histoire religieuse d'Agoué* ([Agoué], 2000).

Schnapper, Bernard, *La politique et le commerce français dans le Golfe de Guinée de 1838 à 1871* (Paris, 1961).

Schramm, Percy Ernst, *Deutschland und Übersee; der deutsche Handel mit den anderen Kontinenten, insbesondere Afrika, von Karl V. bis zu Bismarck* (Braunschweig, 1950).

Sebald, Peter, *Togo 1884–1914: Eine Geschichte der deutschen 'Musterkolonie' auf der Grundlage*

amtlicher Quellen (Berlin, 1988).
——, '7,5 Kilogramm westafrikanische Korrespondenz 1843–1887: Der Foliant der Königsfamilie Lawson, Aneho, Togo', *Sprachkulturelle und historische Forschungen in Afrika; Beiträge zum 11. Afrikanistentag in Köln 1994* (Köln, 1995), 267–81.
Seidel, H., 'Der Fischfang in Togo', *Globus: Illustrierte Zeitschrift für Länder- und Völkerkunde*, 82/7 (21 Aug. 1902), 111–1
Sensbach, Jon F., *Rebecca's Revival: Creating Black Christianity in the Atlantic World* (Cambridge, MA, 2005).
Shumway, Rebecca, *The Fante and the Transatlantic Slave Trade* (Rochester, NJ and Woodbridge, 2011).
Skinner, David, *Thomas George Lawson: African Historian and Administrator in Sierra Leone* (Stanford, 1980).
Smith, Robert S., 'The Canoe in West African History', *JAH*, 11/4 (1970), 515–33.
——, *The Lagos Consulate 1851–1861* (London and Basingstoke, 1978).
Soumonni, Elisée *et al.*, *Le Bénin et la Route de l'Esclave* (Cotonou, n.d.).
——, 'The Compatibility of the Slave and Palm Oil Trades in Dahomey, 1818–1856', *From Slave Trade to 'Legitimate' Commerce*, ed. Law, 78–92.
Spear, Thomas, 'Early Swahili History Reconsidered', *IJAHS*, 33/2 (2000), 257–90.
Spiess, C., 'Ein Beitrag zur Geschichte des Evhe-Volkes in Togo: Seine Auswanderung aus Notsie', *MSOSB, Dritte Abteilung: Afrikanische Studien*, V (1902), 278–83.
——, 'Ein Erinnerungsblatt an die Tage des Sklavenhandels in Westafrika', *Globus. Illustrierte Zeitschrift für Länder- und Völkerkunde* 92, 13 (3 Oct. 1907), 205–8
Spieth, Jakob, *Die Ewe-Stämme; Material zur Kunde des Ewe-Volkes in Deutsch-Togo* (Berlin, 1906).
Sprigge, R. G. S., 'Eweland's Adangbe: An Enquiry into an Oral Tradition', *THSG*, 10 (1969), 87–128.
Strickrodt, Silke, 'A Neglected Source for the History of Little Popo: The Thomas Miles Papers *ca.* 1789–1796', *HiA*, 28 (2001), 293–330.
——, 'Afro-Brazilians on the Western Slave Coast in the Nineteenth Century', *Enslaving Connections: Western Africa and Brazil during the Era of Slavery*, ed. José C. Curto and Paul E. Lovejoy (Amherst, NY, 2004), 213–44.
——, 'British Abolitionist Policy on the Ground in West Africa in the Mid-Nineteenth Century', *The Changing Worlds of Atlantic Africa: Essays in Honour of Robin Law*, ed. Toyin Falola and Matt D. Childs (Durham, NC, 2009), 183–200.
——, 'The Atlantic Slave Trade and a Very Small Place in Africa: Global Processes and Local Factors in the History of Little Popo, 1680s to 1860', *The End of Slavery in Africa and the Americas: A Comparative Approach*, ed. Ulrike Schmieder, Katja Füllberg-Stolberg and Michael Zeuske (Berlin, 2011), 15–26.
——, 'In Search of a Moral Community: Little Popo and the Atlantic Trade in the Mid-Eighteenth Century', *THSG*, new series, 14 (2012), 105–30.
——, 'Aballow's Story: The Experience of Slavery in Mid-Nineteenth Century West Africa, as Told by Herself', *African Voices*, ed. Bellagamba/ Greene/ Klein, 387–403.
Sundström, Lars, *The Exchange Economy of Pre-Colonial Tropical Africa* (London, 1974).
Sutton, I. B., 'The Volta River Salt Trade: The Survival of an Indigenous Industry', *JAH*, 22 (1981), 43–61.
Swanzy, Henry, 'A Trading Family in the Nineteenth-Century Gold Coast', *TGCTHS*, 2 (1956), 87–120
Thornton, John, *Africans and Africans in the Making of the Atlantic World, 1400–1800* (1992, 2nd ed. Cambridge, 1998).
——, *A Cultural History of the Atlantic World, 1250–1820* (Cambridge, 2012).
Turner, Jerry Michael, 'Identidade étnica na África-Ocidental: o caso especial dos afro-brasileiros no Benin, na Nigeria, no Togo e em Gana nos séculos XIX e XX', *Estudos Afro-Asiáticos*, 28 (October 1995), 85–99.
Valsecchi, Pierluigi, *Power and State Formation in West Africa: Appolonia from the Sixteenth to the Eighteenth Century* (New York and Houndmills, Basingstoke, 2011).

Van Dantzig, Albert, *Les Hollandais sur la Côte de Guinée à l'époque de l'essor de l'Ashanti et du Dahomey 1680–1740* (Paris, 1980).
——, 'English Bosman and Dutch Bosman: A Comparison of Texts – V', *History in Africa* 6 (1979), 265–85.
——, 'Some Late Seventeenth-Century British Views on the Slave Coast', *Peuples du Golfe du Bénin*, ed. de Medeiros, 71–85.
Verger, Pierre, *Les afro-américains* (Dakar, 1952).
——, *Notes sur le culte des orisa et vodun à Bahia, la Baie de tous les Saints, au Brésil et à l'ancienne Côte des Esclaves en Afrique* (Dakar, 1957).
——, *Flux et reflux de la traite des Nègres entre le Golfe du Bénin et Bahia de Todos os Santos de 17è au 19è siècle* (Paris, 1968).
——, *Trade Relations between the Bight of Benin and Bahia from the 17th to the 19th Centuries* (Ibadan, 1976).
——, *Os libertos : Sete Caminhos na Liberdade de Escravos da Bahia no Século XIX* (São Paulo, 1992).
Vogt, August, *Westafrika in vorkolonialer Zeit: Freuden und Leiden eines Bielefelder Kaufmanns vor fünfzig Jahren in Togo, der früheren Sklavenküste in den Jahre 1873–77* (Bielefeld, n.d. [1926]).
Vogt, John, *The Portuguese Rule on the Gold Coast 1469–1682* (Athens, 1991).
Ward, W. E. F., *A History of Ghana* (London, 1966).
Wariboko, Wabinte E., 'New Calabar: The Transition from Slave- to Produce-Trading and the Political Problems in the Eastern Delta, 1848–1891', *Ports of the Slave Trade*, ed. Law/Strickrodt, 153–68.
Wendl, Tobias, 'Slavery, Spirit Possession and Ritual Consciousness: The *Tchamba* Cult among the Mina of Togo', *Spirit Possession, Modernity and Power in Africa*, ed. Heike Behrend and Ute Luig (Oxford *et al.*, 1999), 111–23.
Westergaard, Waldemar, *The Danish West Indies under Company Rule (1671–1754)* (New York, 1917).
Westermann, Diedrich, 'Kinderheitserinnerungen des Togonegers Bonifatius Foli', *MSOSB, Abteilung: Afrikanische Sprachen,* 34 (1931), 1–69.
——, *Die Glidyi-Ewe in Togo: Züge aus ihrem Gesellschaftsleben* (supplement to *Mitteilungen des Seminars für orientalische Sprachen an der Universität Berlin* 38, 1935).
——, *Wörterbuch der Ewe-Sprache* (Berlin, 1954).
Wilks, Ivor, 'The Rise of the Akwamu Empire, 1650–1710', *THSG*, 3/2 (1959), 99–136.
——, 'Akwamu and Otublohum: An Eighteenth-century Akan Marriage Arrangement', *Africa: Journal of the International African Institute*, 29/4 (1959), 391–404.
——, *Asante in the Nineteenth Century: The Structure and Evolution of a Political Order* (Cambridge, 1975).
——, *Akwamu 1640–1750: A Study of the Rise and Fall of a West African Empire* (Trondheim, 2001).
Williams, Raymond, *Keywords: A Vocabulary of Culture and Society* (London, 1988).
Wilson, Seth, 'Aperçu historique sur les peuples et cultures dans le Golfe du Bénin: le cas des "Mina" d'Anécho', *Peuples du Golfe du Bénin*, ed. de Medeiros, 127–50.
Wright, Donald R., *The World and a Very Small Place in Africa: A History of Globalization in Niumi, The Gambia* (1997, 3rd ed., Armonk, NY and London, 2010).
Valsecchi, Pierluigi, *Power and State Formation in West Africa: Appolonia from the Sixteenth to the Eighteenth Century* (New York, 2011).
Yarak, Larry W., *Asante and the Dutch, 1744–1873* (Oxford, 1990).

Unpublished theses

Aguigah, D. A., 'La Site de Notsé: Contribution a l'archeologie du Togo' (thèse de Doctorat de troisème cycle, Université de Paris I, 1985).
Akibode, Imbert O., 'Contribution à l'étude de l'histoire de l'ancien royaume Agoué (1821–1885)' (mémoire de maîtrise, FLASH, Université Nationale du Bénin, 1988–9).
Gayibor, Nicoué Lodjou, 'L'aire culturelle ajatado des origines à la fin du XVIIIè siècle', 3 vols (thèse de Doctorat d'État, Université de Paris I, 1985).
Kassa, Jérôme Koffi, 'Le Foyer Xwla de Xwlagan: Migrations et traits de culture (des probables origines au XVème siècle)' (mémoire de maîtrise, FLASH, Université Nationale du Bénin, 1993–94).
Nangbadi, Djamoudja, 'Histoire d'une capitale africaine: Lomé des origines à nos jours' (thèse de doctorat, Université de Poitiers, 1994).
Sorensen-Gilmour, Caroline, 'Badagry 1784–1863: The Political and Commercial History of a Lagoonside Community in South-West Nigeria' (PhD thesis, University of Stirling, 1995).
Soumonni, Elisée Akpo, 'Trade and politics in Dahomey 1841–1892, with particular reference to the house of Régis' (PhD thesis, University of Ife, Ile-Ife, June 1983).
Turner, Jerry Michael, 'Les Brésiliens: The Impact of Former Brazilian Slaves upon Dahomey' (PhD thesis, Boston University, 1975).

Other unpublished material

Jones, Adam, 'Between Three Stools: The Lawsons, their Rivals and the Europeans, 1869–1887', unpubl. paper presented at the colloquium 'Il y a plus que trois cents ans, nassait le pay guin' in Aného/ Togo, 18–20 Sept. 2000 (publ. in French translation in *A l'écoute de l'histoire*, vol. 1 of *Le tricentenaire d'Aného*, ed. Gayibor, 137–58).
Juhé-Beaulaton, Dominique, 'History of a Controversy between Social Sciences: The Origin of the Dahomey Gap (Togo-Benin) or the Complementarity of History and Archaeology', unpubl. paper, conference 'Common Ground, Different Meanings: Archaeology, History, and the Interpretation of the African Past' (Syracuse University, 8–10 Oct. 2009).
Law, Robin, 'The Earliest European Descriptions of Little Popo, 1680s-1690s', unpubl. paper presented at the colloquium 'Il y a plus que trois cents ans, nassait le pay guin' (Aného/ Togo, 18–20 Sept. 2000, publ. in French translation in *A l'écoute de l'histoire*, vol. 1 of *Le tricentenaire d'Aného*, ed. Gayibor, 2 vols, 33–58).

Index

Abeokuta 178
Aboré/Abree/Abrow, alternative names for Little Popo 6, 94, 95, 96
Abson, Lionel 124, 149–51
Accra, kingdom 58; conquest by Akwamu of 29, 75–7; immigration from, to Little Popo 73, 79–81, 85–9, 154, 166
Accra, town 17, 18, 29, 34, 56, 60, 69, 72, 79n.85, 95, 99, 104, 106, 116, 122, 125, 128, 131, 140, 214, 219; links with Little Popo 5, 9, 18, 22, 29, 88, 112, 122, 136, 140, 146, 147–8, 161, 197–8, 217, 228; European trade at 97, 100, 149, 195, 197–8, 218
Ackwaw, Prince, see: 'Aqua'
Ada 56, 76, 85, 118, 121, 122, 135–6
Adafia 34, 143 n.71, 204, 207, 214, 226, 227 n.10
Adaku 154
Adamé 43, 142–3, 144
Adams, John 40, 52–3 (and n.142)
Adandozan, King of Dahomey (1797–1818) 162
Adangbe, town 84–5
Adangme-speaking people: on Gold Coast 76, 77–8; on western Slave Coast: immigration 1, 25, 29, 30, 75–8; settlements 82–88, 90n.155, 151–2; and war 25, 80, 90, 92–94, 99, 102–3; and trade with Europeans 94–5, 98, 99, 115 (also: 'Anlo', 'banditry')
Adanliakpo 154–5 (also 'Fantekome')
Adikpi, Ouatchi hunter 81
Adiner Cooma: see 'Elmina Chica'
Adja Kpodji, quarter of Glidji 51, 81
Adja-honoue 43

Adjido 59, 72, 87, 163, 174, 190, 199–200
Adjigo, clan 72, 73 (and n.44), 75, 153, 157n.2, 165, 170, 177n.111, 178n.116, 181; cult 166; alternative name for Agoué 166
Ado, King of Akwamu (1689–1702) 93–4, 102–3
Aduaduí, ancestor (Anlo) 82
Adwoma, caboceer of Little Popo 107, 117
Afegame 84
Aflao 3, 34, 45, 46, 51, 53, 83, 84, 91n.155, 105–6, 118, 123, 134, 136, 138, 141, 143, 151n.118, 204, 226; European trade at 106, 113, 138, 139, 144–5, 146, 148, 149n.103, 150, 214
Afro-Brazilians: see 'Agoué, Brazilian immigration to'
Agaja, King of Dahomey (c.1716–40) 118–20
Agave, people 76, 77, 82 n.104, 118, 121
Agbanaken, Hula capital 33, 43–4, 47, 48, 54, 63, 104, 108–9, 142, 184, 222, 223–4, 232
Agbanaken, market place 60–1 (also 'Glidji-Kpodji')
Agbanon II, Fio, 24, 78–9 n.82, 80 (and n.90), 83–4 (and n.113), 87–8 (and n.139), 107 n.23, 117–8 n.86, 122 n.112, 125, 136 n.16, 143, 154–56 (and n.139) & 150, 157 n.2, 161 n.20, 165, 170–1, 175, 185–6 (and n.160), 193
Agbodrafo: see 'Porto Seguro'
Agbosome ('Some'), 139, 143, 226
Agome 23
Agonglo, King of Dahomey (1789–97) 142

Agotime 83–5 (and n.119)
Agou, mountain 30, 85; Adangme settlement 85
Agoué 167–9, 170, 171, 176–83, 227, 228, 235; foundation of 157–66; Brazilian immigration to 9, 18–19, 21, 23–4, 168–9, 179–93, 200–1, 233; and slave trade 197–210; and 'legitimate' trade 213–4, 218–24; war with Little Popo (1860–66) 184–66; and colonial partition 231–32, 234
Agouégan 45n.104, 61, 110, 118, 166, 232
Agouna 142, 144
agriculture 20, 52, 55–58, 59, 60, 74, 81, 90, 125, 197, 215, 219, 223, 224; implements 44, 149; introduction of new crops 1, 7, 57–8; local trade in agricultural produce 44, 52, 60–2, 232; export of agricultural produce 2, 7, 8, 26, 44, 58, 125, 197, 210–24 (also 'provisions', 'palm oil')
Aguégué 45
Aguinerweh/Agin-no-hay 143 (and n.71), 204
Ahanta 69
Ahémé, lake 33 (and n.19), 36, 48, 54, 107, 109, 235 n.51
Ahkurst, John Henry 177, 213, 215, 220
Aho, river 48, 50, 63, 107
Ahossi/ Ahosi Zanglanmio, 163 n.32
Aité, 167–9, 179
Aja, language 51; -speaking people 46, 51, 52, 60, 81
Akan, language complex 56n.165, 58 (and n.175); names 73, 104–5, 153, 165, 166, 177n.111, 178n.116; -speaking people 1, 13, 25, 29, 36, 45, 69–70, 72 (and n.40), 79n.85, 81, 83n.108, 88, 153 (see also 'Fante', 'Mina')
Akibode, Imbert 13
A-kien, chief (Porto Seguro) 171
Akinjogbin, Ade 12, 142
Akitoye, King of Lagos (1841–45, 1851–53) 183
Aklaku, market town 62, 119; river: see 'Gbaga, river'
Aklapa, channel 35
Akoi, caboceer at Little Popo 88, 151–3 (and n.117), 163 (also 'Aqua'?)
Akuapem 83, 121, 123, 124–5, 136; hills: see 'Togo-Atacora, mountains'
Akue: see 'Akoi'
Akuete Zankli: see 'Lawson family of Little Popo: George Lawson'
Akwamu 58, 110–11, 112, 118, 128, 142; conquest of Accra and Ladoku 29, 75–8, 83, 95; interventions on western Slave Coast 93–4, 102–4, 105–6, 113, 121, 123–5, 134, 137–8, 139, 140; relocation on Slave Coast (1730) 106
Akwonno, Akwamu ruler (1702–25) 103
Akyem 94, 102, 106, 115, 121, 122, 123, 123–5, 134, 138
alcoholic drinks, locally produced 56 (and n.166); imported 68n.15, 114, 115, 127–8, 133, 146, 168; tax paid in 63
Al-lee-far, King of Grand Popo (c.1860–?) 183–4, 208, 215
Alampo, kingdom: see 'Ladoku'; people: see 'Adangme'
Alfaiate, José: see 'dos Santos, José Francisco'
Allada 12, 17, 43, 66–8, 69, 70–1, 74, 92, 101, 103, 107, 110; control of Grand Popo 46, 67–8, 89; relations with Little Popo 91, 93 (also 'Offra')
Allongo 54
d'Almeida, Antonio 23–4
d'Almeida, Joaquim 23–4, 168, 179, 180, 185, 200–1, 202, 206
d'Almeida, Manoel Joaquim 200
d'Almeida, Pedro Felix: see 'Ayi Yovonou'
Ama Adakoo, notable (Little Popo) 156 (and n.150)
Amegadje, founder of Degbenu 153
Amenumey, D.E.K. 50–1
America/ American: see 'USA'
Americas (also 'Brazil', 'Cuba', 'USA') 5, 14, 31, 41n.79, 70; imports from 1, 57, 197; export of slaves to 3, 4–5, 28, 94, 161
Amma, King of Little Popo (c.1767–???) 122–3 (and n.119)
Amoni, caboceer at Little Popo 123
Amu, Akwamu general 106 (and n.20)
Amutinu 34
Ando, caboceer at Little Popo 111
Aneho, quarter of Accra, 72; township/ quarter of Little Popo 72–3, 81, 87, 88, 162
Aného: see 'Little Popo, town'
Anfro 90
Angola 71
animal husbandry 20, 55–6, 58–9, 232; introduction of new breeds 1, 59 (also 'provisions')
Anlo 56, 59n.185, 143; Adangme immigration to 77–8, 82–3; wars with Little Popo 92–4, 99, 103–4, 106–7, 120–1 (Nonobe War), 123–4, 134–7 (Sagbadre War), 138–9 (Keta War/Some War); relations with Akwamu 102–3, 105–6, 123–4, 140; other wars and

foreign relations 106, 117–18, 139–40; British annexation 183, 203, 226 (also 'Adangme', 'Keta')
Anloga, capital of Anlo 59n.185, 94n.182, 105, 135–6, 149
Anomabo 70, 132 n.181, 146
Ansa Sasraku, Akwamu ruler (-1689) 93
Ansa, John 158–9, 163–6, 167–8 (also 'Komlagan'?)
Ansah, William, 132n.181
Antonio, Joaquim 202
Apa 45, 46 n.106
Aplaviho, original quarter of Little Popo 43 (and n.93), 45, 74n.44, 86–7 (and n.135)
Aqua, son of Ashampo 5, 131–3 (also 'Akoi')
architecture and housing 85–6, 126, 129, 146, 162, 175, 176, 181, 200, 202n.41, 203n.45, 207, 211, 213, 214, 221–2, 223n.180, 224, 226n.5; barracoons 167, 202, 204; multi-storey houses 9, 134, 151 (and n.117), 152, 167, 211
Ar-con-tee, chief (Porto Seguro) 171
Ardra: see 'Allada'
Asante 20, 121, 125, 134, 139–42, 143, 225n.1, 226n.5
Ashampo (1), King of Little Popo (c.1737–c.1767) 5, 26, 102, 117–23, 125–33, 152
Ashampo (2) ('Okannia Assiambo'), prince (Little Popo) 151
Ashampo (3) ('Little Assiambo'), prince (Little Popo), 151
Ashampo (4) ('another smaller Assiambo'), prince (Little Popo) & pawn 151
Ashampo (5) ('Al-sham-bo-gar-gai'), prince (Little Popo), 175 incl. n.99
Ashampo (6) ('Al-sham-bo-Douavee'), prince (Little Popo), 175 incl. n.99
Assina ('le Forban') 110
Assou/ Ossue, Hueda chief 108–9
Ata Ayi 154–5 (and n.139)
Atahounlé/Atanlé, caboceer of Agoué (1873/4–?), 193–4
Atakpame 38, 62, 219
Atitsogbi: see 'de Lima, Geraldo'
Atogbo 54
Atoko, 137, 199, 203
Atta-catri-ger, caboceer of Agoué 181
Attome 85–6, 96n.201, 104
Augo: see 'Agou'
Augoja 84, 105, 138–40
Augona: see 'Anloga'
Aumane, trader (Little Popo) 115, 123n.119
Avlékété 46

Avlêkpon, Hula ancestor 43–4
Avlo 55
Awey: see 'Woe'
Awouna: see 'Anloga'
Ayi Manko 168 n.60
Ayi Yovonou 168–9

Ba, Hula clan name 46
Badagry 18, 20, 45, 46; civil wars in 194; raids by Dahomey on 142; trade at 59n.184, 125, 130–1, 142, 150, 163, 199, 203, 212–13, 221n.152
Badji 72, 87, 161–2, 171, 191, 211
Baeta/Baêta, João Gonçalves, 203 (and n. 45 & 46), 204, 206, 207–8, 209
Baguida 3, 23, 33, 37, 199, 204, 226–7, 231
Baguida Beach 23, 226–7, 231
Bahia 9, 15, 24, 167, 179, 185, 203, 207; trade to 200, 201, 203, 207
Bajado: see 'Baguida'
banditry 68, 82, 89, 102, 107, 109, 110, 113, 118, 119, 128, 166,
Banks, Samuel 164, 168, 196
Baquaqua, Mohammah 6n.13, 198–9n.17
Barbot, John, 16, 33n.20, 36–7, 45n.104, 47–8, 51, 67–8, 69, 71, 76–7, 79, 89, 94–5, 116
Bareste, U.V., French Vice-Consul, Sierra Leone 228
Bassora/ Bassard, John, 183–4
Basua, Akwamu ruler (1689–1699) 93–4
Bauduchiron 16, 124, 135, 144
Bayly, C.A. 8n.20
Bé 51, 80, 151n.118
Bé Beach: see 'Lomé'
Bell, Captain, 99
Benin Gap 28, 29–30
Benin, Bight of 21, 34, 59, 178, 199, 200, 203, 209–10, 212, 216, 219–20,
Benin, kingdom 34, 45, 65–6, 71, 196
Bénin, Republic 1, 2, 14, 22n.89, 27, 200
Bernasko, Peter William 176, 181–2, 185–8, 190
Bewu 154
Biafra, Bight of 10, 53, 189, 194, 233n.44
Biørn, A.R., 42n.82, 83–4, 85n.123, 117n.86, 122, 123n.119, 135–40, 151–3
Bismarck, Otto von, Chancellor of the German Empire, 227, 234
Blekesu, 34, 35, 139, 143n.71, 169n.63, 203, 204
Blockhouse: see 'Blekesu'
Boko, river 32
Bold, Edward 196, 197
Bonesee 111

Bonny 189, 194, 212
Borghero, Francesco 19, 32n.18, 46, 50, 179, 181–2, 187, 190, 209
Bosman, William 16n.52, 52, 72n.40, 74–5, 82–3, 89–94 passim, 98–101 passim, 104, 115
Bouche du Roi 2–3, 36–7, 38–40, 43, 44, 46–50, 54–5, 65–6, 183, trade at: see 'Grand Popo'
Bouche, Pierre 19, 24, 42, 46–7, 72–3, 157–166 passim, 169–70, 178, 179, 181, 182n.140, 184–6, 193–4, 209n.79, 219, 223, 224n.185
Bouët-Willaumez, E. 212, 216
boundaries 1, 2–3, 28n.1, 38, 48–50; colonial 203, 226–7, 232, 234–5 (also 'taxation: toll stations')
Bowden, William 182–3, 207–8
Bowdich, Thomas Edward 20, 83, 85, 141–2, 143, 165
Bowen, Thomas J. 19
Brand, G., British Consul, Lagos 185, 187–8
Brandão, Tobias Barretto 201
Brandenburg, trade/traders, traders 67, 70, 97, 98, 99, 101; records 14, 17
Brásio, António 14
Brazil, Brazilian trade/traders 5, 23–4, 25, 59, 100, 115, 162, 168–9, 179, 199–206, 208, 209; immigration to western Slave Coast 5, 8, 9, 179 (also 'Agoué, Brazilian immigration to'), records 14–15, 23–4 (also 'Bahia')
Bremen 220, 226
Brew, Richard 128, 129
Britain: see 'Great Britain'
Brokosu: see 'Blekesu'
Brooks, George E. 17
Bruce, James, chief at Porto Seguro 171, 214
Burton, Richard 39, 122n.114, 163n.32, 186–7
Byl/Byll, trader at Agbanaken 222
Byll's Town 222

Cameroon 44, 62
Campbell, Benjamin, British Consul, Lagos 202
Cana 12
canoes, canoemen 1, 3, 13, 21, 25, 36, 53, 75, 85, 105–6, 221; in lagoons 3, 6, 33, 34, 37–8, 53, 61, 62, 73–5, 86, 108, 111, 126, 189–90, 198, 214, 214, 216, 217; in coasting trade 71, 72, 73, 196; in European trade 29, 31, 33, 37, 68–71, 72, 73–5, 88, 112, 124, 126, 137, 150–1, 164, 183, 196, 198, 207, 218
Cantaloup, Joseph, 230
Cape Coast 9, 18, 70, 96, 182, 221, 236
Cape Coast Castle, English/British headquarters 15, 21, 67, 70, 96, 121, 127–8, 130, 132, 137, 139, 146, 148, 151, 155, 177, 210, 219, 225n.1
Cape St Paul 34, 196, 199, 203, 209, 214
Cape Three Points 67, 69
Carolof, Henri 67, 68–9, 71
Carter, John 15, 69n.25, 70, 74, 78–9, 81, 85–6, 91, 96–7, 104
de Carvalho, Elias Domingo 201
do Carvalho, José Pereira Monteiro 204–5
de Carvalho, Manoel Joaquim 204–5
cash-trade 195, 197, 218–19
Catraya: see 'Komlanvi'
de Champagny, M. de 16, 137, 145, 148–9, 153, 155–6
chess 167
children 18, 73n.44, 82, 108, 131–3, 160, 163, 165, 168n.58, 172, 175, 181, 186, 187, 220; enslaved for export 200
Chouin, Gérard L. 8n.20
Christaller, J.G. 58n.175, 79n.85, 80, 83n.108, 89n.147, 141
Christianity 5, 133, 176; Capuchin mission 17; Moravian mission 5, 18, 133; Roman Catholic mission/church 17–19, 179 (and n.75), 185; Wesleyan Methodist mission 18, 172, 175–6, 181–2, 185, 213n.105 (also 'missionaries')
Christiansborg, Danish headquarters 5, 17, 18, 76, 78, 111, 112, 127, 135, 151
Clapperton, Hugh 20, 143, 159–60, 164–5, 166, 184
cloth, manufacture of 59, 60, 61, 110, 167; Popo cloth 60, 167, 219; as present 60, 205; regional trade in 71; tax paid in 63; imported by Europeans 7, 44, 67, 68, 95, 114, 115
Coécoé 94
Coelho, Antonio Caetano 200
Cogio, Pedro: see 'Kodjo, Pedro'
Cole, John 179
Cole, S. B. 73, 226
Comlagan: see 'Komlagan'
Comlanvi Toutouyê Dêgnon: see 'Komlanvi'
Compagnie des Indes Occidentales (French) 67
Companhia União Africana (Brazilian) 204
Company of Merchants Trading to Africa (African Company) (British) 34, 131–3, 145–7, 222n.176

Congo, river 66, 71
Congress of Vienna 195
Coparan, Joao, caboceer of Agoué 167–8
Costa da Mina 65
Costa Soares, Samuel da, 207–8
Cotonou 46, 80, 203, 227, 235
cotton 53, 60; cultivation of 56, 215, 219; raw for export 218, 219, 223 (also 'cloth')
Coumin-Aguidi: see 'Kumi Aguidi'
cowry/cowrie shells 120n.96; as currency 52, 63, 150, 187, 197, 216, 219; as present 205; export of 145, 150; import of 7, 44, 64, 67, 68, 95, 216, 219; tax paid in 52, 63–4
Crakou, caboceer at Little Popo 104–5, 117
credit 10, 131, 133, 134–5; credit protection mechanisms 10–11, 130–2, 133 (also 'marriage')
Crepee/ Creepee: see 'Krepi'
Cuavi, John: see 'Quarvee, John'
Cuba, Cuban trade/traders 5, 8, 206–10; immigrants from, at Agoué 19, 207
Cudjoe: see 'Kodjo, Pedro'
Cudjovee: see 'Jehowey aka Kodjovi'
Curtin, Philip 6, 10
Cyprien Fabre et Cie (French) 223n.180, 230

Dahomey Gap: see 'Benin Gap'
Dahomey, kingdom 3, 7, 10, 21, 18, 29, 48, 63, 115, 162, 174, 187, 200, 223, 225, 277; conquest of Hueda (1727) 33n.19, 54, 105, 107–9, 110, 142, 143–4; wars with Little Popo 4, 25, 102, 117–22, 124–5, 129, 134, 135, 137–8, 141, 142–3, 147; relations with Grand Popo 50, 125, 143–4, 183; and European trade 7, 10, 101, 126, 130, 149, 200, 209, 219, 227; historiography 12–13, 42 (also 'Ouidah', 'de Souza family of Ouidah')
Dahomey, French colony 13–14
Dalzel, Archibald, 124
Dan 235
Danes, Denmark, Danish trade/traders 16–17, 34, 35, 42, 67, 68n.15, 76, 83, 88, 100–1, 110–12, 120–1 (and n.231), 123, 126, 127, 129–31; 136, 137, 144–5, 146, 148–9, 154, 196, 210; forts/factories 3n.3, 17, 26, 75n.57, 76, 78 (and n.77), 88, 123n.119, 125–6, 127, 131, 134, 135–9, 144, 145, 146, 148, 131, 153, 155, 183, 196, 203; diplomacy/intervention in local politics 60, 76, 78, 112, 121, 122, 126, 131, 134–41; records 14; West Indies 5
Dawson, Joseph 185, 187, 190, 191, 221–2
Decorsa, Philip, acting caboceer (Agoué) 177
DeCorse, Christopher R. 8n.20
Degbenu 72, 87, 105, 153
Dekpo 84, 216
Delbée 46, 47n.113, 67–8, 89
Denkyira 103
Densu, river 30, 69
Denu 34, 143n.71, 204, 226
Dettmar, Andrew Lewis and John, 127, 182
Dixcove 132n.181
Djalloukou 235
Djeken, name/title 54n.151; kingdom 130 (also 'Jakin')
Dôdômê 43
Dodowa 85
Dolben, W.D.M. 187, 188–9, 228
Dondo, Akwamu general 103
Duala 44
Duncan, John 19–20, 21, 38, 40, 53–63 passim, 161, 162, 169, 172–3, 179, 180, 198–201 passim, 211, 214, 215–16, 219
Dutch trade/traders 16, 34, 48, 66–71, 83, 97–101, 104–5, 107, 110, 112, 113, 115–18, 125–6, 127–32, 144, 146–8, 150, 164–5; forts/factories 3n.3, 67–8, 70, 76, 89, 91, 97, 98, 101, 106, 110, 112, 115–16, 117–18, 125–6, 128, 129, 132, 146–7, 148, 222, 225; diplomacy/intervention in local politics 76, 91–2, 117–18, 122, 131, 139–40; records 14, 16
Dzelukofe 208

East Africa 7, 9n.20, 11n.31
Edina: see 'Elmina'
Edjenowah: see 'Aguinerweh'
education, in Africa 172, 175–6 (and n.104), 181–2, 205; in Brazil 186, 199; in Europe 5, 131–3 (and n.181), 154, 160, 161; on slave ships, 154, 205
Egbiffeemee (= Agbosome?) 143
Ekpoui 220
Ekué Agbanon I, King of Little Popo (1849–1852) 175
Elia, river 32
Elmina Chica 59n.184, 72n.41, 144n.71, 204, 208
Elmina, as Dutch headquarters 66, 69n.25, 70, 105, 110, 164; town 9, 27, 66, 69, 71, 73, 147–8, 182, 208, 235; immigration to western Slave Coast 68–71, 164 (also 'Mina')

England/ English: see 'Great Britain'
Epe 130–1
Ewe 46, 50–1, 56–62, 74, 79–89 passim, 103, 105–6, 109, 118, 121, 123–4, 143, 149, 158, 173 (also 'Krepi'); 'Eweland' 51
Eytzen, Philip von 34, 59n.185, 83, 104–5, 112–13, 114, 117

Faloim: see 'Ouidah'
Fante, language 88, 178n.116; people 53, 72 (and n.40), 88, 154–5, 165 (also 'Akan-speaking people')
Fantekome 72, 83, 85–7, 153, 155
Fetu 76, 78
firearms 68n.15, 108, 115, 126, 131, 135, 149; artillery 76, 122; 139, 142–3, 203n.43
fishing 1, 31, 33, 38–9, 40, 44, 45, 52–3, 56, 62, 73, 88, 101, 136, 138, 166; methods and utensils 38, 53; rights 121; fish trade 52, 56, 60–2, 69n.24, 101; sea-fishing 31, 53, 72
Fishtown: see Gunkope
Foli Bebe: see Ofori (03) ('Offerry Bembeneen')
Foli Dekpo 156 n.150
Foli Gbosu: see Ofori (08) ('Ofoly Bossum')
Fon 1, 42, 43, 48, 54, 71n.32, 142, 92; immigrants at Agoué 179
Forbes, Frederick E. 22, 160–1, 174, 180, 200n.24, 202
Forbes, Thomas George 21, 54, 174–5, 180, 181, 183–4, 204–5, 215, 226n.7
France, French trade/traders 16, 67–9, 90, 91, 97, 98, 101, 104, 108, 112–14, 116, 124, 126–7, 128–9, 135, 137, 144–5, 148–50, 155–6, 173, 184, 203, 205, 221, 222, 224, 226, 227–8, 230–1 (also 'Barbot, Jean'); factories 67, 114, 149 (and n.103), 205, 221, 222, 224; missionaries: see 'Christianity, Roman Catholic mission/church'; intervention in local politics 89–90; imperialist intervention/ annexation 1, 3, 194, 227–33; colonial rule/officials 13, 36, 42, 235; records 14, 16, 22n.89, 24, 50
Fraser, Louis, British Vice-Consul, Ouidah 21, 37, 40, 42, 204, 219
Freeman, G. Stanhope, British Consul, Lagos 209n.79
Freeman, Thomas Birch 18, 160, 172, 176–7, 181, 198, 199, 224
Freetown 9, 22
French Guyana 94

Friedrich M.Vietor (Söhne) (Bremen) 226

Ga-Adangme languages 1, 82–3 (and n.108), 89 (and n.147) (also 'Adangme, language')
Gaba, Kue Agbota 170, 171
Ganli Seddo, King of Little Popo (1854–56) 175
Gayibor, Nicoué Lodjou 13, 85n.116, 142n.63, 159n.10
Gbaga, river 33, 48, 56, 62, 119
Gbe-speaking peoples 28, 40–51
Gbego Sokpa: see 'd'Almeida, Joaquim'
Gbome 33n.18, 38, 62, 216
Ge: see Little Popo
Gedzi 79–80
Genyi 2, 79, 174, 223 (also 'Little Popo')
Germany, German trade/traders 8, 173, 226, 227, 229, 230, 234; Christian missions: see 'Christianity: Moravian mission'; imperialist intervention/ annexation 3, 171, 227, 230–2, 233, 234; colonial rule of 13, 32n.18, 234–5, records 14, 15, 22–3 (and n.89), 24
Ghana 3, 8n.20, 14, 83, 84, 236
Glehue, indigenous name of Ouidah: see 'Ouidah'
Glele, King of Dahomey (1858–89), 169 n.62
Glidji, capital of Little Popo 9, 18, 30, 37, 51, 56n.162, 60, 63, 73, 78–81, 83–4 (and n.116), 86, 88, 89n.147, 93, 106, 115, 117–25 passim, 134–8 passim, 142, 149, 151–6 passim, 157n.2, 163n.32, 165–76 passim, 180–1, 184, 185, 216, 219, 227, 228, 233
Glidji-Kpodji 60–1n.197 & 200, 87, 216
Godomé 46, 203, 209 (also 'Jakin')
gold, as currency 64; as jewellery/treasure 159, 167, 182; trade in 7, 76, 95, 100, 114, 115, 197, 219
Gold Coast, region 3, 9, 12, 13, 19, 20, 21, 29, 30, 56, 57, 116, 121, 122, 124, 134, 215; European trade on 3, 5, 6, 33, 42, 45, 65–7, 96, 110–11, 112, 113, 127–8, 130, 132, 133, 140, 144–5, 146, 148, 150, 151, 155, 172, 195, 208, 216, 219, 220, 221–2; immigration into western Slave Coast 31, 53, 58 (also 'Accra', 'Adangme', 'Elmina'); incursions into western Slave Coast from 123; trade between Slave Coast and 71, 219
Gold Coast, British colony: see 'Great

Britain, imperialist intervention/ annexation'
Gomaluta: see 'Gunkope'
Grand Popo, kingdom 2–3, 40–50, 75, 89–90, 110, 116, 142, 148, 183–4, 196, 198, 235 (also 'Hula'); origins/foundation of 43–6; and European trade 1, 65–6, 67–8, 71, 94, 104, 113–14, 184, 198, 202, 209, 215, 221, 222–4, 228; control by Allada 46, 89; relations with Hueda exiles (1727–33) 107–9, 125; relations with Dahomey 143–4, 183, 209; relations with Little Popo 61, 75, 93, 142–4, 156, 183; and colonial partition 228–9, 231, 232; and French colonial rule 235
Grand Popo, town 31, 36, 46–8, 232, 235
Great Accra, capital of Ga kingdom 75, 76
Great Britain, British (England, English) trade/traders/factories 42, 53, 63, 66–7, 69–70, 71, 76, 77, 94–100, 105, 108, 111, 112–13, 114–15, 118, 122, 124, 127–9, 130–3, 137, 141, 142–3, 144–51, 153–5, 156, 160, 161–2, 163–4, 173, 175, 183, 195–7, 199 (also Cape Coast Castle); 'legitimate' trade/traders 8, 210–21, 222; intervention in local politics 76, 90, 91–2, 122, 137, 139–40, 182, 185, 187–9, 190–3; Christian missions, see 'Christianity, Wesleyan Methodist Mission'; campaign to suppress slave trade 4, 8, 14, 182–4, 195, 197–9, 201, 203–10, 215, 217, 218; imperialist intervention/annexation 3, 203, 225–9, 231, 234; records 14, 15–16, 18, 19–22, 23, 77n.65; West Indies 128, 160
Great Popo: see 'Grand Popo'
Greene, Sandra E. 17, 83n.113, 120, 123, 192
Greve 137
Grivot, R. 36, 54, 55
Gun Kope Tonu 80
Gunkope, 204, 214, 234
gunpowder 68, 122, 126, 133, 135, 141, 147, 149, 152, 181
Guyana, French colony 94

Haho, river 20, 23, 33, 37–8, 84
Hahoté 23, 38, 216
Hakoué 48, 54
Hanson, James W. 178, 220
Hanson, Walter 220 (and n.152)
Hanto-Tona, caboceer of Agoué (1846–1858) 181, 182 n.140
Hargreaves, John D. 230
Harqueng: see 'Hakoué'

Hausa, immigrants at Agoué 179
Havie, Miss, 182 (and n.14)
St Helena 21
Henrici, Ernst 23, 24, 39n.66, 51, 59, 73 (and n.44), 74, 84, 87, 89n.147, 155n.139
Henrique, Mr 214 (and n.110)
Herrnhuter Brüdergemeinde: see 'Christianity: Moravian mission'
Hévé 47, 107, 204; French factory at 205, 221, 224
Hilakondji 232
Hlihoué 54
Ho 103
Hoko 200
Honga, Captain, Allada official 70–1
Hoolwerff, Isaac van 91, 97
Hopkins, A.G., 7, 9, 10, 232–3 (and n.44 & 45)
Houéyogbe, capital of Hueda-Henji 109
Houtson, John 21n.81
Hueda 12, 33, kingdom (pre-1727) 3, 48, 66, 89–90, 91–3, 94, 103, 104; conquest by Dahomey 105, 107; Hueda community in exile (post-1727), 54, 107, 109, 110, 120, 121–2, 124, 125, 144; Hueda-Henji 109
Huesu Agbo, founder of Agbodrafo 45
Hufon, King of Hueda 107–9
Hula 1, 2, 3, 13, 33, 38, 40–50, 52–6, 74, 75, 80–1, 83, 85, 86, 88, 90n.155, 93, 108, 125, 142–3, 144, 166n.51; local economy 52–6, 57, 59–64 (also 'Grand Popo')
Hutton, A. Calvert 221
Hutton, Thomas 21–2, 177–81 passim, 183, 210n.89, 213–14, 219, 220–21
Hutton, W.M. 211, 212, 219, 220

Ijebu, kingdom 41, 65
Ingram, late Governor in the Gambia 214 n.110
Iroko, Félix 13, 43n.91, 51n.135
Isert, Paul Erdmann 17, 35, 40, 42, 58, 61, 62, 75, 86, 135n.9, 136, 137, 138n.34, 144, 152–5, 161, 205n.57
Islam 179
ivory 2, 7, 105, 111, 114–15, 117, 120, 125, 127, 128, 137, 145, 146, 147, 150, 152, 158, 195–7, 211, 218, 219

Jack, John, chief of Porto Seguro 169
Jakao, chief (Agoué) 178
Jakin, title 54n.151; town 46, 104, 115, 116n.75 (also 'Djeken')
James Town ('British Accra') 217 (also 'Soko')

Jehowey aka Kodjovi 73n.44, 173, 228
Jella Coffee: see 'Dzelukofe'
Justesen, Ole 17

Kassa, Jérôme Koffi 13
Kea, Ray 17, 71n.36, 123, 135, 138, 140, 141, 151–2n.118
Kedzi 138n.34, 143n.71, 203, 214
Keta, state: see 'Anlo'
Keta town 34, 35, 59n.184 and 185, 77, 81n.100, 84, 120, 121, 138, 143, 224, 229n.25; relations with Little Popo 3n.3, 17, 120, 121, 123–4, 134–7, 138–9, 143; European trade at 17, 29, 94–7, 98, 100, 105, 106–7, 112–13, 114, 115, 117–18, 120, 125–9, 131, 136–7, 145–6, 149, 150, 196, 199, 203–4, 208, 213, 222, 226; forts at 3, 117–18, 125, 136–7, 138, 139, 146, 160, 183, 196, 203, 208; British annexation of 3, 183, 203, 226 (also 'Anlo')
Keta Fort, British 3, 183, 203, 208
Keta lagoon 33–7, 137 passim, 226, 229n.25
Kiøge, Jens Adolf 136, 144, 149
Klein-Popo: see 'Little Popo'
Kliko 139
Klose, Heinrich 23, 38, 40n.66, 57, 62, 219
Kodjo Agbosu: see 'Sedjro Agboku/Agbosu'
Kodjo-Dahoménou, caboceer of Agoué (1844–46) 178
Kodjo, Pedro aka Kodjo Landjékpo aka Pedro Pinto da Silveira 73n.44, 87, 176, 184–93
Kodjovi family of Little Popo 231 (also 'Jehowey aka Kodjovi')
Komlagan, chief at Little Popo, founder of Agoué 158, 163, 165–6, 168, 170, 181, 184 (also 'Ansa, John'?)
Komlanvi aka Catraya, caboceer of Agoué 166, 168, 181, 184
Kongensten, Danish fort (Ada) 136, 137
Kosoko, King of Lagos (1845–51) 183
Kouasi-Gazouza, English caboceer (Agoué) 194
Kouenta 54
Kouffo, river 33, 51
Kpalime 32, 83
Kpandu 103
Kpeme 89
Kpengla, King of Dahomey (1774–89) 149
Kpessi 62, 149
Kpétou 54
Kpodji-Agué 45
Kpokpo, King of Tado 41

Kpone 76, 77
Kpossi, King of Grand Popo 44
Krepi 50, 58, 83, 105–6, 110, 118, 123, 137, 141–2, 143, 149, 151, 155, 179, 201–2 (also 'Ewe')
Krobo 121, 123
Kuadjo Kanli, founder of Agoué 166
Kumi Aguidi, caboceer of Agoué (c.1859– 73) 181–2 (and n.140), 185–93 passim
Kwadjovi, Pedro, chief (Little Popo) 73n.44 (see also 'Jehowey aka Kodjovi')
Kwahu 106, 115
Kwam: see 'Quam'
Kwavi/Ouavi Hauta 191

La, town 71, 76, 77, 83, 84, 98
Labadi, see 'La'
Ladoku, kingdom 29, 71, 75, 76, 77–8, 83, 85; capital 76 (also 'Adangme')
Laffitte, Irenée 19n.73, 189
Lagos 9, 21, 178, 182–3, 185, 187, 188, 194, 218n.136, 221, 222, 225, 229, 230; reports by British Consul at 197, 201, 205, 207, 222; trade at 73, 145, 150, 167n.54, 196, 198, 203, 209, 212, 217, 220n.152
Lagos channel 28, 30, 34, 39n.63, 40, 65
Lampi, kingdom: see 'Ladoku'; people: see 'Adangme'
Landjékpo, Kodjo: see 'Kodjo, Pedro'
Late Awoku: see 'Lattie/Lathe'
Latebi, kingdom 83
Latham, A. J. H. 194n.208, 233n.44
Lattie/Lathe aka Late Awoku 88, 134, 142–3, 146–7, 151 (and n.117), 153, 154–6, 160, 161, 163, 164
Law, Robin 12, 15n.49, 41, 51, 66, 73, 78, 89, 90n.155, 91, 95, 96n.186, 108
Lawson, Captain George, British trader 147n.94, 161
Lawson family of Little Popo 5, 23, 153–4, 165, 170, 174, 175–6, 184, 191, 205, 213, 217–18, 227–9, 231, 233; Alexander Boevi Lawson 222, 228, 229; Daniel Cummings Lawson ('George Akwete Lawson III') 229–30; Edmund Lawson 229n.21; Edward Lawson 228; Frederick L. Lawson 176; George Latty Lawson 22, 23, 161, 174–6, 183, 184, 201–2, 211, 214, 215, 217, 218, 220, 221, 228; George Lawson aka Akuete Zankli 5, 23, 154, 158–65, 168n.61, 169–75, 183, 191, 199, 211, 212, 217, 218, 221; James W. Lawson 191; Sashey Lawson, 211

(and n.94 & 95), 217–18, 220; Thomas George Lawson 176, 188, 189, 194, 228, 229, 234; Tobi Lawson 191; William Helu Lawson 163–4; William Lawson aka Boy Salvador 204; William Thomas George Lawson, report by (1879) 22, 32n.18, 33–4, 35, 37, 38, 40, 42, 47, 48, 50, 54n.155, 56, 63n.218, 79n.86, 86, 165, 166, 169, 173, 204, 216, 223–4, 227, 229; as agent for British at Little Popo (1883) 229, 230
Lay: see 'La'
Le Herissé, Auguste 42–3
Lepunguno: see 'La'
de Lima, Cesar Cequeira, 208
Lima, Geraldo de ('Atitsogbi') 226, 234
Lind, Lieutenant, 34
Little Popo, kingdom 2–3, 5, 8–9, 15, 17–24 passim, 83–4, 85–9, 90–4, 109–10, chapter 5; foundation of 78–81; and European trade/traders 22, 23, 94–101, 107, 110–13, 114–17, 125–40, 143, 144–51, chapter 6, 226; internal politics 78–9, 116–17, 119, 151–6, 157, 172–3; 157–66; mercenaries from 91, 104, 119; links with Accra 5, 9, 18, 22, 29, 88, 112, 122, 136, 140, 146, 147–8, 161, 197–8, 217, 228; wars and foreign relations 91–4, 99, 102–4, 105–7, 109–10, 117–25, 135–44; and colonial partition 227–36
Little Popo, town 6, 9, 31, 85–7, 104–5, 183, 224; foundation of 72–5; civil war (1823) 157–66, 169–76; war with Agoué (1860–66) 184–66
Little Vo: see 'Vo-Kutime'
Lomé 23, 35, 227, 231, 235
Luanda, Court of Mixed Commission at 21, 195

M'Leod, John 34, 141, 147n.98, 149–50, 196–7
Madail, Felis Cosme 200
Madeira 57, 207
Mahi 122; immigrants at Agoué 179, 186, 200; slaves from 149
Manning, Patrick 13
markets 60–62, 63, 216; market-cycle 60
Marman, Gerard Wilkins 220
Marman, John 22, 23, 175, 183, 210–20
marriage 11, 87, 88, 154, 163, 168n.58, 169, 211 (and n.95), 218 (also 'women')
McCormack, John 176
Medair, Seçar 200
Medeiros, Francisco José de 180, 186n.160,

191, 207–10
Mefe 35
Mensa, caboceer of Porto Seguro 170–1
Miles & Weuves (London) 15, 145–7, 150, 152, 153, 155, 156
Miles, Richard, Governor-in-Chief (1777–85) 145–7, 150, 155
Miles, Thomas 142, 143, 145–7
Miller, Joseph 6
Mina, town on Gold Coast: see 'Elmina'; community/people at Little Popo 13, 27, 72–5, 81, 87n.133, 88–9, 91, 96n.201, 104–5, 109–10, 116–17, 151, 153, 162, 164, 166, 173, 194, 228 (also 'Akan-speaking people', 'Adjigo')
missionaries 9, 17–19, 41, 133, 160, 172, 175–6, 179–190 passim, 221, 228 (also 'Christianity')
Mlapa, King of Togo (town) 231
Mono, river 1, 13n.38, 33, 41, 43–4, 47, 51, 54, 85, 94, 95, 142, 144, 150, 216, 223; as trade route 37–8, 62–3, 125, 223; as colonial boundary 232; outlet into Atlantic Ocean: see 'Bouche du Roi'
Monrad, H. C. 19, 40, 59
Monroe, Cameron 12
de Moore, Pieter 126
Mouléro, Th. 42, 43, 45, 54 (and n.151), 57, 64
Mustiche/Musticke, Domingo 201–2

Nachtigal, Gustav, German Imperial Commissioner 230–1
Netherlands: see 'Dutch'
Newbury, C. W. 12, 227n.10, 212n.99
Nieser, Hendrik 147–8 (and n.98)
Nieser, Jan 147–8
Ningo 76, 77, 83
Nokoué, lake 35n.35, 45,
Norman, Neil 12
Norris, Robert 34, 36n.39 & n.40, 118–19 (and n.89), 120n.98 & n.101, 122
Notsé 13, 50–1
Nyive 139

Obly: see 'Ofori (09)'
Ocoy 118
Odo, caboceer (Little Popo) 151
Odom, caboceer (Little Popo) 151, 152
Offra 46, 69, 75; destruction by Little Popo force 91–2, 98, 99; European trade at 66, 67, 70, 97, 101, 110
Offra Lade: see 'Aflao'
Ofori (01) ('Great Ofori'), King of Little Popo 76–7, 78–9, 86

Ofori (02) ('Little Ofori'), King of Little Popo (d.1693/4) 78–9, 86, 90–93, 99–100
Ofori (03) ('Offerry Bembeneen'/Foli Bebe), King of Little Popo (c.1694–1727) 79, 88, 93, 100, 102–4, 105–6, 111–12, 115
Ofori (04) ('Aufferre'), caboceer of Little Popo (May 1731) 106, 115 [?], 116–17 [?]
Ofori (05) ('Affoery'), Akwamu general [and King of Little Popo: Ofori (4) and/or (6)?] (Nov. 1731) 106
Ofori (06) ('Ofolie'/'Affory'), King of Little Popo [= Ofori (4)?] (– c.1737) 106–7 (and n.23), 115 [?], 116–17 [?], 118, 119 (and n.95)
Ofori (07) ('Affurrey'), son of Ashampo (d.1763) 122 (and n.114)
Ofori (08) ('Ofoly Bossum'/'Bussu'), prince (Little Popo), 135 (and n.9), 136–7, 142–3, 151–2
Ofori (09) ('Obly'), King of Little Popo (d.1786) 135n.9, 138, 152, 155–6
Ofori (10) ('Offoli-adjalu'), King of Little Popo (c.1788–?) 138, 142–3 [?], 152, 156
Ofori (11) ('Offoli'), prince (Little Popo), 151
Ogie Koram ('Great Ogie Koram'), caboceer (Little Popo) 151
Ohaittee, defeated candidate for succession (Little Popo) 138, 144
Okai Koi, King of Accra 76
Old Arqua 152 (also 'Akoi')
Old Calabar 53, 194 n.208, 233n.44
Olympio (da Silva), Francisco 209
Oöogloobooë 143
Osu 72 (and n.41), 76, 217
Osudoku 76
Oto Brafo, chief of Accra 136
Ouatchi 51, 56n.162, 61, 81
Ouidah 2, 3, 4, 5–6, 9, 15, 18–27 passim, 33, 34, 37, 39, 42, 46, 52, 53, 55, 58, 59, 60n.197, 61, 63, 71, 72, 74, 75, 91, 104–5, 107, 151, 155, 173, 188, 204, 223; 236; European trade at 66, 67, 68, 69n.25, 70, 78, 90, 91, 94–5, 96–101, 105, 110–1, 112, 113–14, 116, 126, 129, 142, 144–5, 148, 149, 150; as centre of 'illegal' slave trade 162, 163, 168, 169, 174, 180, 181, 183, 186–7, 190, 196, 197–200, 201, 202, 208, 218, 224; palm oil trade at 211, 212, 217, 218, 220, 221, 234; raided by exiled Hueda 108; raided/threatened by Little Popo forces 92, 110, 118, 119–20, 122, 124, 135; British Vice-Consulate at 179, 204, 219; Roman Catholic mission/church at 185, 189, 190
Owosu ('Ursue'), Akyem ruler 106
Oy 45 n.104
Oyo 29, 101, 119, 120, 126

Paine, Captain Sylvanus 96
palm kernels 55, 216; trade in palm kernel oil 61, 216, 223
palm oil trade 8, 16, 22, 23, 26, 37, 61, 64, 159, 174, 177, 187–8, 203, 206, 207, 210–24; production of oil for 215–16
Paokahnee, alternative name for Little Popo 6, 99
pawns/ pawnship 10, 112, 131, 151
panyarring 109, 133
Pazzi, Roberto 54
Peda/ Pedah, people: see 'Hueda'; river, see 'Aho, river'
Peile, M.S.L. 192
Peki 50, 103, 106, 118, 123
Pélofy, Isidore 19
Pepple, King of Bonny 189
Pereira, João Soares 207–8
Phillips, Thomas 69, 70, 71
Phipps, Thomas 95n.189
Pickaninee Popo, alternative name for Little Popo 74
Piti 46
Pla, people: see 'Hula, people'
Poccahonna, alternative name for Little Popo 6, 98
Poeselwit, Johan 97n.203
Pomeh: see 'Gbome'
Popo: see 'Grand Popo', 'Little Popo'
Porto Novo 29, 40, 101, 146, 198, 205, 208, 209, 225, 227
Porto Seguro 2, 14, 27, 32, 190, 204, 227; reports to 18–21 passim; foundation of 26, 45, 169–71; European trade at 31, 169, 199, 203–4, 207, 209, 213–23 passim, 225, 226; and colonial partition 228, 231–2
Portugal, Portuguese trade/traders 1, 8, 14, 41, 44, 45, 65–6, 69, 76, 78, 98, 100, 101, 114, 115, 124, 126, 128, 129, 137, 144, 145, 154, 159, 161, 173, 174, 191, 204, 207, 208, 209, 223 (also 'Brazil'); language 167, 169, 187; missionaries: see 'Christian missions: Roman Catholics'; Portuguese immigration to Agoué: see 'Agoué: Brazilian immigration'; and suppression of slave trade 195, 197–8; records 14–15

Pottebra 35, 136 (and n.16), 138–40, 150
Prampram 76, 77, 83
Prindsensten, Danish fort (Keta), 136–7, 138, 139, 146, 196, , 203, 205n.57
Protten, Christianus Jacob 5, 18, 119n.95
provisions 74, 90, 108, export of 3–4 (and n.4), 52, 56, 58, 59, 74, 137, 144n.76, 146, 149, 150, 155, 159, 193, 195, 197, 210, 216–17, 218, 223, 224 (also 'agriculture', 'animal husbandry')

Quadjo, Pedro: see 'Kodjo, Pedro'
Quadjovi: see 'Jehowey aka Kodjovi'
Quahoe: see 'Kwahu'
Quam Desu, ancestor of Adjigo people 73, 117
Quam-Dessou, local historian 170, 171
Quam (1), caboceer (Little Popo, 1732) 116–17
Quam (2), caboceer (Little Popo, 1770s-1790s) 146, 151, 152, 153, 155
Quaminagah/Quamina Gang, 165
Quarvee/Quarver/Quarvil, John, English caboceer at Agoué 168, 177, 178, 180, 181–3, 187, 194, 234
Quashie Corley, notable (Agoué) 177
Quashie Gah, notable (Agoué) 177
Quashie Sooquoo, chief (Agoué) 177
Quenum (Houénou), Azanmado 202
Quitto: see 'Keta'

Randad, Heinrich 231
Rask, Johannes 56n.166, 58, 64
Reindorf, Carl Christian 80, 135n.9
religion 1, 9 (and n.23), 13, 38, 42n.89, 44, 75, 82, 83n.113, 87–8, 143, 144, 156n.150, 152, 166, 186 (also 'Christianity', 'Islam', 'Sakumo')
Reynolds, T.D. 188 n.175
Richelieu, Johan Daniel 111
River of the Popos: see 'Bouche du Roi'
Roberts, John, RAC Chief Agent at Cape Coast Castle (1750–52) 127–8, 130, 131–3
Robertson, G. A. 15–16, 42, 58–9, 141, 144, 145, 149, 156, 173, 197
Rømer, Ludewig Ferdinand 17, 24, 35, 79n.82, 107n.23, 120, 121n.108, 126 (and n.142), 127, 133, 135
Rottmann, M. 226 n.5
Rowe, Sir Samuel, Governor of Gold Coast Colony 228n.21, 229
Royal Adventurers Trading into Africa, English 67
Royal African Company, English (RAC) 15, 67, 69n.25, 70, 78, 85, 90, 91, 92, 95–100, 105–6, 107, 109–10, 112–15, 116, 121, 123n.119
Royal Geographical Society, British 19–20
Royal Navy, British 4, 20–1, 54, 59, 144n.71, 162n.24, 173–5, 182–4, 185, 187–9, 190–3, 196, 197–9, 200, 201, 203–10, 211–12, 215, 217

Sagada 216
Sakumo, lagoon 69, 75; cult 87 (and n.139), 88 (and n.143), 89n.147, 156n.150
salt, salt-making 1, 40, 44, 52, 53–5, 56, 62, 72n.40, 82; regional trade in 52, 56, 60–2, 141; imported from Europe 44, 62, 235
Sampayo, Joseph Moreyra 200
de Sandoval, Alonso 41, 66
dos Santos, Antonio Verra 200
dos Santos, José Francisco ('Alfaiate') 24, 186, 201 (and n.33), 206 (and n.63)
São Jorge da Mina, Portuguese 66 (after 1637: 'Elmina, Dutch headquarters')
São Tomé 14, 18, 66
Sasi Aheba 186
Savi, Hueda capital 92, 109
Sebald, Peter 13, 18n.63, 226n.5
Sedjro (Seggiroe/ Sagrow) Agboku/Agbosu aka Kodjo Agbosu 169 n.63, 170–1 (and n.76 & 77), 191
Segbohoué 235 n.51
Sekko 199, 206
Sekpon, chief of the beach (Little Popo) 163, 186
Seva 61
Seva Beach: see 'Anyogboe'
Seward, H. 212–13, 219
Shai 76, 85
Sierra Leone, British colony 21–2, 51n.134, 176, 189, 218, 220, 228; Court of Mixed Commission at 21, 195, 206, 209; immigrants from 19, 178–9, 188, 194, 222, 226, 228–9; region 10n.28 (also 'Freetown')
Silveira, Domingo Francisco da, 186
Silveira, Pedro Pinto da, see: 'Kodjo, Pedro'
Singelenburg, Dutch fort (Keta) 3n.3, 117–18, 125
slave vessels: Christianus Quintus 111–12; Ciceron 209; Dahomey 209; Duc de Bretagne 126; Fauconburgh 99; Galère d'Afrique 127n.149; George 97n.205; de Goude Leeuw 97; Goude Put 115–16; Hanover 207; Københavns Børs 100; La Perle 95; Lydia Gibbs 207; Pepita 204;

Pepito 201; William Clarke 205
smuggling 226–7, 231, 234
Snelgrave, William 108–9, 119
Société des Missions Africaines, Lyon: see 'Christianity: Roman Catholic mission/church'
Soko 76 (also 'James Town')
Some: see 'Agbosome'; Some War: see 'Anlo'
de Souza family of Ouidah 19, 87, 169–70n.10, 200; Antonio Felix 'Kokou' de Souza, 163n.32, 200 (and n.24), 203, 215, 220n.152; Francisco Felix de Souza 59, 87, 158, 162–3 (and n.32), 164, 167–9, 173–4, 180, 183, 186, 199–200 (and n.24), 202, 211–12, 218; Ignacio de Souza 163n.32, 200n.24; Isidoro de Souza 163 (and n.32), 199, 202–3 (and n.41), 202–3; Maria de Souza 163 n.32; Norberto de Souza 163n.32; San Anthonio de Souza 200 n.24; Simone de Souza 19, 163n.32, 200n.24
Sowu, King of Little Popo 171
Spain, Spanish trade/traders 159, 179, 198, 200n.23, 201–2, 205 n.57; missionaries 31, 41
Spieth, Jacob 57, 81
Sprigge, R.G.S. 84
Steirmark, Johan Joost 117–18, 119
Stockwell, Richard, RAC Governor on the Gold Coast (1749–50) 127
Strahan, George, Governor of Gold Coast Colony (1874–76) 227
Struvé, Ferdinand 21, 38, 39, 53, 63, 173–4, 175, 202–3n.41
Stubenrauch, Captain Wilhelm 230
Sugru: see 'Porto Seguro'
Swanzy, Francis & Andrew (London) 222 (and n.176)

Tado, 28, 41, 43, 46, 51, 76
Takoradi 69
Taparica, José de 200
Tary: see 'Grand Popo'
taxation 42, 63, 67, 69n.25, 73, 75, 113, 116, 130, 143, 153, 156n.147, 159, 164–5, 194, 215, 223, 226–7, 228, 230, 232–4; toll stations 42, 48–50, 53, 62–4, 226n.7
Tchamba 33, 62; cult 9 n.23
Tegbesu, King of Dahomey (1740–74) 120, 124, 126–7
Tegbi 136–7
Tema 75, 76
Tetetu 85
Tette-Obrim 151, 152, 153

textiles: see 'cloth'
Tilleman, Erich 100–01
titles: Ata 154–5 (and n.139), 181; dootay (Ewe dutɔ́) 172–3; Djêken 54n.151; Fidalgo 41, 153, 155; Fio 27; Fettera/Fiterre/pheter 116; Hulaholu 27; yovogah 173
tobacco 100, 114, 155
Todegereapu 194
Togo-Atacora, mountains 29, 30, 101
Togo, lake 20, 21, 32–8 passim, 51, 56, 61, 62, 63, 84, 216, 219
Togo, Republic 2, 15, 22n.89, 27, 83
Togo, town 51, 61, 63, 170n.71, 169, 170–1
Togoland, German colony 13–14, 23, 32n.18, 230–2, 234–5
Ton/Tonu 80
Topoy 107
Toyi, caboceer of Agoué (1835–44) 178
Tshegbo 216
Tsiame 213
Twi, language/language complex: see 'Akan'

Ursue: see 'Owosu'
USA 14; anti-slave trade squadron 195; missionaries 19; trade/traders 17, 164, 196, 205–8 17

Valkenburgh, J. 73
Verger, Pierre 15n.46, 24, 200n.28, 206n.63
Victor Régis (Marseille) 16, 184, 201, 205, 221, 224
Vidal (Barcelona) 201
Villa Franca 45
Villa Longa 45
Vo-Kutime 61
Vogan ('Vo') 60, 61, 216
Volta, river 28–40 passim, 51, 54, 58, 66, 74–8 passim, 80, 82n.104, 85, 89, 94–8 passim, 102, 103, 105, 106, 117–18, 123, 135–42 passim, 144, 145, 146, 150, 209; fishing in 40, 121; trade at 65, 105, 114–15, 120, 121, 125, 136

W.B. Hutton & Sons (London) 210–21
Ward, G.T. 214
Wariboko, Wabinte E. 194 n.208
Watchikope 81
Wesleyan Methodist Missionary Society: see 'Christianity: Wesleyan Methodist mission'
West, William 176, 182
West India Company (WIC) (Dutch): see 'Dutch trade/traders'

Westermann, Diedrich 24, 39–40, 58, 60–1, 79–82, 84, 88n.143, 139
Weta 139
Whara, ward of Badagry 46
Whydah: see 'Ouidah'
Wilks, Ivor 76–8, 94, 102–3, 106n.20, 141–2
William's Fort, English (Ouidah) 122, 123n.115
Wilson, Seth 13
Winniett, Sir William, Governor of British Possessions on Gold Coast 203
Woe 34, 59n.184, 136, 149, 199, 213
Wogba 143
Wölber & Brohm (Hamburg) 231
women 5, 11, 76, 79, 88, 118, 153, 154, 156, 163 (and n.32), 169, 182, 186, 210n.89, 211, 218, 220–1 (also 'marriage'); enslaved for export 202
Wortley, John 91–2
Wrisberg, Philip Wilhelm 196
Wyborne/Wybourne, Petley 91–2, 94–8

Yoruba-speaking peoples 28, 41, 178, 179
Young, Tom 151

Zalive 63, 219
Zio, river 33, 34, 35, 37, 51
Zoki Azata, see: 'Joaquim d'Almeida'
Zokikome, quarter of Agoué 179, 200–1
Zöller, Hugo 23, 32n.18, 33–4, 36, 37–8, 38n.66, 42, 63, 84, 186, 194, 223, 224
van Zütphen, C. H. 15, 71n.28, 167–9, 179, 182, 195–6

www.ingramcontent.com/pod-product-compliance
Lightning Source LLC
Chambersburg PA
CBHW051605230426
43668CB00013B/1995